PUFFIN BOOKS
THE PUFFIN HISTORY OF THE WORLD
VOLUME 1

Roshen Dalal is the author of *Religions of India: A Concise Guide to Nine Major Faiths*, *Hinduism: An Alphabetical Guide*, *The Illustrated Timeline History of the World* and the best-selling two-volume *The Puffin History of India for Children*. She has an MA and PhD in Ancient Indian History from Jawaharlal Nehru University, New Delhi. She has worked on various research projects, taught at school and university level, and written numerous articles and book reviews. She lives in Dehradun.

Read more in Puffin by Roshen Dalal

The Puffin History of India for Children
Volume 1 (3000 BC to AD 1947)
The Puffin History of India for Children
Volume 2 (1947 to the Present)

The Puffin History of the WORLD VOL. 1

Roshen Dalal

Illustrations by
Kallol Majumdar

PUFFIN BOOKS

PUFFIN BOOKS

USA | Canada | UK | Ireland | Australia
New Zealand | India | South Africa | China

Puffin Books is part of the Penguin Random House group of companies whose addresses can be found at global.penguinrandomhouse.com

Published by Penguin Random House India Pvt. Ltd
7th Floor, Infinity Tower C, DLF Cyber City,
Gurgaon 122 002, Haryana, India

Penguin Random House India

First published in Puffin by Penguin Books India 2013

Copyright © Roshen Dalal 2013
Illustrations copyright © Kallol Majumdar 2013

The views and opinions expressed in this book are the author's own and the facts are as reported by her, which have been verified to the extent possible, and the publishers are not in any way liable for the same.

All rights reserved

10 9 8 7 6 5 4 3 2

ISBN 9780143331575

Typeset in Goudy Old Style by Eleven Arts, New Delhi

Printed at Repro Knowledgecast Limited, India

This book is sold subject to the condition that it shall not, by way of trade or otherwise, be lent, resold, hired out, or otherwise circulated without the publisher's prior consent in any form of binding or cover other than that in which it is published and without a similar condition including this condition being imposed on the subsequent purchaser.

www.penguin.co.in

Contents

Introduction ix

1. The World Today 1
2. The Origins 17
3. The First People 27
4. Changing Patterns of Life Across the World 39
   50,000–10,000 BCE
5. The First Villages and Towns 48
   10,000–5000 BCE
6. The Rise of Cities: Mesopotamia 60
   5000–1500 BCE
7. Early Egypt 70
8. India 82
   3500 BCE–500 BCE
9. Early China 91
10. Ancient Greece 101
11. Alexander: King of Macedonia 115
12. Ancient Europe 121
13. The Roman World 129

14.	West Asia and Central Asia: The Early Period	148
15.	Christianity	156
16.	Empires of Iran (Persia): Achaemenids, Parthians and Sasanians	162
17.	Africa: Up to CE 500	176
18.	Early North America	184
19.	Early South and Central America	191
20.	China: Early Mongolia and Korea 221 BCE–CE 581	201
21.	India: Great Empires 500 BCE–CE 500	212
22.	Japan: Up to CE 794	223
23.	Europe CE 500–1000	231
24.	A New Religion: Islam	242
25.	Great Britain and Ireland: Up to CE 1000	251
26.	Warriors of the North: Scandinavian Vikings CE 750–1100	262
27.	India CE 500–1000	270
28.	China: Mongolia and Korea CE 581–1000	276
29.	Africa CE 500–1000	284
30.	Europe CE 1000–1500	292
31.	Europe: Kingdoms, Wars and Conflicts CE 1000–1500	304
32.	Europe: Art and Culture CE 1000–1500	321

33. Great Britain and Ireland CE 1000-1500	331
34. The Mongols CE 1200-1500	343
35. Russia CE 1000-1500	352
36. India CE 1000-1500	365
37. West Asia CE 750-1500	376
38. West Asia: The Turks	386
39. China CE 1000-1500	392
40. Japan CE 794-1500	404
41. Southeast Asia: Myanmar, Thailand, Laos, Cambodia, Vietnam	415
42. Southeast Asia: Philippines, Malaysia, Indonesia	427
43. North America CE 1000-1500	436
44. South and Central America CE 1000-1500	443
45. Africa CE 1000-1500	457
46. Southern Africa CE 1000-1500	467
47. Australia and New Zealand: Up to CE 1500	471
Conclusion	485
Index	486
Acknowledgements	528

Introduction

WHAT IS HISTORY?

History is a story of the past, of the people in the world and the way they have lived. It is also the story of the land and of everything that lives and grows, as all life is connected. All the events of the past are not included in history. History includes only those aspects of the past that we think are important, those that we choose to remember. There are different types of histories. There are histories of kings, wars and conquests. There are histories of ordinary people, or of one category of people, such as women or children. There are histories of art, of music, or of sports such as cricket, of education, or even of a single school. There are histories of individual countries, or of regions within a country. Each type of history tells a different story.

CHOICE OF FACTS

In every kind of history, the historian, the person who writes the history, has to decide what to include. Even if someone decides to write the history of one school, perhaps your school, there are so many things that have happened that not everything can be included. Maybe you had a maths test yesterday. Should the history include the marks of everyone who took the test?

Should it include how you felt nervous but finally did well? Should it include the story of everyone in your class? Should it have the story of each of your teachers? If your school has existed for fifty years or one hundred years, can the story of each test, and of every person, both students and teachers, who ever went to the school, be included? It would not fit into one book, perhaps not even into ten books. Hence every time anyone writes a history of anything, he or she has to decide what is important.

CHANGE IN HISTORY

Very often we hear the statement 'the past does not change' or 'facts are facts'. Both statements are correct, but 'the past' is not the same as history. History, as we have seen, is only those aspects of the past that we choose to remember. Another factor is that we really do not know everything about the past. Everyday there are new discoveries of early people, of art and craft and of other different aspects of the past. Though the past does not change, the information we have about it, and the way we look at the past, constantly changes.

APPROACHES

There are different approaches to history, that is, different ways of looking at the past. One historian might like to focus on the psychology of the people of the past, another on economy, others on something else. There are also different trends. At the time of the world wars, everyone was thinking about wars and battles. They saw how cities and even countries were destroyed by war. When they tried to understand the decline of civilizations of the past, they thought that those too might have been destroyed by invasions, wars and battles. Today everyone is concerned about the environment. Hence often when they look at the decline of past civilizations they think it could be because of the destruction of the environment, or because of natural disasters like drought. To decide which the more likely theory is, one has to analyse different types of evidence.

HOW WE KNOW ABOUT THE PAST

We know about the past through material remains and various kinds of records. Material remains are the things people leave behind, which are somehow preserved for centuries and can still be seen. Records are writings of different kinds. All these items are analysed by a number of different scientists and experts.

Material remains include:

Fossils: Fossils are the remains of very ancient plants, animals or people. The term fossil is used for remains that are more than 10,000 years old. Paleontologists are scientists who study fossils.

Bones of people and animals: While very early bones turn into fossils, later bones can be found in graves or excavations. Sometimes entire skeletons are found.

Remains of seeds, plants, trees and pollen: These, as well as pollen analysis can help in understanding environments of the past.

Remains of things people have made: These include buildings, tools, coins, art, pottery. Sometimes entire cities are preserved, as at Pompeii and Novgorod.

Records include:

Histories of various kinds
Inscriptions
Writings of any sort

Archaeology

Archaeology and history are two related subjects. Archaeology examines and analyses the material remains of the past.

Excavations are an important part of archaeology. Excavations involve a systematic way of looking for things buried underground. Sometimes buildings or cities are deserted. They crumble and fall to the ground. Over time, as the wind blows and the rain falls, they get covered in mud, and can no longer be seen. The archaeologist carefully digs and finds the ancient remains. Archaeologists also look for things that have been deliberately buried. These may be graves, or items in graves, or hoards of various items buried in times of war or disaster. Once the archaeologist has uncovered or found these objects, several specialized scientists are involved in analysing and dating them.

An archaeological culture is a term used to refer to material culture, with similar pottery, tools, houses and other items that occur within a particular period of time and within a certain area.

Dating techniques

There are several different dating methods used. Documents and inscriptions often have a date written on them. Coins sometimes have dates, or have names of kings whose dates are known. But there are numerous items found through archaeological excavations that either belong to a time before writing was used, or have no clear indications of a date. Various methods are used for dating these. Among them are:

Stratigraphy: This is a system of relative dating. During an excavation a site or place is carefully excavated by removing one layer at a time. The higher layers or levels belong to later dates, the lower to earlier. If a higher level can be dated through some item found, then the dates of the lower levels can be estimated.

Radiocarbon dating: This is a chemical process which measures Carbon 14 in any part of an organism that was once alive. After the death of the organism, Carbon 14 diminishes at a certain fixed rate.

Thermoluminescence dating: This is another chemical method that can be used to date objects that have been subjected to heat, for instance, pottery.

Dendrochronology: This is used to date old trees. It is based on the analysis of tree rings. These growth rings are found in the trunk of a tree, and usually one ring is added every year.

Seriation dating: This is another method of relative dating, which can be used where the stratigraphy is not clear. It is based on determining a logical sequence in which artefacts and styles change over time. Statistical methods are used for this.

Obsidian hydration dating: Obsidian, a type of stone, grows a rind at a fixed rate when it is exposed after breaking or cutting it. Measuring this can provide a date.

Genetics and DNA

Genetic studies are increasingly being used to understand the people of the past, or the origin of present people. This is a useful technique. For instance, analysing the genome of a finger bone and two teeth led to the identification of a different, and so far unknown early human species, the Denisovan. However, when used to understand the origins of present people, it has its limitations, as generalizations are often made based on very few samples.

ABOUT THIS BOOK

This book is the first of two volumes about the history of the world. This volume begins with an overview of the countries that exist today. How did these countries come into existence? What was there before their present boundaries were formed? How did people reach these areas? In fact, how did people or even the world originate? These two volumes answer these and other related questions. The first volume provides a history of the world up to CE 1500. The second volume begins in 1500 and continues till the present.

These books are especially for young people, though anyone can read them. The various chapters are on different regions of the world, and you can choose what interests you and what you would like to read.

As we had said above there are different types of histories. So much has happened in the world that everything cannot be included here. This book provides a broad framework of political history, along with the main economic, social and cultural aspects. It includes information on animals and plants; the beginnings of agriculture; great civilizations and empires; stories, epics, myths and legends; architecture, arts and crafts; religion and philosophy; temples, mosques, churches and other monuments; trade, travel and adventure; wars and conquests; theatre, music and dance; language, literature and poetry; interesting personalities; clothes, food, houses and lifestyles; climate change and scientific developments.

BCE and CE

BCE and CE are the abbreviations used in this book for dates. BCE stands for 'Before Common Era' and CE for 'Common Era'. The Common Era is the calendar we generally use. These abbreviations are now increasingly used in all parts of the world instead of BC and AD. BC refers to 'Before Christ', and AD to Anno Domini, that is, after his birth (literally 'the year of our lord'). As Christ was not born in AD 1, the use of BC and AD is not that accurate, and it is better to use BCE and CE. In terms of dates, 100 BCE is the same as 100 BC, and CE 200 is the same as AD 200. 1 BCE is one year before CE 1. If this year is CE 2013, 1 BCE was 2014 years ago.

A note on dates in this book

Many dates for archaeological cultures and for people of the past remain uncertain. In this book, different sources have been consulted to choose the most likely and most authentic date.

Sometimes, before a date you will see 'c.'. This 'c.' stands for circa. Circa comes from a Latin word 'circum' that means 'around' or 'about'. It indicates that the date is not exact, but somewhere around what is given.

We often use terms such as 4th or 5th century CE or 5th century BCE. The 5th century CE indicates any date from CE 401–500. The 5th century BCE indicates a date from BCE 500–401. That is because we count backwards for BCE dates.

Spellings used

So many different languages are used across the world. Some of their sounds have no equivalent in English. For European names the English equivalent is often used in this and other history books. Chinese names have their own rules for English spellings. Sometimes earlier methods of Chinese spellings are given in brackets. For other languages we have used the most accepted spellings, without adding accents.

1
The World Today

We live in the world. The world as we know it today has large areas of land known as continents, surrounded by water. The land amounts to about 35 per cent of the whole area of the earth. This land area includes the continental shelves, the sloping land that is below water on the ocean shores of continents.

The continents are Asia, Africa, North America, South America, Antarctica, Europe and Australia. Europe and Asia actually form one continent—Eurasia—but are considered two for convenience. Within the seven continents there are a number of different countries. These countries were formed at different times and some are quite recent. Each continent also has several islands, some of which are separate countries. We will have a brief look here at the continents and countries that exist today.

THE CONTINENTS

CONTINENT	AREA
Asia	4,49,36,000 sq km
Africa	3,03,43,578 sq km
North America	2,47,10,000 sq km
South America	1,78,40,000 sq km
Antarctica	1,42,00,000 sq km in summer; in winter it is double this, as ice forms and extends the area.
Europe	1,05,25,000 sq km
Australia	76,14,500 sq km

THE OCEANS

We live on land, but water covers about three quarters of the earth's surface, and in some areas the water is very deep. Mountains, trenches, volcanoes, canyons, plains and plateaus are beneath the water. Oceans are full of plants and aquatic life, which are used by people who live near the coasts. The oceans together cover an area of 36,11,00,000 sq km.

The four main oceans are:

The Pacific Ocean, which is the largest. Its area is more than the land area of all the continents together.

The Atlantic Ocean, the Indian Ocean, and the small, icy Arctic Ocean surrounding the North Pole, are the others.

The Southern or Antarctic Ocean is sometimes considered the fifth ocean. Others think that parts of the Atlantic, Pacific and Indian Oceans are actually in this region, and there is no fifth ocean.

Both land and oceans, and everything that lives and grows on and in them are very important in our lives. We cannot live without them, and in different ways they affect us and our history.

To start with, we will look at the countries that exist today.

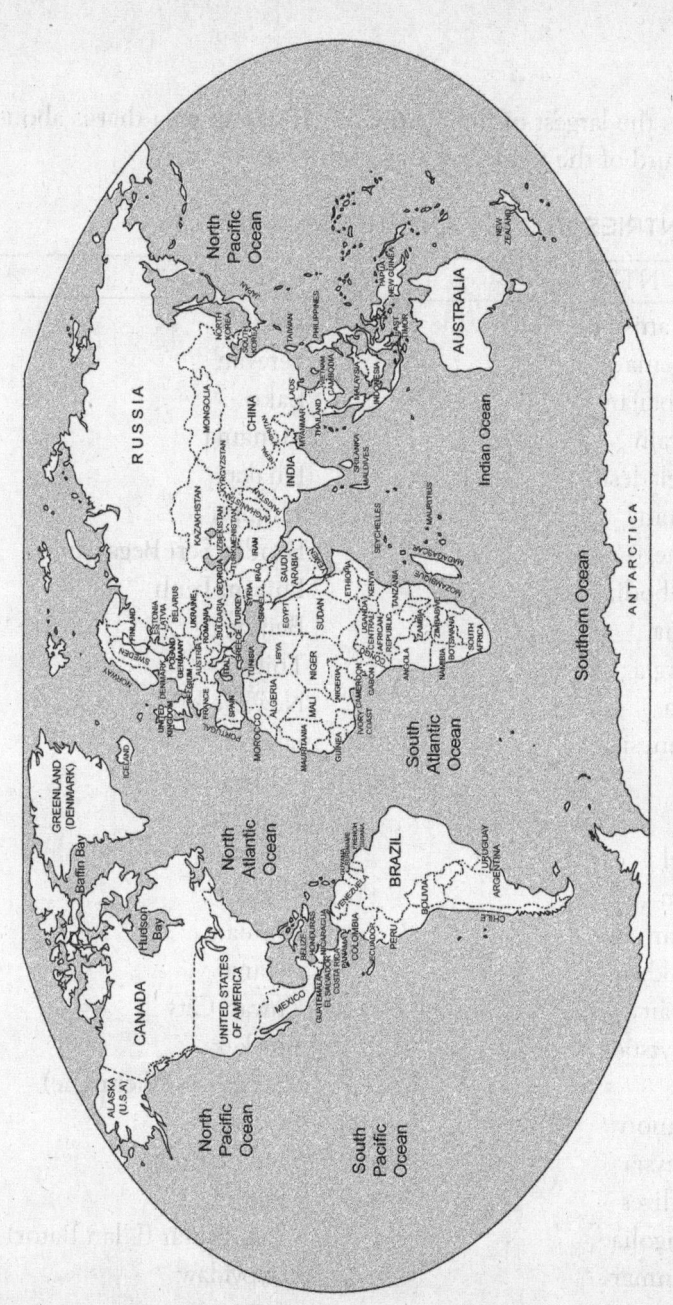

The World: Continents, countries and oceans

ASIA

Asia is the largest of the continents. It has an area that is about one-third of the total land area of the world.

COUNTRIES IN ASIA AND THEIR CAPITALS

COUNTRY	CAPITAL
Afghanistan	Kabul
Armenia	Yerevan
Azerbaijan	Baku
Bahrain	Manama
Bangladesh	Dhaka
Bhutan	Thimpu
Brunei	Bandar Seri Begawan
Cambodia	Phnom Penh
China	Beijing
Georgia	Tbilisi
India	New Delhi
Indonesia	Jakarta
Iran	Tehran
Iraq	Baghdad
Israel	Jerusalem
Japan	Tokyo
Jordan	Amman
Kazakhstan	Astana
Kuwait	Kuwait City
Kyrgyzstan	Bishkek
Laos	Viangchan (Vientiane)
Lebanon	Beirut
Malaysia	Kuala Lumpur
Maldives	Male
Mongolia	Ulaanbaatar (Ulan Bator)
Myanmar	Naypyidaw

Nepal	Kathmandu
North Korea (Democratic People's Republic of Korea)	Pyongyang
Oman	Muscat
Palestine	intended capital—East Jerusalem
Pakistan	Islamabad
Philippines	Manila
Qatar	Doha
Russia	Moscow (Russia is in Asia and Europe)
Saudi Arabia	Riyadh
Singapore	Singapore
South Korea (Republic of Korea)	Seoul
Sri Lanka	Colombo
Syria	Damascus
Tajikistan	Dushanbe
Thailand	Bangkok
Timor Leste	Dili
Turkey	Ankara
Turkmenistan	Ashgabat
United Arab Emirates	Abu Dhabi (UAE is a federation of seven Emirates)
Uzbekistan	Tashkent
Vietnam	Hanoi
Yemen	Sanaa

EUROPE

Europe, as we saw earlier, is actually part of the joint continent of Eurasia, and forms its western part. It is considered a separate continent mainly because its languages and culture are different. It is the second smallest continent.

COUNTRIES IN EUROPE AND THEIR CAPITALS

COUNTRY	CAPITAL
Albania	Tirana
Andorra	Andorra la Vella
Austria	Vienna
Belarus	Minsk
Belgium	Brussels
Bosnia-Herzegovina	Sarajevo
Bulgaria	Sofia
Croatia	Zagreb
Cyprus	Nicosia
Czech Republic	Prague
Denmark	Copenhagen (Greenland and Faroe Islands are self-governing territories of Denmark.)
Estonia	Tallinn
Finland	Helsinki
France	Paris
Germany	Berlin
Greece	Athens
Greenland, territory under Denmark	Nuuk (Godthab)
Hungary	Budapest
Iceland	Reykjavik
Ireland, Republic of	Dublin
Italy	Rome
Kosovo	Pristina
Latvia	Riga
Liechtenstein	Vaduz
Lithuania	Vilnius
Luxembourg	Luxembourg
Macedonia	Skopje
Malta	Valletta
Moldova	Chisinau (Kishinev)

Monaco	Monaco-Ville
Montenegro	Podgorica
Netherlands, The	Amsterdam
Norway	Oslo
Poland	Warsaw
Portugal	Lisbon
Romania	Bucharest
Russia	Moscow
San Marino	San Marino
Serbia	Belgrade
Slovakia	Bratislava
Slovenia	Ljubljana
Spain	Madrid
Sweden	Stockholm
Switzerland	Bern
Turkey	Ankara (part of Turkey is in Europe)
Ukraine	Kiev
United Kingdom of Great Britain and Northern Ireland	London
Vatican City	Vatican City

EURASIA

Two countries are spread across Asia and Europe. One could say they are in Eurasia. Though they are already listed above, Russia under Europe and Turkey under Asia, they belong to both continents.

COUNTRIES IN EURASIA AND THEIR CAPITALS

COUNTRY	CAPITAL
Russia	Moscow
Turkey	Ankara

Roshen Dalal

Another interesting country is the island of Cyprus. Cyprus is considered part of Europe historically and politically, but is really on the border between Asia and Europe.

AFRICA

Africa is the second largest continent in the world. It includes islands which are located quite a distance away from the main continent.

COUNTRIES IN AFRICA AND THEIR CAPITALS

COUNTRY	CAPITAL
Algeria	Algiers
Angola	Luanda
Benin	Porto Novo
Botswana	Gaborone
Burkina Faso	Ouagadougou
Burundi	Bujumbura
Cameroon	Yaounde
Cape Verde	Praia
Central African Republic (CAR)	Bangui
Chad	N'Djamena
Comoros group of islands	Moroni
Congo, Democratic Republic of the	Kinshasa
Congo, Republic of	Brazzaville
Cote d'Ivoire	Yamoussoukro
Djibouti	Djibouti City
Egypt	Cairo
Equatorial Guinea	Malabo (on Bicko islands); Bata on mainland is the administrative capital.

Eritrea	Asmara
Ethiopia	Addis Ababa
Gabon	Libreville
Gambia, The	Banjul
Ghana	Accra
Guinea	Conakry
Guinea-Bissau	Bissau
Kenya	Nairobi
Lesotho	Maseru
Liberia	Monrovia
Libya	Tripoli
Madagascar	Antananarivo
Malawi	Lilongwe
Mali	Bamako
Mauritania	Nouakchott
Mauritius	Port Louis
Morocco	Rabat
Mozambique	Maputo
Namibia	Windhoek
Niger	Niamey
Nigeria	Abuja
Rwanda	Kigali
Sahrawi or Saharan Arab Democratic Republic (declared independence but is disputed territory)	El Aaiun is claimed as capital but is under Morocco; BirLehlou is the temporary capital; Tindouf, Algeria, is the administrative capital of the exiled government.
Sao Tome and Principe	Sao Tome
Senegal	Dakar
Seychelles	Victoria

Sierra Leone	Freetown
Somalia	Mogadishu
South Africa	Pretoria: administrative capital; Cape Town: legislative capital; Bloemfontein: judicial capital
South Sudan	Juba
Sudan	Khartoum
Swaziland	Mbabane: administrative capital; Lobamba: royal and legislative capital
Tanzania	Dodoma
Togo	Lome
Tunisia	Tunis
Uganda	Kampala
Zambia	Lusaka
Zimbabwe	Harare

Comoros and Madagascar are islands in the Indian Ocean. Further east are Mauritius, Reunion Islands and Seychelles. Reunion Islands is under France.

NORTH AMERICA

The third largest continent is that of North America. It includes:
1. Canada, the USA and Mexico
2. Central America and the Caribbean Islands, which are considered part of the North American continent, though they have their own culture and history
3. Islands or territories on the continental shelf: Greenland, Newfoundland, Nova Scotia, the French territory of St Pierre and Miquelon and some Arctic islands

CANADA, USA AND MEXICO

COUNTRY	CAPITAL
Canada	Ottawa
USA	Washington DC
Mexico	Mexico City

CENTRAL AMERICA

COUNTRY	CAPITAL
Belize	Belmopan
Costa Rica	San Jose
El Salvador	San Salvador
Guatemala	Guatemala City
Honduras	Tegucigalpa
Nicaragua	Managua
Panama	Panama City

CARIBBEAN ISLANDS

The Caribbean Islands, located east of Central America, are usually considered a subregion of North America. The hundreds of islands form 27 territories. Out of these, 13 territories are independent, the others under various European powers. The independent territories are:

COUNTRY	CAPITAL
Antigua and Barbuda	St John's
Bahamas, The	Nassau
Barbados	Bridgetown
Cuba	Havana
Dominica	Roseau
Dominican Republic	Santo Domingo

Roshen Dalal

Grenada	St George's
Haiti	Port-au-Prince
Jamaica	Kingston
St Lucia	Castries
St Vincent and the Grenadines	Kingstown
St Kitts and Nevis	Basseterre
Trinidad and Tobago	Port-of-Spain

Some of the other Caribbean islands are listed below:

British territories: Anguilla, British Virgin Islands, Cayman Islands, Montserrat, Turks and Caicos

Dutch territories: Aruba, Netherland Antilles

American territories: Puerto Rico, United States Virgin Islands

French territories: Guadelope, Martinique, St Barthelemy, Saint Martin

There are other Caribbean Islands too. Each island has its own unique cultural heritage.

TERRITORIES ON THE CONTINENTAL SHELF

Greenland, though on the North American continental shelf, is a territory under Denmark and is listed in Europe. Newfoundland forms part of the province of Newfoundland and Labrador, which is part of Canada. Nova Scotia is a province of Canada.

Some Arctic islands are also technically a part of the continent of North America. These islands come under Canada and USA.

SOUTH AMERICA

South America is the fourth largest of the continents. It has a mainland region and some islands.

COUNTRIES IN SOUTH AMERICA AND THEIR CAPITALS

COUNTRIES	CAPITALS
Argentina	Buenos Aires
Bolivia	La Paz is the administrative capital; Sucre is the legal capital and the seat of the judiciary.
Brazil	Brasilia
Chile	Santiago
Colombia	Bogota
Ecuador	Quito
Guyana	Georgetown
Paraguay	Asuncion
Peru	Lima
Suriname	Paramaribo
Uruguay	Montevideo
Venezuela	Caracas

AUSTRALIA

Australia is the smallest continent. However, the country of Australia is bigger than the continent as it includes thousands of islands.

COUNTRY	CAPITAL
Australia	Canberra

Australia has 8222 islands within its maritime borders. Among the largest are: Tasmania; Melville Island; Groote Eylandt; Bathurst Island; Fraser Island; Flinders Island; King Island and Mornington Island.

Whitsunday Islands are 74 islands of Australia, surrounded by the Great Barrier Reef.

Roshen Dalal

Like other countries, Australia also has some other territories. These are: Australian Antarctic Territory, Christmas Island, Cocos Islands, the Territory of Heard and McDonald Islands, Norfolk Island, Ashmore and Cartier Islands, and the Coral Sea Islands Territory.

ANTARCTICA

Antarctica is a continent almost totally covered in ice. Once it was a continent free of people. Now scientists and their assistants live there, for purposes of research. There are no trees there, but lichens, mosses, algae and a few other plants grow in some areas which are without ice. There are some insects and birds. Penguins are the most important bird inhabitants of Antarctica.

The scientists who live in Antarctica belong to many different countries.

ISLANDS

Across the world, there are thousands of islands. We have already looked at some of them. Here are some others.

In the Pacific Ocean there are more than 25,000 islands. Among these there are several independent countries. Each country consists of a number of islands.

COUNTRY	CAPITAL
New Zealand	Wellington
Fiji	Suva
Kiribati	South Tarawa
Nauru	Yaren
Papua New Guinea	Port Moresby
Samoa	Apia
Solomon Islands	Honiara
Tonga	Nuku'alofa
Tuvalu	Funafuti
Vanuatu	Port Vila

SOME OTHER ISLAND COUNTRIES

COUNTRY	CAPITAL	
Federated States of Micronesia (4 states, 607 islands)	Palikir	Independent, in free association with United States
Palau (250 islands)	Melekeok	Independent, in free association with United States
Commonwealth of the Northern Mariana Islands (15 islands)	Capital hill at Saipan	Self-governing part of United States
Marshall Islands	Majuro (Delap)	Independent republic in free association with the United States
Cook Islands	Avarua	Self-governing, in free association with New Zealand
Niue	Alofi	Self-governing, in free association with New Zealand

SOME OTHER IMPORTANT ISLANDS LOCATED IN VARIOUS OCEANS

ISLAND	BELONGS TO
Easter Island	Chile
Hawaii	USA
Pitcairn Islands	UK
Falkland Islands	UK
Aleutian Islands	Alaska, USA
Galapagos Islands	Ecuador
Channel Islands	UK
Isle of Mann	UK

There are thousands of other islands. Some islands in the Arctic Ocean are on the Eurasian continental shelf, and form part of Europe or Asia. A number of these islands are under Russia. Several other islands are controlled by Denmark, Norway and Iceland.

CHANGE AND GROWTH

Countries continuously change. New ones are formed over time. Some join together, others separate. Their boundaries and type of government too change. But did you know that the whole earth and the continents too are constantly changing? In the next chapter we will look at how the earth came to be what it is today, and how life emerged.

2
The Origins

The history of the world is not just the history of the people who live in it. It includes the history of the land, water, plants, trees, insects, birds and animals. The constantly changing land and climate influences all life. Plants and animals existed long before people. Later, people influenced the land and all living creatures, and were in turn influenced by them.

In this chapter we will look at how the land formed and changed over time, and how the first living beings emerged, and the first plants and animals came into being.

IN THE BEGINNING

Once, long ago, at a time you can hardly imagine, there was an empty space. Then there was a big bang, and then very, very slowly the earth began to be formed. This big bang, according to scientists, took place 13-14 billion years ago. It released some gases which laid the base for further developments. Around 12 billion years ago, the first stars and galaxies of our universe were formed. Next followed the first supernovae, and the creation of new elements. Around 4600-4500 million years ago the sun, earth and solar system were formed. There was no life then, and the earth, too, was not as it is today.

The sun, earth and planets

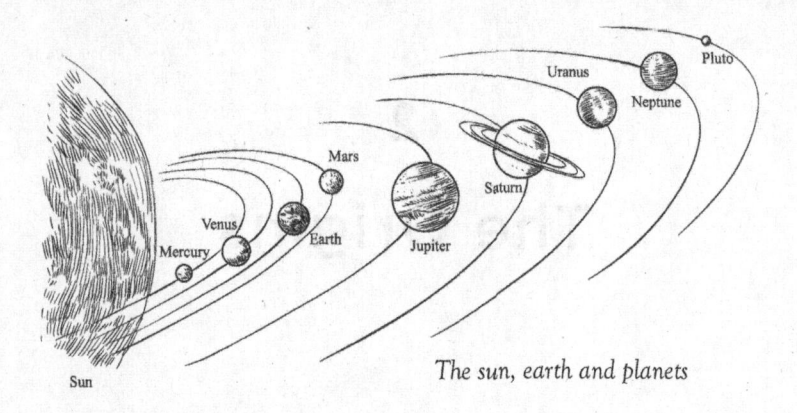

THE FIRST FORMS OF LIFE

Gradually oxygen was formed. The earliest forms of life began around 3800 million years ago. Then as oxygen began to increase in the atmosphere, single-cell organisms began to grow, and later multicellular living things. All life, including plants, animals, birds and people, gradually evolved from these first living cells. How they developed and changed is explained in the theory of evolution, given below.

EVOLUTION

Evolution means that something changes and grows over a period of time. But this is not the same as a plant growing from a seed to a tree, or a baby growing and becoming an adult. It means that a certain type or species of creature changes. For example, over millions of years, an ape gradually changes into different types of monkeys, or a simple type of human becomes more advanced, the type of human being we know today.

Charles Darwin (1809–1882) first put forward this theory.

Darwin's main ideas:

All life comes from one or more early types of organisms (single cells with life).

Different species or types of living beings then evolve or develop over millions of years.

Gradually there are millions of species or different types of living beings.

Species change and evolve over time. Some disappear.

'Natural selection' is the process by which species change and survive or die out.

The theory of 'natural selection' means that the living beings which have characteristics that give them the best chance of survival are those that evolve.

Since the time of Darwin many scientists have studied the process of evolution, to understand it better. How evolution actually happens is a very complex process. Some of the additional ideas apart from natural selection are:

Endosymbiosis: this explains how different types of organisms can join together to form new ones.

Mutations, random mutations and **genetic drift**: these refer to changes in the DNA of an organism, or in gene frequencies. These can lead to genetic changes across a whole population.

Population bottlenecks: a sudden decline in population resulting from environmental factors, leading to changes in genes.

Fossils help in understanding evolution. So does DNA. It is interesting that about 97 per cent of DNA sequences of chimpanzees and people are the same.

THE CHANGING EARTH

At the same time, as life grew and evolved, the earth too was changing. There were many stages over hundreds of millions of years, before the earth became as it is today.

The centre of the earth is very, very hot. Around it are liquid and solid layers. Above this is a thick crust called the lithosphere. On this are the continents and oceans. The lithosphere is in several pieces known as 'plates', which move and bang into one another. This causes the continents and the oceans to move.

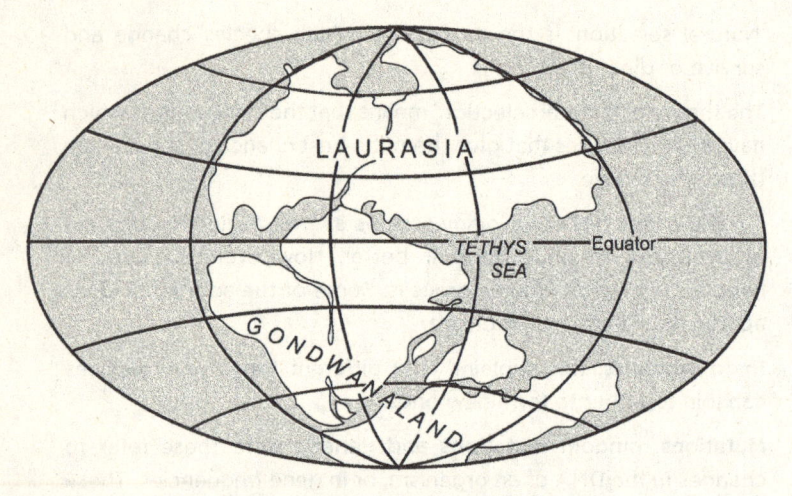

Laurasia and Gondwanaland

Once there was a huge supercontinent that scientists have named Rodinia. Before this there was another supercontinent that has been called Columbia, which was formed 2.1-1.8 billion years ago.

FROM RODINIA TO TODAY

Rodinia formed around 11,000 million years ago and broke up into three continents around 800-750 million years ago. These again joined together to form another supercontinent called Pannotia. But soon after it was formed, about 560 million years ago, Pannotia broke up into four main continents, Laurentia (North America), Baltica (northern Europe), Siberia and Gondwana.

These land masses again joined together to form one large continent. This continent has been named Pangaea. Pangaea means 'all lands', or 'the whole earth'. Two hundred million years ago, there was only one large continent—Pangaea, and one ocean, Panthalassa, which means 'all seas.'

Then once again Pangaea began to break up around 180 million years ago, into two large areas, named Gondwanaland comprising later areas of South America, Africa, Australia, Antarctica and India, and Laurasia including North America, Europe and most of Asia. Gradually these separated into the continents as we know them today. Thus the continents took hundreds of millions of years to reach their present location and form. There was so much movement that even the earth's magnetic field changed. Around 7,80,000 years ago, a compass needle would have pointed to the South Pole, instead of the North Pole, as it does today.

Even now the continents do not remain in one place, and are continuously moving. The plates continue to move a few centimetres a year. Some day, it is thought, all the continents could join together again.

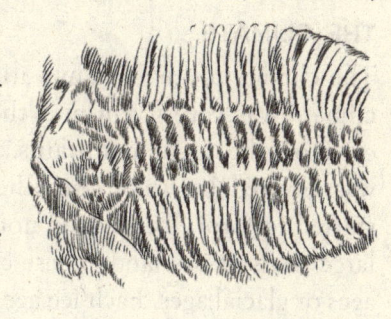

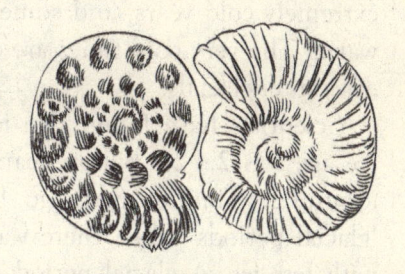

Some fossils

The movement of the plates affects us, as it creates earthquakes and volcanoes.

> Studying fossils helps in understanding the break up and joining of land masses as well as the changes in the land and oceans. For instance, marine shell fossils in the Himalayas indicate that the high mountain ranges were once a sea. Dinosaur bones found in Antarctica show it was once in a tropical zone.

THE CLIMATE

The climate too had many variations over time. At times the climate was very warm and there was no ice anywhere, not even on the high mountains. Then, more of the land area was covered by water. At other times it grew cold and ice started to form. Ice covered not only the mountains, but even large parts of the land. These cold periods were known as ice ages or glacial ages. Each ice age lasted a long time. It had some extremely cold years, and some which were less cold or even warm. The very cold times are called glacials and the warmer ones inter-glacials.

Scientists have found five ice ages in the past. The first ice age was 2.4-2.1 billion years ago. The most recent began around 2.58 million years ago. From then onwards, there were 'glacial periods' when there was more ice, and inter-glacials, with less ice. A glacial period could last 40,000 to 1,00,000 years. In Chapter 3 we will see that the time of the last ice age is when the first human-like beings had evolved. The glacial and interglacial periods had an effect on what people did and how they lived.

Apart from ice ages, there are tornadoes, hurricanes, winds, and periods of more or less rain, or volcanoes, that have an effect on life. All life is interconnected, hence anything that affects the land, animals and plants, affects people too.

PLANTS AND TREES

Around 500-435 million years ago, plants began to grow on land. But they were not the sort of plants we know today. Plants which had seeds, roots and leaves, and the first real trees, developed by the late Devonian period (about 415-350 million years ago). Flowers began about 130 million years ago.

INSECTS, ANIMALS, BIRDS, REPTILES

Insects, animals and birds also gradually evolved. Initially, life was in the ocean, then it moved on to land. Simple vertebrates, that is, animals with backbones, existed around 485 million years ago. Reptiles came into being 300 million years ago; mammals, 215-200 million years ago; and birds, 200-150 million years ago.

DINOSAURS

Though there were animals and birds living on the earth, dinosaurs were prominent from around 230-65 million years ago. Dinosaurs were a type of reptile. There were many different kinds of dinosaurs. More than a 1000 types are known. Some ate meat, others only vegetables. Some walked on two legs, others on four. Some had a kind of bony armour on their bodies which protected them. A few had horns and crests. There were dinosaurs that could fly.

Dinosaurs roamed the earth 65 million years ago

A GREAT DISASTER

Then the dinosaurs, many other larger animals and most of the birds disappeared around 65 million years ago. New types of animals began to evolve around 60 million years ago. There are different theories of this great disaster. One main theory is that an asteroid, 10 km wide, hit the earth. It landed in the present region of Mexico and created a huge crater. Dust and moisture filled the atmosphere and affected the earth's climate. This caused dinosaurs and many animals and birds to die out. There would have been huge tsunamis, earthquakes and volcanoes. There are some suggestions that a few dinosaurs survived.

Not everyone agrees with the asteroid theory.

> An asteroid is an object that orbits the sun, but is smaller than a planet.

NEW PLANTS

Grasses evolved around 35 million years ago. By 10 million years ago there were grasslands and savannahs. New types of trees and plants continued to develop.

NEW ANIMALS AND BIRDS

(Mya=million years ago; these dates are only approximate)

Here is a brief list of when some main types of animals, birds and insects evolved.

55 mya: some modern types of birds, first whales, early rodents, early mammals, including primates.

52 mya: first bats.

50 mya: tapirs, rhinoceros, camels, among others; primates diversify.

40 mya: Simiiformes, a primate group from which humans later evolved.

37 mya: *Paraceratherium*, the largest land animal.

35 mya: several modern mammals, ground sloths, dogs; among birds, the first eagles and hawks.

30 mya: earliest pigs and cats.

25 mya: first deer.

20 mya: first giraffes and giant anteaters; more types of birds.

15 mya: first bovids and kangaroos.

10 mya: diversity in insects; horses become larger; grassland mammals and snakes diversify.

5 mya: first tree sloths; hippopotamuses; grass-eating animals diversify; large and small meat-eating animals evolve; there were new types of birds.

4.8 mya: first mammoths. Mammoths were something like large hairy elephants. They had tusks and were about 3 metres tall.

4 mya: *Stupendemys*, the largest freshwater turtle.

2.5 mya: earliest species of *Smilodon* (sabre-toothed cat).

2 mya: *Bos primigenius*, ancestor of cattle, evolves in India.

Stupendemys: the largest freshwater turtle

Paraceratherium, the largest terrestrial mammal

A woolly mammoth

Roshen Dalal

> Paraceratherium, the largest land animal that ever existed, weighed 20 tonnes and had a height of 5.5 metre. It is also known as Indricotherium and Baluchitherium, and had many different species. It looked somewhat like a huge rhinoceros but had a long neck. It died out around 23 million years ago.

> **PRIMATES**
> Primates include various types of monkeys, apes and humans. Early primates were their ancestors.

PEOPLE

People were also evolving at this time, and we will look at them in the next chapter.

3
The First People

How did people come to be what they are today? Scientists believe humans evolved from a common ancestor of chimpanzees and humans. They search for fossils that will help them to find this ancestor. They also look for the ancestors of modern human beings.

IDA
A fossil dated 47 million years ago called *Darwinius masillae* (nicknamed Ida) was thought to be the common ancestor of apes and humans (found in 1983 at Messel Pit, Germany). Analysis however showed this was not correct.

The Ida fossil

TOUMAI AND MILLENIUM MAN
A fossil called *Sahelanthropus tchadensis* by scientists, and nicknamed Toumai was discovered in Chad in Africa in 2001,

and dated between 7.2 and 6.9 million years ago. Another early fossil found in Kenya in 2000 was called *Orrorin tugenensis* and nicknamed Millennium Man, dated to 6.5–5.9 million years ago. Some scientists believe these were early ancestors of humans, but others disagree.

EARLY ANCESTORS

There are many fossils of later dates that could be early ancestors of humans.

Some of them are:

Ardipithecus, with two main types:

Ardipithecus kadabba dated to 5.8–5.2 million years ago, and *Ardipithecus ramidus*, dated to 5–4.4 million years ago.

Ardipithecus types had small brains. They lived mainly on trees but could walk on two legs.

Another type is called Australopithicene or Australopithecus. There were many Australopithecus types which can be dated between 4.2 and 1 million years ago. This species were smaller than modern humans, but had some similarities. They walked on two legs.

AFRICA

Most scientists believe that all early people originated in Africa and moved from here to the rest of the world. At the time of ice ages Africa had the best climate.

HANDY MAN

After these and other early species, around 3–2 million years ago the early Homo species developed. Homo is very important, as it is the direct ancestor of modern humans. Around 2.5 million years ago a type of Homo that has been called *Homo habilis* developed. *Homo habilis* actually means 'handy man', and this name was given because he was the first human type to start making simple tools out of stone. Now instead of only using teeth and claws, these pre-humans also used tools held in their hands. Other types of humans of the Homo category too developed.

HOMO ERECTUS AND OTHER EARLY HUMANS

One type called *Homo erectus* evolved around 2-1.5 million years ago. Another was *Homo ergaster*, though some think the two are the same. All these types first developed in Africa. Groups of people of the *Homo erectus* type began to move out of Africa, and came to Asia and Europe. In Europe the earliest datable specimen of *Homo erectus* is found at Dmanisi in Georgia, dating to about 1.8 million years ago. Here there were grasslands with ostriches and giraffes, as well as other animals such as wolves and Megantereon, the sabre-toothed cat.

By one million years ago other Hominid (early human) species also spread from Africa to Asia and Europe. *Homo ergaster, Homo antecessor* (known as Pioneer Man), and *Homo heidelbergensis* were other types found in Europe. (Some scientists believe the last two are actually the same.) Early fossils and stone tools were discovered at many sites in Spain, southern France and Italy. Later these early people moved to northern Europe. Within 5,00,000 years, they were settled in the Mediterranean region.

In Britain, sharp flint tools, discovered at a beach in Norfolk have been dated to between 8,40,000 and 9,50,000 years ago. They must have flowed down an ancient course of the river Thames, and hunter-gatherers must have lived in the flood plains. At this time the animals which inhabited Britain included sabre-toothed cats, hyenas, primitive horses, red deer and southern mammoths. The climate would have been a few degrees colder than at present. There were probably thick forests, and a few hundred or a few thousand people would have lived in Britain.

These early inhabitants must have crossed to Britain by a land

Recreation of a Homo erectus and a Neanderthal man; this recreation is based on actual skulls.

bridge, connected to mainland Europe. This early population may have died out or returned to the mainland.

In Asia, early pebble stone tools dating to more than 2 million years ago have been found in Israel, Pakistan and south China. A fossil skull has been unearthed at Pemung Peninsula in Java, dating to 1.8 million years ago. More stone tools of later dates have been located in Asia, as well as fossils of *Homo erectus*. The Zhoukoudian caves of China contain fossils that indicate that *Homo erectus* people lived here from 7,50,000–2,50,000 years ago.

Animals in Southeast Asia at this time included pigs, a large vegetarian ape known as Gigantopithecus and a sort of elephant that has been named Stegodon. Bones of a gigantic hyena have been found in the Zhoukoudian caves.

There were bamboo forests in Southeast Asia, and tools may have been made of bamboo.

NEANDERTHALS (2,50,000–30,000 YEARS AGO)

Neanderthals were another Homo type, also called *Homo neanderthalensis* or *Homo sapiens neanderthalensis*. Their name comes from the Neander valley in Germany. The first Neanderthal fossils were found here. They lived in many parts of Europe and Asia. They were a species of early humans, who at first used stone tools. As the Neanderthal type was present for more than two hundred thousand years, many gradual changes occurred in their way of life. They began to wear clothes made from animal skins, and to bury the dead. They lived in caves and natural shelters, and also built simple houses. They hunted wild animals and ate their meat. They also ate wild plants, fruits and berries. They knew how to use fire.

DENISOVANS

Denisovans were another type of early humans. Their DNA has been reconstructed from a finger bone and two teeth of a girl found in Denisova cave in Siberia. They had some things in common with Neanderthals and may have interbred with other early humans. The date of the bone and teeth was somewhere between 30,000 and 80,000 years ago. Denisovans may have separated from the main evolutionary line between 1,72,000 and 7,00,000 years ago.

MODERN HUMANS

Modern humans have some differences from these early types. *Homo sapiens* is the term used for early types of modern humans, who developed by around 5,00,000 years ago. There were different types of Homo sapiens. Around 2,50,000-1,00,000 years ago, *Homo sapiens sapiens*, that is the type of people known today evolved. It is believed that these too developed in Africa. From here they went to Asia and Europe. New evidence suggests they reached Australia before 1,00,000 BCE, though earlier it was thought they reached by 60,000 BCE. In Asia and Europe they gradually replaced the earlier Neanderthals and *Homo erectus*. But there were some connections between these groups and *Homo sapiens sapiens*. They may have lived together and intermarried.

OUT OF AFRICA

Why did people move out of Africa and travel to Asia and Europe? Early people lived in groups and moved from place to place. They did not settle down in one area. Perhaps they travelled looking for food. Many of them followed migrating herds of animals, as animals were one of their sources of food. Initially people walked across the land. It is believed that they crossed a strait in the Red Sea, where at that time the water level was low, and reached Arabia. From Arabia they could walk into Asia and Europe.

Later they travelled by both land and sea. They probably used rafts and later small boats. Sea travel took place by 60,000 BCE. Recent evidence from Crete, an island located near Greece, suggests that people may even have crossed the sea much earlier, around 1,30,000 years ago. Axes and other tools of this date have been found on the southern coast of Crete. As Crete had separated from the mainland 5 million years ago, people must have reached here by sea from Africa at this time.

One has to imagine how they travelled in groups, men, women and children. Young children must have been carried. Did they take a few things with them wrapped in animal skins? From the earliest times, even 2 million years ago, they took some tools with them. Later, when early humans began wearing clothes, perhaps they carried a change of clothes as we do today?

TOOLS

All these early people used tools of stone. They may have used some other implements too, but these have disappeared with time. Because they used stone tools, the time that they lived is sometimes called 'Palaeolithic'. 'Palaeo' means old and 'lithic' means stone. At first they used large pieces of stone. These early tools were made by banging two stones together, or by hitting a smaller stone against a rock. They shaped the stone into different tools like choppers and axes. Later they made smaller and better tools. Sometimes they attached these to wood or bone handles. They used these tools to clear small spaces of trees and grass, or at times to kill animals, or to cut plants and fruit to eat.

The Palaeolithic or Old Stone Age is divided into Early, Middle and Late periods.

OLD STONE AGE	DATE	TOOL TYPES
Early	2.5 million years ago to 1,50,000 years ago	Choppers, handaxes and cleavers, flake tools
Middle	1,50,000–40,000 years ago	Points, scrapers, flake tools, microliths
Late	40,000–10,000 years ago	A variety of tools

Middle Palaeolithic: starting dates and tool types are different in different areas. In Europe the Middle Palaeolithic is thought to begin 1,80,000 years ago.

SOME COMMON TERMS

Olduwan: An archaeological term for the earliest type of stone tools.

Acheulian: An archaeological term for a type of stone tool dating from 1.5 million years ago. Handaxes are a typical Acheulian tool.

WHERE AND HOW THEY LIVED

In early times people did not make houses for themselves. They lived in caves or under rocks which projected out from the sides of a hill. These are called rock shelters. They

A CHOPPING TOOL

A chopping tool was one of the earliest types of tools made. It was made from a heavy round stone (a large pebble). The base remained round and could be held in the hand. On the top, two or more sides were chipped off to create sharp edges. These edges were used to chop and cut.

The chipped off pieces are called flakes. They could also be used as tools.

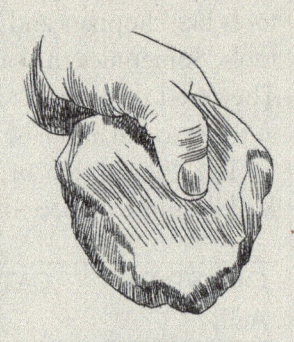

A pebble chopper

THE HANDAXE

The handaxe was a more complicated tool than the chopper. It was used for more than a million years. It was not an axe of the type used later, but a piece of stone shaped somewhat like a long triangle. The long sides and the pointed end were sharp.

With the handaxe food could be chopped better. The skin of animals could be smoothed out and used, perhaps as coverings. (It is not clear when skins were first used to make clothes.)

A handaxe

The people of Africa took the handaxe with them when they travelled to different places. And they must have crafted new ones too.

Handaxes were made in Africa 1.6 million years ago. Before one million years ago they reached Europe and Asia.

may have made simple shelters by pulling branches of trees together. They lived together in groups. They did not stay in one area, but moved from place to place. Often, they followed the herds of wild animals, which migrated during the year as the seasons changed. Sometimes they killed and ate these and other animals. At other times they ate large animals which were already dead.

Early people also ate wild fruits and plants that grew naturally. They did not grow food for themselves.

FIRE

Early people used fire to warm themselves, and later to cook food. At first they must have used fire that occurred naturally. Fire might have spread from lightning, or from dry leaves burning

OLDUVAI (OLDUPAI) GORGE

Olduvai Gorge is a ravine in east Africa, located in northern Tanzania. Its correct name is actually Oldupai, which is the name of the sisal plant that grows wild there. Here there are the remains of *Homo habilis* or handy man, and another early type of human, *Paranthropus boisei*, as well as of *Homo ergaster* (1.8 million years ago). Around this time, they killed and ate a large elephant (*Elephas recki*). Its skeleton and bones were found here, along with the bones of smaller animals. There was a butchering site and pebble stone tools such as choppers and flakes. The succeeding level, also of *Homo ergaster*, probably dating to 1.75 and 1.2 million years ago, had early handaxes. Stone tools and fossil bones continued in successive periods up to 6,00,000 years ago. Later the site was occupied by modern humans and had different tools.

in the sun. Later they learnt how to make and use fire whenever they wanted. When was fire first used for cooking? Perhaps it was around 1.5 million years ago. Burnt animal bones of this time have been found at Swartkrans, Africa.

CLOTHES

Over time their bodies changed. At first the early people were covered with fur like animals, then most of it dropped off. When they left Africa and reached Europe, they must have started feeling cold, and must have worn some kind of clothes, perhaps made from animal skins. This might have been at a very early date. Scientists have found evidence that people wore clothes from at least around 1,70,000 years ago, but they could have worn them earlier too. They discovered this from studying the DNA of lice. They found that clothing lice diverged from head lice, at least 1,70,000 years ago. And clothing lice could only exist when humans started wearing clothes.

LANGUAGE

When did people learn how to speak? How did they tell one another what they wanted? At first they must have used sounds and touch, like animals do. No one knows exactly when they learned to speak. Some scientists feel it may have been one million years ago, others, that it was much later.

Scientists have studied which part of the brain is used when tools like the handaxe are made. The same part of the brain is used when speaking. Hence scientists feel people began to speak full sentences at the time they made the handaxe, that is, at least one million years ago. At first sentences must have been short and simple. Then gradually people could speak more complicated sentences and share their thoughts and ideas.

EARLY ART
A sculpture?
There is possible evidence of an early carving of a woman on a stone pebble, from the site of Berekhat Ram in Israel. It is about 2,50,000 years old. The pebble itself is naturally shaped like a woman and some incised lines have been added. It may have been the earliest sculpture. There are other possible instances of early art. The Deipkloof rock shelter in South Africa has ostrich shells carved with designs dating to 60,000 years ago.

Painting at Blombos cave
Blombos cave is located near Cape Town, South Africa. The cave was occupied by people between 1,40,000 and 70,000 years ago. One hundred thousand years ago, there is evidence of two types of paint, red and yellow ochre, being made and used here. Ochre is a substance found in rocks. The rock had to first be broken, and the ochre removed from it and crushed. The remains at Blombos cave show that quartzite stones were used to crush the ochre into a powder. This was then mixed with charcoal, burnt and broken bone pieces, and some liquid. The paint was stored in large shells of abalones, or giant sea snails. A long bone was dipped in it, and then used for painting. It is not clear what this paint was used for, but these remains show how the paint was made. This is the earliest evidence of painting.

Geometric designs carved on ochre pieces, and mollusc beads have also been found at Blombos cave.

Australian art
In north-west Australia there are carvings on rocks that date back to before 60,000 BCE. There are also paintings of this date.

According to some scholars, modern humans, rock art and ochre seem to be present in Australia even earlier than this, 1,00,000–75,000 years ago.

QUESTIONS
Many questions remain about how exactly modern humans evolved, and the relationship between earlier humans and these modern humans. Genetic research and new discoveries could lead to a better understanding of how present humans evolved.

A GREAT CHANGE
Around 50,000 years ago, a change started taking place in the way people lived. We will look at these changes in the next chapter.

4

Changing Patterns of Life Across the World
50,000–10,000 BCE

Around 50,000 years ago, there were new developments in the world, though at the same time there was continuity with earlier days.

CLIMATE

The climate was still changing. Some parts of the world were covered in ice. Around 20,000 BCE it grew even colder, and there was more ice. In 14,000 BCE it started to grow warm, but another cold period followed from 11,000–10,000 BCE.

ANIMALS

Around 50,000 years ago there were a number of giant animals (megafauna).

After this many animal species began to die out. A few of them are mentioned here:

40,000 years ago: Megalania, giant monitor lizards die out.
15,000 years ago: last woolly rhinoceros.

11,000 years ago: all Equidae (horse family) become extinct in North America; giant short faced bears (Arctodus) vanish from North America; giant ground sloths die out.

10,000 years ago: last mainland species of woolly mammoth die out, and the last Smilodon.

PEOPLE

Homo sapiens sapiens, as we saw earlier, had already developed in Africa. They had started moving out of Africa, and before 50,000 BCE had reached Australia, Europe and Asia. Evidence from Brazil suggests they had even reached South America. At the same time, Neanderthals, *Homo erectus* and some other types of early people lived in various parts of the world. The new *Homo sapiens sapiens* mixed with these earlier people, but by 10,000 BCE, only they survived. Both *Homo erectus* and Neanderthals disappeared around 30,000 years ago.

America

Homo sapiens sapiens were probably the first people to reach America. The date when they reached there is not clear; it could be sometime after 30,000 BCE, though an earlier occupation is possible. At Pedra Furada in Brazil are rock shelters which seem to have been occupied from 60,000-32,000 years ago. Sierra da Capivara in Brazil has stone tools and charcoal dating to 50,000 years ago. These and other early sites suggest a route of coastal migration. In North America too there are some sites that suggest early occupation. Topper, in South Carolina, has a possible date of 50,000 years ago, while Meadowcroft, in Pennsylvania has a date of 16,000 years ago.

At first it was thought that people reached America around 13,000 BCE by crossing the Bering Strait from Siberia. At that time it formed a land bridge which people could walk across. But now it is clear that occupation in America took place earlier. The land bridge, connecting Siberia and Alaska, probably existed even 50,000 years ago and people may have walked across it, or they may have reached the Americas by sea.

Canada too had early settlements. Among the earliest is that of Old Crow Flats where people lived from 20,000-11,000 years ago. The site of Bluefish Caves in Yukon Territory has an occupation date of 15,000 years ago.

Pacific islands

Several Pacific islands were occupied by 30,000 BCE. At this time many of the islands were connected by land to Indonesia and to Australia, as water levels were lower because of the ice age. Two continental shelves, the Sunda Shelf of Southeast Asia which has the western Indonesian islands, and the Sahul Shelf of Australia which has some other Pacific islands, were not under water. People therefore could walk across land and reach these islands, even though sea travel was already known.

The hobbit

One type of early human, *Homo floresiensis* existed on the island of Flores in Indonesia till around 12,000 years ago. They were rather small and were only one metre tall. They have been nicknamed 'the hobbit'.

Cro-Magnon and others

Early *Homo sapiens sapiens* are known from their fossils. They were given different names depending on where their fossils were discovered.

Cro-Magnon man is named after a place in France. Here bones of five people were found, who lived about 30,000 years ago. Near them were bone and flint tools, ornaments made of seashells and animal teeth, and other items. Mungo Man was found near Lake Mungo, Australia, dating to 42,000 years ago. Minatogawa Man was found on Okinawa Island, Japan, dating to 19,000–17,000 years ago. Many more fossils have been located in different areas.

LIFESTYLE
Houses

Soon people started making homes for themselves, though they still lived in caves and natural shelters.

In eastern Europe and parts of Russia, early houses have been found made out of mammoth bones. Some of these date back to at least 25,000 BCE, while others were built later. Stones were laid to make a floor, and then mammoth bones were used to make a kind of tent, which was covered in skins. Some of the houses were quite large. At Timonovka on the river Desna, houses had roofs of logs, as well as hearths and chimneys. Inside, soft stone was cut to make a sort of a lamp, where burning fuel could be placed.

A mammoth bone hut

In some other areas, simple houses were made with tree branches or posts, mud, and clay.

Food

People hunted and ate wild animals. Among these were mammoths, bears and horses as well as small animals. They also ate birds and fish. Different types of plants too were eaten. In some areas, from around 25,000 BCE people not only ate wild plants, fruits and seeds, but began to water wild plants, remove the weeds from them, and later even to harvest them and store the grain obtained.

Towards the end of this period some animals were domesticated, that is, they were tamed.

ABRIC ROMANI—AN EARLY MEAL

Abric Romani is a place near the village of Capellades in Catalonia, Spain.

Here, in 44,000 BCE, there is evidence that a group of people who were Neanderthals, together ate a cooked meal of horse and red deer meat.

Burials

Some people began to bury their dead. Sometimes red ochre was put on the bones and various items were placed in the grave. This shows that people already had some idea that there may be life after death. In Australia, at Lake Mungo there is evidence of cremation and burial.

TESHIK-TASH: A NEANDERTHAL OR HOMO SAPIENS CHILD

In Teshik-Tash, south of Samarkand in present Uzbekistan, is the grave of a Neanderthal child that still exists, after all these years. The child was a boy, nine or ten years old. He had a large head, strong arms and shoulders, but somewhat short legs. Horns of wild goats were placed around the body. Perhaps the people believed that the child would live in another world after death. The horns must have been for his protection. Teshik-Tash has been dated between 57,000 and 24,000 years ago.

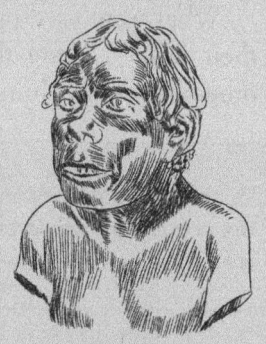

The boy from Teshik-Tash, recreated

> Another child, four years old, was buried in Abrigi do Lagar Velho, Portugal, with pierced shell and red ochre, dated to around 22,000 years ago.

Clothes and shoes

We know that clothes were worn by about 1,70,000 years ago, if not earlier. There is evidence that shoes were worn at least 70,000–40,000 years ago.

ART

We saw in the last chapter that the earliest evidence of art can be dated to 1,00,000 BCE. After 50,000 BCE more paintings were done. People painted on the walls of caves, and made small carvings or sculptures. It was not easy to paint inside caves because the interiors were dark. Some kind of a torch, like a burning log of wood, had to be used to provide light for painting inside. Paints had to be made, and some kind of a brush or implement was needed to paint with.

What were cave paintings used for? Were they to decorate their homes? Were they to communicate in some way with others? Were they hunting magic or some other form of religion?

> Painting a hunting scene and focusing on it, with the hope that the actual hunt would be successful, is a form of hunting magic. It is also called sympathetic magic.

Cave paintings have been found at many other sites. Among the more famous are: the cave paintings at the Apollo site, Namibia, Africa, dated 25,000–24,000 BCE; at Lascaux,

CHAUVET CAVE: THE FOOTPRINT OF A CHILD

The Ardeche is a river that flows in France. In its old course, there are gorges and caves in the Ardeche region of southern France. Many of the caves were occupied a long time ago. Among them is the Chauvet cave, 400 m long.

The walls of the cave are covered with paintings, which date back to 30,000 BCE. There are hundreds of paintings of animals.

The animals painted include horses, reindeer, cattle, cave lions, mammoths, rhinoceros, cave bears, bison, ibex, red deer, aurochs, Megaceros deer, musk-oxen, panthers, cave hyenas and owls.

Lines and dots were also painted on the walls. Hands, with red ochre on them, were pressed against the cave walls, leaving handprints.

Some examples of Chauvet cave paintings

In the soft clay floor of the cave, there was a footprint of a child, dated to about 25,000 BCE. At some time, bears too lived in the cave, and there are bear footprints and bones.

Dordogne, France, dated 15,000–10,000 BCE; and at Altamira in Spain, dated 14,000–12,000 BCE. In northern Australia, there are paintings on rocks that date back to at least 60,000 BCE.

Roshen Dalal

Sculptures

In the Swabian Alb region (Germany) are caves which have items carved from mammoth ivory. These include a female figurine, called the Venus of Hohle Fels (Hohle Fels is the name of the cave where it was found), a lion-headed figure and a flute. These items date between 40,000 and 30,000 years ago. Near the village of Willendorf in Austria, another female figurine was found, dated between 24,000 and 22,000 BCE. It was carved from limestone. There are other such examples of early sculptures.

Early mathematics and astronomy?

In South Africa a baboon bone has been found with marks on it. It may have been used for counting. This dates to 35,000 BCE.

At Blanchard, France, there are early carvings on bone that seem to be showing the phases of the moon.

Language

As we saw in the last chapter language may have developed one million years ago, or somewhat later. By 50,000 BCE there may have been the beginnings of different languages.

Music

As people began to speak, perhaps they also began to develop music.

Bone flutes have been found that date back to 40,000 years ago in Germany and 36,000 years ago in France. There are reports of an even earlier bone flute from Divje Babe in Slovenia. Scholars feel there may have been early musical instruments of wood and reed that have not survived. There is also a theory that stone flakes could have been used to create musical sounds.

OTHER ITEMS

People at this time used better stone tools, making them finer and more painted. They also made tools from bone and antler.

The bow and arrow was invented. They used these weapons to kill animals and even to fight with one another.

There were many different archaeological cultures at this time, which have been given various names by archaeologists. Among them was the Chatelperronian culture located in Spain and France. Arcy-sur-Cure was a site of this culture. Here, bone tools as well as teeth and pieces of ivory and bone were found. The teeth and bone and ivory pieces were carved and had small holes in them. They could be used as beads on a necklace. There were other similar sites of this culture.

A cave of Bruniquel, France, seems to have a stone structure containing a burnt bone of a bear, dated to c. 46,000 years ago.

Dyed flax fibres were found at a cave in Dzudzuana (Georgia) dating to 30,000 years ago. These may have been used for clothes.

The earliest evidence of pottery is from Xianrendong cave in China dating to about 20,000 years ago.

A MODERN LIFESTYLE

By 10,000 BCE people were doing a lot of things they do today.

They wore clothes and shoes, cooked some of their food, created art, spoke different languages, and played music.

5

The First Villages and Towns
10,000–5000 BCE

By 10,000 BCE a period of warmer weather began. Ice began to melt in many areas. The water from melted ice flowed into rivers and oceans, and covered some of the low-lying areas. This process had already started earlier. The Bering Bridge, connecting North America with Asia was covered with water around 13,000 BCE. England became an island a little later, around 8000 BCE. Before that it was connected by land to Europe, but then water submerged the land connection.

New plants grew. Forests emerged in previously ice-covered areas.

PLANT AND ANIMAL MIGRATION

There were different plants growing in the various continents and regions, depending on the climate, soil and height of the land. There were different animals too. Like people, animals and plants, too, move to different regions. Plants can be deliberately exported, or travel by chance, with seeds clinging to the clothes of people, the fur of animals or to some other item.

Animals move across land, both by themselves and along with people, and sometimes are deliberately exported or imported.

NEW WAYS OF LIFE

We saw that earlier people had been collecting wild plants and perhaps removing the weeds and watering them. In some areas they had already started planting seeds and growing plants themselves. Some people had already tamed the dog, because they found it useful. Now plants were planted and grown in many areas, and more animals were tamed or domesticated. Many of the earlier wild animals became extinct. As we saw earlier, woolly mammoths were among those that disappeared.

All over the world, small groups of people began to settle down in villages, though at the same time many continued to hunt wild animals and to collect and eat plants that grew wild. In coastal areas and near rivers, they caught and ate fish. Village settlements emerged in Asia, America, Africa and Europe. In these settlements simple houses of different kinds were built. People used stone and wood tools, as well as tools of bone and sometimes ivory. These tools were better than what they used earlier.

Many groups made pottery from clay, that is, various types of cups, bowls, vases, plates and big containers. These were baked to make them hard, and some were painted in different colours. People learnt to use copper and to make copper tools. They made small figurines of people and animals. They harvested their crops and began to store grain. Life became a little easier as they did not need to hunt for food every day. People must have spoken different languages. Some carved or drew types of symbols or lines, which had a meaning. These are called petroglyphs, and existed before writing appeared.

Music developed further. We saw that some bone flutes have been found dating back to 40,000 years ago. More advanced bone flutes dating to 7000–5700 BCE were found at the Jiahu site of the culture in China. Even after so many years, these can actually be played. Drums were also made. One was found in Moravia, dating to 6000 BCE.

Cave paintings and carved objects continued to be made. Burials were found in different regions along with grave goods.

SOME EARLY FOOD PLANTS

FOOD PLANT	REGION WHERE IT WAS FIRST GROWN	EARLIEST DATE WHEN IT WAS PLANTED
Wheat	Turkey; Iraq	9000 BCE
Chickpea	Turkey; Iraq	8500 BCE
Potatoes	Andes mountains of Peru	8000 BCE
Bottlegourd	Asia	8000 BCE
Millet	China	8000–6000 BCE
Rice	China; India	6000 BCE
Barley	Abu Hureyra; Syria	7000 BCE
Bananas	Southeast Asian islands	5000 BCE
Beans	Central America	5000 BCE
Pomegranate	Iran	3500 BCE

The Puffin History of the World

ANIMALS DOMESTICATED

Some of the earliest animals domesticated are mentioned below:

ANIMAL	PLACES WHERE IT WAS FIRST DOMESTICATED	DATE
Dog	Germany; Utah; China; Israel	12,000–6000 BCE
Sheep	West Asia; Afghanistan	8500 BCE
Cat	Cyprus	7500 BCE
Goats	Iran; Turkey; Afghanistan; Pakistan; Syria, Israel	8500–7500 BCE
Pigs	Turkey; Central Asia	7000 BCE; 11,000 BCE
Horse	Saudi Arabia; Central Asia	7000 BCE; 5500 BCE
Cattle	Israel; India; Africa	9000–7000 BCE
Guinea pig	Peru	6000 BCE
Chicken	Thailand; China	6000 BCE
Donkeys	North-east Africa	4000 BCE
Llama	Peru	3500 BCE
Alpaca	Peru	1500 BCE
Reindeer	Siberia	1000 BCE

CATTLE

Aurochs were an early and large form of wild cattle (*Bos primigenius*). Aurochs existed in India two million years ago. Some aurochs were domesticated in Mesopotamia in 10,500 BCE. Aurochs spread through Europe, Asia and Africa, but later were only found in Europe. The last auroch died in Poland in 1627.

Cattle (*Bos indicus*, humped cattle, known as zebu) were domesticated in the Pakistan region around 7000 BCE. In Africa there is early evidence of early domestication from Egypt and in the Sahara region. At this time the Sahara was not a desert as it is today. It had grasslands and there were wild cattle, gazelle, giraffes and zebras. As the climate began to grow dry, the animals moved away. Cattle were probably domesticated here at this time.

Taurine cattle (*Bos taurus*) were in Europe, but may have originated in the Fertile Crescent (the region of West Asia and the river Nile). Cattle were a form of wealth, and moved across the world along with people.

At first cattle may have been used for meat, or to carry things. Later they were used for milk and milk products, and for ploughing. The human digestive system had to change over time, in order to digest cow's milk, which was not a natural food for people. Later, the cow was considered sacred in Egypt and in India.

Cattle genome: The cattle genome has 22,000 genes. Of these, 80 per cent are found in humans.

EARLY SETTLEMENTS

West Asia had some of the earliest village settlements. There were also early settlements in Afghanistan, north-west India/Pakistan, China, Japan and other areas in Asia. In Europe farming began around 7000 BCE and spread to many areas. Africa had early village settlements in the region of the Nile valley, in the Sahara region, and in South Africa. North and South America, too, had early farming cultures.

We will look at some of the interesting places of this time.

ABU HUREYRA

One interesting place is Abu Hureyra on the banks of the River Euphrates in present Syria. This has some of the earliest evidence of agriculture. It was occupied from the Stone Age. Around

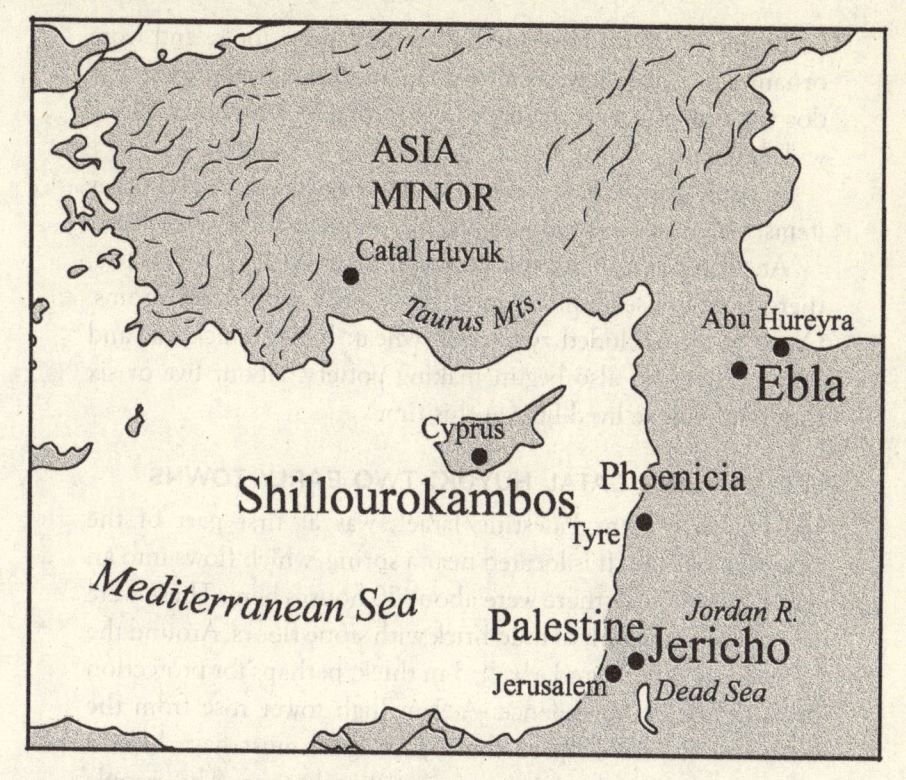

Abu Hureyra, Catal Huyuk, Jericho and Shillourokambos were among the early sites in and around West Asia.

12,000 BCE, the hunter-gatherers who lived here began to improve their way of life. They built simple houses, which at first were partly in pits below the ground. They killed wild animals for meat and collected seeds and fruit which they ate. They grew rye, lentils, and possibly wheat. The climate grew cold again, and the wild plants they ate died. Then another warm period started, and people built new houses above the ground. Abu Hureyra is part of what is called the Natufian culture. Many sites of this culture were in this region of the eastern Mediterranean, which included the present countries of Israel and Syria.

People of this culture used stone and bone tools, and wore ornaments. They made small animal and human figurines. The dog was domesticated. Pet dogs were buried in some graves along with humans.

In some graves there were a number of ornaments and other items. One grave of a woman had 50 complete tortoise shells.

At a later period at Abu Hureyra, between 7000-5000 BCE, there were houses built of mud brick, each with many rooms. Crops grown included rye, lentil, wheat, barley, chickpeas and beans. They had also begun making pottery. About five or six thousand people lived here at this time.

JERICHO AND CATAL HUYUK: TWO EARLY TOWNS

Jericho, in present Palestine/Israel, was at first part of the Natufian culture. It is located near a spring, which flows into an oasis. By 8500 BCE there were about 70 houses here. These were round and were built of mud brick with stone floors. Around the houses was a ditch, and a wall, 3 m thick, perhaps for protection from floods or for defence. A 9 m high tower rose from the wall, and steps led up to the top of it. It must have been a watchtower. The people grew wheat, barley and pulses, and hunted and ate wild animals.

Around 7000 BCE there were new developments. Rectangular houses were made, more crops were grown, and sheep and goats were domesticated.

There may have been some ancestor worship, that is, prayers to the

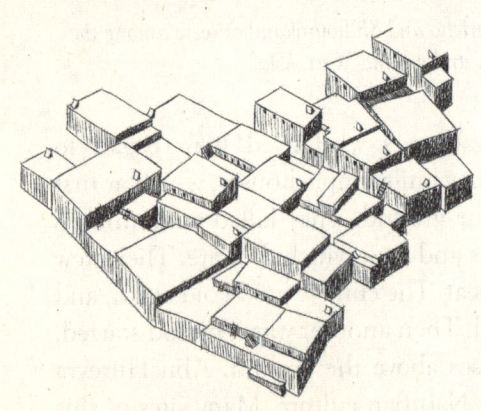

A recreation of houses at Catal Huyuk: a view of the roofs

dead. Skulls were covered in plaster to look real, and cowry shells marked the eyes.

Catal Huyuk in Turkey was another early town. It was first settled around 8000 BCE. By 6000 BCE it covered an area of 13 hectares. Houses were made of wood and mud brick, and were close together without any doors. Entry and exit was through the roof, and a ladder was used for this. Inside, the walls and floors were plastered. Reed mats covered the floor. Clay platforms and benches were in the main room, where people must have sat. There was a hearth for cooking.

Cereals, pulses and flax were grown, and linen was woven from flax. People were buried beneath the floor of the houses. Some houses had shrine rooms with paintings on the walls. At Catal Huyuk there were objects of different kinds, made of turquoise, copper and shell, as well as of wood and bone. Baskets and pottery too were made.

MAQAR CULTURE

The Arabian peninsula has early settlements. Recent excavations indicate that there was a civilization there, which is called the Maqar civilization or culture. It is named after the site of Maqar, near Abha in Saudi Arabia. Maqar probably dates back to 7000 BCE, and has the first evidence of domesticated horses. Other items found there include mummified skeletons, arrowheads, grinders to grind grain and tools of various kinds including those used for spinning and weaving.

SHILLOUROKAMBOS—A PET CAT

Cyprus is an island, about 70 km south of Turkey. It had some early village settlements. These include those at Kastros, Shillourokambos and Tenta. The houses in the villages were round; the floors were made of burnt lime. Water wells in western Cyprus date back to at least 8000 BCE, the oldest in the world. At Shillourokambos are the remains of a grave of a person, along with a cat, of about 7500 BCE. It is the earliest evidence of a domesticated cat in the world. The cat or kitten was about eight months old and the human buried with it was around 30 years old. The grave also contained a seashell, a polished stone pendant, an ochre fragment, flint tools and two stone axes. Cat remains have also been found in other Cyprus villages of the same period. They were not associated with human graves and must have been untamed cats.

Cyprus was settled by farmers from the mainland who brought with them both plants and animals. Cats, pigs, goats, dogs, sheep and cattle were all transported to Cyprus and are not native there.

Foxes and Persian fallow deer were also introduced by settlers, and were unknown before on the island. It is not known how these animals reached here. Perhaps they came by boat, in a sort of Noah's ark. The local animals, which were dwarf elephants and pygmy hippos, gradually died out with the arrival of people and animals from the mainland.

AMERICA: CLOVIS CULTURE

This culture is named after a town in New Mexico, USA. It dates from around 11,000 BCE. Clovis tools included fluted spear points, spearheads, bone points and flake tools. Fluted points are considered typical of the Clovis culture.

These tools were used to hunt mammoths and early large forms of bison, mastodon, sloths, llama and other animals. The Clovis culture lasted about 500 years. Clovis sites are found all over the USA, northern Mexico and southern Canada. Some of the important sites are Gault in Texas, Murray Springs in Arizona, Cactus Hill in Virginia, Blackwater Draw in New Mexico, East Wenatchee in Washington, Shawnee Minisink in Delaware and Charlie Lake Caves in British Columbia. Gault is the largest site.

There were pre-Clovis sites from which the Clovis probably developed. It was once thought the people of the Clovis culture were the first occupants of North America but recent discoveries show that this is unlikely.

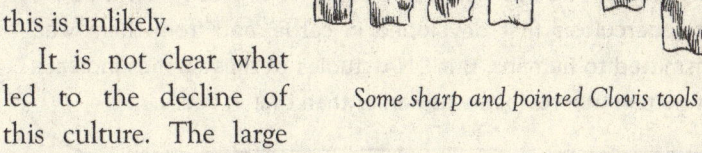

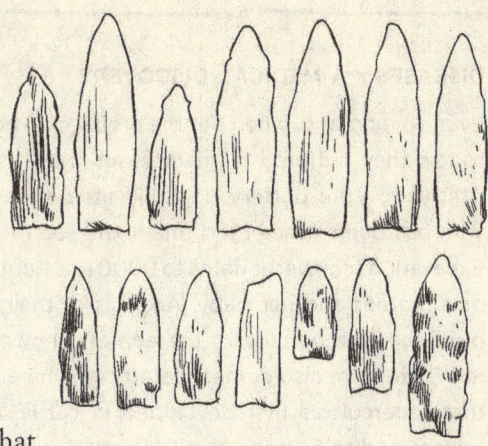

Some sharp and pointed Clovis tools

It is not clear what led to the decline of this culture. The large animals seem to have suddenly died out, possibly through over-hunting. A shortage of animals to hunt may have contributed the end of the culture. Several sites end with a 'black mat' or black covering of organic matter. One theory is that an asteroid hit Canada. This led to fires in the dry regions of North America, causing this mat.

There were many other villages and settlements across the world.

COPPER—THE FIRST METAL USED

There were different stages in the world in the use of metals. Copper was the first metal to be used. A copper pendant of north Iraq dates to 8700 BCE.

Copper smelting sites date back to about 4500 BCE in the Middle East, present Egypt, Israel and Jordan. Copper was known in Iran and India around the same time.

DISEASES—A MEDICAL DISCOVERY

Even so long ago, when people probably lived a healthier life than today, they suffered from diseases. Here is one example from Atlit-yam, a pre-pottery Neolithic site on the coast of Israel. Atlit-yam has been submerged under the sea for thousands of years. Excavations showed it dates to 9000 BCE. Here there were skeletons of a mother and her baby. Analysis of their bones indicates the presence of tuberculosis, the earliest known evidence of this so far. There were also domesticated cattle here. Usually, it is thought that tuberculosis first developed in cattle, and from them was transmitted to humans. But DNA studies of these bones indicate that human tuberculosis was earlier than that in cattle.

MEGALITHS

A megalith is a large stone (mega=large; lith=stone). In Europe and in other parts of the world, large stones were used in buildings or graves or for other purposes. Some were in memory of things that had happened. Sometimes tall stones were placed in a circle.

There are different types of megalithic structures.

A menhir is a single large standing stone.

A stone circle has several large stones in a circle.

Chamber tombs were graves made of large stones where people were buried. These

An early megalith from Gobekli Tepe, Turkey

included single graves, called dolmens; passage graves where the tomb was approached by a passage; gallery graves, which were long and rectangular. The earliest megaliths are in Turkey, dating to between 9000 and 8000 BCE. Gobekli Tepe is one of the main megalithic sites in Turkey. Here there are about 20 stone circles. The stones are carved with various creatures including boars, foxes, lions, birds, snakes and scorpions.

Why did people erect megaliths? Some have seen them as aspects of a widespread religious movement. Others analyse them to show the builders knew about mathematics and astronomy. Another theory is that they may have marked community boundaries.

6

The Rise of Cities: Mesopotamia 5000–1500 BCE

Across the world people still lived in different ways. Some lived in caves and rock shelters, or made very simple houses. As they had done earlier, the people hunted a few animals, and ate plants and fruits that grew in the wild. Other were living in villages, growing crops and keeping animals. In a few areas, towns had already developed. Some of these towns became cities.

WHAT IS A CITY CIVILIZATION?

A city: To start with we have to understand what a city is. A city is actually a large town. Both towns and cities are places where people live, who have different occupations, that is, they do different types of work. These people may be may be officials or administrators, soldiers, or merchants, weavers or carpenters. Farmers too may live there, and some crops may be grown, but usually there is no large-scale agriculture in a city.

Villages exist some distance away from the city. There too

people have different occupations, but many of them are farmers. Farmers grow crops such as wheat, rice, vegetables and cotton, harvest them and send the grain to the city. In return, they get money or something else as payment.

Civilization: Civilization is a term that refers to an advanced or 'civilized' way of life. People know how to read and write, and can appreciate art and culture.

A city civilization is thus a way of life where people lived in both cities and villages and had an advanced type of culture.

The first city civilizations were in Mesopotamia, Egypt, India-Pakistan, China, Greece, Mesoamerica and along the Mediterranean coast, though there were towns and cities in other areas too. These city civilizations did not suddenly appear, but gradually grew from villages. We will look at each of them in turn, and then see what they had in common.

HOW CITIES DEVELOP

Usually, cities and towns develop when the people living in villages grow or produce plenty of food. When there is more food than villagers can eat, they store the grain from the harvest. They do not have to go looking for food every day. Then some people start doing different things, like making jewellery, pottery, copper objects and other items. There is more time for people to get together to talk, eat, listen to music or to watch dances and plays. Buildings and common areas are made for all this, and thus a town or city develops. Four of the early city civilizations were in fertile river valleys, as it is in such land that more food could be produced. Some villages became cities because they were centres on the routes of trade.

MESOPOTAMIA

Mesopotamia is the old name of a region between the Tigris and Euphrates rivers. It included the area where the country of

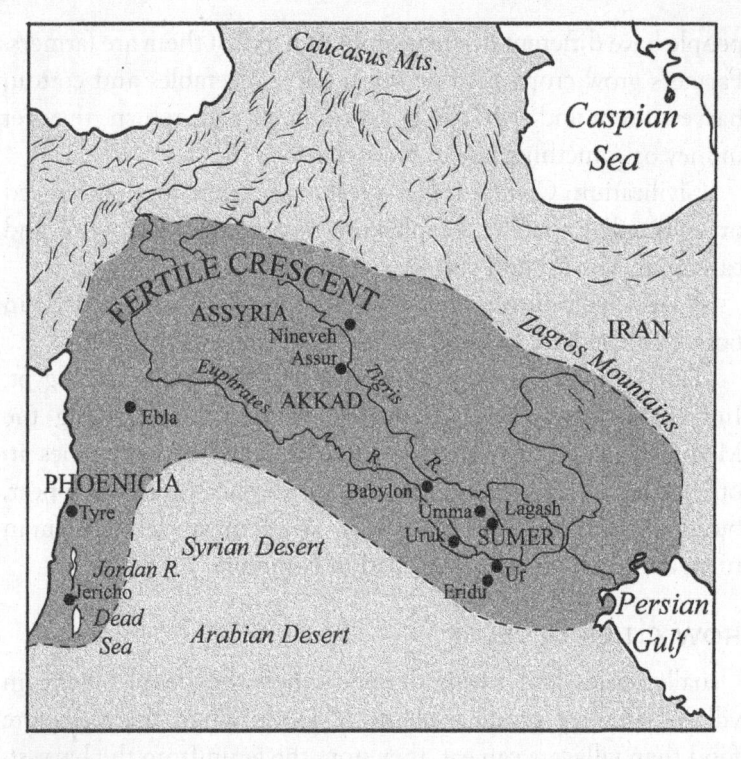

Mesopotamia with main cities

Mesopotamia: the region and main cities

Iraq is located today, as well as part of Turkey and Syria. The Tigris and Euphrates start in Turkey, and flow into the Persian Gulf. In Iraq they are about 150 km apart, with fertile land between them.

In this area there were farming villages even before 10,000 BCE. Pottery was made and used by around 7000 BCE. Gradually the villages grew larger, and some became towns and cities. Among the early cities of Mesopotamia, some were in the north and others in the south. In northern Mesopotamia, early cities were at Tell Hamoukar and Tell Brak, among other places.

SUMER

The southern region came to be known as Sumer, as the Sumerians were the main people there after 3250 BCE. But cities existed even earlier. The city of Uruk was flourishing by 3500 BCE. Between 3000 and 2500 BCE, Ur and Nippur were other important cities. Sumerian cities are known as city states, as each was a separate state, with its own government. Initially there may have been some kind of democratic government, but later, from around 2900 BCE there were dynasties of kings. Each city state had its own dynasty. The city state included some farmland around it. The cities had a number of buildings. In the centre was the ziggurat, a temple with its chief god. There were different gods in every city. Around the temple there were public buildings. Then there were houses for the people who lived there. Important people lived in buildings with two storeys, others in single-storied houses. All these buildings were made of sun-dried bricks. Some buildings were very large and had columns and terraces.

Priests, merchants and traders, shopkeepers, craftspersons and government officials lived in these buildings. Ordinary labourers, farmers and fishermen lived in poor structures.

These city states often fought against one another. Sometimes one state became powerful and took over other states.

Barley, wheat, millet and sesame were among the crops grown. The land in the region was fertile, but irrigation too was used. The food grown was enough for all the people.

ITEMS MADE

In this region, different types of pottery were made. Some were made with the potter's wheel. By 3000 BCE, the wheel began to be used for transport.

There are no sources of metal in Mesopotamia. Metal or metal objects were obtained from trade with Syria, Iran, Bahrain and India. By 2500 BCE supplies of tin from places nearby were exhausted and weapons were then made from copper.

Among other items made were carved cylinder seals, objects of copper, such as copper sculptures, vases, and daggers, and stone sculptures. Flax was woven and made into linen.

Sculptures and paintings depicted everyday life or various events. There are battle scenes, victory scenes and illustrations of processions and banquets.

The Standard of Ur (c. 2700 BCE)

Beautiful items have been found in the graves of Mesopotamia. 'The Standard of Ur' was discovered from the royal graves at Ur by an excavator named Leonard Wooley. He thought it may have been carried in battle, but no one really knows what it was used for. It is actually a narrow, tapering wooden box. Both the front and the back have three rows of illustrations. Some scenes show tribute being paid to a king; others show processions of some kind. Shell, lapis lazuli and various stones have been inlaid to create these scenes.

The Standard of Ur

The golden goats

Another beautiful sculpture discovered from the royal cemetery at Ur is of two goats near a golden tree. Gold, silver, shell and lapis lazuli were used to make the goats.

Religion

There were many gods and temples. Enlil was the god of air. He separated heaven and earth, with air between them, and created the universe. He was also the god of storm and wind. Anu and Enki were other male gods. Anu was the father of other gods including Enlil. Enki was the god of wisdom and of sweet waters.

A typical ziggurat

The ziggurat or temple consisted of a platform and a stepped tower. They were built of sun-baked mud bricks and decorated with coloured and glazed bricks.

Writing, language and education

Cuneiform writing gradually developed in Sumer, by around 3300 BCE. It was one of the first writing systems in the world.

Even before this, cylinder seals were made with pictures or drawings on them. The earliest writing, consisting of pictograms, was found on clay tablets, written in the Sumerian language. These pictograms mainly listed goods or were records of receipts. The cuneiform developed from this. Cuneiform means 'wedge-shaped'. A reed pen was used for writing. This gave a wedge shape to the lines forming the letters. The reed pen carved the letters on clay tablets, that is, on pieces of clay. These were then dried in the sun or baked, and because of this the writing has remained for thousands of years.

Now the government could keep records. Even stories could be written.

> Pictogram: a picture or drawing that has a meaning.

Edubba

Schools were known as edubbas. Edubba means 'House of tablets'. Boys from rich and wealthy families went to these schools and learnt to read and write on clay tablets. Some girls from rich families also studied in these schools, though they were very few. Students sat on brick benches. Apart from reading and writing they learnt grammar and geography. Students attended these schools for many years.

THE EPIC OF GILGAMESH

Gilgamesh was a king of Uruk in Mesopotamia. He ruled in about 2650 BCE. His life and adventures are described in a story written on clay tablets. There are many versions of this story or epic, about this great king. The earliest version was written in around 2000 BCE.

According to the story, Gilgamesh was the son of King Lugalbanda and the goddess Ninsun. When Gilgamesh became the king he built the strong walls of the city of Uruk. He also constructed the temple of the god Anu and the goddess Ishtar in the city.

But Gilgamesh became very proud and dominating, hence the gods sent Enkidu to teach him to behave better.

Enkidu was created by a goddess and looked and behaved like a wild creature. He saved and protected all the animals in the forest. But after he was attracted to a priestess, he became like a human being and forgot about saving animals.

Enkidu and Gilgamesh were good friends. Together they had many adventures. Gilgamesh wanted to be immortal. He found a plant that would make him young again but finally lost it.

He understood that he had many strengths and powers, but that no one could live forever.

This epic is a mix of fact and fiction.

SARGON I

Mesopotamian city states fought wars against one another. In 2334 BCE, Sargon I of the city of Akkad, conquered Mesopotamia. The Akkadians had their own language which they introduced in the region. Under the Akkadians the area was more united. After about 200 years, the Akkadians were defeated.

CONFLICT AND CONFUSION

Many other people fought for control in this region. For a brief period there was another Sumerian dynasty, before it too was defeated.

BABYLON

Hammurabi of Babylon ruled from 1792 BCE and unified the whole region of Mesopotamia. Among the cities at this time were Nineveh and Nimrud on the river Tigris, and Mari on the Euphrates. A great palace was built at Mari which had more than 300 rooms.

Hammurabi created a code of law which had 282 articles or statements on different topics. These laws were engraved in stone and set up in different places. The laws promised justice to all.

MARDUK

Marduk was the main god of Babylon. Soon he became the most important god in Mesopotamia.

Marduk is described in the *Enuma Elish*, a book first written on clay tablets around 1000 BCE. According to this, Marduk was the son of the gods Ea and Damkina. He was born fully grown. He had four eyes and four ears, to see and hear everything in the world. There were halos around his head. This book or epic describes how Marduk became the most powerful of all the gods.

Hammurabi's successors ruled till about 1590 BCE. The Hittites, another dynasty, conquered Babylon at this time. Other kings and dynasties ruled in different areas of Mesopotamia.

ASSYRIANS

Around 1000 BCE the Assyrians became the main ruling dynasty.

Ashurbanipal (ruled 668–627 BCE) was an important Assyrian king. His territory extended beyond Mesopotamia to Egypt, and the present regions of Iran and Turkey.

LIBRARIES

Today, libraries have books, and sometimes Internet and computers.

Long ago libraries consisted of clay tablets, on which books, records and stories were written.

King Ashurbanipal had a library at Nineveh. It contained more than 30,000 clay tablets with writing.

There was another library in the city state of Ebla, which had 20,000 clay tablets. Ebla is modern Tell Mardikh in Syria.

SCIENCES

Mathematics and other sciences developed in the region from the time of the Sumerians. Fractions, algebra, quadratic equations and geometry were known.

Astronomy and the position of the stars were studied. By 1000 BCE, lunar eclipses were predicted.

During this long period the cuneiform script developed in different ways. At first it was pictographic, but gradually became syllabic.

CONTINUITY IN ART AND CULTURE

Though there were so many different dynasties in the region, there was continuity over this long period in art, culture and trade.

METALS—THEIR USE IN THE WORLD

We saw that copper was the earliest metal used.

Gold and silver were first used to make items between 4000 and 3000 BCE. Gold items of this date were found from the Nahal kana cave cemetery in Israel and from the Balkans. Silver slag from surface mining has been found in Asia Minor and Aegean Sea islands from the fourth millennium BCE.

Bronze, consisting of copper alloyed with tin, was used from around 3000 BCE.

Iron began to be used from around 3500 BCE, but its use became widespread after 1500 BCE.

7
Early Egypt

Egypt in north Africa, in the fertile plains of the river Nile, had a great civilization. The Nile begins south of Egypt, in the mountains of Ethiopia. It flows northwards 1000 km to the Mediterranean Sea.

THE EARLY PERIOD

The area of Egypt can be divided into two regions, of north and south. By 5000 BCE craftsmen of south Egypt were making copper objects and fine pottery. These and other items were bought and sold at market centres. People here knew how to make boats from papyrus, and to use hard materials like basalt. Around the market centres, there were villages. By 3500 BCE, Egypt traded with other areas, mainly with Mesopotamia. Sculptures and bas reliefs began to be carved, and the use of copper objects spread. Egyptian hieroglyphic writing was known. There were two separate kingdoms in north and south Egypt.

KING MENES

In about 3100 BCE, King Menes of the south conquered the north and Egypt was united. A period of great development began.

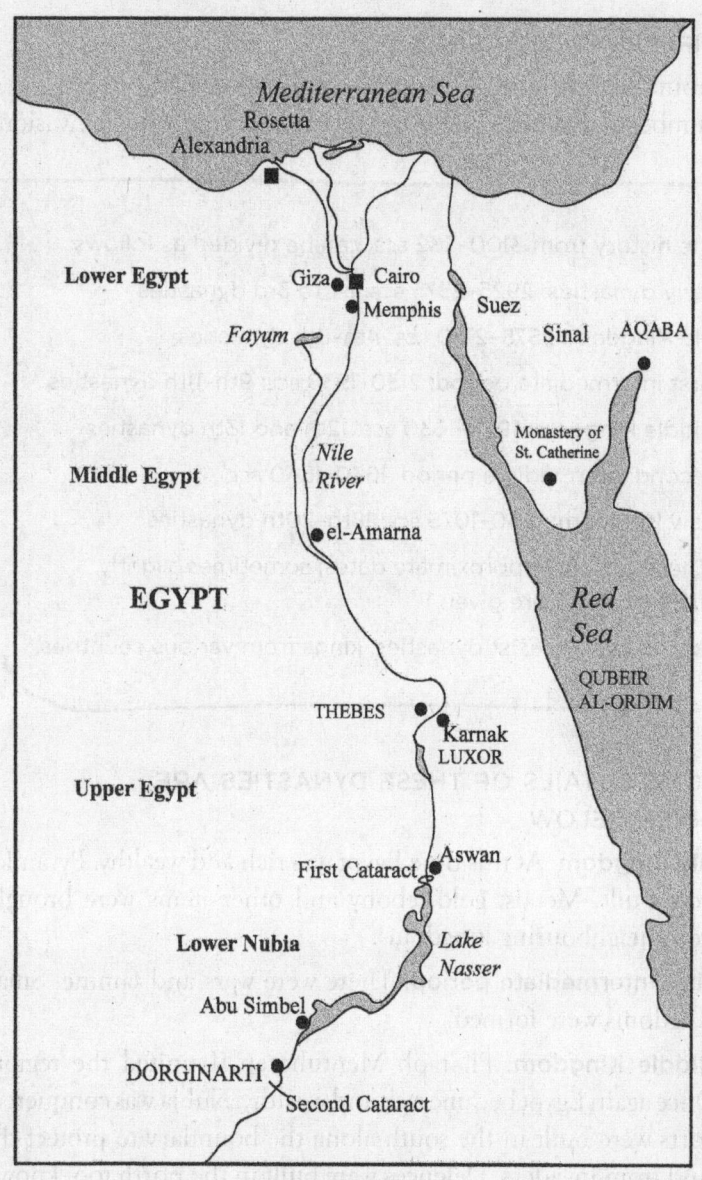

Ancient Egypt

DIFFERENT DYNASTIES

From this time until Alexander's conquest of Egypt in 332 BCE, a number of dynasties ruled, and there were some foreign invasions.

> The history from 3100–332 BCE, can be divided as follows:
>
> Early dynasties: 2925–2575 BCE: 1st to 3rd dynasties
>
> Old Kingdom: 2575–2130 BCE: 4th–8th dynasties
>
> First intermediate period: 2130–1938 BCE: 9th–11th dynasties
>
> Middle Kingdom: 1938–1630 BCE: 12th and 13th dynasties
>
> Second intermediate period: 1630–1540 BCE
>
> New Kingdom: 1540–1075 BCE: 18th–20th dynasties
>
> (These are only approximate dates; sometimes slightly different dates are given.)
>
> Later days: 21st–31st dynasties: kings from various countries.

SOME DETAILS OF THESE DYNASTIES ARE GIVEN BELOW

Old Kingdom: At this time Egypt was rich and wealthy. Pyramids were built. Metals, gold, ebony and other items were brought from neighbouring kingdoms.

First intermediate period: There were wars and famine. Small kingdoms were formed.

Middle Kingdom: Pharaoh Mentuhotep II united the region. Once again Egypt became rich and wealthy. Nubia was conquered. Forts were built in the south along the boundary to protect the land from invaders. Defences were built in the north too, known as the Walls of the Rulers. Egyptian traders reached Syria and Palestine. They also crossed the Red Sea in ships.

Second intermediate period: Then again there was civil war and foreign invasions. The Egyptians called the invaders Hyksos, meaning 'kings of foreign lands'. Later the Hyksos were defeated and the new kingdom began.

New Kingdom: This was the best time, when Egypt was the most rich and prosperous. Egypt again conquered Nubia in the south. Canaan (Israel-Palestine region) too was conquered. Great buildings were made, and there were new developments in religion. There was trade with Greece, Crete, Syria and Phoenicia. Silver was among the items imported. It was very precious to the Egyptians, as it was not found in Egypt.

Later days: A decline followed. There were numerous invasions from Nubia, Assyria, Babylon and Iran. Finally Alexander reached here. He defeated the Persians who were then ruling the region and Egypt came under the Greeks. We will look at the history of Egypt after Alexander in Chapter 13.

THE KINGS

Egyptian kings were considered gods. 'Pharaoh' was a title given to them during the New Kingdom, but now it is used for earlier kings too. Before the New Kingdom, pharaoh, meaning 'great house' referred to the royal court and palaces.

The pharaohs were helped by nobles, hundreds of administrators and scribes (official writers), who wrote and recorded events.

Some important pharaohs:

Menes: the first king. Narmer may be an earlier king, or it could be another name of Menes.

Zoser: a king of the 3rd dynasty.

Khufu: a king of the 4th dynasty, known for his great pyramids.

Amenemhet I: a king of the 12th dynasty; he reunified the country from Thebes.

Ahmose I: founded the 18th dynasty in 1540-39 BCE, and unified the region.

Tuthmosis I: a king of the 18th dynasty, ruled 1493–c.1482 BCE; he made the first underground tombs.

Amenhotep II: ruled c.1426–1400 BCE; he built a temple at Luxor dedicated to the god Amun-Re.

Amenhotep IV: took the name Akhenaton. He ruled from 1353–1336 BCE. Akhenaton made the worship of the sun god Aton important. He built a new city called Akheteton (Amarna). His chief wife was Queen Nefertiti. She was very beautiful. Many sculptures and engravings of her have been discovered. Nefertiti and Akhenaton had six daughters.

Tutankhamun: ruled c.1332–1323 BCE; a boy king of the 18th dynasty. Akhenaton's son-in-law, Tutankhamun became king at the age of nine. During his reign three gods, Amon, Re and Ptah were prominent. Tutankhamun is famous because of his rich tomb.

Hatsheput: queen of the 18th dynasty.

Rameses II: a king of the 19th dynasty, ruled from c.1279–1213 BCE; he built a temple at Abu Simbel. The temple has sculptures of the seated king.

Tutankhamun

Seated statues of Rameses II at the entrance of a temple at Abu Simbel. The temple was carved around 1250 BCE.

> DNA tests suggest that Tutankhamun's wife, Akhesenamun was his half-sister. His parents were brother and sister. But some scientists do not agree with these test results.

DISTRICTS

There were 42 nomes or districts in Egypt. Each had its own officials and its own gods.

CITIES

Memphis, the capital of the Old Kingdom, and Thebes, the capital of the new kingdom, were among the great cities. The cities had huge public buildings built of stone, which included palaces. A number of temples too were built.

Houses of ordinary people were built of mud brick. They were plastered on the outside and the inside. Within, the walls were often painted in different colours. The rich lived in big houses surrounded by gardens. Their houses were often furnished with beds, couches and tables.

PYRAMIDS AND TOMBS

Pyramids were among the greatest buildings. They were triangular shaped, soaring above the ground. Within them were tombs for the kings. Nearby there were other buildings, where it was believed that the king would live after his death. There was thus a clear belief in life after death. Before being put into the tombs the dead were embalmed. Embalming was a process of preserving the bodies. The embalmed bodies were known as mummies. The mummies were put in decorated wooden coffins and then in stone sarcophagi (tombs) and buried in the pyramids. At least 80 pyramids have been found in different places.

MUMMY

Why are the embalmed bodies called mummies? Mummy is an English word. It was not a term used in Egypt. It comes from the Latin word *mumia*. This is from the Persian word 'mum' which means wax and the Arabic and Persian word *mumiyah* for bitumen. This means a body preserved in wax or bitumen. This was not the method used in Egypt for preserving bodies. In the long process of embalming, the early Egyptians used natron, a mineral salt, along with oils and other items.

Apart from people, more than one million animal mummies have been found in Egypt. They include hippopotamuses, gazelles, crocodiles, dogs, lions, donkeys, hawks, ibis, but mostly cats. Cats were worshipped. Usually, people were not allowed to kill cats. They were punished if they did so. But at the same time, kittens and cats were offered in sacrifice to the cat goddess, Bastet. Thousands of cats were sacrificed to the goddess. Hundreds of thousands of cat mummies have been found.

The earliest mummies are not from Egypt. They are found in the Atacama desert of Peru and date back to at least 5000 BCE.

At Giza: the Great Sphinx. This and one of the pyramids in the picture were constructed by the Pharoah Khafre; the other pyramid was made by the Pharoah Khufu.

THE PYRAMID OF PHAROAH KHUFU

At Giza some great pyramids were built. Among the greatest is the pyramid of Pharaoh Khufu (also known as Cheops). It was made of two million blocks of stone, which together must have weighed five to six million tonnes. This huge pyramid has sides which are 232 m long. Near this pyramid a 43-m-long boat with oars was found. Perhaps it was believed that the Pharaoh could use this to travel to the other world.

Along with two other pyramids here, this pyramid was considered one of the seven wonders of the ancient world.

THE VALLEY OF KINGS

At the time of the new kingdom, the pharaohs' tombs were cut into rock, in a place near Thebes, known as the Valley of the Kings. The rich grave of Pharaoh Tutankhamun is located here.

TUTANKHAMUN'S TOMB

Tutankhamun's tomb is entered through a passage, leading into four rooms or chambers. The walls of the rooms are covered in paintings. The rooms contain fine furniture, chariots, weapons, statues and other items. Tutankhamun's mummy was inside three coffins, which were in the shape of his body. The outer coffin was made of wood, covered with gold foil, decorated with gods, goddesses, leaves and flowers. The second coffin too, was of wood covered with gold foil, and profusely decorated. The third and innermost coffin was of gold. Tutankhamun's face was covered with a gold mask. Today his mummy is displayed in a glass box within his original tomb.

LIFESTYLE

Around the cities were villages, where crops were grown. The Nile deposited rich silt, making the area fertile, but it would sometimes flood. Canals brought water to the fields. The main

> **SEVEN WONDERS OF THE ANCIENT WORLD**
>
> Early travellers, particularly Greeks, listed some monuments that they thought were the best in the world. These were:
>
> The great pyramids at Giza; the Hanging Gardens of Babylon; the Temple of Artemis at Epheseus; the statue of Zeus in Olympia; the Mausoleum at Halicarnassus; the Colossus of Rhodes; the Pharos lighthouse in Alexandria.

crops grown were vegetables, barley, wheat and flax. Beans, chickpeas, lentils, dates and fruits including figs and grapes were also grown. Cattle were used for ploughing the fields. Because of irrigation, two or more crops could be grown throughout the year.

Cattle, sheep, pigs, goats and chickens were kept. Some of these were used for food. Fish, found in the river Nile, was also eaten. Wild animals like gazelle were hunted. Wine was brewed and drunk. Donkeys were used to carry items on land. Boats were used for transport on the river. Boats had sails and oars.

There were crafts of all kinds. There was fine pottery, jewellery, items of metal, glass and stone. Flax was woven to make cloth.

Men wore short wrap-around kilts, while women wore long dresses and tunics. Both wore jewellery.

There were many holidays and festivals. Dancing and music was popular. Flutes, trumpets, harps and lutes, and clappers were used.

Wrestling and boxing matches were organized, as well as races.

People visited beerhouses, where along with food and drink, there was dancing, music and games.

OCCUPATIONS

People had different occupations. Administrators and scribes were the most important. Scribes were those who wrote the records.

> **A SPECIAL MEAL**
>
> Ordinary people usually ate simple food such as bread made from ground grain. The rich ate differently. From a noble's grave, this menu was found for his funeral feast: porridge, quail, pigeon, boiled fish, beef, kidneys, bread, cakes, stewed fruit and cheese.

Priests of the temples were powerful.

Most ordinary people were farmers or farm labourers. Others were craftsmen or traders. There were boatmen for the boats on the river. Women generally looked after the house but some also wove textiles. Some women were entertainers. They danced and played music.

SCRIPT AND WRITING

Egypt had two types of writing: hieroglyphic and hieratic. The hieroglyphic, which had picture symbols, was used on monuments. The hieratic was a more simple script. Papyrus reeds were made into sheets like paper, and were used to write on. Egyptian hieroglyphics, over 5000 years ago, were the world's first script. Evidence suggests it existed by 3250 BCE, at least 150 years earlier than the Sumerian.

EDUCATION

Scribes studied in special schools to learn how to write. Only children of rich people were educated. Simple mathematics, science, astronomy and medicine were also studied. A 365-day calendar was known.

TRADE AND COMMERCE

Trade was through barter, that is, the exchange of goods. Egypt exported grain, linen and papyrus. Wood for building

> **MATHEMATICS IN EGYPT**
>
> A papyrus scroll, later called the Rhind Papyrus, dated to 1650 BCE, is a text for teaching basic mathematics. It includes 84 problems along with their solutions. One problem is given below:
>
> Problem 79: There are seven houses. In each house there are seven cats. Each cat has killed seven mice. Each mouse has eaten seven grains of barley. Each grain would have produced seven hekat of barley. What is the total of all these?
>
> Answer:
> Houses: 7
> Cats: 49
> Mice: 343
> Grains of barley: 2401
> Hekats of barley: 16807
> Total: 19607
>
> (Another way to solve the problem is also given.)

and furniture was brought from Lebanon. Copper came from Cyprus. Semi-precious stones were brought from different places, including far away Afghanistan. Silver, monkeys and incense were among other imports.

ART

Egyptian art was quite realistic. Paintings on walls of houses, tombs and temples, show scenes from everyday life. Sculptures were carved.

RELIGION

Large temple complexes were attached to the pyramids. The Egyptians had a number of gods and goddesses. The sun god Ra or Re, later Amon-Re, was one of the most important. Some

An illustration of the gods Anubis and Thoth from an early painting

gods were associated with animals, and were shown with animal or bird heads. Each city and village had its own gods. Some of the important gods were:

Ptah: god of creation
Osiris: god of the underworld
Isis: goddess, wife of Osiris
Mut: goddess of the sky
Horus: god of the sky; associated with the falcon
Anubis: god of the dead; associated with the jackal
Thoth: god of the moon, associated with the ibis
Bast or Bastet: goddess of love and fertility, associated with the cat.

8
India
3500 BCE–500 BCE

India and Pakistan, known as India to the Greeks, was occupied from the Stone Age. It had early farming settlements dating back to 7000 BCE.

A CITY CIVILIZATION

Between 2600–1900 BCE a great city civilization developed. This has been called the Harappan civilization, named after the city of Harappa, or the Indus civilization, because the cities that were first discovered were in the Indus plains. It is now also called the Indus-Sarasvati civilization, as a number of other settlements have been found along the ancient river Sarasvati.

These cities emerged in the north-west plains, where the river Indus flows, and extended south and east. In the west, its outposts reached Afghanistan. Covering an area of 1.3 million sq km, it occupies the largest area of any ancient civilization. The whole civilization has similarities in terms of pottery, types of items used and house styles, though at the same time there were some regional and local variations.

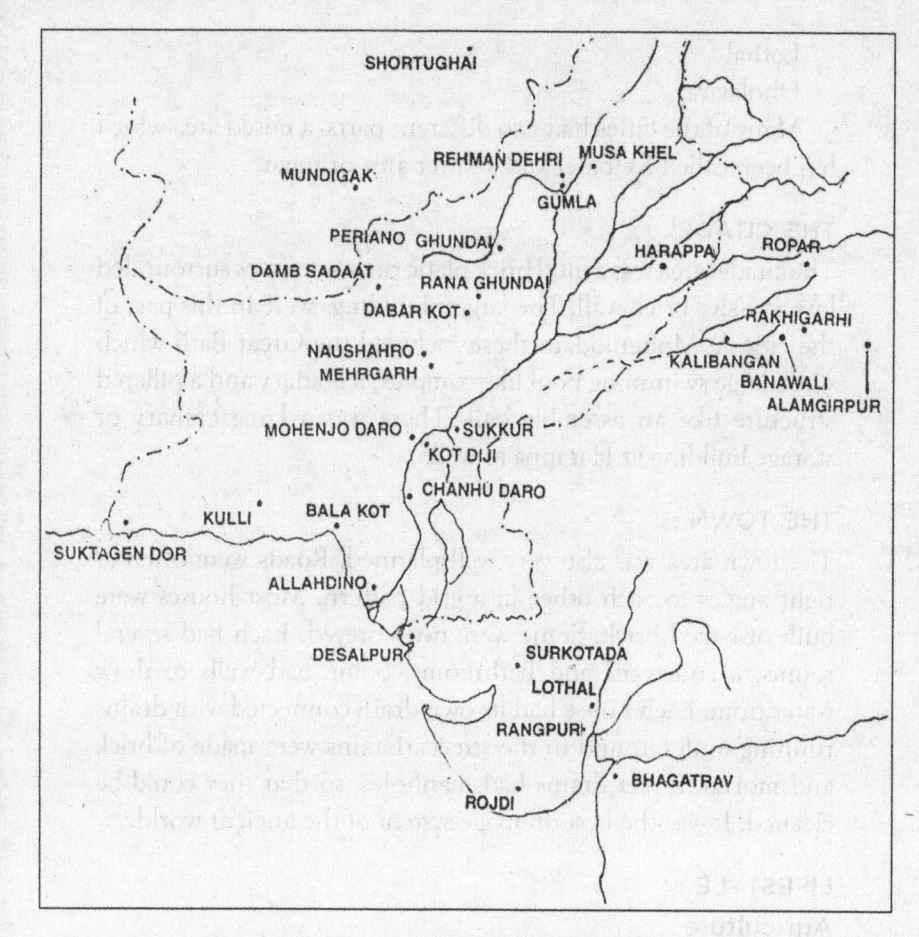

The Harappan Civilization

THE CITIES
Some of the main cities are:
- Harappa
- Mohenjodaro
- Ganweriwala
- Kalibangan

Lothal
Dholavira

Many of the cities had two different parts, a raised area which has been called a citadel and a lower area or town.

THE CITADEL

The citadel area was a mud brick platform, sometimes surrounded by a massive brick wall. The largest buildings were in this part of the city. At Mohenjodaro these included the Great Bath which was a large swimming pool like complex, a granary and a pillared structure like an assembly hall. There was a large granary or storage building at Harappa as well.

THE TOWN

The town area was also very well planned. Roads were often at right angles to each other in a grid pattern. Most houses were built of baked brick. Some were two-storeyed. Each had several rooms, a courtyard and bathrooms. Some had wells to draw water from. Each house had its own drain connected with drains running underground in the streets. Drains were made of brick and mortar. Street drains had manholes, so that they could be cleaned. It was the best drainage system of the ancient world.

LIFESTYLE
Agriculture

In the floodplains were planted wheat, barley, mustard, sesame, peas and cotton. Rice was grown in western India. The plough, probably made of wood, was used. At Kalibangan, there is evidence of a ploughed field belonging to pre-Harappan times.

Animals

Domestic animals included cattle, buffaloes, goats, sheep, pigs, dogs, asses and camels. In the forests they came in contact with elephants, tigers, monkeys, rhinoceros and deer.

Crafts

The people here made stone and bronze tools, including axes, saws, knives and spears. There was wheel-made pottery, shiny red with black painting, as well as plain red pottery. Baked bricks were in standard sizes. Some stone sculptures have been found. The best is one of a bearded man, wearing a shawl. They also made some bronze images and wove cloth from wool and cotton. Jewellery was made from gold, silver and semi-precious stones. Boats and carts with wheels were constructed for long-distance trade. Weights and measures were used. Weights were usually in multiples of 16. If one weight was 16 units, the next would be 32 units. Terracotta figurines were made.

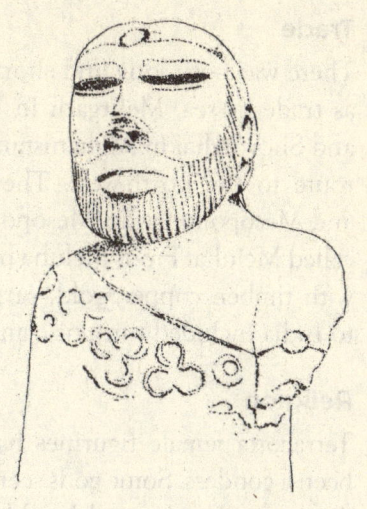

Stone image of a bearded man

Entertainment and games

Several terracotta toys have been discovered. While children played with toys, adults played dice or an early form of chess. Dance peformances were probably held. A beautiful bronze image of a dancing girl has been found. The image is only 9 cm high.

Seals

Intricately carved stone seals were made. The seals were small tablets, usually of steatite stone, which left an impression when pressed into a soft substance like clay. They were carved with some kind of writing, and depicted various animals, trees, and possibly deities.

Roshen Dalal

Trade

There was both long and short-distance trade over land, as well as trade by sea. Mehrgarh in Baluchistan near the Bolan Pass, and Shortughai in Afghanistan, were halting places on the trade route to the north-west. They traded with Afghanistan, Iran and Mesopotamia. In Mesopotamian records, India is probably called Meluha. From Meluha boats went to Mesopotamia loaded with timber, copper, gold, carnelian and ivory objects. Imports to India included turquoise and lapis lazuli.

Religion

Terracotta female figurines have been found, which may have been a goddess. Some gods seem to have been carved on the seals. A man with a horned headdress, surrounded by animals, was probably a god. Some strange looking animals and half-human, half-animal deities may also have been worshipped. Many seals depict what looks like a unicorn. Trees were also worshipped. There is evidence of worship of fire from a series of 'fire-altars' at Kalibangan. The Great Bath at Mohenjodaro may have been a sacred tank where people took a dip or wash before praying. One structure in the citadel area of Mohenjodaro looks like a temple, but this is not certain.

Writing

Short inscriptions were carved on the seals, and have also been found on clay and pottery. Though there are many different theories, no one has successfully been able to decipher the writing. There are about 400 different symbols. Some say each symbol represents a picture or idea, others that it represents a sound, or that it was a combination of both. Some feel the language is like the Dravidian languages of south India, others that it is like the Sanskrit of north India. It could even be of two or more different languages. In Mesopotamia the same script was used for different languages. As the writing cannot be read, no one actually knows who ruled the area or who the inhabitants were.

DECLINE

After 1900 BCE the city civilization began to decline. Once again there were villages in the area. Writing disappeared and was not known again till the 3rd century BCE.

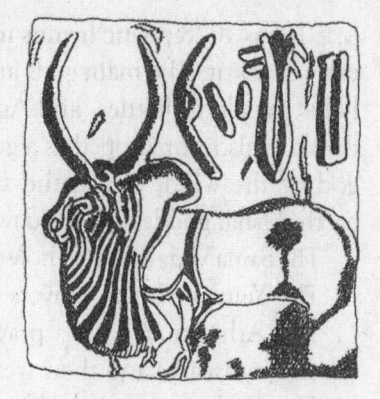

Seal depicting a humped bull with short inscription

Why the civilization ended is not clear. There may have been floods or earthquakes, a change in climate, or a decline in trade. At one time it was thought invaders destroyed the cities, but there is no evidence of this.

OTHER DEVELOPMENTS

By the time the Harappan civilization declined there were village settlements in most parts of India. From around 1000 BCE there were megalithic monuments in some areas including south and central India. New cities emerged in north India by around 600 BCE. Coins too began to be used.

RELIGIONS

Three early religions of India are Hinduism, Buddhism and Jainism.

Hinduism: The Vedas

Hinduism has a long development over time. Its first texts are the four Vedas, of which the Rig Veda is the earliest. The date of the Rig Veda is uncertain. Usually it is dated between 1500 and 1000

BCE. It has 1028 poetic hymns to various deities, and is written in early Sanskrit. The main gods are Indra, god of thunder, who also helps people in battles, and Agni, god of fire. Soma, the divine drink, is also worshipped as a god. Some other deities were Vayu, god of the wind; Surya, the sun god; Prithivi, goddess of the earth; Usha, goddess of the dawn and Aditi, mother of the gods.

The Sama Veda indicates how the verses are to be sung and chanted. The Yajur Veda has prayers to be used in rituals.

The Atharva Veda has prayers, spells and charms, and also describes diseases and their treatment.

The Brahmanas, Aranyakas and Upanishads are later texts associated with these four Vedas. The Upanishads contain philosophical discussions.

A prayer from the Atharva Veda

> As heaven and earth are not afraid, and never suffer loss or harm,
> Even so, my spirit, do not fear.
> As day and night are not afraid, and never suffer loss or harm,
> Even so, my spirit, do not fear.
> As sun and moon are not afraid, nor ever suffer loss or harm.
> Even so, my spirit, do not fear.
> * * *
> As what has been and what shall be are not afraid, and never suffer loss or harm,
> Even so, my spirit, do not fear.

Buddhism

Buddhism is based on the concept of the Buddha. Buddha is a term for any 'enlightened' person, that is, a person who has understood the true nature of life and death. Siddhartha Gautama founded the religion of Buddhism. He was born in 563 BCE in a garden in Lumbini in Nepal, while his mother Mahamaya was on her way to her mother's house. His father, Shuddhodhana was a king of the Shakyas. Siddhartha grew up in luxury, sheltered from the evils of the world. He married, and had a son.

One day, riding in his chariot, he came across three disturbing sights—a sick man, an old man, and a dead man, surrounded by weeping people. He understood that all people grow sick and old and die, and felt that life was full of sorrow. Then he saw an ascetic, a holy man, walking on the path, with a happy, peaceful expression. Siddhartha wanted to understand the secret of his happiness. Leaving home, he fasted and meditated, and finally discovered the truth. He had become enlightened, a Buddha. For the next 45 years, he conveyed his understanding of the true path. His basic teachings are the Four Noble Truths, stating that life is full of suffering caused by desire, by a longing for what one did not have. He said one should lead a balanced life. He called this type of life the Eightfold Path. This path consists of Right Views, Right Thought, Right Speech, Right Action, Right Mode of Livelihood, Right Effort, Right Mindfulness and Right Meditation.

Later, Buddhism spread to different parts of the world, and acquired different forms.

Jainism

Jainism was founded by Vardhamana, who was born around 599 BCE in Kundagrama in Bihar (India). He was actually the 24th in a long line of teachers called Tirthankaras (ford-makers, as they showed people the way to enlightenment). According to some accounts, he too was married and had a daughter, before he left home to discover the truth. After he had understood the truth of life and death, he was called Mahavira, the great one. He said one should live a very simple and disciplined life, and should not harm any living being, not even an insect or a plant. One should give up all desires, even finally the desire for food.

Then one would go beyond life and death.

No gods
Neither Buddha or Mahavira spoke about god or worship. But later prayers and worship became a part of both religions.

SIX SYSTEMS OF PHILOSOPHY
At about the same time as Buddhism and Jainism, six systems of Hindu philosophy were developing. These were: Nyaya, Vaisheshika, Mimamsa, Samkhya, Yoga and Vedanta. Nyaya and Vaisheshika use logic and experience to analyse the world. They said the world is composed of atoms (*anu* or *paramanu*).

Mimamsa is based on the divine knowledge contained in the Vedas.

Samkhya sees the world as a result of two principles, passive and active.

Yoga deals with uniting the individual self with the divine.

Vedanta is based on the Upanishads.

9
Early China

China had been occupied from ancient days. It is a huge country with a varied habitat. The main rivers are the Huang (Yellow River) and Yangtze. Finds of early humans known as *Homo erectus* date back here to 7,50,000 BCE.

China had several early developments. Around 10,000 BCE farming settlements began. China began to raise silkworms and to produce silk by 3600 BCE. By 2700 BCE they cultivated tea.

There were many different Neolithic or village cultures spread over different parts of China. Among them is the Cishan culture in north China near the Huang river.

CISHAN CULTURE

Cishan is an early village of this culture that existed from 8000 BCE. Here there were a number of round houses, sunk a little below the ground. Millet was the main crop grown. By 6000 BCE chickens were domesticated. Bones of pigs, dogs, tortoises, fish, clams and other animals have been found, indicating that these were eaten. Walnut shells have also been discovered, suggesting they were grown in the region. There were at least 500 underground storage pits where millet was stored. Some of these were 5 m deep and could contain a 1000 kg of grain.

Similar cultures existed nearby.

EARLY DYNASTIES

Three early dynasties of China were the Xia, Shang and Zhou. Their starting dates are approximately put at 2100 BCE, 1600 BCE and 1100 BCE. The Zhou dynasty ended in 221 BCE.

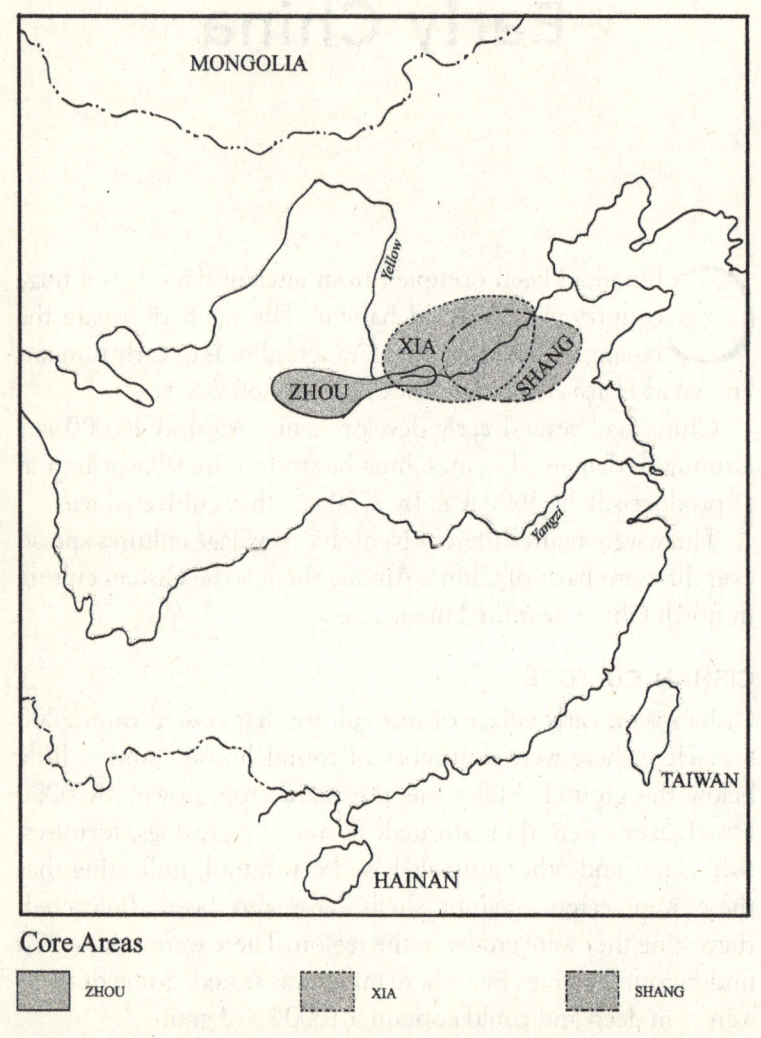

The core regions of the Xia, Shang and Zhou kingdoms

ERLITOU CULTURE (1900-1600 BCE)

Erlitou is the site of an early city in China. It is located on the Yi river, which is a tributary of the Luo river, 10 km south-west of Hanshi city in Henan province. The city was quite large, measuring 2.4 x 1.9 km. It was occupied by 3500 BCE, abandoned in 2500-2000 BCE and reoccupied and developed into a city by 1900 BCE. It had palaces, royal tombs and paved roads. Eight palaces have so far been discovered. One palace complex was 150 m long and had three courtyards. There were other buildings and smaller houses. Some buildings seem connected with religious sacrifice. Wagon tracks indicate that wagons were used. There were areas for different crafts. There was a bronze smelting workshop, pottery and bone workshops, and a workshop just for making objects from turquoise. Nearby there were 400 tombs.

Among the other items found here were vessels of bronze and jade. The earliest bronze vessels of China have been found here. The first bronze vessels were made for religious rituals in which wine was consumed. The wine may have been brewed from rice or wild grape.

According to traditional Chinese history, the Xia dynasty was ruling at this time. Erlitou may be Zhenxun, the ancient capital of the Xia dynasty. Another possibility is that it was an early Shang capital.

The city declined after 1600 BCE. By 1300 BCE the palaces were deserted.

SHANG DYNASTY

The Shang was the next major dynasty after the Xia. They are also known as the Yin dynasty. We know about the Shang from their tombs, oracle bones, various remains and later historical texts.

The approximate starting date of this dynasty can be taken as 1600 BCE, but it has been dated earlier (1766 BCE) or later (1480 BCE). Twenty-eight or 29 kings of this dynasty ruled. Their centre of power was in the Huang river valley, though they also occupied some sites of the Erlitou culture. They expanded their territory over central China extending southwards to the river Yangtze. There were cities and villages in their territory. The last Shang ruler, Zhou Hsin, was overthrown in 1046 in the battle of Muye.

The Shang dynasty had different capitals.

The last capital is said to have been located at Yinxu in Anyang in north China. This site has been named Huanbei Shang city. Here the kings' graves have been found, buried in deep pits. Within them was not only the coffin of the king, but also the coffins of slaves and various animals, including horses and dogs. They may have been owned by the king, and were killed and buried along with him when he died. Chariots, furniture, food and other things he may need in the next world, were also buried with him.

The people who lived at this time grew millet, wheat, barley and some rice. They kept cattle, sheep, pigs, horses and dogs. They also hunted wild animals. They made silk from silkworms and wove linen. They also made black and red pottery, vessels of white stone, and weapons of various materials, including iron. Weapons they used included halberds and bows. (A halberd consisted of an axe head and hook attached to a long pole.) They carved items of jade, wood and ivory. This period is best known for beautiful bronze items, including different types of bronze vessels. People followed a lunar calendar.

PREDICTING THE FUTURE—ORACLE BONES

The Chinese had a form of writing and believed they could predict the future. They wrote their questions

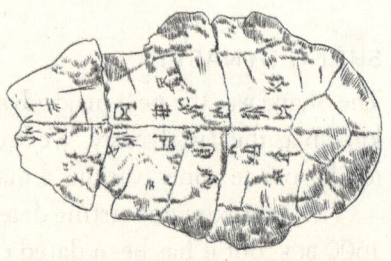

An oracle bone of the Shang period

> An oracle is something (or someone) through which the future is predicted.

on tortoise shell or bone, and then heated these till they cracked. The answers to their questions depended on where the cracks appeared. Thousands of these oracle inscriptions have been found.

RELIGION

The Shang worshipped spirits of dead kings, nature gods, guardian spirits and ancestors. The main god was known as Shangdi. They performed various ceremonies, including human sacrifices. There were ceremonies to communicate with ancestors and get their guidance. Bronze vessels for food and wine were used in these ceremonies.

At the same time as the Shang, there were other cultures in various parts of China.

ZHOU DYNASTY

The Zhou dynasty was the next major power in China. The Zhou were tribesmen from western China. Traditional dates for the Zhou are approximately 1046-221 BCE. This can be divided into three periods.

1. The Western Zhou, 1046-771 BCE

King Wen was the founder of the dynasty. He was followed by King Wu who defeated the Shang ruler. The Zhou ruled in the Wei and Yellow river valleys, and in parts of the Yangtze and Han river regions. The capital was at Hao near modern Xian. The area became too large for the king to rule directly. Hence there were local rulers or lords under the main kings. Each lord ruled a small area. Around 771 BCE the Zhou were pushed out of their western territories. When they left the western regions and fled to the east, they left behind hoards of bronze vessels.

2. The Eastern Zhou, c. 771–481 BCE
The Zhou now ruled in the east. They had a new capital called Luoyang. The states under local rulers grew stronger. Each ruler tried to expand his territory. There were hundreds of small states.

3. The warring states: 481–222 BCE
At this time the Zhou were still officially in power (up to 256 BCE), but in reality, the kingdom broke up into various states, which fought against one another. Among the states were Wei, Han, Qin and Zhao. Though the states were at war, a number of items, including those of iron, were made. Coins were used and there was long-distance trade.

CITIES
The Zhou had different capitals.

The Feng river valley has several sites of the Western Zhou. The Feng is a tributary of the river Wei. Zhangjiapo is a residential site of the Western Zhou dynasty, located in Fengxi, Changan City, Shanxi province. It is near the Feng river, south-west of Xian. Its remains are connected with the Zhou capitals, Feng and Hao. It has 15 underground rooms or soil pits. South of Zhangjiapo are 1500 tombs. North of the present village of Mangwancun is a huge palace complex. There are more sites between Doumenzhen and Fenghaocun across the river Feng.

Yan was one of the vassal states of the Zhou, whose ancient capital, named Pingming, was discovered in Lulihe town, Fangshan district, Beijing.

LIFESTYLE

The Western Zhou had tombs similar to the Shang. Some pit graves contained remains of horses and chariots. Delicate arrowheads of horn and copper were made, as well as copper knives, jade and bronze items and glazed stoneware.

ZUN

Zun was the term for a kind of wine vessel. Zun had different shapes. The foal zun was made in the form of a foal, with horns and wings.

WRITING

Writing developed further. By 1000 BCE Chinese calligraphers began to use a pen.

Zun in the shape of a foal

MUSIC

China has a long history of musical instruments. Flutes made of bone date to 7000 BCE.

During the Shang period there were chimes, bells, drums and other instruments. In one grave of the Zhou period, 125 musical instruments of different kinds were found, forming an entire orchestra. They included bells, flutes, pipes, mouth organs, zithers and drums.

RELIGION

The Zhou religion had ancient traditions. There was reverence for heaven and for ancestors.

Kings believed they had a divine right to rule, and had been asked to do so by heaven (tien or dien). Tien replaced the earlier supreme deity Shangdi. Many other deities were worshipped.

There were gods of agriculture and of nature. Bones were still used to discover the future.

CHINESE PHILOSOPHY
Yin-yang

Yin-yang are two principles. They can represent female and male, dark and light, freezing and boiling, sunny and shady, or other similar opposites. When joined together they create harmony. Once there was a separate yin-yang philosophy, but later it became a part of other Chinese philosophies.

Confucius

Confucius (551-479 BCE) or Kongfuze was a great philosopher of China. His thoughts and ideas can be read in a book called *The Analects*. He said that good behaviour was very important. One should be polite, loyal and unselfish. Order should be maintained in society by respect of elders and seniors. They in turn should behave justly and correctly. Confucius said that though there was a Supreme Being, there was no point in worshipping god if one did not help and serve others. One should learn and acquire knowledge and appreciate art and culture.

Confucius' tomb is at Qufu, Shandong, in China. At the time of the Han dynasty, emperors paid tributes at his tomb. Even today Chinese society is influenced by his ideas.

Mencius (372-289 BCE) and Xunzi were some of the later writers on Confucianism.

Dao

Dao, meaning 'the way', was a different philosophy that developed at this time. Dao believed in living a natural life.

Two main Daoist books are the *Daodejing (Tao-tse-Ching)*, said to be written by Laozi (Lao-Tzu), the founder of Daoism, and the essays of Zhuangzi (Chaung-tzu). Laozi probably lived in the 6th century BCE though sometimes he has been placed later in the 5th or even the 4th century BCE. Zhuangzi lived in the late 4th century BCE. Laozi described Dao in this way:

> There is a thing confusedly formed
> Born before heaven and earth
> Silent and empty,
> It stands alone and does not change.
> It goes around and does not get tired.
> It is the mother of the world.
> I do not know its name,
> I call it Dao, the way.

Legalism

Legalists believed that all aspects of life should be controlled by laws. The king should be strong and powerful, and even he should follow the laws. Han Fei, who lived in the 3rd century BCE (d.233) was the founder of this system.

Literature—Wu Ching

Between 1050 and 479, the Wu Jing (Wu Ching) or five classics of Chinese literature were composed. They were said to have been composed by Confucius, but they must have been compiled by various authors.

Among them were:

Yijing (I Ching) or The Book of Changes: this has a method of divination, that is, of predicting the future and providing guidance.

Shujing (Shuh Ching), The Book of History: this has writings and speeches of early kings.

Shijing (Shih Ching), The Book of Poetry: this contains 305 poems which were set to music and sung on different occasions.

Chunqiu (Chun Chiu/Chunqin), The Spring and Autumn Annals: a record of the state of Lu, from 722-481 BCE. This deals with the history of the Eastern Zhou.

Liji, or The Book of Rites: this describes ancient customs and ceremonies.

(Alternative spellings are in brackets.)

MEGALITHS

Megaliths are numerous in Southeast Asia. The earliest are in north-east China, dating between 1500 BCE and 850 BCE. From here they spread to Korea. Around 30,000 or more megaliths are found in Korea.

10
Ancient Greece

Greece (Hellenic Republic) today includes part of southeast Europe, the southernmost part of the Balkan peninsula, as well as several islands in the Aegean and Ionian seas. In ancient times there were different states and kingdoms in the region, but still all had something in common.

MINOAN CIVILIZATION

Crete is one of the Greek islands. We earlier saw that the island of Crete was occupied from at least 1,30,000 BCE, and that people reached here by sea. Much later, Crete had a great civilization known as the Minoan civilization. This lasted from 3000 BCE-1450 BCE. The beginnings of this civilization can be traced back to 7000-6000 BCE. The site of Knossos was occupied from this time.

The Minoans lived in Crete and in other nearby islands, including Kea, Kythera, Milos, Rhodes and Thera. Their early kings were buried in round vaulted tombs. Beautiful stone vases date to this time. Grand palaces were built from around 2000 BCE. Around 1700 BCE, most of these were destroyed by earthquakes, but were soon restored.

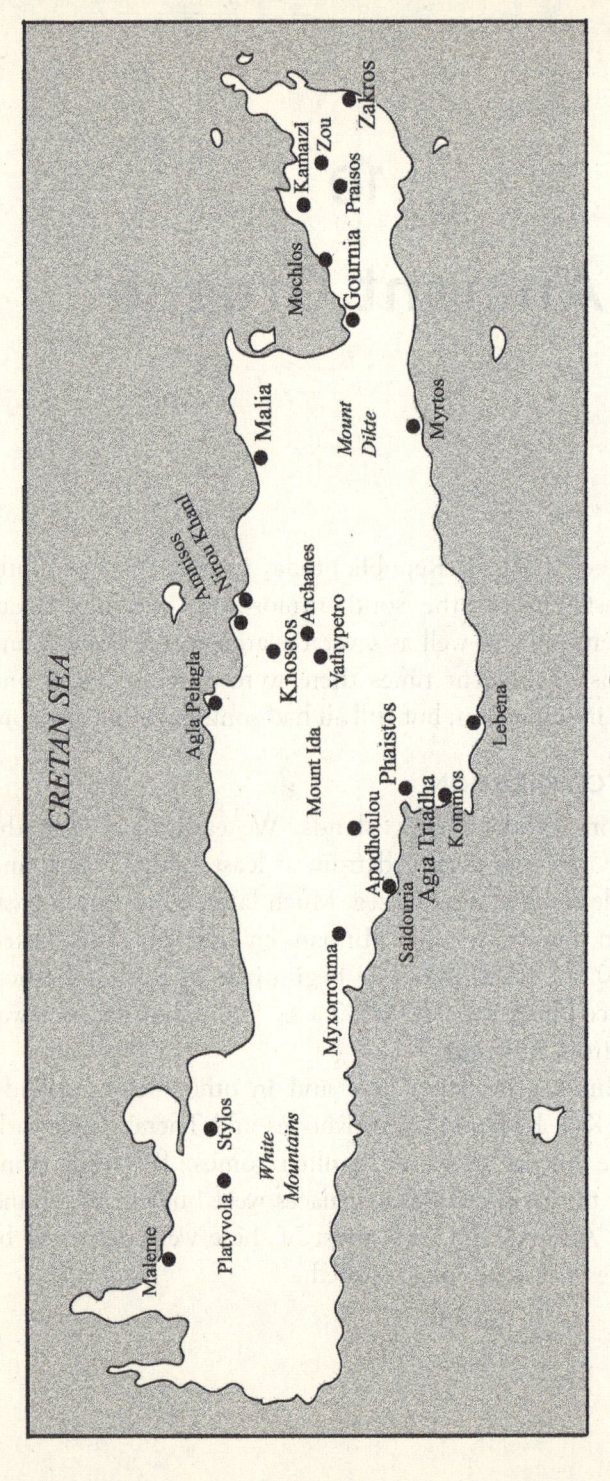

Minoan Crete

Thera—a volcano

Around 1700 BCE a huge volcano erupted on the island of Thera. A tsunami followed and many of Crete's ships, which were used to guard the island, were destroyed. Some areas were destroyed by fire, but were rebuilt, and a period of prosperity followed.

Palaces

Palaces were built at Knossos, Malla, Phaistos and Zakro, the greatest being at Knossos. On the palace walls there were frescoes, that is, wall paintings. There were paintings of gardens wild goats and monkeys, dolphins and griffons, goddesses, and processions.

Ruins of the palace at Phaistos. This corridor led to the royal chamber; an irrigation channel was in the centre.

Phaistos had a multi-storeyed palace built of stone. There was an excellent drainage system. The queen had her own bathroom, and a toilet that could be flushed with water.

Gods and goddesses

Potnia was a great goddess. Her symbol was a double axe. She was worshipped with offerings of honey. There were other nature goddesses, of mountains, trees and wild animals. There were some gods, including a bull god.

Temples

Huge temples were built. One such temple located at Knossos was called The Labyrinth. It was 150 m wide, and had 300 rooms.

Other items

Fine pottery, gold jewellery and bronze items were among the items made.

Roshen Dalal

Trade

Minoans had trade contacts with Egypt, Cyprus, Anatolia and other areas. Sea trade made the civilization rich and wealthy.

Writing

Minoans knew how to write. They had their own script. The earliest form of writing was hieroglyphic, found on seals. Later a script called Linear A developed. It has not yet been fully deciphered. There were short inscriptions in Linear A which may have been names and dedications to a god or goddess. Linear B was an even later script. This script was used for administrative records at Knossos. Its language was early Greek. Linear B may have been introduced by the Mycenaeans.

Last days

Mycenaeans from Greece captured Knossos and the Minoan civilization began to decline around 1450 BCE.

THE STORY OF KING MINOS

The Minoan civilization is named much later, after the mythical king, Minos. It was thought that the palace of Knossos may have belonged to this king. In Greek myths Minos was the son of the god Zeus and was the king of Knossos. Bull sacrifices were common during this time, and Minos once refused to sacrifice a beautiful snow-white bull, sent to him by the god Poseidon.

According to one story, Poseidon made the bull a fierce animal. The Greek hero Heracles captured it, brought it to Tyrins and freed it.

According to another story, the god Poseidon made Minos' wife Pasiphae fall in love with the white bull. As a result of their union, a Minotaur, a half-bull half-man was born. The Minotaur was kept in a labyrinth, a maze of rooms. Every year he ate seven girls and seven boys, who were brought from Athens as tribute to the king. But finally the Minotaur was killed by Theseus from Athens.

MYCENAE

Other areas in Greece had early farming settlements. By 2500 BCE, grapes, olives and grain were being grown in northern Greece. Bronze items were made. By 1600 BCE towns emerged. Among them was Mycenae. Mycenae controlled the neighbouring areas. It even occupied Crete.

The early kings of Mycenae were buried in shaft graves. In these graves there were items of gold, silver, bronze, crystal, alabaster and clay.

Mycenaeans seem to have been warlike. Bronze daggers and armour have been found at Mycenaean sites. Military scenes were depicted.

A Mycenaean vase

After occupying Crete, Mycenaeans were more prosperous. In the towns, metalwork, pottery and other items were made. In Mycenae, the kings lived in huge palaces decorated with frescoes. Tombs were in large, round

Part of a gold necklace, Mycenaen period

buildings called tholoi. Trade was widespread and new ports were established.

Mycenaeans had beautiful pottery and made perfumed oils. These were exported to different countries and sold at high prices. Mycenaeans too knew how to write. They used the Linear B script (referred to above). They probably created this script, by modifying the Linear A of the Minoans.

By around 1200 BCE this culture began to decline. New people reached Greece, of whom the Dorians began to take over some cities. There were also groups who fought against one another.

Homer

A great poet, Homer wrote an account of these times in two great epics known as the Iliad and the Odyssey. Though everything described in these epics was not true, some parts of it were based on real events.

Trojan war

Homer and other writers have described the Trojan war. According to the story, Helen, wife of King Menelaus of Sparta, ran away with Paris, a Trojan. She was happily married to Menelaus, but Paris was helped by the goddess Aphrodite to make her fall in love with him. Paris was the son of King Priam of Troy. Agamemnon, king of Mycenae, was the brother of King Menelaus. He led an army to Troy to bring Helen back. Many Greek heroes fought in the war. Troy was besieged for ten years. Then the Greek warriors made a huge wooden horse. They kept it outside the gates of Troy and hid inside it. The soldiers of Troy did not know the Greeks were hiding inside. They brought the wooden horse inside the gates. The Greek soldiers came out at night and killed most of the people of Troy.

Menelaus fought with Paris, but he escaped. Menelaus and the beautiful Helen returned to Sparta and lived happily. They had a daughter named Hermione.

No one knows if this story is true. But a place in Turkey, Hissarlik, is thought to be the ancient Troy. Archaeological evidence shows it was destroyed around 1260 BCE, which is the approximate date for the battle that destroyed Troy.

CITY STATES

After 1200 BCE there was a decline in Greece. But Greek city states began to be formed from about 800 BCE. These were known as polis, the term for city. Each polis included some land around the city. Though there were separate states, they

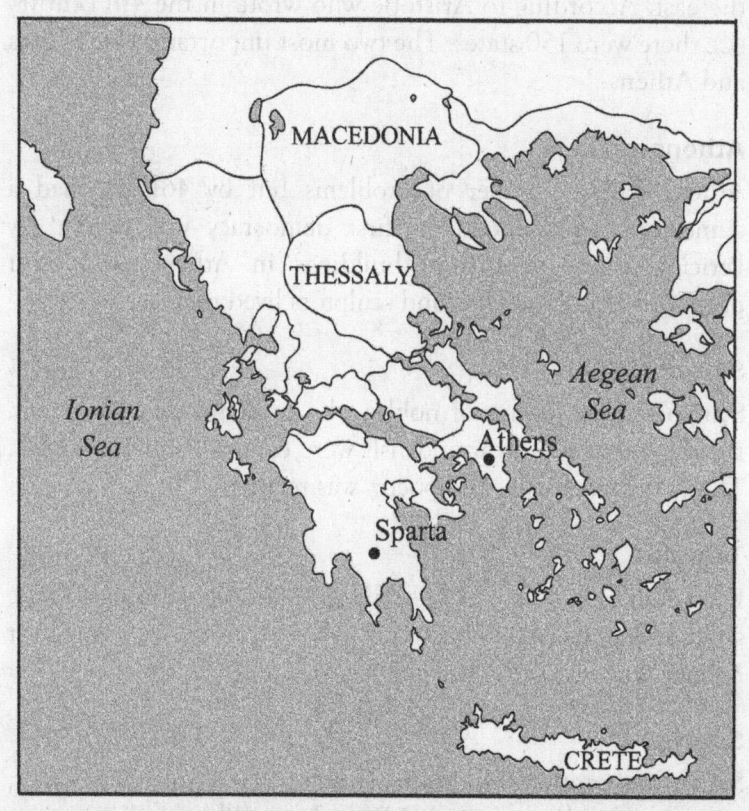

Athens and Sparta, the two main city states

had some common aspects. The term used for the whole Greek world was Hellas. Different types of Greek were spoken in this region. Ionic was the language of many Greek islands. Attic developed from this. It was the language of Athens, and soon became the most important. A new form of writing, the Greek script, developed.

At first many states had kings, but by 650 BCE most of them were ruled by groups of rich and powerful citizens. There were several such states including Athens, Sparta, Olympia, Corinth, Delphi, Argos, Thebes, Syracuse in Italy, Miletus in the east. According to Aristotle who wrote in the 4th century BCE there were 150 states. The two most important were Sparta and Athens.

Athens

Athens had a number of problems but by 461 BCE had a democratic government. Its first democracy was headed by Pericles. There were huge buildings in Athens, and great philosophers, playwrights and sculptors lived there.

Symposia

Symposia were groups of nobles who met and dined together. Bread, vegetables, meat and fish were eaten. Wine was drunk. There was much talk, and poetry was recited.

Temples

Each polis or city state had its own temples. A large temple to the goddess Athena was built at the Parthenon on the high area near Athens, known as the Acropolis.

Sparta

Sparta was another important city state. It was not a democracy, but was ruled by a few individuals. It was like a military state.

All the male citizens received military training. Infantry (foot soldiers) were developed who were very strong in war, almost undefeatable. The soldiers remained separate from their families. They lived a simple life together, and trained to become good warriors.

Sparta conquered many Greek states.

WARS

Numerous wars led to the decline of the city states. The states fought against one another. Persia too attacked the Greeks. The Persians were defeated in three main battles: Battle of Marathon in 490 BCE; Battle of Salamis, in 480 BCE; and the Battle of Platea in 479 BCE. To defeat Persia the Greek states united for some time. Then the local wars began again.

Athens and Sparta became leaders of groups of Greek states. Athens headed the Delian League of Greek states and Sparta the Peloponnesian League. Sometimes one group won, sometimes the other.

Macedonia was a state to the north of Greece. It was somewhat different from other Greek states. Macedonia was ruled by a hereditary king, and did not have a polis-type of government. However, Macedonians claimed to be Greek and spoke a Greek dialect. By 338 BCE most of the Greek city states had been conquered by Philip II, king of Macedonia.

ITEMS MADE

Fine pottery, jewellery and furniture, were among the items made in these states.

CULTURE

Greece had a great culture. There were advances in literature, philosophy, art and architecture, and science. Most of the developments took place in Athens, but also in other city states.

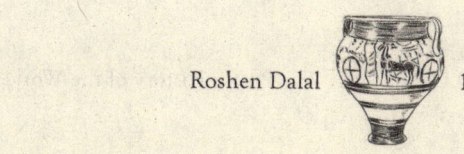

Literature

Among the great poets was Pindar (518-438 BCE). Sappho was a great woman poet (c.650-590 BCE). Playwrights included Sophocles (496-406 BCE), Euripides (484-406 BCE) and Aeschylus (525-456 BCE).

The works of these poets and playwrights can still be read today. Here are some verses from a poem by Pindar:

> If ever a man strives
> With all his soul's endeavour, sparing himself
> Neither expense nor labour to attain
> True excellence, then must we give to those
> Who have achieved the goal, a proud tribute
> Of lordly praise, and shun
> All thoughts of envious jealousy.
> (from Isthmian Odes, trans. Geoffrey S Conway)

Philosophers

There were different types of philosophy and many philosophers in the Greek world. Some tried to understand the world and matter. Others looked for life beyond the world. Perhaps the three greatest Greek philosophers were Socrates, Plato and Aristotle.

Socrates (c.469-399 BCE) lived in Athens. He tried to understand the world through dialectics, that is, a method of asking questions. He said that by asking question after question, one would reach the truth.

Plato (424-348 BCE) was a disciple of Socrates. He was a philosopher and mathematician. He founded an academy of learning in Athens. In his book *The Republic*, Plato wrote about an ideal state.

Aristotle (384-322 BCE), a philosopher, was a disciple of Plato. Born in Stageira, a Greek city, he went to Athens to study with Plato. Later he lived in Macedon and taught Alexander, but

PYTHAGORAS

Pythagoras (c. 582-500 BCE) was a great mathematician and philosopher. Even today people study the Pythagorean Theorem, which is named after him. He applied mathematics to music and to nature. The movement of the planets and the stars could be written down mathematically. And these could be equated with musical notes. He was born in the Greek island of Samoa but travelled to different places and later moved to Crotona in southern Italy. He believed in reincarnation, i.e. that the soul is reborn in different bodies. He believed it was wrong to eat meat, as the soul was first born in animals, and later in people. Hence he said animals should not be killed and eaten. Pythagoras had a number of followers.

then again returned to Athens. Aristotle wrote on many subjects including physics, zoology, geography, politics, economics, religion and literature.

Art and architecture

Two styles in architecture were reflected in the Dorian and Ionic style pillars. Dorian pillars rose straight up from a flat floor. Each pillar was fluted, that is, carved with concave grooves. Ionic pillars had a base and were thinner. Buildings had carved and painted decorations. There were frescoes or wall paintings and mosaics. Great sculptors included Phidias, Scopas, and Praxiteles. Phidias made the statue of the god Zeus at Olympia, and of the goddess Athena at the Parthenon. Zeuxis and Apelles were among the great painters.

Science

The Greeks knew different sciences. Hippocrates (460-370 BCE) was a physician and is called the father of medicine. He put

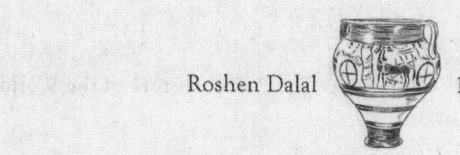

> **COLUMNS OR PILLARS**
>
> Tall columns or pillars are found in many parts of the ancient world, and had different purposes. They were used in temples or buildings, or sometimes just stood by themselves. Columns usually had three parts, a base, the shaft or main pillar, and a capital at the top.

together different theories of medicine, and wrote a book, *The Complicated Body*.

Some other great scientists of Greek origin lived in later times.

Euclid (323-283 BCE) is called the father of geometry. He lived in Alexandria in Egypt, and wrote several books on geometry and mathematics. One book called *The History of Mathematics* was studied even in the 19th century.

Archimedes (287-212 BCE) lived in Syracuse in Sicily, but was educated in Alexandria in Egypt. He was a mathematician and inventor.

> Why was Euclid called the 'father of geometry' and Hippocrates the 'father of medicine'? Generally it means they made the earliest or greatest contribution in that subject.

> **PARCHMENT**
>
> Around 200 BCE the Greeks began using parchment for writing, instead of papyrus.
>
> Parchment was used elsewhere from 1500 BCE, and was made from the skin of sheep, goat and calves. A finer type of parchment, vellum, was made from skins. It is not the same as the parchment of today which is a type of paper.

Historians

Herodotus (c. 484-425 BCE) and Thucydides (460-400 BCE) were great historians.

Herodotus was a Greek born in the region of Turkey. Later he went to Athens, and finally settled in a Greek colony in south Italy. He is called the father of history, as he wrote a very long work called *History*. Later it was divided into nine volumes. The word history comes from a Greek word meaning 'inquiry'.

Strabo (63 BCE-CE 24) was a later Greek historian and geographer. His *Geographica* in 17 volumes contains information about geography and history.

Games and sports

The Olympic Games that are held today had their origin in Greece. The first Games were held in 776 BCE at Olympia in Greece, and every four years after that. They continued till CE 393. Men who spoke Greek could enter the Games. All the Greek states stopped fighting when the Games were held, so that citizens could participate. Usually women did not participate, but sometimes they did. One woman, Bilistiche, won two horse races in the 264 BCE Games.

Other games were also held in the Greek islands. These were the Pythian Games at Delphi, the Isthmian at Corinth and the Nemean at Nemea.

RELIGION
Greek gods and goddesses

There were many Greek gods and goddesses. Among the main gods who lived on Mt Olympus were:

The god Zeus, sculpted in marble. This is a later image of the 1st century CE.

Zeus: king of the gods
Apollo: sun god
Ares: god of war
Dionysus: god of wine
Poseidon: god of the sea
Hermes: god of trade
Hades: god of the underworld
Athena: goddess of wisdom
Aphrodite: goddess of love
Artemis: goddess of the hunt
Hera: goddess of the family
Hestia: goddess of the hearth

Titans

The Titans were the earlier gods. Among them were Gaea, Uranus, Atlas and Prometheus.

Rhea and Cronus were Titans, the mother and father of the Olympian gods.

Temple of Artemis

The temple of Artemis, at Ephesus, Greece, was one of the seven wonders of the world. It was destroyed in CE 262 by the Goths, a Germanic tribe.

11

Alexander: King of Macedonia

As we saw earlier, in Greece there were wars between the city states. By 338 BCE, the king of Macedonia, Philip II had conquered most of Greece. He wanted to defeat the Persian Achaemenid empire. However, Philip did not live long enough to fulfill his dream.

After Philip II's death in 336 BCE his son Alexander became the king.

ALEXANDER
Early life

Alexander was born in Pella, the capital of Macedonia around 356 BCE. His mother was Olympias, the third wife of King Philip II. Alexander studied with the great philosopher Aristotle. Among Alexander's friends was Hephaestion, the son of Amyntor, an important person in Philip's court. Hephaestion met Alexander when he was still young, and they probably studied together at Aristotle's school at Mieza. Mieza was a place in Macedonia.

Alexander was 20 years old when he became the king. He was very ambitious and wanted to create a world empire. He decided to start by attacking Persia. At this time Persia was under the rule of King Darius III of the Achaemenid dynasty. The Persian empire extended through West Asia to parts of Central Asia and to Egypt. Though this empire faced internal problems and was declining at this time, it was still the largest empire of those days. (See Chapter 16)

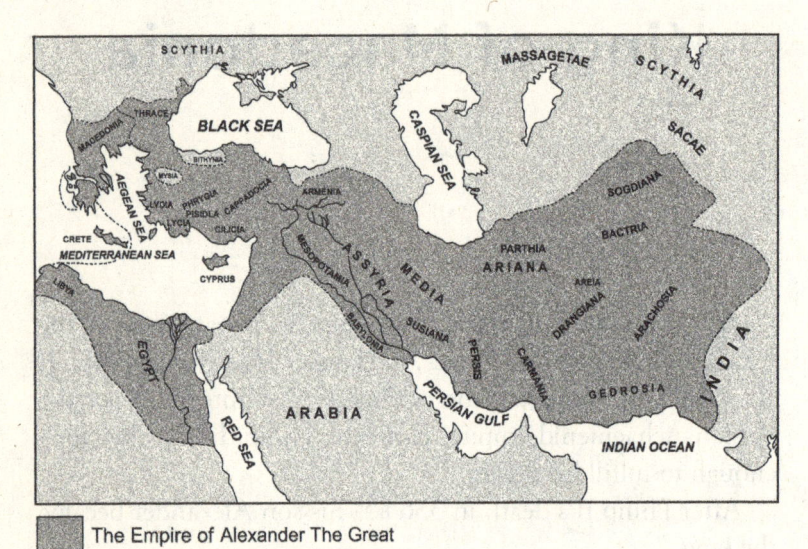

The Empire of Alexander The Great

The extent of Alexander the Great's empire

His conquests

Alexander first put down rebellions in Macedonia and in the Greek states, and then began to march against Persia. He defeated the Persians near the river Granicus in present north-west Turkey. Next he conquered some more areas of Turkey which were under Persia. He defeated the army of Darius III at Issus, and went on to conquer Tyre and Gaza. In 332 BCE he seized Egypt.

Alexander then crossed the river Euphrates and defeated Darius III in the battle of Gaugamela. Next he conquered Babylon and then Susa.

He crossed the high Zagros mountains through a pass known as the Persian Gate, and reached the Persian capital of Persepolis. Darius III was trying to gather an army again, but meanwhile he was murdered.

Alexander crossed the Hindu Kush and defeated Bessus another Persian leader. Next Alexander attacked Spitamenes, who had started a revolt in Sogdiana. (Sogdia or Sogdiana included parts of present Uzbekistan and Tajikistan.) Again crossing the Hindu Kush, he reached Kabul, Swat, and finally in 326 BCE the river Indus in north-west India. He won battles here too, defeating Omphis (Ambhi), king of Taxila, and King Porus (Puru) on the banks of the Jhelum.

The journey home

But now his soldiers refused to go further. They were tired and homesick, and really couldn't see the point of all these conquests. Alexander began the journey home. In 324 BCE he reached Persepolis and then Susa.

The wedding ceremony

Alexander wanted the areas he conquered to be united. At Susa, in Persia, a grand marriage ceremony was organized, where Macedonians married Persian women. Alexander thought this would help the Persians to accept Macedonian rule. The ceremonies lasted for five days. Dancers and musicians came all the way from Greece to entertain the guests.

Decline and death

Persia was temporarily pacified, but revolts had started in the other areas Alexander had conquered. In 323 BCE he returned to Babylon, where he fell ill and died. His brother Philip Arridaeus succeeded him as king, but as Philip was mentally slow, a regent was appointed to rule.

SOME OTHER ASPECTS OF HIS LIFE
Alexander's marriages
During his Sogdian campaign, Alexander married a Sogdian princess named Roshanak or Roxane in Greek. A few months after Alexander's death, Roxane gave birth to a son who was named after his father. At the grand marriage ceremony held in Susa, Alexander married two more princesses, Barsine, a daughter of Darius III, the Persian emperor, and Parysatis, a daughter of Artaxerxes III, who was an earlier Persian emperor. Barsine was renamed Statira after her mother, the wife of Darius III.

Alexander's wife Statira was murdered soon after his death in 323 BCE.

Alexander as depicted on a coin

Roxane and the child Alexander, who was given the title Alexander IV, went to Macedonia. There they were killed in 311–310 BCE, before the young Alexander could actually become the king.

Alexander's best friend
Hephaestion (c.357–324), his best friend died at Ecbatana in 324 BCE. Alexander was present there at the time, and was shocked and filled with grief. Hephaestion had accompanied Alexander in many of his campaigns and always remained his loyal friend, even when others deserted him. At the Susa wedding ceremony, Hephaestion had married Drypetis, another daughter of Darius III. In Ecbatana, Hephaestion fell ill after a drinking party and died. He was cremated in Babylon.

Boukephalus, his horse

Alexander's favourite horse Boukephalus died after the battle against King Porus. It is not clear if the horse died of wounds, or of old age. Alexander mourned him deeply. He founded a city that he named Alexandria Boukephalus on the river Jhelum.

Alexandrias

Alexander founded a number of other cities named Alexandria, in the present regions of Iran, Iraq, Afghanistan, Pakistan, Turkmenistan and elsewhere. Most important was the city of Alexandria in Egypt, which is still known by that name. It became a great city with palaces, museums and a huge library (see Chapter 17).

AFTER ALEXANDER

Alexander did not expect to die so young. He had not made any plans about who would take care of the empire he had created, when he was not there.

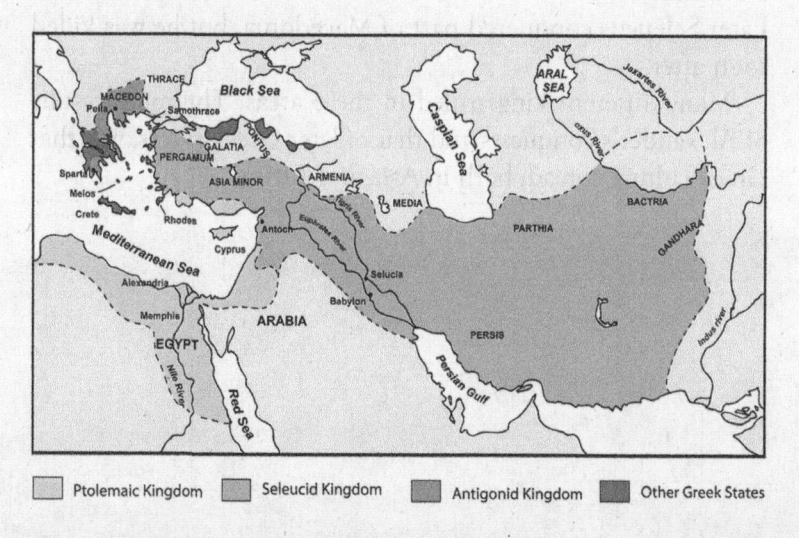

The later Hellenic kingdoms

As Alexander was dying his friends and soldiers gathered around him. They asked him who should succeed him. He said that the strongest person should rule.

His son Alexander IV and his half-brother Philip III Arridaeus became kings in name, but one was too young and the other too incapable to actually rule.

Perdiccas, a general of the army, controlled Babylon; Antipater took charge in Macedonia; Ptolemy ruled in Egypt; Antigonus held power in Asia Minor; Seleucus Nikator governed the eastern territories. They all began to fight to gain control over all the territories. Antigonus conquered several regions including Macedonia. Seleucus was also gaining power. In 321 BCE he became governor of Babylon, and in 312 BCE, the king of Babylon.

A great battle was fought at Ipsus, in present Turkey, in 301 BCE. This was between Seleucus and his allies on one side and Antigonus on the other. Seleucus won. He became king of Syria. Egypt became independent under Ptolemy. Macedonia was a separate kingdom was under Demetrius, son of Antigonus. Later Seleucus conquered part of Macedonia, but he was killed soon after.

Many different kings ruled in these areas. The main results of Alexander's conquests and that of later Greek rulers, was that Greek culture spread, both in Asia and Africa.

12

Ancient Europe

Europe had different types of settlements and many different groups of people. We will look at some of them here.

FARMING AND AGRICULTURE

We saw that there were farming settlements in Europe from 7000 BCE. These soon increased in number and spread to different areas. Each area had some special features, such as a particular type of pottery, houses, or other items. Based on these features, and the region where they were located, archaeologists have given them different names. Among the earliest were:

- the Proto-Sesklo and Sesklo cultures in Greece
- the Starcevo Cris cultures and the Comb Ceramic culture in south-east Europe
- the pre-Cucuteni and Cucuteni cultures in Romania
- the Hamangia culture in Romania and Bulgaria
- the Karanovo culture in Bulgaria, and many others.

Out of these we will look at one culture, where copper was used.

Vinca copper culture

The Vinca culture, dating from about 5500-4000 BCE, named after the site of Vinca Belo Brdo on the river Danube, in Serbia, was one of the earliest cultures in Europe to use copper. This culture was mainly located in Serbia, but extended into parts of Romania, Bulgaria, Macedonia, Greece and Montenegro. Apart from Vinca, other sites included Plocnic, Potporanj, Selevac, Valac and many others. Some of these sites are quite large, and it is suggested that these were not villages, but early towns. Houses of two or three rooms were built along streets, within these larger settlements. The people grew wheat, oats, flax and barley. They domesticated animals, though they also hunted and ate wild animals and used some wild plants for food. They made pottery, figurines of all kinds and copper items. They fixed painted skulls of cattle inside their houses. Perhaps these were considered guardians. People of Vinca used symbols which may have been an early form of writing.

A figurine from a Vinca site

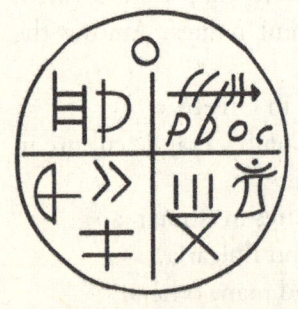

Vinca symbols on a clay tablet from Romania. This can be dated to around 5000 BCE.

Bird goddess

The Vinca people probably worshipped various gods and goddesses. Among them was a bird goddess, who was depicted like a bird-woman. There are figures of women on vases and separately, which have some birdlike features. For instance, there could be a bird's beak and wings or a bird's tail on a woman's body. There was also a bear god.

MEGALITHS

There were other types of cultures associated with megaliths (large stones). We had looked at the different types of megaliths in Chapter 5.

More than 50,000 chamber tombs as well as other types of megaliths, have been found in Europe.

At Evora in Portugal is an early stone circle dated to 5000 BCE.

The most famous stone circle is at Stonehenge in Britain. The construction of Stonehenge began around 3000 BCE. It consists of upright rectangular stones arranged in concentric circles. A single stone stands in the centre.

Why were megaliths made? There were many different reasons, along with the different types. Some were related with astronomy, others were graves. Some large stones were placed to indicate routes used by pastoralists. Others marked boundaries of agricultural land or farms.

TRADERS—THE PHOENICIANS

The Phoenicians lived on the Mediterranean coast from about 2500 BCE. The land of Mesopotamia was nearby. Tyre, Sidon and Byblos were among their cities. They first traded with Greece, crossing the seas, and later with other areas. They controlled the coastal regions of north Africa and founded a city there known as Carthage. Between 1200 and 800 BCE the Phoenicians became wealthy and powerful.

The murex snail and other items

The murex was a sea snail found in these coastal areas. The Phoenicians extracted a purple dye from its shell, and selling this made them rich. They were famous for this dye, and this led them to be

The murex snail was used to make a purple dye.

called 'Phoenicians', from the Greek word 'phoinios' which means 'purple'.

The Phoenicians also made glass, textiles, wine and bronze objects. They trained and sold hunting dogs.

Religion
There was a temple in every city. Baal, meaning lord was the name of many of their gods. Astarte was a goddess.

Writing
Writing already existed in Mesopotamia, Egypt and Greece. But the Phoenicians created a new simple alphabet on which the later Greek and other European alphabets were based.

THE CELTS
Among the different types of people in Europe were those who have been called Celts. Celt is a term for those who spoke Celtic languages. These were a number of different languages. Between 1300 and 500 BCE there were many Celtic groups in Europe. The Celtic Hallstatt culture (800-500 BCE), named after Halstatt in Austria, occupied a large area in eastern and western Europe. They became rich through trade in salt, tin, copper and iron. They built forts on hills, and wealthy people were buried in graves. Jewellery, swords, pottery, clothes, bronze vessels, wagons with wheels and other items were buried with the Celts. More than a thousand rich graves of this culture have been found.

Celtic languages
Early Celtic languages include Gaulish and related languages, spoken in large parts of early Europe. Among these were: Celtiberian; Goidelic, including Irish and Scottish Gaelic; Brythonic,

A Celtic helmet

including Welsh, Breton, Cornish and Cumbric, with Pictish as a related language.

Heuneburg

Heuneburg fort, on a hill near the town of Herbertingen in south-west Germany, was an important Celtic settlement, and a centre of trade. Nearby a tomb was found which had a floor made of oakwood. Among the items in this tomb were gold and amber jewellery.

There were several other hill forts, with graves where wonderful items were buried along with the people.

La Tene

The next Celtic phase (500 BCE–1 BCE) is known as La Tene, named after a place in Switzerland. The Romans called these Celtic people the Gauls. The Celts at this time used iron weapons and were more warlike. They invaded Italy and Greece, and attacked Rome. They also settled in Britain and the region of present Turkey.

But the Romans defeated the Celts in Italy and France, and by the 1st century CE, occupied Britain. Celtic languages and customs survived in western France in a region known as Brittany, in Wales, Ireland and part of Scotland, as well as to some extent in Britain.

In CE 410 after the Roman empire collapsed in Britain some Celtic kingdoms remained. Though Christianity soon reached the area, Celtic culture was still important. Typical Celtic stone and metalwork continued to be made. Manuscripts were illustrated in Celtic styles.

Celtic life

The Celts included a number of tribes, each ruled by a king. After some time, in parts of

Celtic coins

Europe they had elected leaders instead of kings. In each tribe there were nobles, warriors, farmers and craftsmen.

In their hill forts, there were different types of buildings, both large houses and small huts. The forts were enclosed with high walls and a moat around them. The Celts were said to be very ferocious fighters. While fighting they coated their bodies with blue paint in order to terrify their enemies.

Religion

They worshipped many gods. Celtic gods were known by different names in different regions. Cernnunos was a horned god worshipped by all Celts.

Celtic priests were called druids. Druids were said to be very wise and to have special powers. Some types of trees, animals and birds were also considered sacred.

Detail from a silver cauldron found at Gundestrup in Denmark. This cauldron could be of Celtic origin and has been dated between the 2nd century BCE and 1st century CE.

THE ETRUSCANS

The Roman empire with its centre at Rome, in present Italy, was one of the largest empires of Europe. Before Rome became powerful, Italy had several early settlements and a number of different groups of people.

Among them, around 1000 BCE, were a people known as Etruscans. They lived mainly in northern Italy and had a number of kings who ruled over city states. The city states combined with each other in times of war. They fought several wars and had a powerful navy.

The cities were surrounded by stone walls. Vetulonia and Tarquinia were two of the early cities. Caire and Vulci were other cities. Within the cities there were houses and temples. Early temples were built of brick and wood, and later of stone. The temples contained statues of their gods. Etruscans worshipped many deities including the gods of nature. Catha was the sun god; Tiv was the god of the moon. Voltumna was an important goddess. Above these gods and goddesses were 'nameless powers'. Located outside the cities were cemeteries which contained tombs. Some of the tombs were like houses with many rooms. The walls of the tombs were painted with murals and frescoes.

Within the tombs were items made of amber, silver, gold and gems, brought from different parts of the world.

Etruscans created beautiful sculptures of terracotta, bronze and limestone. They made fine painted pottery and gold, silver and ivory jewellery. They traded with Greeks and Phoenicians.

On the coasts of southern Italy, Greeks settled by the 8th century. Greek culture influenced the Etruscans. The Etruscan script was developed from the Greek script, though the Etruscan language was different.

Etruscans were powerful in the 6th century BCE, but after that their power declined. The Latin people also lived in Italy. The Etruscans were gradually replaced by the Romans (Latins).

By 283 BCE Rome had conquered most of the Etruscan areas. In 393 BCE the city of Veii was captured by Rome after a ten-year siege. But Etruscans too contributed to Rome. Three of the early kings of Rome were probably Etruscans. Etruscan religion and culture influenced the Romans.

MALTA

Malta consists of some islands near Sicily, to the south of Italy. People from Sicily settled here around 5000 BCE. In the islands of Malta there are some very ancient structures made from huge blocks of stone. These may have been temples. The temples were constructed between 3600 and 2500 BCE. Among them are the Tarxien temples. One of them has relief carvings of spiral designs and animals, including goats, bulls, pigs and a ram. These may have been domestic animals. Some of them may have been sacrificed. Other temples include the Mnajdra temples and the Hagar Qim temples.

Around 800 BCE Phoenicians occupied the islands of Malta. In 218 BCE, they were conquered by Rome.

An early temple from Malta. This Tarxian south temple dates to around 3000 BCE.

OTHER CULTURES

In this chapter we have looked at some of the main cultures of early Europe. There were many others.

128   The Puffin History of the World

13
The Roman World

Rome, today the capital of Italy, was once the centre of a huge empire that stretched across Europe, and extended into Africa and Asia. In Italy at that time there were Etruscans, Latins and other groups of people. The Latins lived near the river Tiber. This area was known as Latium. The city of Rome was located in Latium.

The site of Rome was occupied from 1500 BCE or earlier. But according to a story, Rome was founded much earlier in 753 BCE.

A statue showing the wolf nursing Romulus and Remus. This statue is located on the Capitoline hill in Rome. Its date is uncertain; the wolf is dated to the 13th century CE, or to a much earlier period, the 5th century BCE. The twins were probably added to the sculpture in the 15th century CE.

THE STORY OF ROME

Romulus and Remus were twins, who founded the city of Rome. Their father was Mars, the god of war. Their mother was Rhea Silvia, daughter of Numitor, a king of the city of Alba Longa. Numitor was removed from the throne by his younger brother Amulius, who made himself king. Amulius threw the twins into the river Tiber, so that they would not grow up and claim his kingdom. But the twins were rescued from the river and lived in a cave on the Palatine hill. Here they were nursed by a she-wolf and fed by a bird. Later a shepherd and his wife took care of them. When the twins grew up, they removed Amulius from power and returned the throne to their grandfather, Numitor. Then they thought of establishing a new city, and began to build Rome. But they soon fought over who would be the first king, and Remus was killed. Then, Romulus is said to have become the first king of Rome in 753 BCE.

Was Romulus a real king? No one really knows.

Three periods

The history of Rome can be divided into three phases:
Period 1. The early kings: six more kings ruled after the mythical Romulus.
Period 2. The Roman republic: existed from 509 BCE till 27 BCE.
Period 3. The Roman empire: 27 BCE to about CE 450.

The early kings

The names of these kings and their activities are known from later accounts. The last three were Etruscans. The Etruscans considered the wolf a protector, hence they may have been connected with the story of Romulus.

The king looked after the government, commanded the army,

and was the chief priest. The king was helped by the senate, which consisted of powerful people who advised him. At this time the senate did not have much power, as the king remained supreme.

Lucius Tarquinas Superbus was the name of the last king. He built a temple for the god Jupiter, and fought wars against neighbouring kingdoms. But he and his son were hated for their violent acts, and they were overthrown.

THE REPUBLIC

After the kings were removed, a new type of government was formed. It was a republic, in which the leaders were elected.

The people of the republic

There were different groups in the Roman republic. The two main groups were patricians, the noble and wealthy people, and plebeians, the ordinary people. Apart from these, there were a number of slaves. There were also people who were not considered citizens. They were different from slaves but did not have the rights of citizens.

The government of the republic

The government consisted of two consuls, as well as the senate and the assembly.

The assembly

The plebeians together formed the assembly, which could vote on some aspects of government. Though plebeians were the ordinary citizens, some of them were quite rich and powerful.

The senate

The senate, with 300 members, was chosen by the consuls mainly from the patricians. Those selected remained members of the senate for their lifetime.

The consuls

Two people, known as consuls, were elected every year by the assembly to head the government. The assembly could not elect just anyone, the consuls had to be members of the senate. The two consuls were in charge of the government, and headed the army. They had to agree on all decisions.

How the government worked

The senate could advise the consuls on what to do. The assembly too could demand some policies, but the consuls and senate did not have to do what they wanted. But since the assembly elected the consuls, as well as other government officials, the consuls and senate could not ignore them.

Plebeians, the ordinary people, could belong to the senate, but initially only patricians, the wealthy landowners, could be consuls. Later this discrimination was removed. A new class of nobility came into being, consisting of rich and powerful plebeians and patricians.

The difference between plebeians and patricians was reduced, but that between the rich and the poor remained.

CONQUESTS

The Romans conquered the rest of Italy by 264 BCE. They had to fight wars against many different groups. After this they fought three wars against Carthage. These are known as the Punic wars. Carthage was an independent kingdom in north Africa which controlled the Mediterranean. Finally, Carthage was defeated.

The Romans gained control over part of Sicily, Sardinia, Corsica, Spain and some Mediterranean islands, as well as parts of north Africa, and Pergamum in Asia Minor.

They also fought against Macedonia, Syria and the Achaean League of Greece, and were victorious after several wars. Rome thus created a huge empire through its conquests.

INTERNAL PROBLEMS
Within the republic there were problems and conflicts.

The Optimates and Populares
The Roman aristocracy had two groups known as the Optimates and Populares. The Optimates supported the senate, and did not want ordinary people to become powerful. The Populares were against them. They tried to help the plebeians.

The Marsian war
As we saw, many wars were fought against other countries. The non-Roman soldiers fought for Rome but received no benefits. These soldiers, who felt they were being unfairly treated, started a revolt in 90 BCE, known as the Marsian war. After this they were granted Roman citizenship, though they were defeated.

There were other revolts too.

Sparatacus was a slave and gladiator who escaped. He was joined by many others and led a revolt against the Romans. After some success, he was defeated and killed in about 71 BCE. Books were written about Spartacus. A film was made on him in 1960.

THE TRIUMVIRATE
In 59 BCE three people (the triumvirate) became joint leaders of Rome: Gaius Julius Caesar of the Populares, Pompey the Great of the Optimates and Marcus Licinius Crassus. Caesar, a great general, conquered Gaul (France) and led a Roman army into Britain. Crassus died in 53 BCE and Caesar and Pompey came into conflict. Pompey was defeated at Pharsalus in Greece in

Julius Caeser: A later portrait

48 BCE, and Caesar made himself dictator for life in 46 BCE. The senate was against this and in 44 BCE he was murdered by Gaius Cassius Longinus, Marcus Junius Brutus and other senators.

Second triumvirate

Another triumvirate was formed, consisting of Mark Antony, Octavian and Lepidus, who divided the Roman territories among themselves. But wars soon followed as each tried to acquire more territories for himself. Lepidus tried to take over Sicily. Mark Antony, in love with Cleopatra, wanted his own kingdom in Egypt. Finally Octavian defeated the others and became the emperor (see Chapter 17 for the story of Cleopatra).

THE ROMAN EMPIRE

In 27 BCE, Octavius became the first emperor of Rome. He was known as Augustus. In CE 14, Tiberius became the next emperor. There were many more emperors. Some were from different regions. The emperor Trajan was a Spaniard; Septimius Severus (ruled CE 193-211) was from north Africa.

At the time of the empire, more wars were fought. Because of the confusion at the time of the end of the republic, many areas tried to become independent. Augustus restored order in Gaul and Spain and made peace with the Persian empire which was under the Parthian dynasty. He tried to extend his territories further, but lost a battle against the Germans. The emperor Claudius (ruled CE 41-54) began the conquest of Britain. Britain had earlier been invaded by Caesar. Claudius also conquered Mauritania, the region of present Morocco and Algeria in north Africa. The emperor Nero was killed in CE 68 as his policies were not liked. He was quite eccentric and did strange things. He ignored the welfare of the people. He is said to have played the fiddle while Rome was burning. Civil war followed his death, and finally Vespasian became the next emperor. The emperor Trajan (CE 98-117) conquered more territories, including Dacia, Armenia and Mesopotamia. His successor, the emperor Hadrian (ruled CE 117-138) let go of Armenia and Mesopotamia, and focused on controlling Britain. The emperor Marcus Aurelius (ruled CE 161-180) faced many problems, including an attack by the Parthians and an invasion of the Goths, a Germanic people. More problems were to follow. The emperor Commodus was murdered in CE 193 and there was another civil war. Finally Septum Severus (ruled CE 193-211) defeated all rivals and became the emperor. Between his reign and that of the emperor Diocletian, who came to the throne in CE 284, there were 27 emperors who ruled for short periods of time. At the same time there were many invasions in Europe, while in the east there was a threat from the Sasanian Persian dynasty. The emperor Valerian was even taken prisoner by the Sasanian emperor in CE 260.

Roman empire divided into two

The empire was really very large, and with all the invasions and unrest, it had become very difficult to rule. In CE 285 the emperor Diocletian thought it would be better to divide it into two. He made Maximian a second emperor. There would be two senior emperors (Diocletian and Maximian) and two junior emperors. (This system was called tetrarchy.) Diocletian reorganized the administration, creating one hundred provinces. All his reforms did not last, but gradually the two parts of the empire became separate.

Diocletian had created a new capital at Nicomedia in present Turkey. The emperor Constantine (CE 306-337) moved it to Byzantium, which was then called Constantinople. After CE 395, there were two separate empires, the Byzantine or Eastern empire with its capital at Constantinople, and the Western or Roman empire with its capital at Rome.

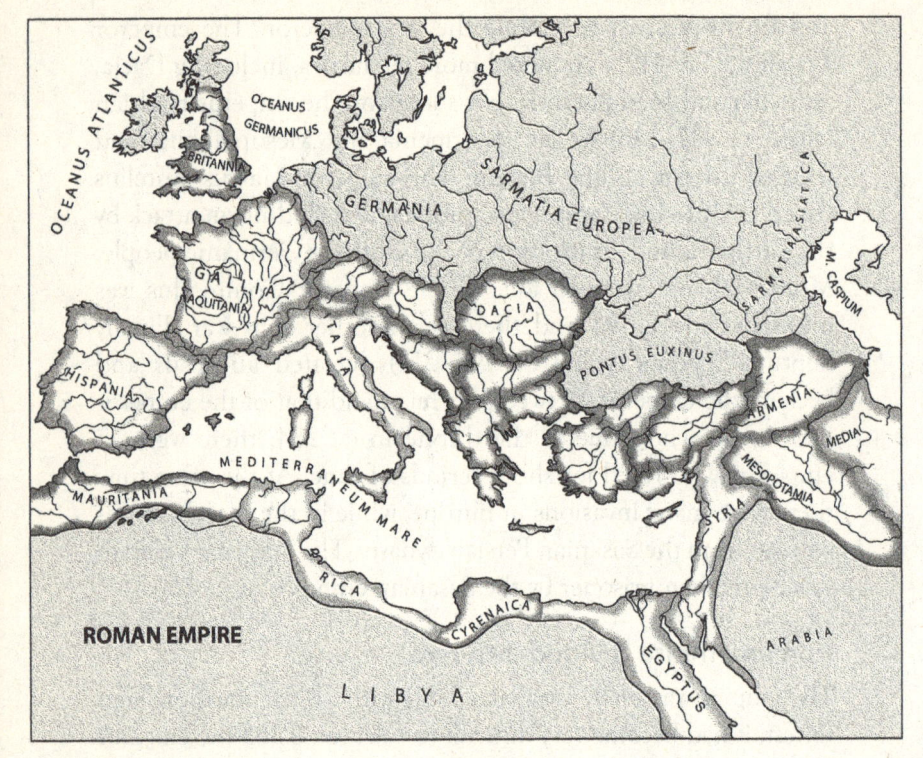

Map of the Roman empire

Invaders

In the 5th century, the Roman empire was invaded by different groups.

These included the Visigoths, Huns and Vandals. The Visigoths were a Germanic group. Led by their king, Alaric I, they won a victory against Rome in 410. Later they established their own kingdom extending over Gaul (France), Spain and Portugal.

The Vandals were another Germanic group, who invaded both Eastern and Western empires. In 455 they destroyed the city of Rome.

The Huns were a nomadic group who gradually formed an

empire. They invaded first the Eastern and then the Western empires.

With all these attacks the Western empire totally declined. The Eastern was able to recover its territories.

SOME EVENTS
Revolts

The Roman emperors had to face several revolts. Among them was the revolt of Boudicca of England, and Gildo of Africa.

Boudicca, the widow of Prasutagus, a local king in England, began a revolt in CE 61, but was defeated.

In CE 397, Gildo, appointed Count of Africa and head of Roman administration there, started a revolt. He was defeated and killed.

A buried city—Pompeii

Pompeii was a city near present Naples in Italy. It came under Rome in 80 BCE. In CE 79 the volcano, Vesuvius erupted. Its ash and lava buried the city. The nearby city of Herculaneum was also destroyed.

Pompeii remained buried for 1500 years. It was first partly excavated in 1748. Later more parts of the city were discovered. Most of the population had managed to leave the city before its destruction. Even so, about 2000 lay dead in the streets and houses. The houses and buildings were preserved under the ash. One can still see the streets, houses, bathhouses and other buildings of those days.

The remains of Herculaneum, which were covered in mud, can also be seen.

ROMAN LIFE

Roman life was similar in the time of the republic and the empire. But during the time of the empire it grew more prosperous.

Provinces

The empire had provinces in Europe, Asia and Africa. The number of provinces changed over time. Between the 1st and 2nd centuries CE, there were more than 30 provinces. The emperor Diocletian created a 100 provinces. Emperors could not personally rule all the provinces. Different types of officials were appointed to govern them. In some of the imperial provinces, where Roman legions (armies) were stationed, legati or representatives of the emperor were the governors. Most of the other provinces were governed by an official known as a proconsul, who was appointed by the senate. Some other provinces had were governed by lower officials known as prefects.

Usually people in the different provinces were allowed to follow their local customs and practices.

Trade

There was trade by land and sea among the various provinces of the Roman empire. There was also trade with other countries, mainly India and China. Though the Romans erected great structures, they did not produce many items for exchange. Trade was mainly in agricultural products, grain, nuts, fruit, oil and wine. Garum, fermented fish sauce, was also traded. Oil, wine and garum were put in a particular kind of pottery vessel called amphorae.

Papyrus scrolls were brought from Egypt for writing books. Spices came from India. Other items imported from India included rubies, diamonds, sandalwood and pearls.

Rome had its own coinage, in gold, silver and bronze. Bronze coins were known as sestertius. Four sestertii were equal to one dinarii, a silver coin. Some of the provinces had their own coinage.

Accurate weights and measures were used.

Roman cities and towns

The Roman empire had a number of cities.

Most cities had a Forum, a space where people could meet. Here they celebrated festivals and watched plays or games. There were large buildings and temples in the Forum, and markets nearby.

The greatest city was that of Rome, but others too were quite large. Cities were planned, with roads in a grid pattern, that is, at right angles to each other.

Roman cities also had bridges. There were aqueducts to provide water. Aqueducts were of different kinds. Some were like canals, others like pipes.

There were bathhouses, where people bathed in the evenings. Many cities had libraries, schools and colleges.

Houses were of different kinds. Wealthy people had houses with many rooms, built around an atrium, a kind of courtyard open to the sky. The walls had paintings or frescoes, and the floors were decorated with mosaic. Some had their own bathrooms and gardens. There was even a heating system. Other people lived in small houses with only one or two rooms.

ROME

Rome had some very grand buildings. Among them were:

The Colosseum

The Colosseum was a huge amphitheatre built in Rome. It was inaugurated in CE 80.

It was circular and had seats in tiers around it, where thousands could sit to watch games or plays. The remains of the Colosseum can still be seen.

The Circus Maximus

Circus was a term for an arena, a large area where chariot races and other games took place. Around it were rows of seats. There were circuses in many cities but the largest was the Circus Maximus in Rome. This was built in 600 BCE and later expanded. It remained in use till about CE 600. It could accommodate an audience of 2,00,000 people. The term Circus also began to be used for the activities that took place in it.

Villa estates

In rural areas there were villa estates as well as other types of villages. A villa estate had a large house or villa. Around it there was farmland, though some were engaged in other activities like mining or making wine. Farming was done by peasants or slaves, who lived in small houses.

A day in a Roman city

Usually the Romans had breakfast, called ientaculum, early in the morning. They ate flat salted bread, but rich people also had milk, honey, fruit and other items. After breakfast they attended to work, and returned home for lunch.

Lunch, called prandium, was a more substantial meal. After lunch was siesta, the time for sleep and rest. Then in the evening they visited the gymnasium and the public baths. Women and men had separate areas for baths. After that it was time for dinner, which could be a grand meal, specially if there were guests. Dinner was called cena. Like today, a good dinner had starters, a main meal and dessert. The starters could be olives, and small tasty eats; the main course had meat, fish and vegetables, and the dessert was usually fruit. Wine was drunk with the meal. Grand dinners could have 22 courses.

The bathhouses

A bath in the bathhouses took quite a long time. There was hot water, steam and cold water used alternately. Bathers were rubbed with oil, which was then scraped off, along with dirt. During the whole process there was time to talk and chat.

Clothes

Women and girls wore tunics. When going out, they also used a shawl. Men too dressed in tunics with cloaks. In winter they wore leggings, to keep the legs warm. But for formal and special occasions, rich and important men wore a traditional garment called the toga. The toga was made of woollen cloth. It was draped around the body. At the bottom was a coloured stripe, indicating the rank of the person. The emperor's toga had a purple stripe.

A legion

The Romans had a very strong army. A legion was a division of the Roman army. It had foot soldiers and those on horses, i.e. cavalry. Altogether there were 3000–6000 soldiers in a legion.

Entertainment

In the cities there were different types of entertainment.

The Romans played both official and non-official games. The games took place in special areas called arenas. Plays were performed in theatres and amphitheatres. Chariot races were very popular.

There were also gladiator contests and wild animal hunts.

Gladiators were people trained to fight. They were slaves, criminals, prisoners of war, or Christians, who were initially not liked. They fought in public in the Roman circuses or amphitheatres. Two armed people fought until one was defeated or killed. Gladiators who won many victories became famous. When the Colosseum was first inaugurated in CE 80 there were 100 days of games. According to various accounts 11,000 wild animals and 10,000 gladiators were killed in these 100 days. The emperor Trajan organized a contest of 5000 pairs of gladiators in CE 107. There were some strange contests. In CE 90 the emperor Domitian made women and dwarfs fight among themselves.

In CE 325 the emperor Constantine stopped gladiator fights, but they still continued to some extent.

Chariot races
Chariot races were popular. In Rome, chariot races were held in the Circus Maximus. They usually took place between four teams. Each chariot was drawn by four horses. The four teams wore different colours: green, red, blue and white.

Wild animals
The Romans liked to watch wild animals fighting. Such fights took place in the arenas.

Wild animals were made to fight with one another, or with people.

Education
Girls generally studied at home with their mothers. They were often married early, by the age of twelve. At the time of marriage they had to give up their dolls and other toys.

Young boys from rich families studied with their fathers, and later went to school or had a special tutor. They learnt Latin and various other subjects, including Greek, geometry, arithmetic, grammar and philosophy. Those who wanted to study further learnt oratory, or public speaking, or law. Some went to Athens and Rhodes (both in Greece) to study. Boys were generally married later than girls, usually after the age of fifteen.

Science
Roman science was mainly borrowed from that of Greece. But the Romans were extremely advanced in the science of construction. They made huge buildings, arches and columns, and very good roads. They used stone, brick and marble in their buildings, as well as a type of concrete. They had heated baths, and aqueducts

to bring clean water. They built lighthouses and constructed useful items like flour mills.

Roman culture

Rome is known for its great literature, art and culture.

The early Romans are thought to have derived their alphabet, numerals, and elements of art and architecture from the Etruscan culture. After the conquest of the Greek islands they were influenced by Greek culture.

Literature

Romans wrote in Latin and Greek.

Many Greek works were translated into Latin.

Among the great literature of Roman times is *The Aeneid*, composed by the poet Virgil (70-19 BCE). *The Aeneid* has accounts of the kings of early Rome. It includes the story of Aeneas.

Many other books were written on different subjects. There were histories, poetry, literature and philosophy, as well as works on architecture and science. A few of them are given here:

AENEAS

Aeneas was a Trojan warrior. After Troy was destroyed, Aeneas was asked by the gods to go to Italy. He set off by ship along with his friends and companions. After six years he reached Carthage, which was then ruled by Queen Dido. Aeneas stayed there for a year, and though Dido wanted him to live there forever, he had to leave. Queen Dido was filled with sorrow and killed herself. After more adventures, Aeneas reached Latium. He married Lavinia, daughter of the king of Latium, and founded a city called Lavinium. Aeneas is considered the ancestor of several people of Rome, including Rhea Silvia and Julius Caesar.

Suetonius, in around CE 121 wrote *De Vita Caesarum*, on 12 Roman rulers from Caesar to the emperor Domitian.

Livy (c. 59 BCE–CE 17), a Roman historian, wrote *Ab urbe condita* (History of Rome) in 142 books. It is on Roman history from 753 BCE up to 9 BCE. Thirty-five volumes are fully preserved, and parts of another 105. These works were prominent up to the time of the Renaissance in the 16th century.

Lucretius (c. 99–55 BCE) wrote a philosophical poem in six volumes, called *De Rerum Natura* (On the Nature of Things).

Ovid (43 BCE–CE 17), a great Latin poet, composed *Metamorphoses*, a long poem in 15 books, as well as other works. *Metamorphoses* deals with history, from the time of creation to that of Julius Caesar.

Pliny the elder (CE 23–79) wrote *Historia Naturalis* in 37 parts. It is an encyclopaedia on various sciences and natural history.

Marcus Vitruvius Polio (lived from 80 or 70 BCE to about 15 BCE), was a Roman architect and engineer who wrote a work in ten volumes, called *De Architectura* (On Architecture). He described four classical architectural types, Dorian, Ionian, Corinthian, and Tuscan, and put forward other principles such as utility and design, as well as practical details on construction.

Gaius Valerius Catallus (c. 84–54 BCE) wrote poems to a woman called Lesbia.

Horace (65–8 BCE) was another great author. Marcus Tullius Cicero (106–43 BCE), a member of the senate, is remembered as Rome's greatest orator. He wrote philosophical, legal and literary works in Latin.

The emperor Marcus Aurelius (ruled CE 161–180) is known for his philosophical work, *Meditations*.

Julius Caesar too was a great writer.

Plubius Terentius Afer, also called Terence (195 or 185 BCE–159 BCE), was a well-known dramatist.

Tacitus (CE 56-117), a historian, and Petronius (CE 27-66) were among some of the many other writers of the empire.

RELIGION
Roman religion

Before Christianity became the main religion, the Romans had many different gods and goddesses. There were about 30 early gods. After the Roman conquests of different lands, new gods were introduced. Some gods and goddesses were similar to the Greek gods, but usually had different names. Among the Roman gods were:

Jupiter, the chief of the gods

Mars, the god of war

Quirinus, an early god

Janus, the god of gates, doorways, beginnings, endings and time; he is depicted with two heads.

Vesta, goddess of the home

Diana, protector of wild animals, goddess of hunting, and later the moon goddess

Minerva, goddess of wisdom

Hercules, son of Jupiter, famous for his strength

Venus, goddess of beauty and love, and of fields and gardens

Apollo, god of the sun; also the god of medicine, archery, and of foretelling the future

Saturn, god of agriculture

Pluto, god of the underworld

Juno, goddess of marriage and childbirth

Diana: this marble statue of the Greek goddess Artemis or the Roman goddess Diana, is of the 1st–2nd centuries CE, originally found in Italy

Neptune, god of the sea
Uranus, god of the sky
Mercury, messenger of the gods, and god of trade and traders

There were also minor deities. The lares and penates were guardian deities. Images of them were often kept in homes.

Mithra or Mithras, originally an Indo-Iranian deity, and the gods Isus and Osirus, originally from Egypt, were also worshipped.

Religious officials

The Pontifex Maximus was the official in charge of all religious activities. The emperor, in his role as religious leader, was the holder of this title. Below the Pontifex Maximus were 16 pontifices to help him.

Jupiter: this marble statue of Jupiter belongs to the 1st century CE. The eagle, staff and statue of victory are of plaster and late additions

Christianity

Gradually Christianity became the main religion. Paul of Tarsus (lived c. CE 10-67), who was earlier called Saul, was at first against Jesus and Christianity. But while crossing a desert he had a vision of Jesus and became his follower. Then he told people about Jesus, and asked them to follow Jesus' teachings. Later, the emperor Constantine become a Christian, and enforced Christianity in parts of his empire. The emperor Theodosius (ruled CE 372-395) made the Nicene Creed of Christianity the official religion, and was the first not to take the title of Pontifex Maximus. Earlier deities and the worship of Mithra declined. A number of temples were built in the Roman empire. Later churches too were erected.

The Pantheon

The Pantheon in Rome was a huge circular temple, covered with a dome. All the Roman gods were worshipped here. On top of the dome is an oculus, a space through which natural light could enter. Around the sides are pairs of columns and sculptures in niches.

Festivals

The Romans celebrated a number of festivals. Many of these were connected with the harvest. One special festival was called Saturnalia. It was held in December to worship the god Saturn.

14
West Asia and Central Asia: The Early Period

West Asia includes the Arab peninsula (Arabia), Iran, Iraq and neighbouring regions. In this region there were kingdoms and cities. And there were two new and different religions.

ARABIA

We saw that Arabia had the early Maqar civilization. Later, there were several early kingdoms and dynasties in Arabia. The Minean kingdom existed from 1200-650 BCE. The Himyarites were another dynasty, who ruled southern Arabia from about 115 BCE to CE 525. The main region of the Himyarite kingdom was in present Yemen, though it extended to other areas of south Arabia. The Sabaean and Nabatean kingdoms were among other kingdoms in Arabia.

SABAEAN KINGDOM

The Sabaean or Saba Kingdom lasted from c. 930 BCE-115 BCE. It was famous and prosperous.

Marib (in present Yemen) was its capital. Trade routes passed through this city, and caravans reached here from distant areas. At Marib, a big dam was built. Irrigation from this helped to improve agriculture. Sirwah was another big city. Grand temples and buildings were built in both cities. Saba took over some coastal areas of Africa, and controlled the straits of the Red Sea. The Queen of Sheba is believed to be of this kingdom. (You can read a story about her below.)

NABATEAN KINGDOM

The Nabatean kingdom existed in northern Arabia, with its capital at Petra in south-west Jordan.

Petra was a rich city. Between 400 BCE and CE 200 it was an important trade centre. The Nabateans carved buildings and tombs into the sandstone cliffs of Petra. Petra means city of rock. It is called Sela in the Bible. Petra is a huge fortress, approached through a narrow passage of rock known as the siq. In some places this is only 3.7 metres wide. Beyond this is the Khaznet Firaun, a temple, also called the treasury of pharaohs. There was a theatre here, where 3000 people could be seated to watch different activities.

Nabatean was conquered by the Romans in CE 106.

IRAN—ELAM

Iran (Persia) had farming settlements from 8000 BCE. Cities existed here by 4000 BCE. Later, there were different types of settlements. Among them was the civilization of Elam. This was located to the east of Mesopotamia, in present south-west Iran extending into Iraq. Before 3000 BCE there were a number of small states which joined together to form Elam in around 2700 BCE.

The main cities in Elam were Susa and later Anshan. Elam had several dynasties of kings, and despite some defeats continued to rule parts of the region till 539 BCE. Elam had its own language written in cuneiform script.

The people of Elam made beautiful sculptures. They worshipped several gods. The main god was Khumban. Inshushinak and Jabru were some of the other deities. Karirisha was a goddess. While Elam was declining the Medes formed an empire around 650 BCE. They in turn were defeated by the Achaemenids.

Shar-i sukhteh—an interesting city

Many villages and cities are known from archaeology in Iran. Among them, an interesting city was Shar-i sukhteh, on the southeast border of Iran, on the bank of the river Helmand. The name means 'the burnt city'. It was occupied around 3200 BCE, and it was burnt down thrice before it was abandoned around 2100 BCE. The city had various, different crafts and a huge graveyard containing graves of around 25,000 to 40,000 people. Trade was important in this city.

Shar-i sukhteh seems to have had an advanced system of medicine. The world's first artificial eyeball was found here. A gold thread held it in place. It was worn by a woman, 1.82 m tall.

THE HEBREWS

The Hebrews were a people whose story is told in the Bible.

The Bible says that Abraham came from Ur to Canaan. Ur was part of Mesopotamia. Canaan was the region of present Israel, Palestine and nearby areas. Abraham was the leader of the people known as Hebrews. Jacob was his grandson. Jacob was also known as Israel. Jacob had many children and Joseph was his eleventh son. Because Jacob loved Joseph best, his brothers were jealous. One day, they sold him as a slave to some traders. The traders took him to Egypt and sold him there. Joseph had many talents. Soon he became a high official in Egypt.

Later, because of a famine in Canaan, Jacob sent his sons to Egypt. After some time, he too went there. Many years passed. Jacob, Joseph and their families died.

Hebrews still lived in Egypt. But some Egyptian pharaohs began to sense a threat from them. The Hebrews also suffered from mistreatment. Moses, one of the Hebrews, escaped and went to the Sinai Peninsula. After living there for many years, he had a divine vision on Mt Horeb (identified with Mt Sinai). God spoke to him from a burning bush, and asked Moses to return to Egypt, rescue the Hebrews who had been made into slaves, and take them back to Canaan. After many problems, led by Moses, the Hebrews began the return journey to Canaan. On the way, Moses again went to Mt Horeb, and received the Ten Commandments from God. These formed the basis for a new religion, now known as Judaism. Later, the Hebrews returned to Canaan.

This is the traditional story, though historians are not sure whether the events described really happened or when they took place. (Abraham may have reached Canaan from Ur around 1800 BCE. The probable date for their return, led by Moses and later by Joshua, is between 1400-1200 BCE.)

After their return

The Hebrews, also known as the Israelites, fought against the Canaanites and Philistines who lived in Canaan, and established their own territory. They had a number of tribes or clans.

Early kings

According to the Bible and other sources, three early kings were Saul, David and Solomon.

A portrait of King Solomon: this is a detail from a larger painting by the French painter Ingobertus. It can be dated c. 880 CE.

King Solomon was famous for his wisdom. He built a temple at Jerusalem in c 950 BCE. His kingdom was very rich, and people from other lands visited him.

> **THE STORY OF QUEEN SHEBA AND A BIRD**
>
> A Jewish text (*Targum Shem*) says that all living creatures used to dance in front of King Solomon. But one day the hoopoe bird did not appear. King Solomon called the bird and asked him why, and the bird said he had found a wonderful new land. It was full of gold, silver and wonderful plants. Its capital was Kitor, it was called Sheba, and it was ruled by a queen. King Solomon requested the bird to ask the queen to visit, and Queen Sheba then visited King Solomon. The Bible says the queen brought gold and jewels as gifts. She had heard of Solomon's wisdom, and came with riddles for him to solve. King Solomon in turn gave her gifts with which she returned to her own land. The land of Sheba is thought to be Saba, a kingdom in Arabia (described above).
>
> According to some accounts, kings of Ethiopia were descended from King Solomon and Queen Sheba.

Two kingdoms

After Solomon's death two kingdoms arose. The northern kingdom was called Israel, and the southern Judah. Ten tribes were located in the northern kingdom of Israel, which was conquered by the Assyrians in 721 BCE. According to tradition, the ten tribes wandered to different places. Later they came to be known as the 'Lost Tribes of Israel'. Judah too came under Assyria in 682 BCE. Israel and Judah were both conquered by a Neo-Babylonian dynasty in 627 BCE. This is also known as the Chaldean dynasty. Jerusalem in Judah was attacked by

Nebuchadnezzar II of Babylon in 587-586 BCE. He captured and took many of the people to Babylon.

Cyrus II, founder of the Achaemenid empire of Iran (see Chapter 16), next conquered the region. He freed the Jewish people in Babylon, and allowed them to return to Jerusalem.

RELIGION

People worshipped different gods. But at this time two new religions were founded. Both of them believed in one supreme God.

Judaism

Judaism was the religion of the Hebrews. Judaism believes in one God, Yahweh. God created the world, and gave his people some rules and laws to follow. The people who follow Judaism are today known as Jews.

The Hebrew Bible is the main text of Judaism. Other texts were written later.

Jewish Bible

The Jewish Bible is also known as the Hebrew Bible, Tanach, or Mikra.

It has three parts, Torah, Neviim and Ketuvim. Torah, or the Law, is the most important, consisting of the first five books or sections of the Bible. These are also known as the Pentateuch or the five books of Moses. The Jews believe they were chosen by God to listen to him and follow his commandments. These, known as Mitzvah, are contained in the Torah. Among them are the Ten Commandments of Moses.

Neviim, or the Prophets, contains eight books on the Prophets, while Ketuvim, or the Writings, has 11 books, including the Psalms, Proverbs and the book of Job. Most of these 24 books were initially written in Hebrew. A Greek translation, the Septuagint was made in the 3rd century BCE.

Torah, in a wider sense, includes other Jewish texts as well.

Zoroastrianism

Zoroastrianism was founded by a prophet known as Zarathushtra (known in Greek as Zoroaster). He lived in Iran around 1500 BCE. He said there was one god known as Ahura Mazda. People should live a good life and help Ahura Mazda to create a better world.

Zarathushtra's words are in a text called *The Gathas*. His ideas influenced Judaism, and later Christianity and Islam.

CENTRAL ASIA—THE REGION

Central Asia includes the present countries of Kazakhstan, Kyrgyzstan, Tajikistan, Turkmenistan and Uzbekistan, as well as some areas around these countries. In this region there are high mountains and passes, deserts and grassy steppes. The main rivers are the Amu Darya (Oxus), Syr Darya and Hari. The Aral Sea and Lake Balkash are in this region.

The early history of Central Asia is known only from archaeology. There were many different 'archaeological cultures' in this region. Among them were the Sintashta culture in the southern Urals and northern Kazakhstan (2200-1600 BCE), where people kept sheep, goats, cattle, horses and dogs. Horse-drawn chariots have been found in graves here.

In Turkmenistan the Djeitun culture, named after a village of that name, had early agriculture dating to 7000-6000 BCE. Later there were cities in the region.

Oxus civilization

The Bactria Margiana Archaeological Complex (BMAC or Oxus civilization), dated to 2200-1700 BCE, is another interesting culture. The BMAC was in present Turkmenistan, northern Afghanistan and Iran, southern Uzbekistan and western Tajikistan.

Some of the places of this culture had multi-roomed structures and were fortified. There was pottery, fine ceramics, jewellery and items of stone, bronze, silver, gold and semi-precious stones. There were seals carved with narrative scenes and amulets with snakes, scorpions, eagles, Bactrian camels and other items. Wheat and barley were among the crops grown, and irrigation was practised.

This limestone goat with blue eyes made from lapis lazuli, belongs to the Oxus civilization.

15

Christianity

Christianity arose in the region where the Hebrews lived. In the previous chapter we have seen that there were two Hebrew kingdoms: Israel in the north and Judah in the south. Samaria and Galilee were part of the northern kingdom of Israel. The people of Israel left the kingdom after its conquests by the Assyrians in 721 BCE. Judah, too, was later conquered by the Assyrians.

After this there were other dynasties and rulers, including the Neo-Babylonians (Chaldeans), the Seleucid Greeks and the Hasmoneans. Finally the region came under the Romans in 63 BCE.

THE ROMANS

Herod

Herod became the Roman governor of Galilee in 47 BCE. In 40 BCE he was named King of the Jews. Helped by the Romans, he captured Jerusalem, which was under Antigonus, a Hasmonean in 37 BCE. Herod became the governor of Judea. He built amphitheatres, palaces and other huge buildings in the region.

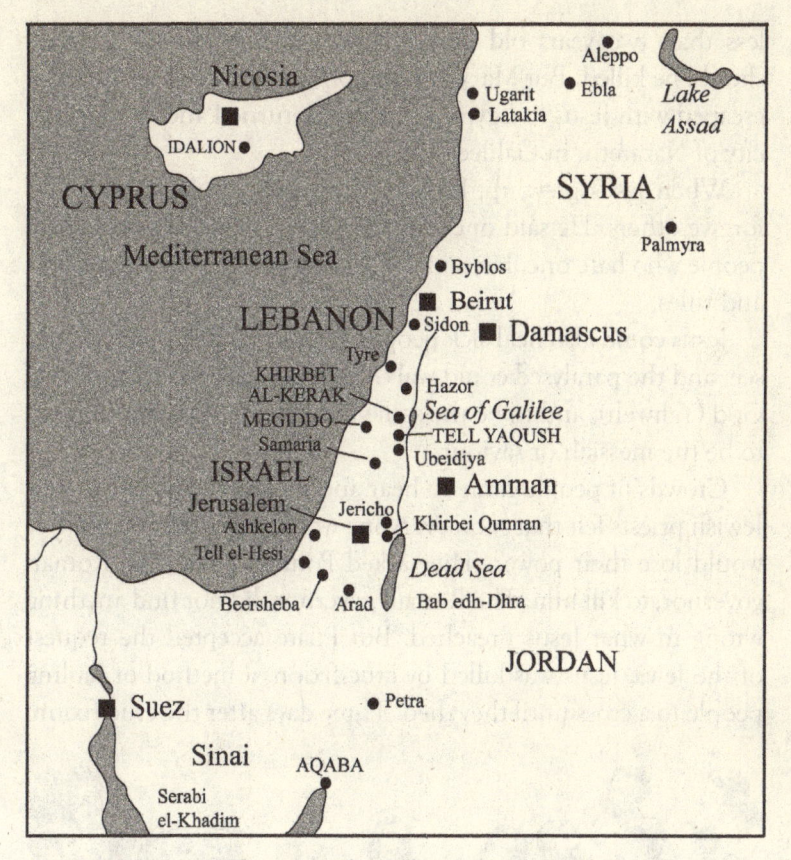

The region where Christianity arose

JESUS

According to stories in the Gospels of the New Testament, which is part of the Christian Bible, Jesus was a Jew born in Bethlehem in Judea (the Roman name of Judah), when Herod was the king. This was around 5 BCE. Jesus was born through a miracle to Mary, who was married to Joseph. Wise men told Herod that a great king was born, and Herod was afraid that this newborn king would grow up and kill him. So Herod ordered that all children less than two years old in Bethlehem and surrounding areas, should be killed. But Mary and Joseph came to know of this and escaped with Jesus to Egypt. Later they returned and lived in the city of Nazareth, in Galilee.

When Jesus grew up, he began to teach people to love and forgive others. He said one should even love one's enemies and people who hate one. He said this was more important than laws and rules.

Jesus could also heal sick people. By his touch the blind could see, and the paralysed could walk. Jesus was said to be the son of God (Yahweh), and to be the same as God. He was also believed to be the messiah or saviour.

Crowds of people came to hear and see Jesus. Some Jews and Jewish priests felt that soon everyone would follow Jesus and they would lose their power. They asked Pontius Pilate, the Roman governor, to kill him. The Roman governor did not find anything wrong in what Jesus preached. But Pilate accepted the request of the Jews. Jesus was killed by crucifixion, a method of nailing people to a cross until they died. Three days after the crucifixion,

A painting of Jesus at the Last Supper

Jesus came to life again and was seen by people. This is called the resurrection. Jesus promised that everyone who followed his teachings would live again after death.

THE APOSTLES

Jesus had chosen 12 people to be his companions and to spread his teachings. They are called the apostles. The twelve apostles were: Simon Peter and his brother Andrew, James and his brother John, Philip, Thomas, Bartholomew, Mathew, James the son of Alphaeus, Simon Zelotes, Judas, brother of James, and Judas Iscariot, who later betrayed Jesus. After the betrayal, Judas Iscariot was replaced by Matthias. The 12 disciples, who were the first group of apostles, were selected when Jesus was around 30 years old.

Some later disciples, such as Paul, also called themselves apostles.

THE POPE

Pope comes from the word for 'father'. The pope was first in charge of the whole Christian Church and later only of Catholics. The Apostle Peter is considered to be the first pope. He was later called St Peter.

APOSTOLIC FATHERS

Apostolic Fathers, is a term for disciples and successors of the apostles. Among them was Clement I of Rome, who was the pope in CE 92-101; St Ignatius of Antioch; and St Polycarp, who was martyred at Smyrna in CE 155.

JEWS AND CHRISTIANS SEPARATE

Jesus was called Christ, which means messiah or saviour. That is why followers of Jesus are called Christians, and the religion is called Christianity.

Early Christians were Jews, but later, by about CE 136, Christianity and Judaism separated. The Jewish temple was destroyed by the Romans in CE 70. At first the Jews resisted Roman rule; later many of them settled in areas outside the Roman empire. Their religious leaders were known as rabbis. New Jewish texts were written, including the Mishnah and Talmud. In CE 380 Christianity became the official religion of the Roman empire. It also spread to other regions and among other people.

THE CHRISTIAN BIBLE

The Bible is the main text of Christianity. The Christian Bible has two parts, the Old Testament and the New Testament. The Old Testament includes all the books of the Hebrew Bible but is differently arranged and divided, the whole forming 39 books. Sometimes additional books are added. It was originally written mainly in Hebrew, with some Aramaic passages. It was probably composed between 1000 BCE and 300 BCE, and was translated into Greek by the 3rd century BCE.

The New Testament was first written in Greek, some time after Jesus died. The most important part of it consists of four books describing the life of Jesus. These are called the Gospels of Mathew, Mark, Luke and John. Another important book is the Acts of the Apostles, which describes what happened soon after Jesus died and was resurrected. In addition there are 22 Epistles or letters, written by various disciples. The last part is the book of Revelation, which reveals the future.

The Bible was translated into Latin in the 2nd century CE. In the 5th century it was translated into the Anglo-Saxon language, and in the 14th century into English. Since then there have been different Bibles in English, as well as in more than 364 languages in all parts of the world.

CONFLICTS IN CHRISTIANITY

Jesus Christ taught that one should lead a simple life and show love and compassion. All Christians agreed to this, but there were a number of philosophical topics on which they had differences. For instance, was Jesus divine? What did the statement that Jesus was the son of God mean? Was he the same as God, or was he different, a human being? These questions and others were debated by scholars, priests, popes and kings over centuries. There were also debates on how Jesus was to be worshipped.

Arianism

Arius, a priest initially from Libya, said that Jesus was not divine in the same way as God, but was made by God. Some followed him but many disagreed. In 379 the Roman emperor Theodosius I (ruled 379-395) banned his teachings but many in Europe still followed them.

The Nicene Creed

The Nicene Creed was first laid down in CE 325. This was later affirmed by the emperor Theodosius. It said that the son, that is Jesus, was the same as the father, that is God.

16
Empires of Iran (Persia): Achaemenids, Parthians and Sasanians

In Iran, which was also known as Persia, there were three great early empires. These empires conquered different regions, and extended far beyond Persia. The ruling dynasties of these empires were the Achaemenids, the Parthians and the Sasanians.

> **PERSIA/IRAN**
>
> Persia and Iran refer to the same region.
>
> The Persian kings mentioned below are usually known by Greek names. Their original Persian names are given in brackets.

ACHAEMENIDS (HAKHAMANISHYA)

Anshan, in south-west Iran, was a capital of the kingdom of Elam. Tiespes (lived 675–640 BCE) conquered Anshan. He was the son of Achaemenes (the Greek form of the Persian word Hakhamanishya), after whom the dynasty was named. In Anshan, Tiespes was succeeded by his son Cyrus I (Kurush), and the next king was his son Cambyses I (Kambuja).

Cyrus II

Cyrus II (Kurush) the Great (ruled 559–c.529 BCE) was the son of Cambyses I. According to an early Greek source, his mother was the daughter of Astyges, king of the Medes. Astyges dreamt that Cyrus would one day overthrow him, and ordered that he be killed. But secretly, Cyrus was given to a shepherd. Astyges found him when he was ten years old, but let him live. Cyrus became king of Anshan in 559. He defeated Astyges and the Medes who ruled in other parts of Persia, and declared himself king of Persia. Next he defeated the Lydians, and the Neo-Babylonians who were ruling in West Asia. He expanded his territory further into Central Asia, but died while fighting against the Massagetae, a nomadic people who lived in the north-east, near the Caspian Sea.

Cyrus II is remembered for having laid the foundations of the Achaemenid empire. He reorganized the administration and divided the empire into provinces. His main capital was at Pasargadae. An earlier capital was at Ecbatana and the winter capital was at Babylon.

Cyrus was known for his tolerance. The Bible records that he allowed the Jews, who had been sent into exile by the Babylonians, to return to Israel and rebuild their temple. He also allowed the Babylonians to worship their own gods and rebuild their temples, too.

Cambyses II, the son of Cyrus, conquered Egypt but soon died.

Darius I

Darius I became the king in 521 BCE. He was the son of Hydaspes (Vishtaspa), who was the governor of Parthia, a province in the

CYRUS CYLINDER

The Cyrus cylinder is a baked clay cylinder with writing on it, found in Babylon (in present Iraq), and composed during the reign of Cyrus. It describes the achievements of Cyrus. It is written in the Akkadian language in Babylonian cuneiform script, and has 45 lines. It includes the following words about the king.

'I am Cyrus, king of the world, great king, powerful king, king of Babylon, king of Sumer and Akkad, king of the four quarters of the earth, son of Cambyses, great king, king of Anshan, descendant of Tiespes, great king, king of Anshan.'

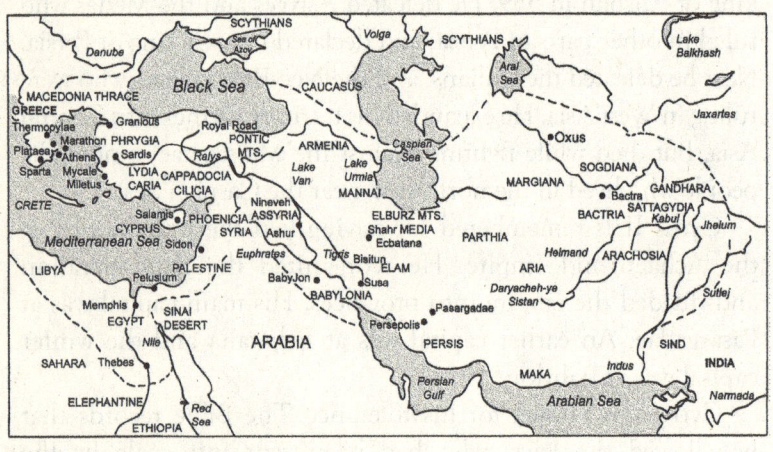

The Achaemenid empire

kingdom. Darius I traced his descent to Ariaramnes, another son of Tiespes, and hence was also an Achaemenid. He was with Cambyses II in Egypt, and after Cambyses' death, he returned to Persia.

Meanwhile Cambyses had left his brother Smerdis (Bardiya) on the throne. Darius killed him and became the king.

Darius conquered new areas including Macedonia, some Greek

> **BARDIYA/GAUMATA**
>
> According to some accounts Bardiya was killed earlier, and a person who looked like him took over the throne. He was called Gaumata. Darius' own inscription states that he killed Gaumata, to become the king.

islands, and north-west India. Soon he had created a huge empire. This extended from Libya in the west to the river Indus in the east, and from the Caucuses in the north to the Persian Gulf in the south. He divided his empire into 20 provinces or satrapies. His capital was at Susa and later at Persepolis. He built roads and canals. Gold and silver coins were used. His inscriptions were mainly in Old Persian, in a modified type of cuneiform script. The Persians became involved in wars against the Greeks. Fighting against the Greeks Darius was defeated in the Battle of Marathon in 490 BCE.

Elamite, Babylonian and Old Persian were among the main languages of the Achaemenid empire.

> **BEHISTUN INSCRIPTION**
>
> Behistun, a village in western Iran, was once known as Bagastana, which means the place of the gods. On a cliff at a height of 100 m, can be seen an important inscription of Darius I, along with a carving of him. This large carving on the face of the rock measures 5.5 m x 3 m and shows Darius, his bow carrier and lance bearer, and ten people (one under Darius' feet) representing those he had conquered. There is also the symbol of Zoroastrianism. The inscription is written on three panels in three languages, Old Persian, Elamite, and Babylonian.
>
> The inscription narrates how the god Ahura Mazda helped him to kill Gaumata, and then his other enemies.

Darius as depicted at Behistun

Xerxes I

Darius' son Xerxes I (Khshayarsha) was the next ruler. He became king around 486 BCE.

Xerxes continued the wars with the Greeks. He won a great battle against Sparta at a place called Thermopylae. Next he invaded Athens which had been abandoned, but later he suffered defeats. The Persian empire became weak under the next few kings. There were revolts in several areas.

Alexander and Darius III

Darius III became the emperor in 336–35 BCE. Despite the weak kings after Xerxis I and the various revolts, the empire was still huge, almost covering the same extent as at the time of Darius I. Finally, Alexander of Macedon ended the Achaemenid empire, defeating Darius III in three battles, the last being the battle of Gaugamela in 331 BCE.

After Alexander's death, the area was under the Seleucid Greeks.

PARTHIANS

As we have seen earlier, Parthia was a region in Iran. It was also known as Parthava. The Arsacid (Arshakani) dynasty rose to power here, and created another huge empire. As they came from Parthia, they are also known as Parthians.

Arsaces I

The first king was known as Arsaces I (Arsaks). His origins are not clear. According to one account, he was a leader of the Parni tribe, who were part of the Dahae, a federation in Central Asia. Other accounts say Arsaces was of Persian origin, or was a local ruler. Whatever his origin, Arsaces became king of Asaak in 247 BCE. It is not known where this was. Around 238 BCE, Arsaces conquered Parthia or Parthava, from the Greeks.

Some other kings

Arsaces was followed by many other kings. Among them were:
   Mithridates I (Mithradata) (c.171-138 BCE), who expanded the empire.
   Mithridates II (c.124-88 BCE), who restored some lost territories and gained control over the northern Mesopotamian kingdoms and Armenia.

Parthian territory

During its long period of existence, Parthia ruled from different capitals including Nisa (Turkmenistan) and Cteisiphon (on the Tigris, near Baghdad in present Iraq).
   The Parthian empire existed for 475 years. At its height the Parthian empire included parts of present Iran, Iraq, Turkey, Armenia, Georgia, Azerbaijan, Turkmenistan, Tajikistan, Afghanistan, Pakistan-north India, Syria, Lebanon, Jordan, Palestine and Israel.

⌐ ¬
¦___¦ **Parthian Empire**

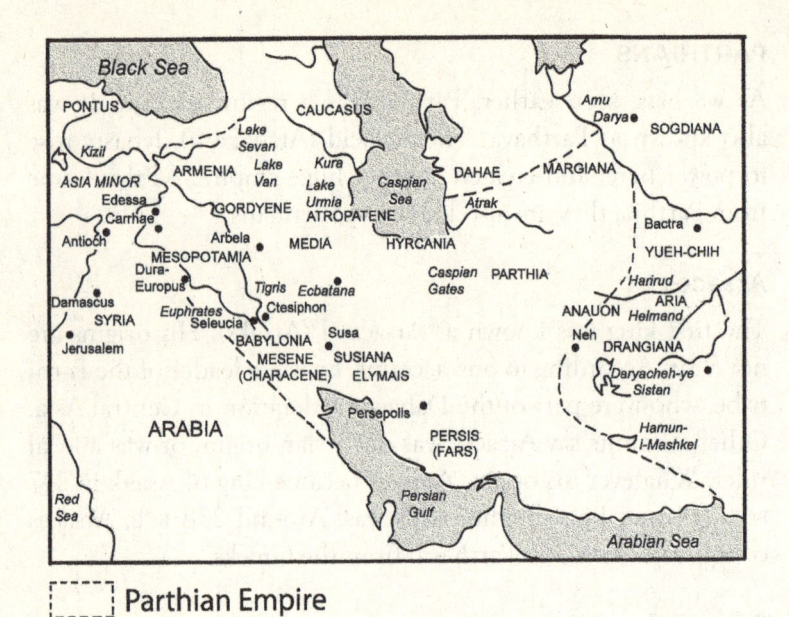

The Parthian empire

Their sub-kingdoms were Characene in southern Mesopotamia, Elymais (Greek form of Elam) and Persis (present region of Fars in Iran). Parthian culture was a mix of Persian, Greek and local or regional cultures. Many languages were spoken in Parthia, including Parthian (an Iranian language), Greek, Middle Persian, Aramaic and Sogdian.

It was not easy to maintain this huge area. Wars were fought against the Seleucids, Romans and others. The Parthians had to defend their frontiers against nomadic tribes.

SASANIANS
Ardashir I
Ardashir was a governor of Persis (Fars) at the time of the Parthians. He defeated the Parthian ruler Artabanus V in CE 224, and gradually gained control over the various Parthian provinces and kingdoms. The last Parthian was Vologases VI,

who ruled till CE 228. In 246 Ardashir I was crowned king at Ctesiphon. He established the Sasanian dynasty. It was named after his ancestor Sasan.

Some other kings

Shapur I (ruled CE 241-272), was the next king and extended the territories through conquest. He conquered Armenia, Georgia, part of present Afghanistan and Pakistan, and extended his territories up to the Gulf of Oman in the south. He fought against the Romans and even captured the Roman emperor Valerian in the Battle of Edessa in 260. The Sasanian empire extended from Mesopotamia to north-west India and Central Asia.

Shapur II (ruled 309-379) had to defend his territories from the Romans and the Huns. During his long reign he further expanded the empire.

Khusrau I (ruled 531-579) defended his territories and reorganized the administration in his empire. He divided it into four parts, each under a *spahbad* or general. Forts and walls were built in the north for defence. Canals helped to improve irrigation and agriculture. New roads, bridges and towns were built to promote trade. His capital was a centre of culture, where scholars and philosophers came from different parts of the world. Greek and Sanskrit books were translated into Pahlavi (Persian of those days).

The succeeding kings faced attacks from the Arabs, Turks and Huns and fought wars against the Byzantine Empire. In CE 642 the Arabs defeated the Sasanian emperor Yazdagird III and took over the empire.

Statues of Sasanian kings

Huge statues of the Sasanian kings were created. Those of Ardashir and Shapur I can be seen at Naqsh-e Rustam, carved on rock. The kings are seated on horses. A statue of Khusrau II is

A rock-cut statue from Naqsh-e Rustam, Iran, of the founder of the Sasanian dynasty, Ardashir. He is depicted to the left, receiving the emblem of kingship from the god Hormuzd, earlier known as Ahura Mazda.

carved in a similar way at Taq-i-Bustan. There is a large statue of a king, found near Bishapur. All these places are in Iran.

TRADE

Important trade routes, both by land and sea, connected the Persian empires with other regions. Mithridates I, the Parthian emperor made an agreement with the Chinese emperor Wudi, in 114 to open an overland trade route, later known as the Silk Route. This route, connecting China and the Roman empire, passed through Persia. There was also sea trade.

Silk, perfumes, spices and other items were imported from India and China.

ARMY

The army included cavalry with bows and arrows, and lances. Horses and archers both wore armour.

COINS

Achaemenid coins often showed a bearded, crowned king carrying weapons. In the time of Darius I there were gold coins called darics, and silver coins known as sigloi. The legends (inscriptions) on the coins were in Old Persian. After the conquest by Alexander, Greek coins were used.

Parthian coins were known as drachma. Coinage was in silver and copper. Silver drachma mainly depicted Arsaces I. Copper coins were of different types. Sometimes deities, horses, stags or elephants were depicted on them. Legends on the early Parthian coins are in Greek, but later Old Persian and Aramaic were used. There were also coins of local dynasties.

Sasanian coins continued the style of Parthian coins, but the drachmas were thinner and larger. Inscriptions were in Pahlavi (Middle Persian). Some of the coins depicted busts of kings or fire altars.

CRAFTS

The three empires were known for their beautiful crafts. In Achaemenid times items were made of stone, gold, silver and semi-precious stones, and of other materials. There was finely decorated pottery and seals made of stone, glass and ivory.

The Parthians wove wool carpets with beautiful embroidery. Their coins had images of kings, as well as of gods and goddesses. They made drinking horns called rhytons from metal and ivory, and some in silver, gold and glass. These were decorated with figures of animals including rams, horses, bulls, ibexes, supernatural creatures, wild cats and goddesses. They also painted frescoes. Parthian pottery included large jars. Jewellery was crafted and large statues were made in bronze, and some in terracotta. One statue of a woman shows her wearing a long, full-sleeved flowing gown, a necklace, bracelets and an elaborate headdress.

In Sasanian times too there was beautiful metalwork including

THE TREASURE OF THE OXUS

Once in the 19th century some traders were travelling by road to India. Along the way, near the river Oxus, they found a hoard of more than 170 gold and silver items. There were bracelets, coins, a beautiful small gold chariot, statues, vessels, and many other items. Some were decorated with glass and semi-precious stones. The traders were very excited! They packed the treasure in their bags, and continued on their journey, crossing through Kabul. But as they proceeded, they were surrounded by robbers and captured. A British officer rescued them, and they gave him one of the precious items. The officer realized that these items were more precious than they knew, as they were ancient, of the time of the Achaemenid dynasty.

The traders sold the items in the markets in India. British officers bought them, and most are now in the British Museum.

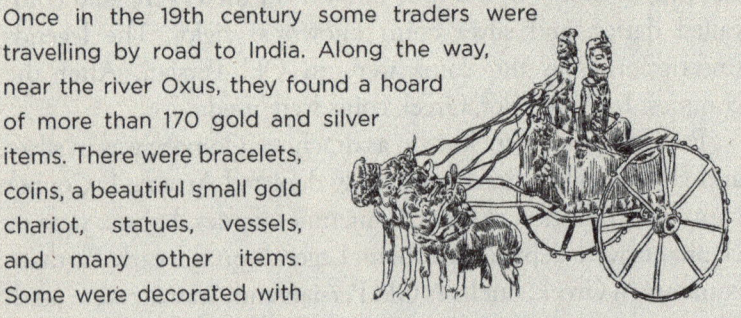

This tiny gold chariot, drawn by four horses, was part of the Oxus treasure. It is now in the British Museum.

silver cups and engraved bronze vessels. Birds, animals, plants and court scenes were depicted on them. Silk was woven with intricate patterns of plants, animals and other items. Sasanian silks and metalware were famous. Glassware, fine pottery, and woollen textiles, as well as carved stone seals, were also made.

Both Achaemenids and Arsacids embalmed their kings and placed them in royal tombs.

Achaemenids and Sasanians specialized in making huge carvings on rocks and cliffs.

SOME IMPORTANT CITIES
Pasargadae
Pasargadae was once a great capital of Cyrus II. Remains of those days include two palaces, apart from the tomb of Cyrus and some other structures. Around the palaces were gardens, and inside were large halls and rooms. The walls were of mud brick, but there were tall stone pillars in the halls, and stone foundations. The ancient city is located in Iran.

Persepolis
Darius had his capital at Persepolis, where a grand palace was built. At the gateway to the city, two bulls with human heads were carved. Within the palace there were sculptures, carvings and columns. On the doorways and staircases the king and royal scenes were depicted. The pillars had animal capitals. On the outer corners, lions were carved. Darius also built a palace at Susa. At Naqsh-e Rustam near Persepolis are rock-cut tombs. Near the tombs the cliffs are carved with the front of a palace and a king worshipping the gods.

At this time ordinary houses were made of mud-brick, but the palaces were of stone and brick.

THE FRIEZE OF ARCHERS

The frieze of archers is one of the decorated panels from Susa. It has rows of soldiers holding spears and carrying bows. The archers have beards and some have curly hair. They wear boots and long robes. The panel is made of glazed bricks in green, white, brown and yellow and blue.

Susa
Cambyses II built a capital at Susa. Here Darius too constructed a palace. It was decorated with glazed brick panels in different

colours, on which there were soldiers, bulls with wings, sphinxes, winged lions and griffins. Susa is now known as Shush, a city in Iran.

Ctesiphon
Ctesiphon was a capital of the Parthians. Their structures no longer exist, but the remains of a palace built by the Sasanid ruler Khusrau II can be seen. It has an arched entrance and a large vaulted hall. Ctesiphon is located in Iraq.

Other cities
The Sasanians built a number of cities at Firuzabad, Bishapur, Neyshabur and others.

The Sasanians used burnt brick, stone and mortar, vaults and domes in their buildings. The palaces had large audience halls and small rooms. Remains of palaces have been found at Firuzabad, Girra, Sarvestan, Qais, Hira and Damghan, among other places.

RELIGION
Zoroastrianism
Zoroastrianism was the main religion of the three empires. We saw that the earliest text of Zoroastrianism was *The Gathas*. This text asks people to lead a good life and to always choose to do the right thing. In this way a perfect world could be created. It describes the supreme god known as Ahura Mazda, and his six special powers. Many other texts were composed later. In the time of the Sasanians these texts were written down in a special script. All the texts together are called the Avesta. The language they are written in is also known as Avesta. Some minor deities known as yazatas were also worshipped. Among them were Mithra and the goddess Anahita.

In Zoroastrianism, fire is considered sacred and is worshipped as a symbol of the divine.

Other religions

Christians, Jews and Buddhists also lived in the empire. Nestorian Christians were prominent. And there were some who started new religions. Among them were Mani and Mazdak. These new religions had good ideas but did not last long.

Mani

Mani's religion was later called Manichaeism. He began to preach around CE 242 in the time of the king Shapur I, who supported him. Mani wrote some books, including the *Shabuhragan* in Persian, and others in Syriac. He tried to combine the best principles of Christianity, Zoroastrianism and Buddhism. As his religion began to spread, kings and priests felt threatened. Mani was put into prison and died there in 276. However, his religion continued to spread and became known from the Roman empire to China.

Mazdak

Mazdak believed there were two equal principles of good and evil, or light and darkness. To bring light into the world he wanted people to live a simple life. He felt the rich should share what they had with the poor. He was popular with poor people, and the Sasanian king Kavadh I at first accepted some of his teachings. But later the king and the rich felt threatened. Mazdak was killed in CE 524.

Both Mani and Mazdak were against eating meat.

17
Africa: Up to CE 500

Africa had different states and groups. North Africa includes the present countries of Morocco, Algeria, Tunisia, Libya and Egypt. With the Mediterranean Sea to the north, this was the most important region of Africa in ancient times. Western Sahara, Mauritania, Mali, Niger, Chad and Sudan are countries just south of the northern region. East of Sudan are Ethiopia, Eritrea and Somalia.

EGYPT

We have already looked at the history of early Egypt. After Alexander's conquest of Egypt in 332 BCE, he appointed governors to rule there. When Alexander died in 323 BCE, Ptolemy, one of his generals, became the ruler, and called himself pharaoh. He built a great library at Alexandria, a city founded by Alexander. Ptolemy I extended his control to Libya, Syria and Cyprus. He encouraged learning and science.

The great mathematician Euclid lived here at this time.

Ptolemy's son Ptolemy II, and grandson Ptolemy III, were the next rulers. Other Ptolemys ruled after this but were not strong kings. In 51 BCE, Ptolemy XIII came to the throne along with his sister Cleopatra VII. It was an Egyptian practice for the pharaohs to marry their sisters; hence Cleopatra was also his wife. Ptolemy XIII was ten years old at this time, and Cleopatra was 17. Cleopatra ruled as queen.

The Romans were already becoming powerful in the region. Julius Caesar of Rome reached Alexandria in 48 BCE. He and Cleopatra fell in love, and had a son, Caesarion. Meanwhile Ptolemy XIII had died after a battle, and Cleopatra married her younger brother, Ptolemy XIV.

In Rome, Julius Caesar was murdered in 44 BCE. Mark Antony and Octavian both wanted power. Cleopatra was living in Rome when Julius Caesar was killed, and she supported Mark Antony. Soon Cleopatra and Mark Antony fell in love, and the two lived together in Egypt. The people of Rome did not like this. Octavian defeated Mark Antony in a sea battle at Actium, and later in Egypt. Both Mark Antony and Cleopatra killed themselves (30 BCE), and Roman rule began in Egypt.

By this time many Greeks were living in Egypt.

ALEXANDRIA

Alexandria was a city founded by Alexander the Great. He wanted it to be the greatest city and port in the whole world. Pharos, an island was connected to Alexandria, creating a harbour. At Pharos a lighthouse was built, which was considered one of the Seven Wonders of the World. Alexandria had palaces, museums and grand buildings. Philosophers and scholars lived here. By the 3rd century BCE, its great library was stocked with more than 5,00,000 books. It was the biggest library of the ancient world. People from different countries lived in Alexandria. There were markets filled with goods from various parts of the world.

The Rosetta stone

Ptolemy V was six years old when his father died in 205 BCE. He was crowned king only in 195 BCE. During his rule several inscriptions were carved on stone slabs listing various rules and decrees. Among them was the Rosetta stone. This inscribed stone was originally erected at a temple at Sais in Egypt. Later it was moved to the town of El Rashid, later known as Rosetta. In 1798 Napoleon and his army captured the stone. In 1801 it was given to the British. And finally in 1822 it was deciphered.

The stone has the same inscription in three languages: Greek, Egyptian hieroglyphics and everyday Egyptian. It was through this stone that the hieroglyphic script was deciphered and our knowledge about ancient Egypt grew.

The Romans

After conquering Egypt, the Romans built forts and walls to guard their southern frontier. In the 4th century CE northern Africa was divided between the Eastern and Western Roman empires. Thus in CE 395 Egypt came under the Byzantine or Eastern Roman empire.

As the Roman empire began to decline, the Vandals ruled part of North Africa for some time. Then Justinian of the Byzantine empire again took over the region.

At the time of the Romans, Alexandria remained the capital of Egypt and was a prosperous port city. It is believed that Mark, the author of one of the Gospels, came here between CE 42 and 62 and brought Christianity to the region. The form of Christianity practised here is known as Coptic (Egyptian) Christianity. At the same time both Greeks and Romans allowed and even encouraged the worship of Egyptian gods.

CARTHAGE

The Phoenicians built early settlements all along the northern coast of Africa, the main city being Carthage. Later Carthage

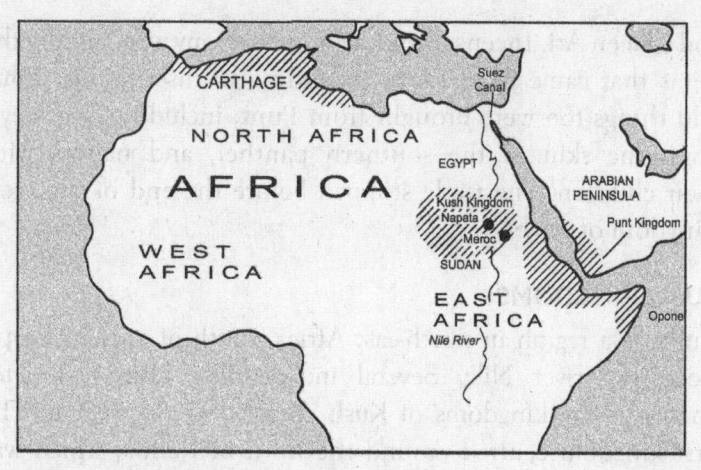

Early Kingdoms of North Africa

Some early kingdoms of Africa

became independent and powerful. It conquered other Phoenician areas. In the 6th century BCE Carthage controlled the northern coast of Africa, up to Egypt in the west, as well as some islands including Malta, Sicily and Sardinia. The empire of Carthage developed different crafts and became rich through trade. They exported silver, lead, jewellery, wooden and glass items. Ivory, gold, and wild animals from the forests were also exported. Carthage fought many wars against the Greeks and Romans. It was conquered by the Romans in 146 BCE. Under Rome, Carthage became a prominent city and a centre of Christianity.

PUNT

The ancient kingdom of Punt or Pwenet is mentioned in Egyptian inscriptions and texts. The first reference dates to 2500 BCE. The location of Punt is not clear, but it was probably in the region of present Somalia, Ethiopia and Eritrea. Egypt traded with Punt and sent ships there. Queen Hatsheput of Egypt visited Punt. At that time it was ruled by King Parahu and Queen Ati. Incense, gold, ivory and ebony were among the items that came from Punt. According to inscriptions, some odd things too were brought from Punt, including 'monkeys, dogs, the skin of the southern panther, and natives with their children'. The trade stopped before the end of the New Kingdom of Egypt.

KUSH KINGDOMS

Nubia is a region in north-east Africa, south of ancient Egypt, along the river Nile. Several independent kingdoms, later known as the kingdoms of Kush emerged in this region. The first kingdom centred around the town of Kerma, which was flourishing from 2400 BCE. The Kerma kingdom was powerful at the time of Egypt's Middle Kingdom, but during the New Kingdom it came under Egypt. From here, Egypt obtained gold, precious and semi-precious stones, ivory and ebony.

After the New Kingdom lost power, another independent kingdom emerged. Its capital was at Napata. Kings of this dynasty even ruled Egypt from c.770–671 BCE, forming the 25th dynasty of Egypt, known as the Kush dynasty. King Taharqa of this dynasty constructed buildings and monuments in Nubia and Egypt. In Egypt the dynasty was replaced by the Assyrians, who conquered the area. But in the Nubian region, Napata continued to exist.

Remains of pyramids of the Kush kindom from Meroe

In the 4th century BCE, the capital was shifted to Meroe. Meroe was a prosperous city and a centre of trade.

The Kush kingdom of Meroe began to decline from the 1st century CE.

Kush culture was influenced by that of Egypt. At the time of the New Kingdom, a great temple was built at Abu Simbel by Rameses II, which was in the Nubian region. Here the gods Amon and Re were worshipped. The Egyptian language and script were used from Napatan times, though a different Meroitic script developed at Meroe.

Under Egyptian influence pyramids were built. Forts, mound graves at Kerma, and pyramids at Napata and Meroe still survive. In a pit in the Nile valley, granite sculptures of early Kush rulers have been found.

AKSUM

Aksum was a kingdom which emerged around 100 BCE in the highlands of Ethiopia. It covered parts of present Ethiopia and Eritrea. There were earlier settlements in the region, along with graveyards. Among them was Ona Nagast, where there was a building partly below the ground, with several rooms.

Aksum is a place on a high plateau after which the kingdom has been named. Around 150 sites of this kingdom have been found. Adulis was its main port. Mai Agam, Matara, Gondar, and Kidane Mehret were other places. There were both towns and villages in the kingdom. Aksum became prosperous through trade. Its exports included gold dust, ivory and perfumes. It traded with Rome, Persia and India.

In the 4th century, a Christian named Frumentius converted the king Ezana to Christianity.

Ezana, also known as Aezianas, spread Christianity in his kingdom. Monasteries and churches were built. Ezana conquered the Kush kingdom of Meroe, and erected 100 stone obelisks.

(An obelisk is a tall, four-sided, tapering pillar). The tallest was 30 m high and weighed more than 500 tonnes. Other kings also erected obelisks. Aksum had its own coins, in gold, silver, and bronze. There were also written records, in their own language, Geez, and in Greek. More than 20 names of kings are known from the coins.

> Frumentius and Edesius were brothers from the city of Tyre. They travelled in a ship with their uncle Meropius to Ethiopia, but on the way, the ship was attacked and everyone but the brothers was killed. They were given as slaves to the king of Aksum, but gained his trust and their freedom. Later Frumentius became a bishop, and after his death, a saint.

NOBATIA

Nobatia was a kingdom in Nubia, in the region of Sudan that existed from c. CE 350-c. 590. Its capital was at Pachoras (modern Faras). Dongola, which may be the same as Makuria, was another kingdom nearby that existed from c. CE 590.

OPONE

Opone in present Somalia was an ancient centre of trade. It has been identified with Ras Hafun. It was prominent in the 1st century CE as the main centre of trade in cinnamon. There were other ancient centres of trade in this region too.

NOK CULTURE

In west Africa, in the region of present Nigeria, is the village of Nok, after which the Nok culture is named. The Nok people lived in villages between c.1000 BCE and the 3rd century CE. By 500 BCE or earlier, they began to make iron tools and weapons, including knives and arrowheads, as well as iron bangles. They made clay figurines, of animals human heads and life-sized people, as well as pottery. Taruga and Samun Dukiya are among the places where Nok type tools and figurines have been found.

UREWE CULTURE

This culture existed in east Africa, near Lake Victoria, between around 500 BCE and CE 600.

The Urewe people made iron objects and pottery. They cultivated finger millet and sorghum, and kept cattle.

WRITING IN AFRICA

A figurine of the Nok culture

In Africa, Egypt had the earliest form of writing. The Meroitic script developed in the Kush kingdom. Geez was a language with its own form of writing in Aksum.

Tifnagh is the script used by the Berbers. An early form of the script was used between 300 BCE and CE 300.

All these scripts were of North Africa. Greek, Hebrew, and Latin, which came from outside Africa, were also used in the region. Arabic was later used.

In West Africa, Nsibidi is another type of script that was used in the region of present Nigeria. Early forms of Nsibidi are known from the Calabar region, where these symbols have been found on pottery dating between CE 400 and 1400. Thousands of Nsibidi characters were divided into two parts: a sacred version and one for general use.

Roshen Dalal

18

Early North America

The huge region of America, including north, central and south America, was occupied by many different groups of people. North America had diverse climatic regions, plants, and animals. The lifestyle of people varied according to these. In the north were the cold Arctic regions where fish and seals were the main food. In the east there were forest regions, where animals such as elk and deer were hunted. In the western grasslands there were large animals which were hunted, such as bison, mammoths, and horses. Mammoths and horses became extinct here around 10,000 BCE. In the south-west there were deserts with smaller animals and plants.

One of the early cultures in North America is known as the Clovis culture, as we have seen earlier. There were many different cultures after the Clovis. We will look at a few of them here.

The early people of North America did not have a system of writing. We know about them from their own traditions, and from archaeology.

ALONG THE MISSISSIPPI

The Mississippi river flows through North America, and has a length of 3779 km. It is joined by several tributaries.

People probably lived in the lower Mississippi valley region from 10,000 BCE. They were nomadic hunters who lived in temporary shelters perhaps made from branches and animal skins. There are several sites with earth mounds in the present USA states of Louisiana, Mississippi and Florida, some of which date back to 6500 BCE. Between the 1st century BCE and the 5th century CE there was settled agriculture in the Mississippi valley and the south-west. Farming and village settlements, with maize as the main crop, spread up to the east coast. Elsewhere hunter-gatherers continued to exist.

OUACHITA RIVER

The Ouachita river flows through Arkansas and Louisiana. Along the Ouachita lived various tribes, including the Washita, Caddo, Osage, Tensas, Chikasaw and Choctaw. Many mounds with the remains of ancient settlements have been found along this river.

Watson Brake and other places

Watson Brake in Louisiana near the Ouachita river dates to 4000–2800 BCE. Here the people began building platforms or mounds around 3500 BCE. Here there are eleven mounds connected by ridges that form a circle which is about 260 m in diameter. The highest reaches to a height of 8 m. The people here are thought to have been hunter-gatherers who used this site as a base. They hunted small animals and ate local plants and fish, as well as snails and other aquatic creatures.

Poverty Point is a larger and later site in Louisiana, covering 2.6 sq km. It has numerous mounds built between 1500 and 500 BCE. By this time there was agriculture in the region. Squash and maize were among the crops grown.

After 500 BCE there were different cultures in the area.

The Marksville culture developed in the 2nd century BCE. The images on their pottery were similar to those of the Hopewell

THE WOODLAND PERIOD

In eastern North America, the Woodland period refers to some cultures dated between 1000 BCE and CE 1000, all of which had agriculture, pottery and burial practices. The Woodland period is divided into Early, Middle and Late.

The Adena culture, named after the site of Adena in Ohio, belongs to the Early Woodland period.

The Hopewell culture belongs to the Middle Woodland period. There were other similar North American cultures of this time, including the Armstrong culture, Marksville culture and Swift Creek culture.

The Late Woodland period is dated CE 500–1000. At this time there was long-distance trade. Crops grown included maize, beans and squash, which are together called 'The Three Sisters'. The bow and arrow was used instead of the earlier weapons of spear and atlatl. There were many different cultures including the Cole Creek culture of Louisiana and the Plum Bayou culture of Arkansas and Missouri.

The Woodland period was followed by the Mississippi culture.

culture in Ohio. The Adena culture of Ohio was earlier than the Hopewell and had burial mounds.

ADENA CULTURE

The Adena culture dates between 1000 and 200 BCE and is known for its earth mounds, which were usually built on graves. These mounds have a diameter between 6 m and 90 m. There may have been a number of different groups that belonged to this culture. The main region was Ohio, but the Adena culture also existed in Indiana, West Virginia and Kentucky, and had links with sites in Pennsylvania and New York.

The Adena people lived near the burial mounds in round houses with conical roofs, made from wooden posts, along with bark and reeds. They hunted animals and birds, gathered seeds and nuts, and grew various crops including pumpkin, squash, sunflower, sumpweed, knotweed, maygrass and goosefoot. Many of these plants initially grew wild in the region. These people were the first to cultivate crops in this area. They made tools and ornaments of stone, bone, antler and copper, as well as pottery. They also made small stone tablets.

Living along the Ohio river they traded with areas along this river, obtaining copper and mica. They made smoking pipes of siltstone. These were tubular pipes. One unique tubular pipe is carved from stone in the shape of a man. The carvings show hairstyles, clothes worn and ornaments. The pipes were actually used for smoking tobacco during special ceremonies.

Later there were different types of economies in the region. The Caddo Indians of north-western Louisiana grew corn, while the Chitimacha Indians of south-western Louisiana based their economy on fishing.

A tubular smoking pipe in the shape of a man. This pipe of the Adena culture is from the Adena mound in Chilicothe.

HOPEWELL PEOPLE

In North America, the Adena culture developed into what is called the Hopewell culture. It is named after Captain Hopewell, on whose land burials of the culture were first found. Sites of the culture, which began around 200 BCE, are found in the present states of Ohio, Illinois and Indiana. Like the Adena, the people made huge earthen mounds and enclosures. They

TOBACCO

Tobacco was first grown and smoked in the Americas. The earliest tobacco found dates back to more than one million years ago, but the tobacco plant as it is known today grew in the region by 6000 BCE. Tobacco leaves were dried and smoked, either wrapped in leaves or in stone pipes. Tobacco was considered sacred, a gift of the Great Spirit (god). It was not to be smoked every day or for pleasure. It was used in religious ceremonies, or for healing and to give relief from pain.

also made stone tools, pottery and other items. Under the mounds were graves where rich people were buried along with items of copper, silver, shell and other goods.

Maize, sunflower and squash were among the crops grown.

An otter-headed pipe from the Hopewell culture, from Mound City, Ohio. This pipe can be dated between 200 BCE and CE 100.

Mann site

Among the many Hopewell sites is the Mann site in Evansville, Indiana, with 20 mounds of the Hopewell type. Items found here include the teeth of grizzly bears and carvings of jaguars and panthers.

Mound city

Mound city in Ohio has 24 burial mounds. In one of them 200 stone pipes for smoking tobacco were found. Stone pipes were found elsewhere too. These pipes were small, flat and rectangular. At one end was a hole for smoking, at the other end an animal or bird was carved. As the pipe was smoked, the person smoking stared at the animal. The smoker then reached a dreamlike state, understanding the aspects and powers of that animal. Sometimes shamans, wise men who knew some magic, received messages and guidance from the spirits of animals in this way. The Hopewell declined by about CE 400-500.

Oasisamerica

Oasisamerica is a name given to a southern region of North America, extending into Mexico. It includes the south-west states of Arizona, Utah, New Mexico, Colorado, Nevada and California in the USA. This region had some early cultures. There were also connections with the southern cultures of Mesoamerica.

Hohokam culture

Hohokam is a name given to a culture that developed in central and southern Arizona, and in the Sonora desert. It existed between 300 BCE and CE 1400. Snake Town, Casa Grande and Red Mountain were some of their main centres. On two sides of the region are the Gila and Colorado rivers. From the rivers, canals were made to bring water to the fields in this dry region. These were often quite deep, and could reach a length of 10 km. In the early period their houses were made of branches, reeds and mud, but later they built pit houses, using posts and adobe. (Pit houses had their floors slightly below ground.) They grew maize, squash, beans, cotton, tobacco and other crops. Pottery, clay figurines, textiles and jewellery were made. They had ball courts, like those in southern America, and traded with Mexico.

Other cultures

There were other cultures in the region. Among them are those called Basketmaker, which developed into the Pueblo culture, and the Mogollon culture. The Basketmaker people were originally nomadic. Later they cultivated maize and squash, wove baskets and lived in pit houses. The early Pueblos also lived in such houses. They made both plain and painted pottery. The Mogollon culture had several different branches, located mainly in New Mexico, Texas and Arizona. By CE 1000, three-storey-high structures were made.

LLAMA

The llama belongs to a group of animals known as camelids. Camelids include camels, llamas, alpacas, vicunas and guanacos. Camelids were once of different types and evolved in North America 45 million years ago. The early types are now extinct. The guanaco and vicuna are thought to be ancestors of the llama and alpaca, which evolved after the domestication of the former. After 10,000 BCE camelids died out in North America. Camelids reached South America about three million years ago, and continued to exist here.

A llama

19
Early South and Central America

In South and Central America there were early farming settlements. By 7000 BCE farmers grew maize, squash and beans in this region. Later, chilli pepper and cotton were planted. We will look at some of the main cultures and civilizations in this area.

THE OLMECS

Around 1500 BCE the Olmec civilization arose.

Olmec, meaning 'rubber people', was a name given to them later; it is not known what they were called in those days. The name was given because these people knew how to make a form of rubber. The Olmec civilization first developed around San Lorenzo Tenochtitlan on the Coatzacoalcos river in present Mexico, and spread to other areas. There was fertile land around the river. San Lorenzo was deserted around 900 BCE, and a new centre arose at La Venta. Here a huge pyramid was made.

An Olmec basalt head

The Olmecs made beautiful items including huge male heads of basalt. The heads that have been found were between 1.47 and 3.4 m high. They carved face masks in jade, and made other items of jade, obsidian, greenstone and magnetite. The stone and other material for these were brought across long distances. They were the first to play the Mesoamerican ballgame. They had developed an early form of writing.

They ate fruits, vegetables, turtles, fish and small animals. The Olmecs traded with different regions. They obtained minerals from Oaxaca in the Mexican highlands.

La Venta declined around 400 BCE.

The ball game

The rubber they made was used to make rubber balls, which were used to play a game. A long court was constructed and players hit the ball mainly with their hips. They wore padded belts or hip guards, as the ball was hard and heavy. The game was not played just for fun. Some of the people who played it were later killed in a religious sacrifice. This game, with many variations, was also played by most of the later cultures in the region.

Religion

The Olmecs had many different gods.

Some of the gods were a rain god, a fire god and a feathered serpent. Gold represented life energy and the sun. The jaguar represented the earth spirit. Jade was considered sacred.

Though the Olmecs declined, their religion remained important.

Sculptures

The Olmecs carved a number of objects. Notable among them was a were-jaguar, that is, a creature that was part-human and part-jaguar. They also carved a jaguar baby, that is, with the face of a human baby, but the long teeth and look of an angry jaguar. Another type of sculpture included a number of different creatures combined, including birds, animals and reptiles.

CUICUILCO

Cuicuilco was an early city in the valley of Mexico. Its name means 'place of colours and songs'. It existed at about the same time as the Olmec civilization, but was not a part of it. First, around 1200 BCE, it was a village. Later it became a city with pyramids and buildings. The main pyramid is circular, 27 m high, and 80 m in diameter. The people of Cuicuilco made pottery, clay figurines, stone sculptures and jewellery.

The city began to decline by 100 BCE. In CE 400 the Xitli volcano erupted in Mexico and destroyed Cuicuilco.

ZAPOTEC CULTURE

As the Olmecs declined other cultures emerged in the Mexico region.

Around 500 BCE the Zapotec culture developed in the Oaxaca valley of Mexico, with its centre at Mt Alban. The Zapotec culture continued to exist till CE 900 and later, and expanded to cover a territory of 2000 sq km, with a population of at least 1,00,000 people. Mt Alban was the main city, but there were other towns nearby. El Palmilo, one of the towns, had a large hilltop palace with about twenty rooms.

Other huge buildings, as well as ball courts were constructed. The Zapotecs made beautiful gold jewellery, textiles and pottery. They also developed a form of writing and a calendar.

Zapotec gods

Their main gods were Cocijo (lightning), a rain god, and Coquihani, the god of light.

Early Kingdoms of South America

Some early kingdoms of South and Central America

TEOTIHUACAN

Teotihuacan was once a great city in Mexico. There were earlier settlements in the area, but the ancient city began to be built from around 200 BCE or earlier. By about c. CE 500, it was the largest city of North and South America. Probably 1,50,000 or more people lived here. The Totonac people say that they built the city, but it is thought many different people lived there, including some from the Zapotec civilization. In the centre was a long avenue and near it was the Pyramid of the Sun, with a height of 66 m, and the Pyramid of the Moon. People, animals, birds and reptiles were sacrificed and buried in this pyramid, which was 43 m tall.

At the end of the avenue was a large area with temples. There were other pyramids, temples, palaces, and more than 2000 houses. In the 7th century CE, the city declined.

CHAVIN CULTURE

The Chavin culture was another early civilization. It was located in Peru in South America, and developed around 1000 BCE.

The people cultivated maize, potatoes and other crops, and domesticated llamas, which were used to carry loads.

This culture was named after the main site of Chavin de Huantar, built at a height of 3000 m in the Andes mountains of Peru. Here there were large stone buildings and temples with courtyards and underground galleries. Some of these had sculptures of gods, people and animals including jaguars, caimans and animal-human figurines. Other sculptures were of huge birds like eagles, and composite feline-humans with serpents. Many Chavin bone and metal objects depict the jaguar, an animal they worshipped. Chavin de Huantar was a great religious centre, visited by people from far-off places.

The Lanzon

Far underground, reached through dark tunnels, stands the Lanzon, a pillar sculpture, showing a god that was half-man and half-animal. It has a feline head and human body and is thought to be the main god of the culture. Other gods include those that have been called the 'Smiling god' and the 'Staff god'.

Items made

The Chavin people made gold items, pottery and textiles. Chavin-type pottery was known even in Ecuador to the north, while their textiles have been found in the Paracas region of Peru.

PARACAS CULTURE

There were several early cultures of Peru. Among them was the Paracas culture named after the site of Paracas. It can be dated

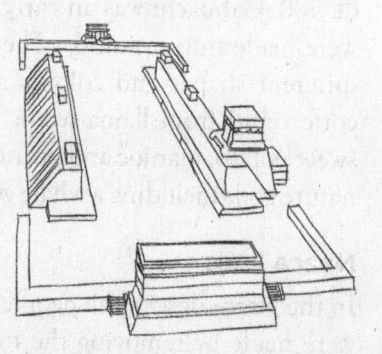

A recreation of the court for the ball game. The ball game was played by all cultures in the region.

between 1000 BCE-CE 400. The Paracas people made beautiful pottery and textiles. Their embroidered textiles are considered the best in the ancient world. They buried the dead in shaft tombs.

MOCHE CULTURE

The Moche culture in the northern coastal regions of Peru lasted from around CE 100 to 800. The Moche made pottery of different types and shapes. Some depicted people and animals, and most were in two colours of cream and red. They also made textiles woven from the wool of vicunas and alpacas, as well as gold items and huacas. Huaca was a term for a large structure including a pyramid. The main city was Moche, where there were two huge pyramids of the Sun and the Moon.

They built irrigation channels to fertilize their crops.

The names of the Moche gods are not known, but one associated with human sacrifices was sometimes in the form of a spider.

NAZCA CULTURE

On the southern coast of Peru was the Nazca culture. It existed between around CE 100 and 800 though it began to decline from CE 500. Cahuachi was an early Nazca centre, where natural hills were made into pyramids. The Nazca made beautiful pottery in different shapes and colours and wove colourful textiles from cotton and from llama wool. They grew maize, squash, beans, sweet potato, manioc and peanuts, and ate fish. They worshipped nature gods including a whale god, who is shown on their pottery.

Nazca lines

In the Nazca desert, the people drew or created long lines. These were made by removing the top red pebbles so that the lighter soil below could be seen. Seen from high above, the lines seem to form drawings of geometric figures, plants, and various creatures, including monkeys, birds, lizards, and spiders. Some of them are over 100 m long. No one knows what these lines were for. According to one theory, they were made so that gods could see them from the sky, or, that they were made for alien visitors from other planets! Other theories are that they were roads, or pathways for ceremonies, or that they marked underground water channels in the dry desert. The lines are also thought to be linked to solar or lunar calendars.

HUARI CIVILIZATION

The Huari or Wari civilization was in the Peru highlands. Huari was the name of the main city. Though Huari was settled by 200 BCE, it became a city and the centre of an empire between CE 600–1100. The city of Huari had large stone buildings. Among these were temples with sculptures. There were large male and female sculptures, along with small figurines made of turquoise. There were masks made of gold and other gold, silver, bronze and copper items, as well as fine pottery. Beautiful textiles were woven. Quipus, bundles of knotted string, were used, perhaps as memory aids. Rich people were buried in stone tombs. Roads connected different parts of the empire.

Among the gods they worshipped is a deity who has been called the 'Doorway god'. This god had a rectangular face, and wore a headdress. Rays radiated from his headdress, indicating the sun.

The Huari laid the foundations for the later Inca empire.

TIAHUANACO

Tiahuanaco (Tiwanaku), near Lake Titicaca in Bolivia, and the surrounding areas were occupied from 1500 BCE. Tiahuanaco grew into a city by CE 550. It began to control neighbouring regions and soon the Tiahuanaco empire covered parts of Peru, Argentina, Chile and Bolivia. It remained powerful till about CE

950. Temples and other buildings were constructed at Tiahuanaco which became a great religious and trade centre. The Akipana, a pyramidal structure, was one of the great buildings here. The Pumapunku is an earthen platform with a raised terrace of stone blocks. The Kalasasaya was a rectangular enclosure with a high gateway. There were numerous other structures which show great skill in stone-cutting and building with huge stone blocks. Among deities, the Doorway god, known from Huari, was also worshipped here.

THE MAYA CIVILIZATION

The Maya civilization was very important in Central America. This civilization originated around 1500 BCE or earlier, but was most powerful between CE 250 and 900. They did not have a kingdom or empire, but had different city states. All these states had a similar culture and lifestyle. This civilization spread over parts of southern Mexico in the Mexican states of Chiapas and Tabasco, the Yucatan peninsula of Mexico, and northern Central America where the present states of Guatemala, Belize, El Salvador and western Honduras are located.

Each city state had its own kings. Some of their names are known from inscriptions. Among the states were Copan, Tikal, Caracol, Palenque and Calakmul. The city states traded with one another, but sometimes entered into wars. At times they fought against the Olmecs, Teotihuacan and other cultures.

In the main cities there were palaces, temples, pyramids and ball courts, as well as plazas or open areas where festivals were held.

Agriculture
Around the cities the Maya people grew different crops such as maize, beans, squash, chilli peppers, manioc, cacao, vanilla and avocado.

COPAN—A CITY STATE

Copan, known as Xukpi in Maya language, was a city state. It was located in Honduras, and was prosperous between CE 400 and 850. One of its early kings who ruled from about CE 426-436 was called Kinich Yax Kuk Mo (Blue Quetzal Macaw) or Mah Kina Yax Kuk Mo (Sun-eyed Green Quetzal Macaw).

Crafts and trade

The Maya made sculptures of stone, wood, jade and obsidian, as well as murals or wall paintings, decorated and carved pottery, textiles and other items. They traded with different areas including Teotihuacan and the Zapotec culture.

Writing

The Maya had a system of writing. Their writing had about 1000 characters. They made books with sheets of paper or leather.

Religion

The Maya had many gods and goddesses and sacrificed humans and animals. They played the ritual ball game that was also played by the Olmecs and other early South American people.

Among the gods and goddesses were:

Itzamna: a supreme creator and moon god

Ix chel (rainbow lady): wife of Itzamna, goddess of medicine, childbirth and weaving

A Maya deity: a detail from a lintel, from the site of Yaxchilan

Ahau Kin: the sun god; at night he became a jaguar and visited the world beneath the earth

Kukulcan: the feathered serpent, also known by different names

Maize god: the god represented food, particularly maize and had different names.

> **THE THREE WORLDS AND THE CEIBA TREE**
>
> The Maya believed there were three different worlds, earth, heaven, and the world below the earth. From far below to high above a Ceiba tree grew. The gods and dead persons climbed this tree to cross to different worlds.
>
> A Ceiba tree is very large and one of the tallest trees in the rainforests.

Calendar

The Maya used many different calendars, to decide on the dates of their festivals and for future predictions. One type of calendar, called the Tzolkin, had 260 days. Another type is known as the Long Count. This calendar began in 3114 BCE, and predicted a change in CE 2012. Making these calendars required a knowledge of mathematics and of astronomy.

Decline

The Maya civilization declined in the southern lowland regions after 900 CE, but continued to exist in the north.

20

China: Early Mongolia and Korea

221 BCE–CE 581

As seen earlier, as the Zhou kingdom declined in China, a number of small states emerged. These fought against one another. The state of Qin gradually began winning against the other kingdoms, and adding them to its territory. By 221 BCE, all the other states were defeated, and a unified empire was created in China for the first time. The new king called himself Qin Shi Huangdi, or 'first emperor of Qin'.

Shi Huangdi realized that to maintain control he had to have a well-organized government. He divided the country into provinces, each under a governor. The whole country had the same type of coins, weights and measures. He created a strong army and introduced strict laws. In the north he invaded Korea. After Shi Huangdi's death in 210 BCE, there were weak emperors and a struggle for power. Rebellions took place in various parts of the empire.

Some warriors of the terracotta army of Shih Huangdi

Terracotta warriors

Qin Shi Huangdi must have believed that he would continue to live after death, in a grand style. Near Xian city in Shanxi province he built a tomb for himself. Under a pyramidal mound, the area of the tomb is huge. Like a palace, it has several rooms, halls and gates. Apart from the main tomb of the emperor, there are tombs of his nobles, servants and other workers. There is a life-size army made out of terracotta, with more than 7000 warriors, along with charioteers and horses, which were buried near the emperor. Each of these terracotta warriors has different hairstyles and features, and they are of different heights, just like real people. These warriors held weapons, and were painted to look real. Another burial near the tomb was in the model of a swamp, with 40 life-size bronze statues of swans, cranes, geese and other aquatic birds.

THE HAN DYNASTY

Liu Bang was one of those struggling for power. He defeated his rivals and made himself the emperor. He was given the title

Gaozu, and was the founder of the Han dynasty. He ruled from 206-195 BCE with his capital at Changan (now Xian). Changan was one of the biggest cities in the world. Liu changed some of the strict laws of the Qin dynasty, and reduced the taxes. He made Confucianism the philosophy of China. There were 13 other emperors of this dynasty. Among them, Wendi, son of Gaozu, ruled from 180-157 BCE. Wudi (ruled 140-87 BCE) expanded the territory into present Korea and Vietnam. Parts of Central Asia, including Farghana, were conquered. Special cavalry horses were obtained from here. This dynasty, known as the Western Han, lasted till CE 9. In the last years there were conflicts and rebellions.

An examination system

Chinese officials were appointed in different ways, usually from rich aristocrats. But right from this time an examination system was set up. Those who wanted to become administrators had to pass an exam in the Chinese classics. A university was established to teach the classics.

The Silk Route

From China a trade route crossed through Central Asia. This was called the Silk Route as along this route silk and other items from China were exported. Among various items, China also exported gold. In return China received wine, spices, grapes, pomegranates, beans, sesame and woollen cloth.

Lacquer ware and other items

Among the many items made at this time were beautiful lacquer bowls and cups. Making lacquer objects is quite difficult. First the bowl or cup is carved in wood. Then sap is taken from a lacquer tree. It is mixed with various substances, and applied on the bowl in layers. The best items had about 30 layers. The final product has a shining finish. Han lacquer ware was decorated and waterproof. Government officials supervised the making of the products, ensuring that they came out perfect. A cup or bowl of the Han period, found at Pyongyang, North Korea lists the following people involved in making it: Yi made the wooden core; Li did the lacquering; the top lacquer coat was made by Dang; the handles were gilded by Gu; painting was done by Ding; the final polishing was by Feng. Then the cup was inspected by Ping and the supervisor-foreman Zong. There were other government officials in charge. They were the government head supervisor Zhang; the chief administrator, Liang, the deputy chief administrator, Feng; the subordinate executive officer Long; and the chief clerk, Bao.

Items of wood, bronze, iron, pottery, were also made.

Literature and history
Literature and poetry were composed at this time. *Shiji* (historical records) was written by Sima Qian (141-86 BCE). It included an account of people living on the outskirts of the empire. Later histories were composed on the same pattern.

WANG MANG—THE XIN DYNASTY
The last Western Han emperor was a young child, and Wang Mang was his regent. Wang Mang took over the kingdom in CE 9. He distributed the land belonging to rich landowners among peasants, and reduced taxes.

But in the north the crops had failed. Some peasants formed a group known as the Red Eyebrows. They joined forces with the angry landowners, and Wang Mang was killed.

EASTERN OR LATER HAN DYNASTY (CE 25-220)
Liu Xiu, later known as the emperor Guangwudi, restored the Han dynasty which came to be known as the Eastern or Later

Han in CE 25. There were 12 later Han emperors. The new capital was at Luoyang, in the province of Henan (Hunan). The Later Han empire extended over China and beyond, and was as large as the Roman empire of that time. It included Annam (Vietnam), Korea and part of Central Asia.

Trade and contacts

Trade continued along the Silk Route. Ambassadors came to the court at Luoyang from Central Asia, Japan and the Roman empire.

THE THREE KINGDOMS AND SIX DYNASTIES: CE 220-589

The Han dynasty declined around c. CE 220 after a civil war. The empire broke up into three kingdoms, Cao Wei (CE 220-265), Shu Han and Dong Wu. But by the end of the 3rd century, all three kingdoms had collapsed.

In CE 280 the Jin dynasty unified part of the area, but there were still many conflicts and small kingdoms.

Finally in CE 589, the Sui dynasty came to power and unified China once again.

THE SIX DYNASTIES—CE 220-589

This period is also known as that of the six dynasties, referring to six dynasties of South China which ruled from Jianye, later called as Jiankang (now Nanjing). These were the Wu (222-280); the Dong or Eastern Jin (317-420); the Liu-Song (420-479); the Nan or Southern Qi (479-502); the Nan Liang (502-557) and the Nan Chen (557-589).

At the same time there were other dynasties in the north. These were: the Bei or Northern Wei, that ruled from Datong (Luoyang) (386-534/5); the Dong Wei (534-550) and the Bei Qi (550-577) that ruled from Ye (Anyang); the Xi Wei (535-556/7) and Bei Zhou (557-581) that ruled from Changan (modern Xian).

NEW DEVELOPMENTS

During the time of the Later Han there were many new developments and inventions.

Art, literature, religion and science continued to develop at the time of the three kingdoms and six dynasties, even though there was so much political confusion.

Paper was first made around CE 100 at the time of the Later Han dynasty. This paper was made from hemp rags and chopped mulberry bark mixed with water and pressed flat. An earlier type of paper was made from 100 BCE. Even earlier silk and bamboo scrolls were used for writing. An early type of wheelbarrow was invented. Water clocks and sundials were used to tell the time. Coal was used for cooking and lighting fires.

Astronomical instruments were made, as well as a seismograph. Huge palaces were built of wood.

In southern China, a beautiful type of pottery, a green-glazed stoneware called 'Yue ware' was made and exported.

There were different types of paintings. There were paintings depicting family life, kings and queens, and Buddhist deities. Some paintings were based on stories. Landscape painting developed at this time. Ku Kai Chi is known as the first great painter of landscapes. Xie He explained the six basic principles of Chinese painting. There were paintings made on silk.

LIUBO—A BOARD GAME

Liubo was a popular board game during the time of the Han dynasty and later. It was played on a square board, and each player had six pieces.

Liubo boards and pieces of this time are still preserved.

TOMBS AND GRAVES
Mingqi
Mingqi or 'spirit vessels' were images of people, animals, mythical creatures and other objects placed in graves during the time of the Han dynasty and later.

Mingqi figures: goats on a farm, in a burial of the Eastern Han dynasty

There are dancers, drummers, dogs, horses, camels, guardian lions and others. In addition entire scenes were created in miniature form. There were farms with buildings, granaries and groups of animals in pens, being fed by their caretaker.

Other items
Other items too, like bronze vessels, were placed in graves. Sometimes there was a shrine nearby, and a pathway led from there to the tomb.

Princess Tou Wen and Prince Liu Sheng
Tombs of this prince and princess were found in Ling Mountain in Hebei province, hidden by heavy stone doors and sealed with iron.

The prince died in 113 BCE, the princess later. The bodies were enclosed in suits of jade. Each suit consisted of about 2000 pieces of jade, sewn together with golden thread. Jade was believed to provide eternal life. In the graves were silk, pottery, bronze vessels, and lacquer ware.

The Jade suit of Princess Tou Wen

RELIGION
Buddhism

Buddhism reached China from India in the 4th century CE. There were new types of architecture, sculpture and painting. Buddhist stories were depicted in wall paintings, and Buddhist sculptures and temples were made. Buddhist texts were brought from India and translated into Chinese.

Daoism

Daoism became popular, and had different forms.

Tso chuan, (Zuo chuan) a Dao text written in the Early Han period, said that from heaven and earth came the two principles of yin and yang, wind and rain, and dark and light. From these came the five elements, the five flavours or tastes, the five colours and the five modes of music. The five colours were green, yellow, scarlet, white and black, and one succeeds the other. These ideas influenced a number of people.

The Dai Ping Dao (Yellow Turbans) was a Daoist religious group that was influenced by these ideas. They said the Han was symbolized by the element wood, and by the green heaven, and now it was time for the yellow heaven, as yellow came after green. They meant that it was time for the dynasty to change. This group preached the equality of all, and was very popular. They started a rebellion in CE 184 in the north-east region of Shandong. They were defeated but the Han dynasty began to decline. Another Daoist group that was against the government was the Five Pecks of Rice, which started a rebellious movement in Sichuan.

LITERATURE

Beautiful poetry was written. Tao Qian, also known as Tao Yuanming (CE 365–427), was a great poet who wrote *Peach Blossom Fountain*.

Around the 3rd to 4th century CE two interesting poems were composed on the beauty of nature. *The Song of Mulan* is the story of a woman, who disguised herself and fought as a soldier. *Southeast the Peacock Flies* is the story of an unhappy marriage. Though the husband and wife loved each other, the husband's mother would not let his wife live in peace, and finally the couple ended their lives. It is said to be based on a true story, on real people named Lui Lanzhi and Jiao Zhongqing, who lived at the end of the Han period. The first few lines of this poem are given here:

> Southeast the peacock flies,
> and every five li it hesitates in flight
>   "At thirteen I knew how to weave plain silk,
> at fourteen I learned to cut clothes;
> at fifteen I played the many-stringed lute,
> at sixteen recited from the Odes and Documents.
> At seventeen I became your wife,
> but in my heart there was always sorrow and pain . . ."
>   (Trans. Burton Watson)

YUEFU—THE IMPERIAL MUSIC BUREAU

As we saw earlier, music in China was well developed.

In the 1st century BCE, the Yuefu or Imperial Music Bureau was set up, to collect and standardize known music, and to organize musical performances at the royal court.

MONGOLIA AND KOREA

Mongolia and Korea were two areas that were closely linked with China's history.

Mongolia

Mongolia is a region to the north of China, which was occupied from Palaeolithic (Stone Age) times. In the 3rd century BCE, the

Xiongnu, Xianbei and other groups of people lived in Mongolia. The Xiongnu are mentioned in Chinese chronicles. Among the Xiongnu was a leader named Toumen, who conquered some areas and founded an empire. The Xiongnu attempted to invade China. The Great Wall of China was extended at this time, joining together existing walls, to prevent invasions. Conflicts between the Xiongnu and the Han dynasty were constant.

Gol Mod

Gol Mod in Mongolia is a place located north of the Khangai mountain range, at a height of 1600 m. From here the land slopes down towards the Khunuin river. Gol Mod seems to have been a place on a route and was occupied from about 2000 BCE. Here graves of the Xiongnu have been found. In the cemetery at least 98 large tombs and 335 smaller graves have been discovered. In the smaller graves there were burials of children, animals and various items. The large tombs had platforms with ramps leading up to them. The largest tomb was 83 m long, on a platform 3 m high. Here there were images of deities similar to those of Greece and Rome, as well as of a unicorn type of creature. A Chinese chariot was found in one of the graves. There were also remains of the Turk empire of the 5th to 7th centuries.

There are other Xiongnu tombs at Noyon uul (Noyn ula), a mountain in north central Mongolia, Tamiryn Ulaan Khoshuu, and other sites, including Tsaaram on the Mongolian Russian border. Finds in various graves include textiles, silk, Chinese lacquer ware, Chinese coins and bronze mirrors.

Later kingdoms

The Xianbei people began to gain power in Mongolia in the 1st century CE, and formed a kingdom in CE 147. They defeated the Han of China and even conquered part of northern China.

Toba, which was a branch of the Xianbei, next formed the Toba Wei kingdom in northern China in 386. This existed till 581.

Korea

Korea's history was influenced by China. China conquered part of north-west Korea in 108 BCE. Koguryo developed as an independent kingdom from around 37 BCE, which expanded over northern Korea. In south Korea, in the 3rd and 4th centuries CE, there were the independent kingdoms of Paekche, Silla and Kaya.

Papermaking and other specialized craft techniques reached Korea by the 6th century.

Buddhism reached Korea in the 4th century from China, and became important. At this time the Korean people worshipped many different gods. The three main deities became part of Buddhism. They were Sanshin, the mountain spirit; Toksong, the recluse; and Chilsong, the spirit of the seven stars (Great Bear). Sanshin depicted as an old man. A tiger sits at his feet. He is still worshipped in Buddhist temples in Korea.

A painting of Sanshin from Taebak-san in South Korea

21
India: Great Empires
500 BCE–CE 500

CITIES AND TOWNS

After the decline of the great Harappan civilization, towns and cities once again arose in India around 600 BCE. Buddhist texts describe 16 great states of northern India, along with their capital cities.

MAGADHA

Among these states, the state of Magadha, in the present region of Bihar, began to grow in importance. Around 360 BCE the Nanda dynasty came to power here. There were nine kings of this dynasty. They ruled till about 321 BCE, and expanded their territory. During their rule Alexander the Great invaded northwest India. He did not proceed further as his soldiers wanted to return home. They were homesick, and also, they had heard of the great army of the Nandas, with 60,000 cavalry and 6000 war elephants. The Greek soldiers did not want to fight this army.

THE MAURYAS

Dhanananda, the last Nanda king, was defeated by a person named Chandragupta, who was helped by Chanakya, his friend

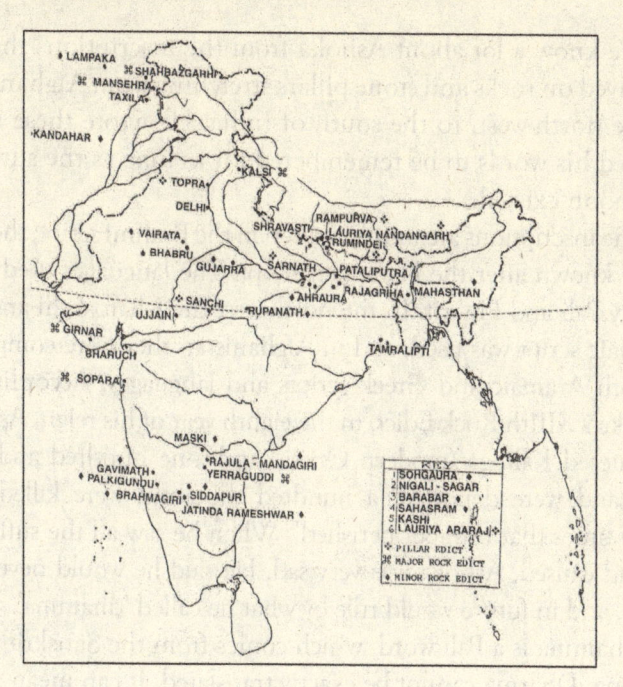

Ashoka's empire

and later his minister. Chandragupta was called Maurya, as according to Buddhist stories, he came from a land where there were plenty of peacocks, known as mora or mayura, from which the name Maurya was derived. Chandragupta founded the Maurya dynasty. Its capital was at Pataliputra (present Patna), in the region of Magadha. Chandragupta conquered part of central India, and fought against Seleucus Nikator, the Seleucid Greek ruler. Then he made a treaty with Seleucus. Megasthenes, a Greek ambassador, came to Chandragupta's court and wrote an account of the kingdom.

Ashoka (ruled 269-232 BCE)

The next king after Chandragupta was his son Bindusara. After Bindusara his son Ashoka came to the throne.

We know a lot about Ashoka from the inscriptions that he engraved on rocks and stone pillars stretching from Afghanistan in the north-west, to the south of India. He wrote these as he wanted his words to be remembered for as long as the sun and the moon existed.

The inscriptions are mostly written in the Brahmi script, the first script known after the Harappan script. The languages used were mostly Pali and Prakrit. In the north-west the Kharoshthi and the Aramaic script was used, and in Afghanistan they were composed in both Aramaic and Greek scripts and languages. According to Ashoka's XIIIth Rock Edict, in the eighth year of his reign, Ashoka conquered Kalinga (modern Orissa) and 'one hundred and fifty thousand were deported, a hundred thousand were killed and many times that number perished'. When he saw all the suffering he had caused, Ashoka was very sad. He said he would never kill again, and in future would rule by what he called 'dhamma'.

Dhamma is a Pali word, which comes from the Sanskrit word dharma. Dharma cannot be exactly translated. It can mean a way of life with truth and justice. Ashoka's dhamma included truth, justice and non-violence, as well as other principles. He wanted all the people in his empire to live according to this dhamma. This meant they should respect their parents, all monks and religious people, and be kind to slaves and servants. They should praise each other's religions, for that showed the greatness of one's own religion. They should not perform unnecessary ceremonies. They should reduce or stop the killing of animals, birds and even insects. A long list was provided of those animals that should never be killed. These included all young animals and their mothers, squirrels, monkeys, parrots, boneless fish and even the queen ant.

DIFFERENT DYNASTIES

After Ashoka the Mauryan empire declined.

In India different dynasties ruled. Among those in the north-west were the Bactrian Greeks and the Indo-Parthians. Other dynasties in the north were the Kanvas, followed by the Shungas.

Around the 1st century CE the Kushans of Central Asia extended their empire into north India. Their greatest king was Kanishka (ruled CE 78-120).

GUPTA DYNASTY

The Gupta dynasty was the next great dynasty of north India. They first ruled in Magadha (Bihar) and expanded their territories from there. The first important king had the same name as the first Maurya king. He was called Chandragupta I and began to rule around CE 320. Samudragupta (c. CE 335-380) created a large empire through conquest. He conquered most of northern and western India. The kings of eastern and southern India, as well as princes from distant lands, paid tribute to him. Samudragupta was not just a warrior and conqueror. He also wrote poetry and played the vina, a stringed instrument. The Guptas declined from about CE 500.

A gold coin of the Guptas

The Satavahanas and Vakatakas were among the dynasties that ruled in central India. In the south were the Cholas, the Cheras and the Pandyas, who ruled between about 400 BCE and CE 300.

LIFE IN INDIA BETWEEN 500 BCE AND CE 500
Cities and villages

During this time there were cities and villages all across India.

In the cities there were markets with shops selling rice and grain, fruit, flowers, jewellery, precious and semi-precious stones, vessels and other items. Many houses in the cities were made of baked bricks. Some were double-storeyed with balconies. In the villages there were simple houses of mud and thatch.

There were ports from where ships sailed to distant lands. Arikamedu, a port in south India traded with Rome. Barygaza, modern Bharuch in Gujarat, is described in a Greek text of the 1st century, as a flourishing port. The text says that special items were imported for the king. These were: 'Vessels of silver, singing boys, beautiful maidens for the harem, fine wines, thin clothing of the finest weaves, and the choicest ointments'.

Agriculture

Rice, wheat, barley, pulses, vegetables and cotton were among the crops grown.

Crafts and trade

Silk and cotton textiles, wood and ivory objects, perfumes, jewellery made from precious and semi-precious stones, items of iron and copper, glass, shell, brass, gold, silver, and terracotta, pottery of different types, were some of the things made. Pearls were obtained from the sea. Oil was produced from vegetable seeds.

Traders and merchants carried the goods to far-off places by land and sea. There were trade contacts with China, Iran, Rome, Southeast Asia, Sri Lanka, Syria, Egypt and Macedonia. India also traded with the Byzantine empire and with kingdoms of Africa.

Coins

Punch-marked coins were among the earliest coin types that existed from the 6th century BCE. These coins were used since Mauryan times. They were mostly made of silver, stamped with different symbols. There were hundreds of symbols, including the sun, rabbits, mushrooms, snakes, elephants, trees, and many others.

Kushans used gold and other coins. At the same time there were coins belonging to local dynasties of north India such as the Mitras.

The Guptas used mainly gold and silver coins. The gold coins were called dinaras. The coins showed scenes from the lives of the rulers. Kings were shown in battle, killing lions and tigers, or even playing musical instruments. Some of the coins had images of gods and goddesses on them.

ART AND ARCHITECTURE
Mauryan pillars and stupas
A stupa was a structure built on some of the ashes or remains of the Buddha. Many stupas were built in Mauryan times. The most famous of these is the stupa at Sanchi that can still be seen.

We saw that Ashoka's edicts were engraved on rocks and pillars. These tall pillars were specially made out of polished sandstone. On top were animal 'capitals'. Bulls and lions were some of the animal capitals.

Kushan Buddhas
In the time of the Kushans, beautiful sculptures were made. There were statues of kings, Buddhas and bodhisattvas. In the north-west the images were made in Greek-Roman style.

Gupta sculptures
At the time of the Gupta dynasty sculpture further improved. Buddha images were carved with serene and beautiful features. Buddhist monasteries and Hindu temples were constructed.

Ajanta and Ellora
Rock-cut caves and temples were made from the 2nd century BCE. Many of these were Buddhist. These can still be seen.

Among the later caves are those carved in the cliffs at

Ajanta and Ellora, near Aurangabad in Maharashtra. At Ajanta there are 30 rock-cut Buddhist temples and monasteries. These date from the 1st century BCE to CE 700. Ajanta caves contain delicate paintings with Buddhist themes. Ellora includes Buddhist, Hindu and Jain rock-cut shrines and temples. These extend for more than 2 km along the cliff face and can be dated between the 2nd century BCE and CE 1000.

Caves at Ajanta

Science

Science, including astronomy, medicine and mathematics developed. Aryabhatta was a great mathematician. Charaka and Sushruta wrote on diseases and their treatment through herbs and by other methods including surgery. Charaka (1st century CE) laid down the basic principles for a doctor. He said: 'You must pray every day on rising and on going to bed for the welfare of all beings . . . You must strive with all your soul for the health of all beings . . . You must not betray your patients even at the cost of your own life.'

Literature

At this time many books were written in different languages.

Sanskrit, Pali and Prakrit were among the main languages of north India. Sanskrit was first used in the Rig Veda but it had developed and changed. It was still a very grammatical and beautiful language. Pali was a simpler form of Sanskrit. Prakrit too was a simpler form and had many different dialects. Tamil was the main language in south India.

THE SANSKRIT EPICS
The Mahabharata

The Mahabharata is an early Indian epic, written in Sanskrit, consisting of 1,00,000 verses. It is still popular today. The Mahabharata, with 18 parvas or sections, each book-length, has a main story and several subsidiary tales. It includes legends, myths and advice on living an ethical life. In fact, it is said there is nothing the Mahabharata does not contain.

The main story is about two sets of cousins, the Kauravas and the Pandavas, and the rivalry between them.

Many years of conflicts between the two groups culminated finally in a great war, in which practically all the kings of Bharata (India) took part, on one side or the other. The god Krishna, in his human form, played a part in the war. The Bhagavad Gita is an important dialogue between him and the third Pandava brother, Arjuna, on the battlefield, as the war was about to start. The Bhagavad Gita is one of the most sacred Hindu texts.

The Ramayana

The Ramayana is another Sanskrit epic, which tells the story of Rama and Sita. There are several versions of the Ramayana, but the earliest is that of Valmiki.

Valmiki's Ramayana has 24,000 verses, divided into seven kandas or sections. It begins with the childhood of Rama and his brothers, sons of Dasharatha, king of Ayodhya. Ayodhya was a city in north India. Rama married Sita, daughter of King Janaka. Though Rama was chosen as heir to King Dasharatha, he was banished to the forest because of a promise King Dasharatha had made to one of his wives. Rama's wife, Sita, and his brother Lakshmana chose to go with him. The Ramayana describes their life in the forest, Sita's abduction by Ravana, and finally her rescue and reunion with Rama. Even after this there are more problems they have to face.

Rama is considered an incarnation of the god Vishnu.

The Ramayana story was rewritten in different versions and different languages in all parts of India, as well as in the countries of Southeast Asia.

Both these epics have an early origin but attained their final form by the first few centuries CE.

Kalidasa

Kalidasa was one of the greatest writers in Sanskrit. Among his many books are *Meghaduta* (The Cloud Messenger) and *Abhijnana Shakuntalam*. *Meghaduta* tells the story of a yaksha, a semi-divine being who was separated from his wife. She lived in the Himalayan mountains in the north, while he was in south India. He sent her a message through a cloud. As the cloud passed over the country from south to north, it described all it saw. *Abhijnana Shakuntalam*, tells the story of Shakuntala, a young girl. She was the daughter of an apsara (divine nymph) and a rishi, a holy man. She was abandoned by her parents, but was found and looked after by another rishi, Kanva. She grew up in his forested ashram (hermitage). She fell in love with a visiting king named Dushyanta, but later he forgot her. Finally Shakuntala and King Dushyanta were united.

Tamil literature

Long ago, it is said that three literary meetings (sangams) were held at Madurai in south India. Some of the works composed or presented at these meetings still exist. They describe life in south India from around 300 BCE to the first few centuries CE. These are called Sangam Literature.

Two Tamil epics were composed some time between the 2nd and 6th centuries CE. *Shilappadigaram* tells the story of Kovalan and Kannagi. Kannagi remained loyal to her husband Kovalan though he loved the dancer Madhavi. When he was falsely accused of theft and killed on the order of the king, Kannagi's powerful anger destroyed the city of Madurai. *Manimekhalai*, the second epic, is the story of Manimekhalai, the daughter of Kovalan and the dancer Madhavi. Manimekhalai was very beautiful. She was loved by a Chola prince, but rejecting the pleasures of the world, she chose the path of Buddhism.

Music and dance

The *Natya Shastra*, written by Bharata, in the 1st century CE, describes drama, dance and music. Its detailed descriptions show that these arts were well developed by this time. In dance it describes movements for every part of the body. Thus there were thirteen movements for the head, six for the nose, nine for the neck, and 32 for the feet. The book describes the hand gestures, as well as methods of depicting different moods and emotions. Musical notes and rhythms are described. These styles in dance and music are still used today.

RELIGION

Buddhism

Ashoka Maurya became a Buddhist after his conquest of Kalinga. He tried to spread Buddhism in India and in nearby countries. In the time of the Kushans, a new form of Buddhism developed, called Mahayana Buddhism. In this form the Buddha was worshipped as a god. Other gods and goddesses too became part of Buddhism and were worshipped. In the earlier form of Buddhism, Buddha was seen as a great teacher, but not a god. This early form came to be called Hinayana. Hinayana Buddhism was prominent in Sri Lanka and Southeast Asia. Mahayana Buddhism spread to several other areas including China, Japan and Korea.

A bodhisattva

A bodhisattva is someone on the Buddhist path, who has not yet attained enlightenment. The Buddha, it is said, had many previous births. In all these births he is considered a bodhisattva. The stories of his lives are collected in books called Jatakas. In his earlier lives the Buddha had sometimes been born as a person, sometimes as an animal. But in all his previous lives he had done his best to help and save others.

A Jataka story

Once there was a king named Sivi. A dove came to the king and asked to be saved from a hawk that was chasing it. The king protected the dove. The hawk then followed and said he was hungry and therefore needed to eat the dove. The king offered the hawk his own flesh to eat instead. In this way, a bodhisattva, or one who is on the Buddhist path, must help every living being, even at the cost of his own life.

Many other Buddhist texts were composed.

Hinduism and Jainism

Hinduism and Jainism were the other major religions in India.

Hinduism had developed and changed from the time of the Vedas. By the 1st century CE, and even earlier, the gods and goddesses worshipped included Vishnu and his incarnations, Brahma, Lakshmi, Shiva, Parvati, Ganesha, Karttikeya, Kubera and many others. Their stories are written in books called the Puranas. There are 18 main Puranas. Brahma, Vishnu and Shiva were at first the most important gods.

Jainism had split into two main sects. The Shvetambaras lived in the north, and wore white clothes. The Digambaras lived in the south and followed strict rules. Those Digambaras who were senior arhats (monks) and had been practising for many years, gave up everything, including food and clothes. They believed this was the ideal, which all should try to reach.

22

Japan: Up to CE 794

Japan consists of thousands of islands. These islands were once joined together in a narrow peninsula connected to Asia, but rising water at the time of the last ice age, around 10,000 BCE, separated them. The four largest islands are Honshu, Hokkaido, Kyushu and Shikoku. Some islands were occupied from around 30,000 BCE. People may have reached Japan from Siberia or the Polynesian islands. Among the early people in Japan were a group known as the Ainu, and the proto or early Japanese.

JOMON CULTURE

Around 10,000 BCE, a type of pottery called Jomon (cord marked) was made. Even earlier fragments of pottery have been found in Japan, dating to about 14,000 BCE. Jomon pottery was made from clay, rolled in strips and then arranged in coils. On top of the coils, reeds or cords were

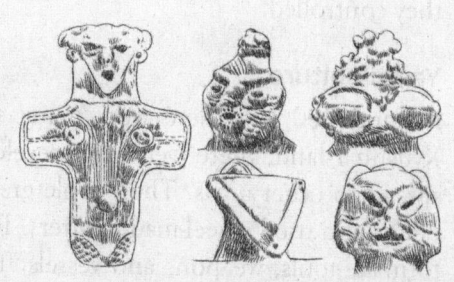

Some examples of dogu images

Jomon pottery

pressed to provide a decorated surface. It could be used for cooking food. The Jomon was among the earliest pottery in the world. (The very earliest comes from China.) The people who made this pottery lived in large huts, which were slightly below ground level. They gathered food from the wild, hunted and fished, and perhaps grew a few crops. They buried the dead. This type of lifestyle continued till about 300 BCE. People also made clay figurines of women that are called dogu. These dogu figurines have large circular eyes and curvaceous bodies. At least 15,000 dogu figures have been found in Japan. They may have been used for magic or healing.

The emperors

According to traditional history, the emperor Jinmu ruled at Kyushu from 660 BCE and then expanded his territory to Yamato, a province in Honshu. Jinmu was said to be descended from the sun goddess Amataresu. Jinmu was followed by the emperor Suizei and many others. These early emperors are considered legendary. It is not known if they actually ruled, or what territory they controlled.

Yayoi culture

Around 300 BCE there were many small states in Japan. In Kyushu Island, there were new developments, which gradually spread to other areas. The people grew rice and irrigated their fields, and used wheel-made pottery. Bronze and iron were used to make tools, weapons and vessels. There were markets where goods were traded through barter. This type of lifestyle is called

the Yayoi culture, named after Yayoi in Tokyo. The Yayoi people too, buried their dead.

Queen Himiko

According to Chinese sources, around CE 200, Queen Himiko (or Pimiko) ruled from her capital, Yamatai, and controlled a number of states. She was said to be unmarried. Her younger brother helped her to rule. She lived in a palace surrounded by towers, high walls and guards. She had a 1000 women attendants and one male attendant. Queen Himiko is not mentioned in traditional Japanese history. The location of Yamatai too is not clear. It was either in Kyushu or Yamato province.

Yamato period: CE 300-710

From around CE 300 Japan began to be unified. The ruling clan came to be called Yamato, named after the Yamato province in Honshu. There were many small areas of local government. Each was under a tribe or clan, known as uji. The Yamato uji or clan gradually began to gain control. The Muraji and Omi were among the other important uji. The Yamato chieftains made Shinto the state religion.

Haniwa sculptures

At this time the rulers and nobles who died were buried in graves covered with earth mounds. Around the earthen grave mounds, many of which were shaped like keyholes, clay sculptures called haniwa were placed. Haniwa included human and animal figurines, and even various objects like hats and houses. Some of the human figurines are shown dancing, some play

Haniwa clay sculptures

harps, others are soldiers. Haniwa are between 30 and 150 cm high. They may have been considered guardians to accompany the dead to the other world. In Japanese the grave mounds are known as 'Kofun'. Hence the early Yamato period is also called the Kofun period.

Chinese influence

Japan was influenced by China and Korea.

Korea had Chinese influence from an early date. Through Korea, Chinese writing, philosophy and literature came to Japan. Buddhism also spread to Japan from Korea, when the king of Paekche in Korea sent Buddhist priests, images and literature to Japan. This was probably in CE 522.

Confucian and Daoist ideas also reached Japan. In Japan, Onmyodo was a system of belief influenced by the concepts of Yin-Yang and of Daoism. Onmyodo rituals were practised to predict the future.

The Soga clan

In CE 592 the Yamato emperor Sushun was murdered by Soga clan members. The Soga were among the uji. The members of the Soga clan acted as regents but were the real rulers. The emperors had little power. They lived in their palaces in luxury. They also regularly performed Shinto rituals.

Asuka

The capital shifted to Asuka valley in the Yamato province. Here the empress Suiko ruled from CE 593-628. Suiko was the niece of Emperor Sushun. She had also been married to a previous emperor. Prince Shotuko, her nephew and regent, wrote the first Japanese constitution in 604. It had 17 principles. According to this, there would be different levels of officials to take care of the administration. The constitution was influenced by the ideas of the Chinese philosopher Confucius.

Shotoku said the people should obey the emperor and follow Buddhist beliefs.

Buddhism became the state religion and spread throughout Japan. Shotoku himself built a huge Buddhist temple at Horyu-ji, south-west of Nara. Yakushi Nyorai, the Buddha of healing, was worshipped here. The original temple was partly reconstructed in 711. Renovations and additions were made later. The temple contains beautiful Buddhist statues and murals.

Emperor Tenji

The Prince Naka no Oe ruled from CE 626-672 and continued Shotoku's reforms. He first ruled as regent and then became the emperor Tenji in 668. In 645 he defeated the Soga clan and increased the power of the emperor and government. In this he was helped by Nakatomi no Kamatari. In 669 the emperor gave Nakatomi the name Fujiwara, which was the place where

A Buddhist temple built by Shotoku at Horyuji

they both planned the attack on the Soga clan. Gradually, the Fujiwara family became powerful.

Taika reforms—Ritsu-ryo system

In CE 646 Naka no Oe helped by Nakatomi, began the Taika reforms. These included a number of political and economic reforms. There were new taxes including a land tax and new laws regarding land ownership.

These reforms were based on the Chinese system of government. The aim was to reduce the power of the uji clans. The clan lands were taken over by the government. A governing council called the Dajokan was set up. The Dajokan appointed governors to rule the different areas. The emperor also organized a national census in 670.

This centralized system was called ritsu-ryo.

Nara period: CE 710-794

In CE 710, the capital shifted to Heiji-kyo (present Nara). Emperor Shomu (ruled CE 724-49) changed the ritsu-ryo system. Instead of all the land being the property of the government, those who developed agriculture in new areas, were allowed to own the land themselves. Soon large temples and important families gained control over land again, and became powerful. Japan had close connections and trade relations with China. Trade along the Silk Route was extended to reach Japan.

Chinese influence could be seen in writing, art and literature. The emperor Shomu constructed a grand Buddhist temple. This was the Toda-ji temple, with a 16-metre-high statue of the Buddha. The temple itself was the largest wooden building in the world. But as Buddhism spread, the Buddhist temples became centres of power. The Buddhist priests tried to tell the emperors what to do. One priest, Dokyo, even tried to become the emperor. To escape from the influence of the priests, the emperor Kanmu (reigned 781–806) moved his capital twice. The first move was to Nagaoka in 784. The second move was to Heian-kyo (later known as Kyoto) in 794. (Though the capital was not at Nara after 784, the ten years from 784–794 are usually included in the Nara period.)

Literature and art

Two histories of Japan were written, *Kojiki* (Record of Ancient Matters, in CE 712) and *Nihon shoki* (Chronicles of Japan, in CE 720). These give an account of traditional history. They probably include both facts and legends. Poems by various poets were collected in a book, the *Manyoshu* (Anthology of a Myriad Leaves). *Manyoshu* contains poems composed at different times from CE 340–760. It was compiled or put together by Otomo no Yakamochi, who was one of Japan's greatest poets.

Buddhist art developed.

Shinto

Shinto is the traditional religion of Japan. It means 'the way of the gods'. The Shinto religion gradually grew and developed. It does not have a founder or any written texts. It has a number of gods who are together called kami. Kami include nature gods and spirits of ancestors. Even some rocks are worshipped as kami. Amataresu, the sun goddess, is the greatest kami. From around the 6th century, the emperor was considered a representative

The Shinto deity Amataresu—a detail from a painting

of the kami. He was believed to be descended from the sun goddess Amataresu and to receive guidance from her and other kami. It was thought Japan would prosper only if the emperor carried out the correct Shinto rituals. These rituals were said to keep away evil and to purify the atmosphere. Shinto and Buddhism had some conflicts but usually coexisted peacefully. Even Buddhists worshipped the kami.

Music

Early Japanese music consisted of chants, used in Shinto rituals and later in Buddhist rituals.

Shomyo or Buddhist chants, and Gagaku, which means elegant music, are two important forms of Japanese music that date back to the 6th and 7th centuries. Gagaku has different styles and types. Gagaku music was used for concerts and for dances. Instruments used in this music included flutes, drums, brass gongs and stringed instruments.

23

Europe

CE 500–1000

Europe at this time saw many changes. The old Western Roman empire was destroyed. But gradually a new Roman empire was formed in western and central Europe. In eastern Europe the Byzantine empire remained in power. There were several independent kingdoms. In northern Europe the Scandinavians had their own history.

Around the Roman empire there were Germanic and other tribes. As the Western Roman empire declined, these tribes began asserting their power. Among them were:

The Ostrogoths: they became rulers in Italy in CE 490.

The Franks: ruled Gaul (France)

The Vandals: took over Spain and the Roman regions of North Africa

Germanic tribes had two main types of religious beliefs. Some worshipped several gods; others practised a form of Christianity called Arianism. As we saw earlier, Arianism was a different form of Christianity. Arians did not believe that Christ was divine.

CLOVIS I—THE MEROVINGIANS

Among the Franks was a family later called Merovingians. The Franks were divided into two groups, Western (also called Salian) and Eastern. Chlodovic, known as Clovis I, became ruler of the Western Franks in 481, and later of the Eastern Franks. He was the grandson of Merovech, a chief of the Salians, who ruled from 448-458. The name Merovingian comes from Merovech.

Clovis conquered many areas. His kingdom covered most of present France and part of Germany. He made Paris his capital. Clovis married Clotilda, a Burgundian princess, in 493. Burgundians were another Germanic tribe.

Religion

At this time, the Christian Church, headed by the pope, was powerful in Europe. According to Bishop Gregory of Tours, who wrote about 50 years after Clovis' death, Clovis and the Franks were worshippers of many different gods. Clotilda was a Catholic Christian. Influenced by her, Clovis became a Catholic Christian in 496.

Some modern historians feel that Clovis may have been an Arian Christian, others believe Gregory's account. Clovis I gained the support of the Church by becoming a Christian. According to Gregory, thousands of other Franks became Catholic Christians after Clovis was baptised.

Clovis I died in CE 511 at the age of 46. His wife Clotilda lived till around 544. Both were buried in the grounds of the Church of St Genevieve which had been built by Clovis. Clotilda was later declared a saint.

Four kingdoms

After Clovis died, the empire was divided among his four sons. The four regions were Austrasia, Neustria, Burgundy and Aquitaine.

King Clotaire I reunited the territories. It was again divided after his death, then reunited under Clotaire II.

Clotaire II was succeeded by Dagobert I, who became king of Austrasia in CE 623, and in 629, king of the Franks. He then took over Burgundy and Aquitaine and became powerful. His capital was in Paris. After his death in 639, the kingdom was again divided among his sons. After him the kings gradually lost their power and the nobles became important, almost like local rulers. From 639 the most important nobles were from a family named Carolingian. In 751, a Carolingian who was the mayor of the palace, removed the Merovingian king Childeric III and founded the Carolingian dynasty. He was known as Pepin the Short.

Merovingian monasteries

Churches and monasteries were built at the time of the Merovingians. A number of people were declared saints, including women.

CAROLINGIANS

Pepin the Short, who started the Carolingian dynasty, had two sons, Carolman and Charlemagne. Both became kings after Pepin died, but Carolman died young and Charlemagne became the sole ruler in CE 771. Charlemagne ruled up to 814. He built a big empire which included present France, Germany, Austria, Switzerland and parts of Italy, Spain and Denmark.

The name Carolingian came from Charlemagne's Latin name, Carolus Magnus, in English, Charles the Great.

A new Roman empire

The pope and the Catholic Church wanted influence and power. They tried to gain this by some sort of association with the emperors of Europe. At the same time, emperors gained support and power through the pope.

Roshen Dalal

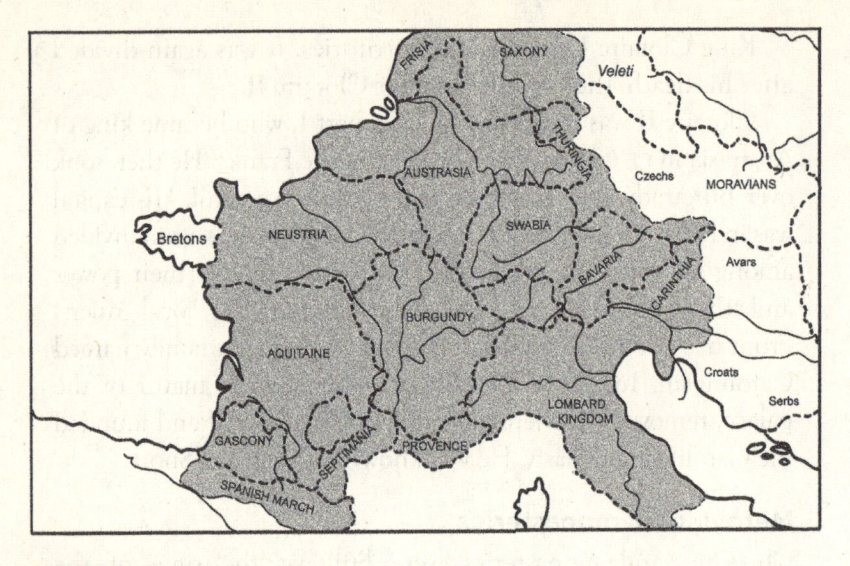

Territory of Charlemagne

Charlemagne's empire, including the dependent territories

After the Western Roman empire declined, the Byzantine or Eastern Roman empire was in name the ruler of the western region too. Some of the Germanic tribes in the west ruled independently but acknowledged the Byzantine emperor as supreme.

The popes recognized the sovereignty of the Byzantine empire as they needed the protection of the empire from the various tribes, particularly the Lombards, a people of north Italy. By the 8th century the Byzantine empire lost some territories and faced threats from the growing Arab power. The Byzantine emperors also angered the pope as they interfered in religious matters and banned the worship of icons, that is, of pictures and images of the saints.

Meanwhile Charlemagne defeated the Lombards and the pope acquired sovereignty over part of Italy. Charlemagne also conquered other territories.

Pope Leo III cut off ties with the Byzantine empire, and gave

Charlemagne the title of Western Emperor on 25 December, CE 800. Thus Charlemagne gained the support of the pope and the Church. The purpose of this was that there would be a new Christian empire in western Europe. It was hoped that it would be as great as the earlier Western Roman empire. Of course the Byzantine empire considered itself the Roman empire, but now it had lost the support of the pope.

Some of the practices and systems of the earlier Roman empire were re-established. Charlemagne granted lands to military leaders, who were known as dukes. Their lands were known as duchies. Several duchies became very powerful. Among them were Franconia, Swabia, Bavaria, Saxony and Lorraine.

Charlemagne's successors also received the title of Western Emperor.

After the death of Charlemagne, his son Louis the Pious, became the emperor. After he died in CE 840, the Carolingian empire in western Europe began to decline.

Carolingian Renaissance

Charlemagne was not just a great conqueror. During his reign there was growth and new trends in literature, education, art and architecture. This continued even later and has been called the Carolingian Renaissance.

Education

Monasteries were the early centres of education in Europe. Schools were also set up in towns and cities and in cathedrals. Studies focused on seven subjects: grammar, rhetoric, logic, arithmetic, geometry, astronomy and music. Textbooks were written on these subjects.

While some studied these subjects, others learnt a craft or trade. There were many others who were peasants, farmers and serfs, who were not educated.

ALCUIN (C.732-804)

Alcuin, originally from York, England, was a great scholar who was head of a school at Aachen (Aix la Chapelle), in the reign of Charlemagne. He was one of the main people who contributed to the Carolingian renaissance. Alcuin encouraged learning and made a new standard curriculum for schools. He wrote on religion, philosophy and education. He developed a new script, which came to be known as the Carolingian minuscule. In 796 he became the Abbot of St Martin at Tours.

Chansons de geste (songs of heroes)

Early forms of French literature, known as *Chansons de geste*, were poems composed in praise of heroes. One of the earliest was *La Chanson de Roland* (Song of Roland). It has different versions but the earliest was probably composed in the 12th century. It has 4004 lines, and tells the story of Roland, nephew of Charlemagne, who had a great sword named Durandel, and a horn called Oliphant. Roland died in Charlemagne's military campaign against the Saracens (Arabs) in Spain in 778, when it was ambushed on the return journey.

A portrait of Charlemagne from an engraving of the 16th century CE

Roland is mentioned by Charlemagne's biographer Einhard, by his Frankish name, Hruodlandus.

The first few lines of this chanson are given below:

The Puffin History of the World

Charles the King, our Lord and Sovereign,
Full seven years hath sojourned in Spain,
Conquered the land, and won the western main,
Now no fortress against him doth remain,
No city walls are left for him to gain,
Save Sarraguce that sits on high mountain.
(Trans. by C. K. Moncrieff)

The Treaty of Verdun

Soon after the death of Louis, the Carolingian empire was divided among his three sons by the Treaty of Verdun (843). Lothair I gained the central territories, Louis II, the east, and Charles the Bald (later Charles II), the west. The eastern region or East Francia, was later called Germany, and the western region, West Francia, later became France. In 870, the central territories were divided between East and West Francia.

THE LATER EMPERORS

We saw that East Francia, a territory created in CE 843, and expanded in 870, later came to be called Germany. East Francia had a number of duchies. Among these were Swabia, Franconia, Bavaria, Saxony and many others.

In 911 the Duke of Franconia, Conrad I was elected as emperor of East Francia. He was succeeded by the Duke of Saxony, Henry I.

Otto I of Saxony was the next important emperor, who ruled from 936. He defended the territory from the Danes of northern Europe, the Slavs and the Magyars of eastern Europe. He conquered many regions of Europe, including Italy. Once again, as at the time of Charlemagne, the pope was keen to have a powerful European emperor. The pope gave the title of Emperor Augustus to Otto the Great in 962. The kings who succeeded

Otto also had this title. Otto is often considered the first Holy Roman Emperor, even though Charlemagne had a similar position earlier, and the term Holy was only added to the title later.

The pope also said that all future popes would be loyal to the emperor. The emperors now began to choose and appoint the popes.

Otto II and Otto III expanded the empire. The present regions of Germany, Austria, Switzerland, the Netherlands and north Italy were the main areas under this new Roman empire. But the territories changed over time. The princes of the different territories voted to elect the emperor.

FRANCE

West Francia was later known as France. Louis V was the ruler of France from CE 967 to 987. After his death, one of his vassals, Hugh, the Duke of Francia came to the throne. As he always wore a cape, he was called Capet. The kings who ruled after him were called Capetians. Other powerful dukes were those of Normandy, Burgundy and Aquitaine, though they acknowledged Hugh as the king.

THE BYZANTINE EMPIRE

While these changes were taking place in western Europe, the Eastern Roman, or Byzantine empire, continued to exist with its capital at Constantinople. The empire had periods of prosperity and decline and lasted until 1453.

Justinian I (ruled CE 527–65), was one of its great kings. He expanded the empire, conquering part of Spain and Italy, as well as Sicily, Sardinia, Egypt and other areas in North Africa. Grand buildings were constructed. Among these, a huge church, Hagia Sophia (Church of the Holy Wisdom), was built during his reign.

At this time the Eastern and Western branches of the Christian

The Byzantine empire and kingdoms of east Europe

Church had differences. Justinian I tried to reconcile them. He also rebuilt Constantinople, after its destruction by fire.

At the same time plagues affected the empire.

In the 6th century, the Lombards, a Germanic people of north Italy, conquered most of the Byzantine territories of Italy, while the Avars, a Turkic group, invaded the Byzantine Balkans. Slavic tribes also invaded the Balkans. In the 7th century, the Arabs conquered the Byzantine territories of Palestine, Syria, Mesopotamia, and Egypt.

The Byzantine army was then reorganized and made more efficient.

From the 9th century, the Byzantine empire began to reconquer lost territory, including Southeast Asia Minor, Greece, Macedonia and Thrace. A Macedonian dynasty began to rule in 867 and continued till 1081. The first emperor of this dynasty was Basil I.

At this time there were new developments in literature, art and science. The Byzantine empire was prosperous under Basil II (CE 963-1025).

OTHER KINGDOMS

There were other regions and kingdoms in Europe. In the north were the Scandinavian countries.

In eastern Europe there were several different groups of people, including Slavs, Magyars and Bulgars. From around the 9th century, separate kingdoms began to be formed.

Magyars

The Magyars were in Romania and Hungary. Stephen I founded the Arpad dynasty and converted to Christianity. The Magyars invaded Germany, northern Italy, and France, but were defeated by Otto, king of Germany, in the Battle of Lechfield, in CE 955.

Bulgaria

The present region of Bulgaria was once under the Roman empire, and later was occupied by Slavic people, and by Bulgars, who were of Turkic origin. The Bulgars gradually created a separate kingdom. Khan Krum, who ruled from 803 to 814, built

> **CYRIL AND METHODIUS**
>
> Thessalonika in Macedonia was an important city of the Byzantine empire. Cyril and Methodius were brothers who belonged to the city. They became Christian missionaries and spread Christianity in Bulgaria and Moravia.
>
> The brothers created the Glagolitic alphabet that was the first system of writing used for Slavic languages. The Glagolitic was first used in Great Moravia. A simplified version known as Cyrillic was first used in Bulgaria.

a strong state. Bulgaria was also powerful in the late 9th and early 10th centuries. At this time Simeon, son of Boris I, ruled.

Simeon defeated the Magyars and Byzantines, conquered Serbia and called himself Emperor of the Greeks and Bulgars. After this, Bulgaria declined. It was attacked by Magyars and Russians. The eastern part came under the Byzantine empire in 976, and the remainder in 1018.

Poland

Mieszko I began the Piast dynasty and set up a separate state of Poland in the 10th century.

Bohemia

Bohemia was the name of a region in east Europe. Near it was a region called Moravia. Both these regions today form part of the Czech republic. In the 9th century Bohemia was a part of the kingdom of Moravia. Vaclav of the Premyslid dynasty founded a separate dynasty in Bohemia in the 10th century. In 950 Bohemia became part of the Holy Roman Empire.

24
A New Religion: Islam

In Arabia there were different kingdoms as well as various groups and tribes. They constantly fought against one another. In this region Muhammad was born in Mecca in CE 570. Mecca in present Saudi Arabia is located to the north-west of the Arabian peninsula.

The Kaba

The Kaba is located in Mecca. The Kaba is a black cube that is considered sacred. Even in those days the Kaba was the centre of pilgrimage for tribals and for city dwellers. About 450 km north of Mecca was Yasrib, later known as Medina. In this area there were Jewish clans, as well as various tribes and Bedouins (Arabs) in the north-west. There were also some Christians. While the Jews and the Christians followed their religious traditions, the tribes worshipped various deities. The Kaba had around it a number of

The Kaba: within the great mosque

idols, including that of the deity Hubal, which were worshipped by the tribes.

Apart from Hubal, Arab tribes worshipped many other deities such as Wadd, Al-Lat, Manat and Uzza.

THE PROPHET MUHAMMAD
Early Life
Muhammad belonged to the Arab Quraishi tribe, and was the son of Abdullah of the Hashemite clan. His father had died before he was born, and his mother died when he was six years old. Two years later, his grandfather, who was taking care of him, also died. Muhammad was brought up by his paternal uncle, Abu Talib. Later, he worked for Khadija, who owned caravans for trade. In 595, he married Khadija. They had two sons, who died in childhood, and four daughters of whom the youngest was named Fatima. (According to some Shiah sources only Fatima was Muhammad and Khadija's daughter, the others being the daughters of Khadija's sister, or of Khadija by an earlier marriage.) Muhammad used to visit Mt Hira (near Mecca) to pray. In 610 the angel Jibril (Gabriel) first appeared to him, and gave him a message from God. The angel said that there was only one God, and that Muhammad, was his messenger or Prophet. The term used for God was Allah. Muhammad began to teach this message. His wife Khadija and his cousin Ali were among his first followers. Muhammad accepted many of the Jewish laws, but the Jews could not accept him as the new Prophet. As Muhammad gained followers, the Quraish in Mecca, who were in positions of power, felt threatened and turned against him.

Hegira
Muhammad went to Yasrib (Medina) along with some supporters, and the date of his departure (Hegira) from Mecca, 622, marks

the beginning of the Islamic era. Muhammad now began to gain more followers. He married women of different groups to bring people together. His daughter Fatima was married to his close disciple and cousin Ali. After a series of successful battles, Muhammad re-entered Mecca in 630, destroyed the idols in the Kaba, and made it as the centre of Islamic pilgrimage. He then sent letters to neighbouring rulers, promising them safety if they became his followers. By the time of his death in 632 most of Arabia was unified. Muhammad had also changed the way of life of the people. He stopped warfare and revenge killings, and women were given a better position.

He continued to receive messages from God, which were collected in the Quran.

ISLAM

The religion founded by Muhammad is known as Islam. Islam in Arabic means 'submission'. This means that people should submit or surrender to the will of Allah or God. One should always follow the laws of God, and not act according to one's own desires. God's laws are contained in the Quran and in the Hadis and Sunnah. Those who follow the religion of Islam are known as Muslims.

The Quran

The Quran is composed in Arabic. It has 114 suras or chapters.

It says that there is one God, Allah, who has made the laws of the universe, and Muhammad is his Prophet. As God is One, no idols should be worshipped. There are angels who are helpers or messengers of God. There is a judgement day, heaven for the good and hell for the wicked. The Quran also describes the basic duties of a Muslim. These include prayer, fasting in the month of Ramzan (the ninth month of the Islamic calendar), charity or helping the poor, and pilgrimage to Mecca, known as Haj. It

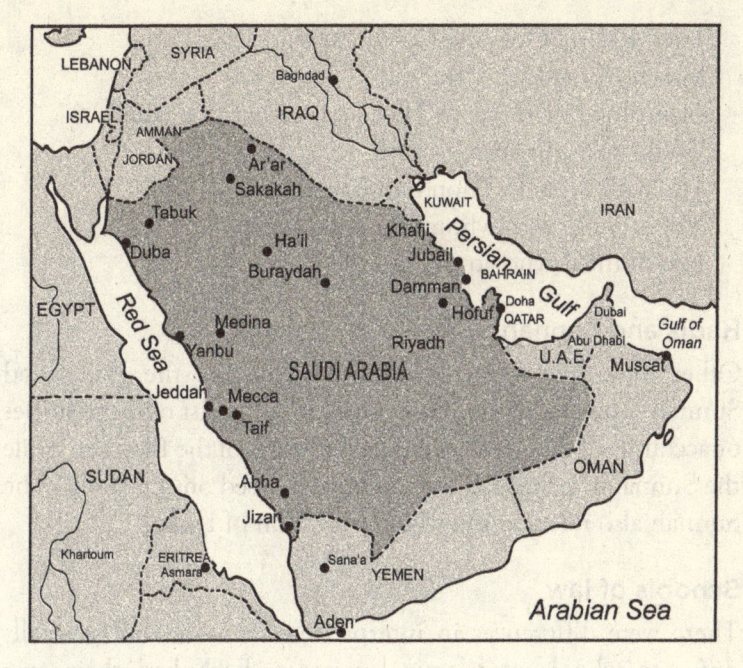

Arabia : Mecca, Medina

The region where Islam arose

also describes the rules to be followed regarding marriage and inheritance, as well as laws for adultery, theft and murder.

The Quran accepts earlier Prophets mentioned in the Bible, including Abraham, Moses and others. It has references to Jesus, Mary and to Christian beliefs. There are numerous commentaries and different interpretations of the text. Though it is normally studied in its original Arabic, it has been translated into a number of languages.

The first chapter of the Quran has the *Fatiha*, a prayer recited at every new beginning, which states:

In the name of Allah, the Merciful, the Compassionate.
Praise be to Allah, the Lord of the worlds,

The Merciful One, the Compassionate One,
Master of the Day of doom.
Thee alone we serve, to Thee alone we cry for help.
Guide us in the straight path
The path of them Thou hast blessed.
Not of those with whom Thou art angry,
Nor of those who go astray.

Hadis and Sunnah

Other important types of texts in Islam are the Hadis and Sunnah. The Hadis/Hadith or traditions consist of short stories or accounts of different incidents in the life of the Prophet, while the Sunnah are the laws that are made, based on the Hadis. The Sunnah also refers to the whole collection of Hadis.

Schools of law

There were differences in interpreting the texts and gradually different schools of Islamic law arose. Each had their own interpretations of what was written in the Quran, Hadis and Sunnah.

Sunni and Shiah

Sunni and Shiah are the two main sects of Islam. The two sects arose soon after the death of the Prophet Muhammad in 632. At this time some of his followers elected Abu Bakr as his successor, who was known as the caliph (khalif, in Arabic, meaning successor). Others felt Muhammad had stated that Ali, his cousin and son-in-law was to be his successor, and so did not accept Abu Bakr. These were known as Shiahs (partisans) of Ali. They also did not accept Abu Bakr's successors, Omar and Osman. The first group later came to be known as Sunnis, the 'people of custom and community' (*ahl-us-sunnah wul-jamaa*). Sunnis form 80 per cent of the Muslim population in the world. Sunnis thus accept the first four caliphs as the rightful successors of the Prophet Muhammad while the Shiahs accept only Ali. Sunnis also accept the Umayyad and Abbasid caliphs, but the Shiahs do not. Sunnis and Shiahs also recognized different Imams or religious leaders.

There are sub sects within Sunnis and Shiahs.

Sufis

Sufis are special types of Muslims who try to find God through various practices. According to one theory, the word is derived from the Arabic suf, or wool as these ascetics at one time wore woollen garments. Other theories are that it comes from suphia, wisdom, or safam meaning purity. Sufis say that their early teachers belonged to an 'inner circle' of disciples of the Prophet Muhammad. He taught them secret and hidden truths, which were not revealed to all. Living with total dedication and devotion to God, they realize God within their hearts, experiencing mystic visions, and uniting with the divine.

The Sufis were divided into different sects.

Some Sufis lived in poverty, others acquired wealth and property. Some sects strictly follow the Sharia (Islamic law); others did so in varying degrees. Some of the saints were involved in the political intrigues of the times, while others lived in isolation as ascetics.

Early Sufi centres were Basra, Kufa, and places in Khorasan and Iran, from where they spread to other regions.

THE CALIPHS

The religious leaders who succeeded Muhammad were known as caliphs. The early caliphs were also rulers.

From 632–661 the early caliphs ruled from Medina in Arabia. Abu Bakr, the first caliph, ruled from CE 632–34. Umar al-Khattab succeeded Abu Bakr, and was caliph from 634–44.

Syria, Palestine, Egypt, Iran and Iraq were conquered at this time. Umar was assassinated in 644, and Usman was elected caliph. However, there was dissension among various groups, and he was killed in 656. Ali was then persuaded to become the caliph, as he had the support of different groups. Ali was married to Fatima, the daughter of Muhammad. Ali too had to face opposition and fight a number of battles, and was finally assassinated in 661. His son Hasan, grandson of Muhammad, was chosen as his successor, but was opposed by Muawiya, governor of Syria.

The Ummayads: CE 661-750

Hasan allowed Muawiya to rule. Muawiya became the next caliph and founded the Umayyad dynasty. He moved the capital from Medina to Damascus. Muawiya was the son of Abu Sufyan, hence the first few Umayyad rulers are known as Sufyans.

Muawiya I (ruled 661-680) further expanded the territories to Khorasan and fought against Constantinople. The caliph was normally elected, but Muawiya nominated his son Yazid as his successor. Husain, another son of Ali and brother of Hasan, was against this. Other important Arabs too did not like this nomination.

The battle of Karbala

Husain went from Medina to Mecca and then travelled towards Kufa, hoping to gain supporters there. But his route was blocked by an Umayyad army. Husain and his small group camped near Karbala. The opposing forces did not allow them to get any water from the river Euphrates for some days. Finally a battle was fought at Karbala in Iraq in 680. Husain and his followers were killed. As this event took place in the Islamic month of Muharram, it is remembered and mourned in this month every year.

Other caliphs

Ibn al Zubayr, son of a companion of the Prophet Muhammad, was also opposed to Yazid I. He established himself in Mecca, and Yazid sent a force to defeat him. Yazid died in CE 683, before Mecca could be reconquered. His son Muawiya II became caliph. Muawiya II wanted peace. When he could not achieve this he abdicated and died soon after in 684. The Sufiyan line ended.

In 684 Marwan I became the caliph, and the rule of the Umayyad Marwans followed. Abd al Malik (ruled 685-705) further expanded the empire. He defeated Ibn al Zubayr and recaptured Mecca. He invaded Spain, and moving to Central Asia conquered Samarkand, Bukhara, Farghana, Khwarizm and Tashkent. He won victories against the Byzantine empire. Arabic was now made the official language. New Arab coinage was introduced. Roads and a postal service connected Damascus to the provinces. Grand buildings were constructed at Damascus. After this a decline started, though there were still some conquests. Sind in India was occupied in 712. However, the Ummayads faced more military defeats. There were also conflicts among different groups. Marwan II (ruled 744-750) was defeated in the battle of the Great Zab river in 750. Umayyad reign ended, but one of the Umayyads, Abd ar Rahman, established an Umayyad dynasty in Spain.

Umayyad architecture

A number of buildings were made in the time of the Umayyad. Palaces were constructed at Jordan, Lebanon, Palestine, and Syria.

Dome of the rock (Qubbat as-Sakrah mosque)

A mosque was erected in Jerusalem. It is built on a rock known as the foundation stone that is sacred to Judaism. The Jewish temple, destroyed in CE 70, was once located here. The mosque was completed in 691 at the time of the Umayyad caliph Abd al Malik, but has been renovated and reconstructed many times. It is richly decorated both inside and outside.

There were other mosques built at Jerusalem and at Medina and Damascus.

Different people

There were both Arab and non-Arab Muslims in Umayyad territories. The Arab Muslims were the rulers, and held a superior position. Christians, Jews, Zoroastrians, and Berbers who worshipped many gods also lived in Umayyad lands. They had freedom of worship, but had to pay a tax. Gradually more and more non-Muslims converted to Islam.

DAMASCUS

The region around Damascus was occupied from about 9000 BCE, and Damascus itself by 2000 BCE. Since then, it saw many political changes. Damascus is mentioned in the Bible. The city was conquered by Alexander. His successors fought over its possession. It came under the Romans and is important in the history of Christianity. Saul, later St Paul, was on the way to Damascus when he saw a vision of Jesus, and then became his follower. Damascus became the centre of a conflict between the early caliphs and the Byzantine empire, but after CE 636 was under the caliphs. Later Muawiya chose it as the Umayyad capital. At this time there were a number of Christian Arabs in the city, and also those who worshipped local gods. The Grand Mosque of Damascus was constructed between 706 and 715. Marwan II moved the capital to Harran, and the Abbasids conquered Damascus in 750. The city then went into decline and came under different dynasties including the Tulunids, Qarmatians and Fatimids, before it once again became a capital under the Seljuk Turks.

25

Great Britain and Ireland: Up to CE 1000

Occupation in Britain dates back to 8,00,000-9,00,000 years ago. But it was around 8000 BCE that with the end of the ice age, and the rising water level, the British islands were created. Before this the land was connected to mainland Europe.

There were a number of farming settlements in Britain by 4000 BCE. By around 3000 BCE megalithic monuments and stone circles began to be built.

THE CELTS

Around the 6th century BCE, or possibly earlier, the Celts reached Britain from Europe. Celtic deities were worshipped. The druids, who were Celtic priests, were prominent. Celtic art included fine work in bronze, gold and silver. Celtic influence continued for a long time. Some of the Celtic people here were known as Britons, Brythons or British. They spoke a Celtic language known as British or Brythonic. There are different legends and accounts about the origin of the Celts in Ireland.

ROMAN BRITAIN

As we have seen earlier, Julius Caesar invaded Britain in 55-54 BCE, but it was the emperor Claudius who began the conquest of the region in CE 43. Wales and Scotland were occupied between CE 70 and 84. Roman conquests brought the Latin language to the region. Towns and cities developed, similar to those in Roman Europe. The towns were like other Roman towns, with forums, markets and baths. By the 2nd century rich people lived in large houses which had mosaic floors and were decorated with frescoes. Forts were built on hillsides. Roman Colchester was one of the first cities in the region.

In the rural areas some Roman type villas were built. But ordinary people continued to live in simple houses made of mud and thatch.

Britain also benefitted from the widespread trading network of the Roman empire. There were new crafts and new products reached the region.

Initially people of Britain had an inferior status. But the Roman emperor Caracalla granted Roman citizenship to all.

Hadrian's wall

Along the northern boundary of Britain, a wall 118 km long was built between CE 122-133. It is called Hadrian's wall, named after

Hadrian's wall; as seen at Greenhead Lough, Northumberland, England

the emperor Hadrian. Northern Britain was often attacked by the Picts from Scotland, and this wall helped to defend the boundary.

Religion

Temples were built to Roman emperors, who were considered divine, and to Roman gods, but Celtic gods were also worshipped. There were also temples to the Indo-Iranian god Mithra and the Egyptian Isis. Both these were important in the Roman empire.

After Christianity became the religion of Rome, it began to spread to Britain.

Roman decline

As the Roman empire collapsed in Europe, its power in Britain declined. By about 409, Romans had left Britain.

ANGLO-SAXONS IN ENGLAND: CE 450-1066

The Angles and the Saxons were Germanic people. From the 5th century, they and other groups began to invade and settle in England. Some Saxons were already living in England, as they had come as mercenary soldiers at the time of the Romans. The Picts from Scotland and the Jutes, who were possibly from Jutland in Denmark, were the other invaders. The Jutes lived in the area of Kent and on the Isle of Wight. By about CE 600, the Angles and Saxons had established a number of kingdoms in England. At first Angles and Saxons may have lived in separate areas, but soon their territories merged. The later name England comes from Angles, and the English language developed from the Anglo-Saxon language. There were a number of Anglo-Saxon kingdoms. Important among these were the seven kingdoms of Mercia, Kent, Sussex, Wessex, East Anglia, Essex and Northumbria. An early text, *The Tribal Hidage*, provides a list of 35 kingdoms or groups of people of Anglo-Saxon times. Mercia was powerful from the 7th to early 9th centuries. Its kings were

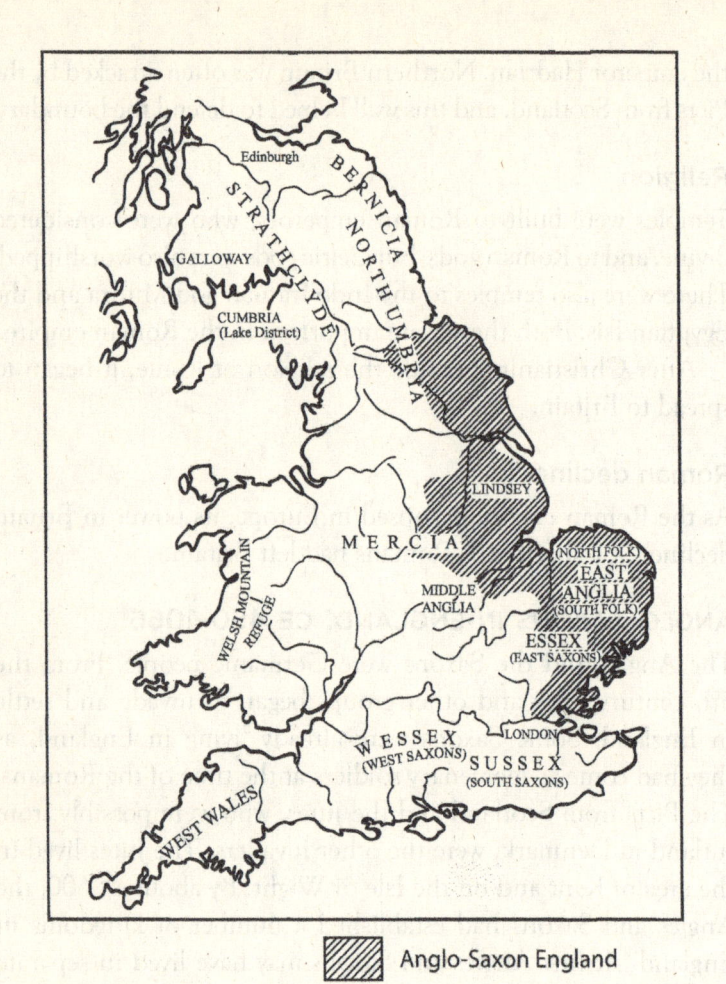

Anglo-Saxon England: the main kingdoms

Angles, and the kingdom reached its height under King Offa (ruled 757–796).

King Offa

King Offa united most of the region and maintained good relations with the pope and with Charlemagne in Europe.

He built Offa's Dyke, as a barrier between the Anglo-Saxon territories and the Welsh kingdoms which were to the west. His portrait can be seen on his coins. His wife, Cynethryth, is also depicted on coins.

The Vikings

In the late 8th century, the Scandinavians or Vikings began to invade England. Among the Scandinavians, it was the Danes from Denmark who reached England first.

In the 9th century, Mercia was defeated first by Wessex and then by the Danes. The east Midlands, Northumbria and East Anglia, came under the Danes.

Wessex

Wessex was ruled by a series of Saxon kings. Among them Egbert (ruled 771-839) defeated Mercia and claimed to be king of all England, but succeeding kings lost territory to the Danes. Alfred I came to the throne in 871, and fought many battles against the Danes.

By the Treaty of Wedmore, England was divided between Alfred and the Danes. Alfred ruled the south and west of England, and the Danes ruled the east and north. The areas where the Danes ruled were known as the Danelaw.

Athelstan, king of Wessex (ruled CE 924-39), a son of Edward the Elder, began to reconquer Dane areas, including East Anglia and the Danish midlands. He conquered Northumbria in 927.

Thus he ruled over most of England. Silver coinage was introduced and the administration was reorganized.

Northumbria was again taken over by Vikings. They established themselves as kings of York. However, king Eadred of Wessex finally defeated them in 954.

In the late 10th century, the Danes again invaded. Cnut (Canute II), king of Denmark and Norway, ruled England. But

Edward the Confessor came back from exile in 1042, and took over the throne. He died without heirs. After his death, in 1066, Harold, Earl of Wessex was made King Harold II of England, but was challenged by William, Duke of Normandy, who then became the king.

Norman rule followed.

Sutton Hoo—a ship grave

Sutton Hoo, a hill on the coast of England in East Anglia, is a burial site which has a number of graves of the Anglo-Saxons. Here there are two ship graves. Kings and chiefs were buried in ships, which were later dragged on to the land. The ships no longer remain, but their nature and size can be understood through impressions in the sand. The larger ship was 27 m long and had 38 oars. It was filled with beautiful objects of gold and other items, including a bronze bowl, helmet, shield and coins. It must have been the grave of a king. But the body of the king has not been found, hence it either dissolved, or this was only a symbolic grave. The ship and other items belong to the 7th century.

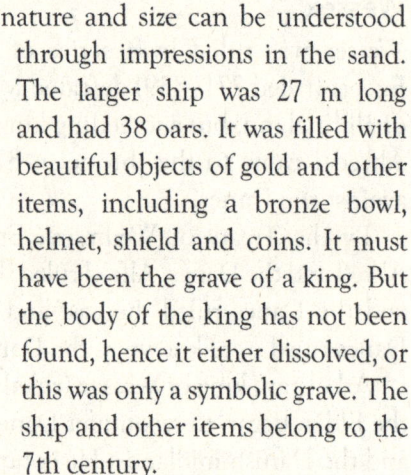

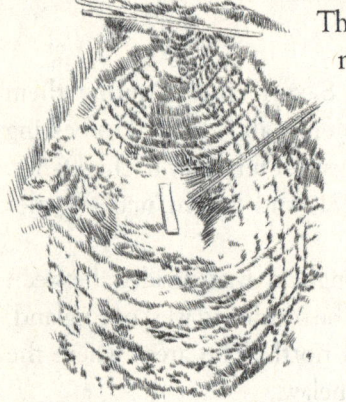

Ship grave at Sutton Hoo; the wood of the ship has not survived but its outline can be seen in the sand.

This grave as well as items found elsewhere indicate that beautiful items were made in Anglo-Saxon times.

TWO TREASURE HOARDS
Treasure at Oglay Hay

Among the many items of Anglo-Saxon times was a hoard (items buried together), of the early 7th century, found in

Oglay Hay in south Staffordshire in the English Midlands. This has 3500 pieces, scattered over about 90 sq m. It was perhaps once buried in a pit. When collected, the pieces amounted to 5 kg of gold and 1.4 kg of silver, as well as a number of gems. The items were mainly fragments of decorations on helmets, swords, caps and other items. There were two Christian crosses, one large and one small, as well as an inscription on a gold strip, which has a quote from the Bible. It says: 'Let god arise and his enemies be dispersed and those who hate him flee from his face'.

Perhaps the items were placed there at a time of war.

Treasure of the Vale of York

Another buried treasure was found near Harrogate in Yorkshire, England. The Vikings had been kings of York and this once belonged to them. The treasure was in a decorated silver bowl. In this there were 600 silver coins. Most of these were Anglo-Saxon coins, but there were some Viking coins as well as coins from Europe, Baghdad, Samarkand and Afghanistan that had been brought by the Vikings through trade or conquest. There were also bits of silver brooches, arm rings, and rings and of silver bars, which the Vikings used as money. This treasure must have been buried in the 10th century, at the time of wars with Athelstan or the later kings of Wessex. It includes a silver coin of Athelstan, with an inscription in which he calls himself 'King of all Britain' (Athelstan Rex totius Brittanaiae).

THE LEGENDS OF ARTHUR

Arthur (Artorius) was a king about whom many stories are told. He was guided and helped by a wizard named Merlin. Arthur had a number of knights who, when they met, sat at a huge round table. He was married to the beautiful Guinevere, but she and Arthur's best knight Lancelot were in love. These and other stories were written much later. Arthur is believed to have been a king who lived in the 5th century and fought against invaders.

LITERATURE

A number of books were written. Some of the most notable are described here.

The Venerable Bede (CE 673-735)

Bede was a Benedictine monk. He lived in Jarrow in Northumbria. He wrote an account of England at the time of the Anglo-Saxons. This is called *Historia Ecclesiastica Gentis Anglorum* (Ecclesiastical History of the English People).

Though Bede focused on the history of the Church, his account also tells us about the life and people of those times. To write this, he used existing accounts as well as legends.

The Anglo-Saxon Chronicle

This narrates the history of England from the late 6th century, when Christianity was introduced, up to 1154. It was written after 1000, but refers to earlier times.

Beowulf

Beowulf is an epic poem, written in Old English. It was probably composed around 750 by an Anglican poet. The poem contains 3182 lines and tells the story of Beowulf, a Scandinavian prince. Grendel, a partly-human wild creature is threatening the Danes. Beowulf defeats and kills him, as well as Grendel's mother, who comes to avenge her son's death.

But 50 years later, Beowulf himself dies in a fight against a dragon.

SCOTLAND

Scotland, earlier known as Caledonia, was occupied by the Romans in the early centuries CE. After the withdrawal of the

Romans, Celts from Ireland invaded the region, followed by the Angles, who conquered part of it and included it in the kingdom of Northumbria. But in 685 the Picts defeated the Angles, and gained control over Caledonia. In the 8th century the Vikings invaded the region. They continued their raids in the 9th century and founded some settlements. By this time the Picts, a Celtic group, Gaels or Scots from Ireland, as well as Britons and Angles lived in Scotland. The Picts, Gaels and Britons spoke Celtic languages.

In CE 843, Kenneth MacAlpin, a Gael, conquered or inherited the lands of the Picts. A new kingdom was formed, that was later known as Alba (Scotland). Under the succeeding kings, particularly Malcolm I of Alba, who ruled from CE 940, more territories were added to the kingdom. By the 11th century, the whole of Scotland was united under Malcolm II (ruled 1005-1035).

WALES

Wales was occupied by Celts, followed by the Romans. After the departure of the Romans, some Brythonic-speaking Celts settled in the Welsh mountains to escape from the Anglo-Saxons. The area had many small kingdoms, but soon four became important. These were called Gwynedd, Powys, Deheubarth and Morgannwg. By around CE 600, the Welsh language had developed from Brythonic. Gradually the kings of Gwynedd became important. The Vikings invaded the region, but Rhodri Mawr (ruled CE 844-878), of Gwynedd, defeated the Vikings in 856, and controlled most of Wales. Rhodri suffered a defeat in 876, and two years later was probably killed in a battle against the English.

Hywel Dda, a later king (ruled 942-950), accepted Athelstan of England as his overlord, while maintaining some independence. Hywell knew Welsh, Latin and English. He issued his own coins and codified Welsh laws.

IRELAND

Ireland had early Celtic settlements. It did not come under the Roman empire. Ireland had a number of small kingdoms known as Tuath, each headed by a king. The ardri or chief king lived at a hill fort at Tara, in the present county of Meah in Ireland. From the late 8th century there were Viking raids into Ireland, as well as Viking settlements. Among the different kings in Ireland was Brian Boru. He became king of Munster and in 1002 was accepted as the High King (chief or supreme king). Brian Boru was killed in 1014 after the Battle of Clontarf. After this, there were again small kingdoms in Ireland.

LEGENDS AND TRADITIONS

Ireland's traditional and legendary history says there were different groups of people occupying the region. According to these legends, in the first age of the world, Ladhra, with his 16 wives, lived in Ireland. He was the first man to die in Ireland, and his descendants too, died in a great flood. The next were the race of Partholon. The Formorians were sea people who attacked the Partholon. In the third age were the divine Nemeds. In the fourth age the Fir Bolg were prominent. In the fifth age there were the Tuatha de Danann. The priests of the Tuatha de were the wise druids. In the sixth age the Milesians came to Ireland.

This traditional account was recorded much later by Irish and Scottish monks, in the *Lebor Gahala Erenn* (Irish Book of Conquests). Though legendary, there may be some truth in it. The Tuatha de Danann were Celts, and worshipped Celtic gods. Milesians too are believed to be a branch of Gaelic Celts.

CHRISTIANITY

In England at the time of the Romans, temples were built to Roman deities, such as Mithra and Minerva. By the time Christianity became the official Roman religion, Rome's power was declining in Britain.

St Patrick brought Christianity to Ireland in the 5th century CE. Here Christianity soon became prominent, absorbing the earlier Celtic religion. Monasteries were set up and Ireland became the centre of Christianity. Christian monks recorded earlier traditions, books were transcribed and written by monks, and beautifully illustrated manuscripts as well as other arts flourished. St Finian of Clonard (470-549) founded a monastic school, Clonard Abbey. St Finian was renowned for his learning and piety, both in Ireland and in other lands. He had 12 main disciples, known as the 12 apostles of Ireland. In the 6th century, Christianity reached Wales and Scotland. In 597 St Augustine was sent from Rome to England to convert Anglo-Saxons to Christianity. He became the first Archbishop of Canterbury.

St Ninian (c.360-c.432) was the first Christian missionary in Scotland. St Colomba (521-597) continued his work. Columba also wrote hymns, transcribed a number of books, and is said to have performed miracles.

THE BOOK OF KELLS

Christianity was often combined with earlier Celtic traditions. *The Book of Kells* is a beautifully illustrated manuscript of the 7th to 8th century, containing the four Gospels in Latin. Many paintings in the book combined Celtic styles with Christian themes.

26

Warriors of the North: Scandinavian Vikings
CE 750–1100

Scandinavia is a region that includes the present countries of Norway, Sweden and Denmark. These three countries speak different but related languages. Finland and Iceland have close connections with these countries and are sometimes included in Scandinavia. The region was occupied from at least 14,000 BCE. But it began to make an impact on other parts of Europe from CE 750.

The way of life
The Scandinavians were basically farmers. They grew various crops including barley and oats, and kept cattle, sheep, goats, pigs and chickens. They caught and ate fish. They made iron tools, were very good woodcarvers, and knew how to write. They lived in a type of long, rectangular dwelling called a longhouse. In their houses, they used furniture, including beds, chairs, tables and stools. They made cooking vessels, bowls, cooking implements, and lamps from stone. The lamps had hollows

which were filled with fish oil, and lit with wicks. On the corners were holes through which ropes were threaded. The ropes were tied to the ceiling, and the lamps hung down providing light. Men worked in the fields or fought wars. Women helped in the fields and also cooked the food. Among the Scandinavians, there were some fierce warriors.

The Vikings

'Viking' is a term used for the warriors of Scandinavia. In the 8th century these warriors began crossing the oceans in their ships, attacking different regions, and bringing back wealth. Some of them were also traders. Later, the Vikings settled in different areas.

A typical Viking ship

Ships

Vikings used two kinds of ships. A langskip (longship) was a special type of ship used for voyages to attack or raid, or for fishing. Knorr was the term for a different and stronger type of ship, in which various produce was carried for trade. The ships were carved out of wood and decorated.

Viking conquests

Vikings reached the coast of England in 793. This was quite far from their home, and they thought of settling on some nearby islands, from where they could attack different places in England. Soon they conquered the kingdoms of Mercia, East Anglia and Northumbria. By the end of the 9th century, the Danelaw was set up, that is, the Danish occupation of part of England. The Danish region was reconquered in the 10th century, but Viking occupation had a long-term influence on society, the names of people and places as well as on other aspects of culture. Trade expanded through the towns established by the Vikings. Among them were York and Lincoln. Norwegian Vikings attacked monasteries in England, Scotland and Ireland, and took away wealth. Trading towns were established in Ireland, at Dublin and other areas.

The Vikings also attacked Europe under the Carolingians, and settled in some parts of the Carolingian empire. Normandy became a permanent Viking settlement. It meant the area of the Northmen.

The Vikings reached Iceland before CE 900, and established settlements there. In Iceland, the *Landnamabok* (Book of Settlements) is a record of the Vikings who settled there. According to this book, the first permanent Viking settler was a chief named Ingolfur Amarson.

After this the Vikings settled in Greenland. They reached Newfoundland and even Russia. Viking raids died out by the end of the 11th century, but some of their settlements remained.

What they made

Vikings made a number of beautiful objects. Some of these have been found in their graves. These consist of furniture, including beds; carts and sleighs for transport; swords and other weapons; jewellery in gold and silver; and carved rune stones. There was also intricate woodcarving of people and scenes, and painted objects.

Ships and other objects were decorated with birds, animals and mythical creatures.

In Norway, many chiefs were buried in wooden ships.

Oseberg ship burial

The Slagen district of Norway has remains of several Viking ship burials. The Oseberg ship burial was one of these. It is named after the town of Oseberg which is nearby. This ship, made mostly of oak, was 21.4 m long and 5.1 m wide. Oar holes indicate that thirty oars were used to row the ship. The hull was carved and decorated. The ship had a number of objects. There were tools, axes, beds, sledges, wagons, and even a loom for weaving, along with textiles. There were remains of animals—dogs, horses and oxen. In the grave chamber were two women. One was over 80 years old, the other more than 50. This showed that people lived quite a long life. An analysis of the wood in the grave through Dendrochronology (dating through tree rings) provides a date of CE 834.

Eirik the Red

Eirik the Red was the name of the Norwegian who established a settlement in Greenland. He lived in the 10th century. There are a number of stories about him, written in Icelandic.

RELIGION
Scandinavian gods and goddesses

From an early period, the Scandinavians had their own gods. The Vikings too worshipped these gods and goddesses. Among them were:

Odin, also called Woden: a wizard and a warrior god; he was the oldest and the greatest god, the ruler of all the other deities.

Viking warrior: this warrior represents Eirik the Red [Eirik Thorvaldsson], who is believed to have founded the first Viking settlement in Greenland. It is reproduced from a woodcut from the book Gronlandia [Greenland], *published in 1688.*

Frigg: a mother goddess, and wife of Odin
Thor: the god of thunder, one of the sons of Odin and Frigg
Njord: god of winds and the sea
Frey and Freya: son and daughter of Njord
Heimdall: god of fire.

Christianity

After about CE 1000, people in Scandinavia began accepting Christianity. But they still liked to hear stories of their gods.

Literature

Early Scandinavian literature consists of sagas and eddas.

The sagas

Stories of the Vikings were written down in Iceland and Scandinavia. These are known as 'sagas' and there are hundreds of them. Though they were written between the 12th and 14th centuries, they were based on earlier stories.

Sagas can be divided into three categories. There are sagas of kings and of other heroes. They may be based on facts, but were turned into fiction. Others are stories of families, based on local history and legends. A third category are stories of the ancient past.

Snorri Sturluson (CE 1172-1241) of Iceland was one of the authors of sagas. He wrote *Heimskringla*, an account of the kings of Norway from the ancient past up to CE 1177.

Other sagas included:

Knytlinga Saga: an account of Danish kings
Egill's Saga: the story of a warrior poet named Egill
Laxdaela Saga: a love story
Gisla Saga: the sad story of an outlaw
Njal's Saga: a story of feuds between two families

More historical sagas were written in the 13th century.

Eddas

Eddas are another category of writings. There are only two eddas. It is not clear what 'edda' means, but the two books are concerned with poetry. Snorri Sturluson, who also wrote sagas, composed a work he titled *Edda*. The main aim of this work was to explain metres used in poetry. This *Edda* includes mythical stories. Among the stories is an account of the visit of Gylfi, a king of the Swedes, to Asgard, where the gods lived.

Later, a text was found consisting of poems about the gods and heroes, some of them similar to Snorri's quotations in his *Edda*. This was given the name of the *Poetic* or *Elder Edda*, and Snorri's text was called the *Prose* or *Younger Edda*. The *Poetic Edda* was written in the 13th century, but has story poems which were

FIMBULWINTER

In Snorri Sturluson's *Edda* is an account of a great winter (Fimbulwinter). It said there would be three winters together, with no summer in between, when snow would spread all around. Snorri was referring to a mythical future event before the destruction of the world. But there is evidence that some such event took place in CE 536–7, for a period of 12 to 18 months. A dust haze or dry fog covered Scandinavia and extended into Europe, Asia Minor and China. Agriculture declined. The worst effects were felt in Scandinavia, where possibly 75 or even 90 per cent of the population died. Was this one of the reasons why Scandinavians began their invasions of other countries about two hundred years later? Were there long-term effects on the land? Some archaeologists think so.

It is not known what caused such a prolonged dust haze. There might have been a volcanic eruption or the earth may have been hit by a comet.

composed between CE 800 and 1100. These books are important sources for Norse myths.

Runes

The Runic or early Germanic alphabet was used all through the Germanic world from around the 1st–3rd centuries CE. There were at least three varieties of this alphabet. The Vikings were among those who used it.

This alphabet consisted of 24 letters, arranged in three rows of eight each. The first six letters were f-u-th-a-r-k. They gave the alphabet its name, Futhark. Each letter is called a rune. The runes were considered magical and sacred. Each was dedicated to a god, who could be invoked through the rune. Invoking the god was different from praying to him. It was like calling the power of the god to be present.

Later other letters were added to the script, and there were different varieties of runes. Over 4000 rune inscriptions and some rune manuscripts have been found, of which more than half are from Sweden. In Norway, the Bryggen inscriptions consist of 670 medieval runic inscriptions of the 14th century and earlier. They include prayers, spells, name tags and longer letters.

An extract from *Voluspo*, on the creation of the world. *Voluspo*, the Wise Woman's Prophecy, is a poem in the Poetic Edda.

Of old was the age | when Ymir lived;
Sea nor cool waves | nor sand there were;
Earth had not been, | nor heaven above,
But a yawning gap, | and grass nowhere.
   Then Bur's sons lifted | the level land,
Midgard the mighty | there they made;
The sun from the south | warmed the stones of earth,
And green was the ground | with growing leeks.
   (Trans. Henry Adams Bellow)

> **Explanation:**
> Ymir was a giant from whom the gods created the world.
> Bur was a god; his sons were Odin, Vili and Ve.
> Midgard is the middle world or earth, where men live.

27
India
CE 500–1000

NORTHERN INDIA

The Gupta empire was declining. The Huns from Central Asia attacked the region. We had seen that Attila, the great leader of the Huns, had led the attack on Rome, and united the Huns. But later they broke up into many groups.

One group of Huns had some success in India. Toramana, a Huna (Hun) leader invaded from the north. He then set up his own kingdom in Malwa in c. CE 500. His son and successor Mihiragula set up his capital at Sakala or Sialkot in the Punjab. Mihiragula was not liked by the people. He aroused terror and hatred by his violent acts. He was finally defeated in c. CE 528, but some Hunas settled in India and were absorbed into the existing culture.

The Sasanians of Persia and the Indo-Sasanians who were connected with them, also had an influence in north India.

King Harsha

One of the important kings of north India was Harshavardhana of the Pushyabhuti dynasty. His father Prabhakaravardhana ruled a kingdom to the north-west of Delhi. Harsha became king when he was 16 years old, after the death of his father and brother. Harsha had to fight against many enemies to rescue his sister Rajyashri. Her husband had been killed, and she had been captured by the king of Gauda. First Harsha rescued her, and then he defeated several other kings and established an empire across north India. Harsha ruled from 606-647.

Kannauj

Harsha's capital was at Kannauj. According to the Chinese traveller Xuanzang, it was a well-defended city with large structures. He said that the city had beautiful gardens and tanks of clear water. Some families were very rich, and the markets displayed objects from distant lands. The people were of a refined appearance and wore clothes of glossy silk.

Buddhism

Harsha was interested in Mahayana Buddhism. He became a Buddhist and asked people of his kingdom not to kill animals, and to be kind to all. He held a huge meeting at Kannauj, where kings from 20 countries came to discuss Buddhism. A large golden image of the Buddha was made, placed in a tower and worshipped.

There were Buddhist monasteries including one at Nalanda. It was a centre of learning where many subjects were taught. Ten thousand Buddhist monks stayed there.

Xuanzang

The Tang dynasty was ruling in China. Xuanzang, a Buddhist, wanted to come to India to learn more about Buddhism.

A portrait of Xuanzang

The emperor of China did not give him a permit to leave, but he left anyway in 629 without telling him. Crossing the high mountains, it took him one year to reach India. Then Xuanzang travelled right across India and wrote about what he saw. After some years he returned to China with a number of Buddhist texts.

Harshacharita

Harshacharita is a book written by Banabhatta who lived at Harsha's court. It is a biography of the king.

Pulakeshin II

Pulakeshin II (ruled CE 608-642) of the Chalukya dynasty was a powerful king in central India. He fought many battles and even defeated King Harsha. Pulakeshin II sent an ambassador to the court of the Sasanian king of Iran, Khusrau II. Xuanzang visited Pulakeshin's kingdom and reported that the soil was rich and fertile, and the people were warlike. Vatapi, Aihole and Pattadakal were the main centres of this kingdom. Temples were constructed here.

The Rajputs

Beginning in CE 700 or a little earlier, there were several kingdoms in north India. Many of these were ruled by the Rajputs (from '*raja putra*', sons of kings). Among the Rajput dynasties were the Guhilas, Pratiharas, Chandellas and Paramaras.

The Rajputs held ideals that were something like those of the knights of Europe. They fought bravely in battle and protected the weak.

SOUTH INDIA

The Pandyas, with their capital at Madurai, and the Pallavas of Kanchi, were among the dynasties in the south. Xuanzang visited Kanchi and provided a description of it. He said there was plenty of grain, fruit and flowers, and precious gems found in the region. Pallava temples can be seen at Mamallapuram. Some of these were rock-cut, that is, carved from rock. The Pallava king Narasimhavarman I defeated and killed Pulakeshin I.

In the 9th and 10th centuries the Chola dynasty became important. Rajaraja Chola and Rajendra Chola were among the important kings.

Shravana Belagola

There were other dynasties in south India. Among them were the Western Gangas. Their kings and many of their ministers followed the Jain religion. Chamundaraya, a minister of Rajamalla IV (977-985), had a huge image of the Jain saint Bahubali carved at Shravana Belagola. According to the story, Bahubali and Bharata were two brothers who lived very very long ago. They fought for a kingdom, and Bahubali won. But after winning he gave up the throne and allowed his brother to rule. Bahubali meditated in a standing pose for several years and finally gained enlightenment.

This image of Bahubali at Shravana Belagola stands on a hill, and is carved out of the natural rock. It is 17 m high, and shows Bahubali meditating, while plants and creepers grow around his feet.

Statue of Bahubali at Shravana Belgola

OTHER KINGDOMS

There were several independent states. The Shahiyas ruled in the north-west (present Afghanistan and Pakistan). They were descended from the Kushans. Kashmir had its own kings and dynasties who sometimes invaded other parts of India. Further north the history of Nepal was influenced by both India and Tibet. Trade between India and Tibet and China passed through the region. In the north-east Kamarupa, in the region of Assam, Manipur and Tripura, were some independent states. In west India, Arabs ruled a kingdom in Sind. There were numerous other small kingdoms, both in the north and the south, the east and the west.

In addition to the small kingdoms, there were feudatories. Feudatories were officials who had been given land by the king. They looked after the land and paid taxes and tribute to the king. The money was collected from the farmers and peasants.

These feudatories lived in great splendour. They wore gold-bordered clothes, rings, earrings and many other jewels. They lived in houses three to five storeys high, and had many servants and attendants.

LIFESTYLE

During this time there was a decline in cities, trade and in the number of coins. At the same time agriculture and local crafts flourished. Cereals including wheat, barley and rice were grown, as well as fruits, vegetables, cotton and sugar cane. Some people ate meat but many were vegetarians. Crafts included pottery, textiles, leatherwork, gold, silver and metalwork.

Across India, a number of books were written. New temples were built.

HINDUISM

Hinduism was growing and developing in different ways. Many gods were worshipped and goddesses such as Durga, Devi or Kali became important. The caste system had divided people. Initially there were four castes based on occupation. These were the brahmanas or priests, the kshatriyas or kings and warriors, the vaishyas, who were farmers, traders and merchants, and the shudras who were supposed to serve others. Within these hundreds of subcastes developed. Each of these had a traditional occupation that they had to follow. They could not choose the work they wanted to do. One caste group did not marry people of another caste. Each caste worshipped different gods.

There were new philosophers and movements that tried to bring unity.

Shankara

Shankara was born in Kerala in the 8th or 9th century CE. He explained the philosophy of Advaita or 'oneness'. This philosophy is part of Vedanta. He said there was only One (known as Brahman), there was no second. God, people, the created world, all were One. People saw differences only because they did not have a true understanding of reality. He said knowledge or wisdom was the only way in which this One reality could be understood. Shankara also introduced the worship of five main gods: Vishnu, Shiva, Durga, Ganesha and Surya.

Nayanars and Alvars

In south India the Nayanar and Alvar saints lived between the 7th and 10th centuries. They worshipped the gods Shiva and Vishnu. They said everyone could reach god through love and devotion. They did not think that caste was important. These saints composed beautiful poems and songs mainly in Tamil.

VAJRAYANA BUDDHISM

By now there were three types of Buddhism.

Hinayana Buddhism followed the basic teachings of the Buddha.

Mahayana Buddhism added new elements including the worship of deities.

Vajrayana Buddhism became important in the 7th and 8th centuries. In this faith there were new methods of worship of different deities and ways to gain power. It was a form of Tantrism.

28

China, Mongolia and Korea
CE 581–1000

After a period of confusion, the Sui dynasty came to power in China in 581. They ruled only till 618 but had some notable achievements. The Great Wall was reconstructed at this time. The major part of the Grand Canal, the longest in the world, was built. A series of short canals were linked together to create this. Ships sailed along the canal, carrying goods and people. The canal also connected a number of rivers. It extended from present Beijing to Hangzhou.

Emperor Yang of the Sui dynasty built a 100 m high wooden pagoda at Changan. This was the tallest pagoda of those times, but it no longer exists.

Tang dynasty: CE 618–907

The Tang dynasty was founded in CE 618 by Li Yuan. It continued up to 907, but was prosperous only up to around 750. Some of the great rulers were: Li Shimin (627–49), son of Li Yuan, who was given the title Taizong after his death (all the Tang rulers were

Part of the Great Wall of China

given apt titles after they died); the empress Wu Zhao (690-705); and Xuanzong (712-756) who had the title Minghuang which meant 'brilliant emperor'. He expanded the empire and made administrative reforms. The empire was prosperous. Literature, art and music flourished. But even a brilliant emperor had his failings. Xuanzong fell in love with a young concubine called Yang Guifei, and stopped paying attention to administration. A revolt in 755 led to Yang Guifei's death. The emperor escaped leaving his capital.

After CE 763 there was peace, but meanwhile millions had died. Small kingdoms under military governors (jiedushi) emerged and the emperor's power was reduced. Another rebellion in 885 soon led to the end of the Tang dynasty.

Under the early Tang rulers, China had a huge and prosperous empire. Its territory included Korea, south Dongbei and north Vietnam, while its influence extended to Japan and across Central Asia up to Afghanistan. Even in the later days of the Tang empire there were new inventions and cultural developments.

Cities

The Tang capital was at Changan (modern Xian). It had broad roads, palaces and large buildings. People from different countries lived here, and there was freedom to practise any religion. At this time the number of cities and towns increased. Trade was widespread both by land and sea. Guangzhou was a major port.

Administration

The administration was centralized. The civil service, that is, the government officials, were appointed through an examination, as earlier, but the system was further improved. Land was under government control, and given for cultivation to adult males in equal portions. Taxation from this made the government rich. The men also had to serve in the military when required.

Crafts

Special items made included glazed pottery, ceramics, and gold and silver dishes. Porcelain began to be made. For this, white clay and feldspar had to be heated at very high temperatures in a kiln. Porcelain figurines were delicate and unique.

Culture

There were great achievements in literature, art, music, and poetry. A large number of poems were composed during the Tang dynasty. Wang Wei, the painter, was also a great poet. Li Bai (Li Po) (701-762) and Du Fu (Tu Fu) (712-770) were among other famous poets.

Stories too were composed, and narrated to audiences or written down in books. Woodblock printing was developed, and paper money and books were printed. Medical texts were written.

Stone pagodas were built and can still be seen. Stone sculptures were carved. There were new styles in painting. Buddhist scenes were painted as well as landscapes and portraits. Wang Wei

These porcelain figurines have a white base and are coloured in green, yellow and brown. One metre in height, they were found in the tomb of Liu Tingxun, an important official of the Tang dynasty.

(699–759) was one of the great artists, who painted snow-covered scenes. Yen Leiben painted portraits of early emperors.

Music, singing and dancing continued to develop. In music, new instruments were introduced from Turkey and elsewhere.

The oldest printed book

A Chinese translation of a Sanskrit Buddhist text, *The Vajrachchhedika Sutra* (Diamond Sutra) dates to CE 868. This is the oldest evidence of a printed book in the world, 600 years before printing started in Europe.

New inventions

In the later years of the Tang dynasty, gunpowder was invented, but at this time it was used only for firecrackers, not for weapons. Another great invention was the magnetic compass.

The magnetic needle pointed north and could be used in ships to find the right direction.

Religion

Buddhism and Daoism were the main religions in the early Tang. The great pilgrim Xuanzang travelled to India and brought back many Buddhist texts. Other religions including Christianity, Judaism, and Islam were also practised in the kingdom. Even Manichaeism was practised. From China Buddhists went to Japan and Korea.

According to tradition, Bodhidharma from India brought Chan (known in Japan as Zen) Buddhism to China in the 6th century. New schools of Buddhism emerged in China.

But as the Tang dynasty declined, Confucianism again became prominent. Some of the emperors turned against Buddhism. In the 9th century thousands of Buddhist monasteries and temples were destroyed. Other religions, too, were no longer welcome.

By 907 the Tang dynasty had ended. For a while there were numerous dynasties and kingdoms in conflict. Then in 960 the Sung dynasty came to power.

TIBET

Tibet is a plateau to the north-east of the Himalayas. It was occupied from around 20,000 BCE. Later there were more migrants to the region. King Songtsen Gampo (CE 608-650) united part of the region. He married Bhrikuti, a princess from Nepal, as well as Princess Wencheng, daughter of a Chinese Tang emperor. Succeeding kings expanded Tibetan control into Central Asia and China. Between 750 and 794, Tibet controlled the kingdom of Nanzhao in Yunnan. From around 850, Tibet lost its power. Small states were formed. Later, Tibet came under the Mongolian Yuan dynasty that also ruled China, though it retained some autonomy. This was followed by the rule of the indigenous Phagmodrupa dynasty from around 1350.

Bon is the local religion of Tibet, but Buddhism reached here from India and China and became the main religion. Buddhism in Tibet includes Mahayana and Vajrayana forms with elements of the earlier Bon religion.

NANZHAO

In the western Yunnan region of China, the kingdom of Nanzhao existed between the 8th and 13th centuries. It was founded by groups of people speaking Tai languages. Nanzhao conquered most of Myanmar, but began to decline after 863. The kingdom was conquered by Kublai Khan in 1253. Meanwhile the Tai

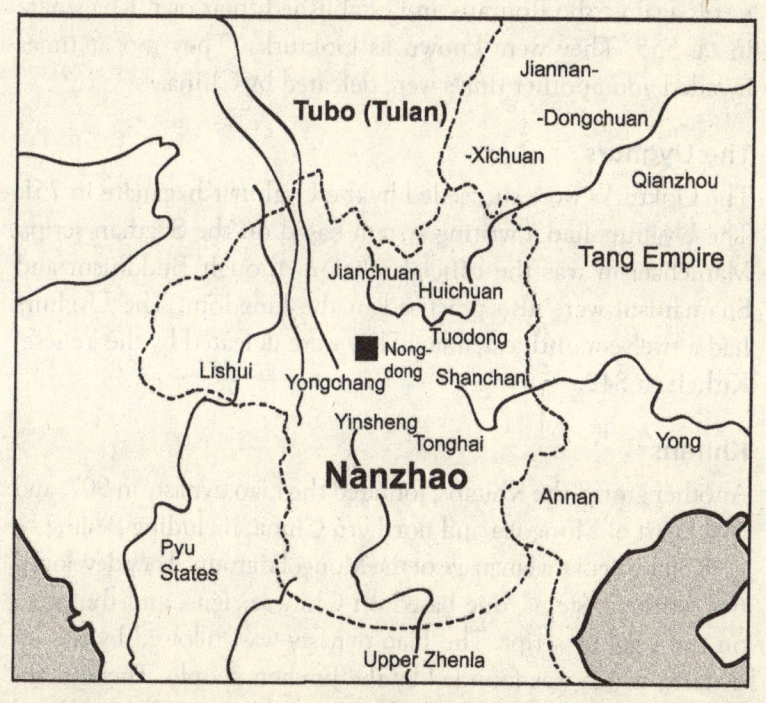

Nanzhao

people moved into Thailand. Tai languages include those spoken in Thailand and Laos.

MONGOLIA
Toba Wei and Rouran

We had seen that the Toba Wei kingdom dominated Mongolia in the 6th century. The Toba Wei were a branch of the Xianbei people. Another branch of the Xianbei were the Rouran, who established the Rouran Khaganate in CE 402. The Toba and Rouran fought wars against each other.

The Gokturks

The Altai Turkics, who lived in the Rouran kingdom, started a revolt against the Rourans and established their own Khaganate in CE 555. They were known as Gokturks. They too at times invaded and at other times were defeated by China.

The Uyghurs

The Gokturks were succeeded by the Uyghur Khaganate in 751. The Uyghurs had a writing system based on the Sogdian script. Manichaeism was the official religion, though Buddhism and Shamanism were also practised in the kingdom. The Uyghurs had a twelve-month calendar. They were defeated by the Yenesei Kirhgiz in 840.

Khitans

Another group, the Khitans, founded the Liao dynasty in 907, and ruled part of Mongolia and northern China, including Beijing.

Khitans spoke a language of the Mongolic group. They developed two writing systems, one based on Chinese signs, and the other on the Uyghur script. The Liao dynasty was followed by the Jin dynasty, which was founded by the Jurchen people. The Khitans moved west and founded the Kara-Khitan khanate (Western Liao) in the present region of Xingjian and part of Central Asia. The next group to dominate Mongolia was the Mongols.

KOREA

Until the 6th century, Koguryo was the most powerful kingdom in Korea. But in CE 668 the state of Silla formed an alliance with China, defeated the kingdoms of Koguryo and Paekche, and united Korea. The Silla kingdom had its own Korean culture, but was influenced by Chinese culture and language. Part of Korea also came under the Tang dynasty of China. Buddhism grew and flourished at this time.

The Silla kingdom began to decline in the 9th century, and the three earlier kingdoms began to revive. A new state named Koryo was established in 918.

WON-HYO AND UI SANG

Among the many great Buddhists in Korea were Won hyo and Ui Sang who lived in the 7th century. They decided to go to China to study the higher aspects of Buddhism. They had to walk, and feeling quite hot, one afternoon they went to sleep. Won hyo woke up thirsty. Nearby he found a vessel full of delicious cold water, and drank it, feeling refreshed. Later he noticed that the vessel was really a skull. He understood that everything comes from the mind; nothing is good or bad in itself. He became enlightened and returned to Korea.

Ui Sang continued on the journey and reached China. He studied there for ten years. He wrote a poem in the shape of a seal. Geometrically its shape symbolized infinity. And the words summarized the essence of a great Buddhist text, the *Avatamsaka Sutra*.

29

Africa
CE 500–1000

As we have seen earlier, northern Africa, with its location close to the Mediterranean and the Red Sea, had many different influences from the earliest days.

ARABS IN AFRICA

In the 7th century, the Arabs began to conquer parts of Africa. In CE 641, Egypt, which was under the Byzantine empire, was conquered by the Arabs. By 648 more regions of north Africa were conquered by them.

In CE 661 the Arab Umayyad dynasty came to power in Damascus (Syria) and continued conquests. More wars were fought against the Byzantines. The Arabs conquered Carthage from the Byzantine empire in 697. Now most of north Africa was under the Arabs. Three Arab provinces were formed—Egypt, Ifriqiya and Maghreb (present Morocco and Mauritania).

Musa bin Nusair, the governor of Ifriqiya, conquered the small north African states of Ibiza, Majorca and Minorca, as well as Algiers.

The Umayyad was succeeded by the Abbasid dynasty. But though the Umayyad and Abbasids controlled north Africa, very often local governors founded their own dynasties and were virtually independent.

With the conquests by the Arabs, the Arab language and culture, and their religion, Islam, spread in the region.

THE BERBERS

Berbers are the indigenous people of a large part of north Africa. They have lived here from the earliest days. At first the Berbers were against the Arabs, but later many of them adopted Islam.

EGYPT

In Egypt, the Arabs appointed governors to rule from Alexandria. Later they created a new capital, El-Fustat, which means 'the tent'. El Fustat, not far from Cairo, became a centre of trade.

Some governors were good, others bad. At times different groups revolted against them.

Tulunid dynasty

In CE 856 the Abbasid caliphs gave Egypt to a Turkish group in Baghdad. A new Turkish governor, Ahmad ibn Tulun, came to Egypt in 868. He paid tribute to the Abbasids, but ruled independently and founded the Tulunid dynasty.

Ahmad ibn Tulun built a new capital, al-Qatai, and constructed a large mosque there. He made Syria part of his kingdom, and had a strong army. Agriculture improved and there was more trade. Brick and plaster were used for the first time in buildings. Art developed.

Ahmad's son Khumarawayh was the next ruler (884–896). The later rulers were weak, and the Abbasids again gained power in the region in 905.

The Fatimids

The Fatimid dynasty became powerful in CE 909, and soon conquered north Africa. They were Shiahs while the Abbasid Caliphs were Sunnis. The Fatimids called themselves Caliphs and wanted to replace the caliphs of Baghdad. They conquered Egypt in 969. The first Fatimid ruler of Egypt was al Muizz. He built a new capital at al-Qahirah (Cairo). Here the first university in the world, the al-Azhar University, was established. A great mosque, too, was built.

The earlier capital of El Fustat too was well developed with markets, buildings and underground drainage. The Fatimids ruled Egypt till 1171. At the same time there were local people and other kingdoms in many parts of Africa.

AKSUM

The kingdom of Aksum was still prosperous. In 525 King Kaleb of Aksum expanded his territory and conquered Yemen. Aksum declined in the 7th century.

IFRIQIYA

Ibrahim ibn al Aghlab was appointed the emir or governor of Ifriqiya (Tunisia and east Algeria) in CE 800 by Caliph Haroun al Rashid. The dynasty he founded was known as the Aghlabid. The Aghlabid dynasty (CE 800-909) ruled almost independently.

The Aghlabids had 11 emirs. Ibrahim was the first. He built the city of al-Abbasiyya. Ziyadat Allah (817-838) put down a rebellion of Arabs and conquered Sicily. Abu Ibrahim Ahmad (856-863) built many public structures. The Aghlabid territory was taken over by the Fatimids.

Kairouan (al-Qayrawan) was their first capital. Later al Abbasiya nearby became the new capital. The great mosque at Kairouan, first constructed in the 7th century, was rebuilt at this time. It still exists today. Kairouan was a centre of learning and a place where poets and scholars lived.

Ifriqiya had fertile agricultural lands and a good system of irrigation. Border defences (rabat) were constructed. It was a centre for trade between various Islamic kingdoms, and between Italy and the Byzantine empire. It had a good navy.

RUSTAMID

In part of Algeria, extending into Morocco, Mauritania and Libya, the, Rustamid dynasty ruled from CE 761-909.

The Rustamid dynasty was founded by an Ibadi Muslim of Persian origin. They built a new capital at Tahert in present Algeria. Tahert was a trading centre. Many different religions were practised here.

They fought against the Aghlabids and were conquered by the Fatimids.

IDRISIDS

The Idris dynasty was founded by Idris I who ruled at Walila (CE 789-791) and later set up a small kingdom in Morocco in North Africa. His son Idris II (ruled 803-828) continued to rule in Morocco and established Fez as his capital. It became an important city. After his death the Idris state was divided and gradually declined.

The last Idrisid king was imprisoned by the Umayyad and killed in 985.

ZIRID

The Zirids were another dynasty which ruled Ifriqiya and Granada (Spain) from CE 972-1175.

GHANA—THE KINGDOM OF GOLD

The kingdom of Wagadou or Aoukar was located in north-west Africa, south of the Sahara. It was also called Ghana, which was a title of the king. In the 8th century, Ghana was known as the land of gold, as it controlled gold mines. The gold trade

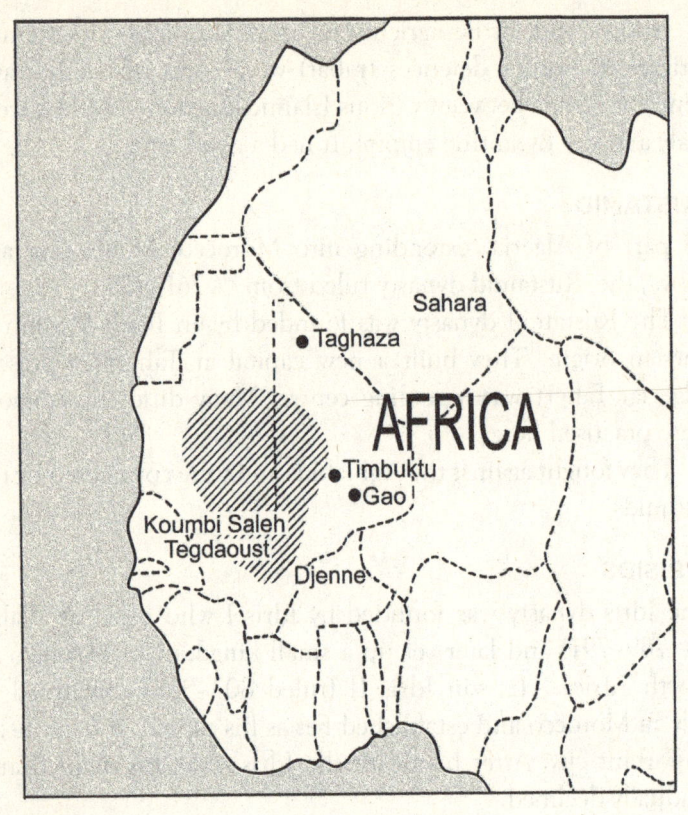

▨ | North Africa, Early Kingdom of Ghana

Early kingdom of Ghana

started in the 5th century. Ghana's capital was at Kumbi Saleh. Ghana was rich through trade and its own gold, and had a strong army and good administration. The geographer al-Bakri reached Kumbi Saleh in the 11th century. There he saw people wearing caps with gold embroidery, and dogs with collars decorated with gold and silver. Horses had gold saddles, and swords and shields had gold edges. Ghana declined after the 11th century.

(It was not connected with the modern state of Ghana.)

> ### *DAUSI*—AN EPIC
>
> The Soninke people ruled Ghana. They composed a number of songs between CE 300 and 1100. Together these form an epic, called *Dausi*. Only parts of this are available today. The epic narrates how Wagadou (Ghana) was destroyed and rebuilt many times. Gassire is one of the characters in the epic. He wanted to kill his father, who was the king. Gassire wished to be famous by becoming the king of Wagadou. He could not do this. He lost seven of his eight sons and had many other troubles. But he attained fame by creating a great battle song, with the lute that he owned.

IGBO

The Igbo are a people of Nigeria. In the 9th and 10th centuries, they made beautiful bronze items and textiles. They grew yam and other crops and traded with different areas.

Bronze and other items of this period have been found at the village of Igbo-Ukwu. Here there were bronze vessels, pendants shaped like human and elephant heads, and other items, placed on a platform. Perhaps it was an early temple.

A grave was also found where an important person was buried. He was placed in a sitting position on a stool, which is how royal people were buried. Along with him there were copper and bronze objects, glass beads, ivory and pottery. Among the Igbo gods is Ala, the earth goddess.

This leaded bronze Igbo vase belongs to the 9th–10th century CE.

NUBIA

In the Sudan region, known as Nubia, both Christianity and Islam existed. As seen earlier, the kingdom of Nobatia declined in the late 6th century CE, and the kingdom of Makuria became prominent. In the 7th century, the two were joined together. At Parachas, modern Faras, a great cathedral was built. Here, between the 8th and 13th centuries murals were painted on the walls, showing bishops, saints, kings and queens.

(Faras was submerged in the Aswan dam, but the murals are preserved in museums.)

SOUTH AFRICA

The Khoisan were the early people of the region. Two main Khoisan groups were the San and Khoekhoe. The San lived as hunter-gatherers over much of the region. The Khoekhoe were pastoralists. The Khoisan people made thousands of rock paintings.

Shamans

A shaman is a person who gains certain powers through rituals. The Khoisan paintings indicate that they had shamans who performed sacred dances to gain this power. It could be a power which was in an animal or bird, like great strength, or the ability to fly.

Bantu people

The Bantu people moved into the region from the north. Some reached southern Africa by around CE 500 or earlier, while others came later. They lived in villages, kept sheep, goats and cattle, and grew sorghum

A Lydenburg head

and other crops. The Bantu people had many different groups, who spoke around 500 different languages.

Lydenburg

Lydenburg, in Mpumalanga province, is a place in east Transvaal. Here some hollow earthenware heads have been found dating to CE 500–700. The clay heads have oval eyes and long necks. Some smaller heads have animal faces with snouts. The heads may have been worn or used in some religious ceremonies. These are the earliest known art of the region. There are traces of white pigment and specularite (a mineral) on the heads.

Phalaborwa

Phalaborwa is a place in eastern Transvaal, in Mopani district, near Kruger National Park. The area was occupied by the Sotho people from around CE 400. The Sotho were a group of the Bantu people. Here the people mined copper and iron, and lived in villages. Ba-Phalaborwa, means 'better than the south', a name given to the place by the Sotho, who moved up from the south.

OTHER KINGDOMS AND PEOPLE

There were many other different kingdoms, peoples and languages, with their own culture, traditions, stories and art. There were also different types of religions in Africa. Both Christianity and Islam were practised, apart from local religions.

30
Europe
CE 1000–1500

In Europe a new type of economic system began to develop, which has been called feudalism.

FEUDALISM

Feudalism was a system of land ownership. It also provided a system of defence. Feudalism existed in western Europe from about CE 800. As there were frequent wars, the king found it difficult to defend and protect his territory. He also found it difficult to collect taxes and to get the money for administration. The king therefore gave large areas of land to high officials and nobles. These lords or officials looked after the land and paid the king rent or taxes. These lords also maintained an army and sent their soldiers to help the king when he needed to fight a war. The landlord ruled like a minor king on the land given to him. The land area given to a lord was called a manor in England, and by different terms in other countries.

The manor included a manor house or castle. Around it there were fields, forest land and one or more villages.

Other people too lived on his land. These included knights, vassals, peasants and serfs.

A 14th-century manor house in Kent, England

A knight was a warrior who fought on horseback.

A vassal was someone to whom the lord sublet part of the land. A vassal could rent part of his land to someone else. Some of the vassals were knights.

A peasant was a farmer who cultivated the land.

A serf had to provide free labour to the lord, in return for some land or a house.

There were also various craftsmen, such as metalworkers or carpenters.

Knights

Knight was a term for the warriors in the army of a lord. Knights were usually the sons of nobles or lords.

Knights began their training at a young age. The young knight-to-be was called a page. He was sent to the castle of another lord, who could be a friend or relative of his father. After learning good manners, basic reading and writing, riding a horse, using a sword, and a few other skills, he was apprenticed or attached to a knight. This took place around the age of 13. In this phase he was known as a squire. He was taught to fight, take care of horses, use weapons, and if necessary go into battle.

Between the ages of 18 and 21, he was made a knight. A knight had to protect his lord's land. He was also supposed to behave in an honest and correct way, and to protect women, and those who were weak. Knights trained for war in tournaments where they fought against one another.

A knight wore heavy armour to protect himself during battle. At first they wore padded clothes and chainmail. Chainmail consisted of vests or tunics made of iron links. In the 14th and 15th centuries, they also wore plate armour. Plate armour consisted of iron plates linked together. A full suit of armour was made for each knight. It had to fit him well, or he would not be able to move and fight. A suit could weigh up to 29 kilos or more.

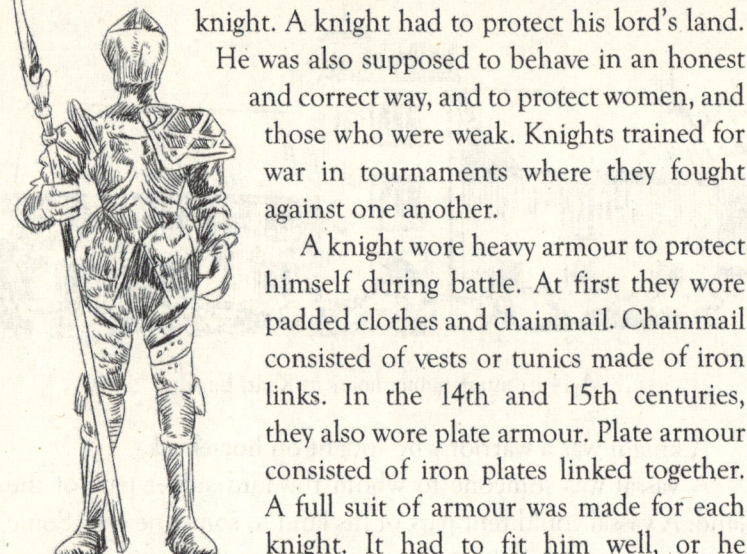

A knight in armour

Knights also wore helmets, and viziers which covered their faces. Thus when dressed for battle, no part of a knight's body could be seen. Each knight or group of knights had a special symbol. These were painted on their armour and shields. Later these were painted on a surcoat, a sleeveless coat worn over the armour. The symbols came to be called 'coat of arms'. Knights could be recognized only through these.

Weapons

Weapons used mainly consisted of swords, daggers, crossbows, battle axe, bows and arrows, and lances. The longbow was developed in Wales and used by the English.

Knight orders

There were military knights who were not vassals of a lord, but were organized into a group or order. Grants of land were made to the whole group. Among such knight orders were the Teutonic Knights, Knights Templar and Knights Hospitaller, and the Order of St Lazarus. There were also chivalric orders, including the Order of St George, the Order of the Dragon and many others.

Castles

A castle is a term for a fortified structure where the lord or king could live in times of war, or even in peaceful times. A castle was built so that it could be well defended if attacked. It could be used to store treasure and weapons, or sometimes as a prison. It was also a centre of administration.

Castles were first built in western Europe in the 10th century, but many more were built from the 11th century onwards. At first they consisted of wooden buildings. These early structures were known as motte and bailey castles.

Motte is the term for the earth mound on which a wooden tower was built. The bailey was a courtyard below the motte. It had a circular ditch around it and a palisade or wooden fence which protected the castle.

Later there were different types of castles. Some were built of stone, with

A stone castle of the 13th century from Antwerp, Belgium. Known as Het Steen, it is on the banks of the Scheldt river.

towers and moats. A moat consisted of water in a deep and wide ditch surrounding the castle. Usually there was no regular bridge across the moat. A drawbridge was used which could be drawn up into the castle with ropes, and let down when necessary. Some castles had concentric walls. Many were built on hills. From the castle, arrows could be shot at invaders, and boiling oil or something else poured on them.

TOWNS

By the 11th century, there were towns and cities across Europe. The number increased by the year 1300. In these towns life was different from that in the lands of the castle or manor. In the towns there were professionals, lawyers, craftsmen, merchants and traders. In Europe there were some towns which had their own governments. Towns or cities were usually surrounded by walls, with guards at the entrance gates. London, York, Paris, Prague, Venice, Florence, Antwerp and Flanders were among the early cities.

These towns and cities emerged because methods of farming had improved. Heavy ploughs were used and new, additional areas of land were cultivated. As food production increased, more people were free to take up other activities. Trade too expanded and there was a huge rise in population.

In the cities all kinds of items were available in the markets. There was entertainment of various kinds. At the same time many cities were overcrowded. Sanitation and garbage disposal were not well planned. While public buildings were often made of stone, up to about 1400, most houses were of wood, and could catch fire. Epidemics took place at times.

In CE 1000 the population of Europe was around 38 million. By CE 1300 it was around 74 million.

Some of the large European cities had populations of 1,00,000 people. But there were bigger cities in other parts of the world, including in India, China and regions under the Arabs.

Money

Coins in gold and silver already existed, but very often goods were exchanged, and not paid for in money. For instance, trade fairs were held in northern France, where furs, woollen cloth, hemp, honey and tin came from north Europe, and were exchanged for textiles, spices and sugar, that were brought here from Italy. And some of these items had reached Italy from distant lands. As trade increased, money began to be used more and more. Profits were made and banks were set up.

Guilds

Merchants and craftsmen in the cities were often organized into guilds. Merchant guilds controlled prices, weights and measures. Each guild had a patron saint and celebrated festivals together. Craft guilds existed for each craft. Craftsmen were of three types. Master craftsmen were the best. Apprentices were the beginners. Journeymen were a higher stage than apprentices. Parents paid money to place their boys with a master craftsman, who then trained them. The apprentices stayed with the craftsmen, who looked after them.

Hanseatic League

The cities and towns were usually along trade routes. With wars and crusades taking place, towns and routes were often not well protected. Towns in many different countries of Europe thus joined together to protect trade, and formed the Hanseatic League. The League was officially formed in 1356, but towns had begun to help one another and form associations even before that. Lubeck in north Germany was the most important trading town. Trade to Scandinavia and Russia passed through here. The League had between 70 and 170 towns at different times.

PEASANTS

Peasants lived in simple houses made of wood, straw and clay, with thatched roofs. Their houses had one or two rooms. The peasants worked all through the year for the lord of the manor. They also planted some crops and vegetables for themselves. Grain, oats, barley, peas and beans were the main crops. Planting and harvesting were the busiest times of the year. Animals like sheep, goats and cattle were kept. Both men and women worked in the fields. In addition, women took care of the household and the children. They also cooked the food.

FOOD

Life was very different for the rich and the poor, even as it is today. The kings, nobles and lords, ate good food and wore fashionable clothes. Of course each country or region cooked and ate different types of food, and wore different clothes, but some general features of life in Europe are given here. The rich ate on plates of gold and silver, the poor on plates made of stone or horn, or pottery. Nobles and lords hunted in the lands they owned and ate the animals they killed, such as boar or deer, as well as wild fowl. The poor were not allowed to hunt. They could be killed if they were caught doing so. After the Crusades (see Chapter 31) the rich of Europe obtained spices from eastern countries. They began to eat rich, spicy and sweet food. The poorer people generally ate bread and vegetable stew or bread and cheese, and occasionally meat. Their bread was made from rye, millet, barley and oats, and sometimes wheat, while the wealthy ate wheat bread. Nuts, fruit and eggs were sometimes eaten. Ale was the main drink, made from grains. Rich people drank wine.

CHRISTIANITY

Christianity and the Church formed an important part of life in Europe.

> Church refers both to a place of worship and to the whole structure and organization of Christianity. It can also refer to a particular denomination or sect of Christianity.

The pope was the head of the Christian Church, that is, the Christian organization in Europe. The Christian Church became part of the whole feudal system. They had some lands of their own known as the Papal States. These were located in Italy. Archbishops, bishops, abbots and other officials were representatives of the Church.

But they were appointed by kings or nobles, and became their vassals. This was known as 'lay investiture'. They had to perform various duties for their lord, including helping him in war. Thus Church officials became administrators and were not very spiritual. In CE 1075 Pope Gregory VII insisted that only the pope should appoint Church officials. King Henry IV of Germany opposed this, and a period of conflict followed between the emperors and popes. An agreement was reached in 1122. A bishop in Germany would be elected by the Church. He would pay homage to the king, who would grant him his worldly power. A representative of the pope would invest him with spiritual power. That is, he would be given the symbols of his spiritual office, a ring and a staff, by a Church official.

Other popes also tried to assert their power over the kings of Europe, while kings made equal attempts to have more power than the pope.

Avignon

In the 13th century there was a conflict between Pope Boniface VIII and Philip IV, king of France. Philip wanted to tax the church officials, while Boniface said this could not be done without his consent. Philip won this conflict, and in 1305 a French pope was elected. Instead of Rome, the pope lived at Avignon in France. This continued up to 1377. At Avignon the popes lived in great luxury and splendour. From 1378-1417, the conflict continued, with two popes being elected, one living at Avignon and the other at Rome. This is called the Great Schism of the Church. Finally in 1417, a Church council met in Switzerland, and a new pope was elected, who was accepted by both sides. The power of the Church and of the pope had by then declined.

Monasteries

Many men and women who wanted to devote their lives to god, joined monasteries, and were known as monks and nuns. Some monks prayed and did all the daily work of the monastery. Others were scholars and teachers. They copied manuscripts, made beautiful illustrations, and wrote down legends and history. Music was composed so that songs of praise could be sung, and new musical styles developed. Monks and nuns also helped the sick and some specialized in learning about herbs and medicines. Monasteries usually owned a lot of land, and were quite rich.

Between the 11th and 13th centuries, there were some new orders of monks and nuns. Among them were the Cistercians, Dominicans and Franciscans. The Cistercians were founded in 1098. The Dominicans and Franciscans were founded in the 13th century. All these orders or groups lived a simple life and tried to spread true Christian teachings among the common people. The Dominicans were founded by Dominic de Guzman, a Spanish priest. The Dominicans were especially against heretical beliefs, those beliefs they considered wrong. The Franciscans, founded by St Francis, were the most popular. Francis was born in Assisi in Italy in a rich family. After some spiritual experiences when he was a young man, he began to live in poverty. He preached the message of Jesus, not just to people but to birds and animals, who, it is said, listened to him. Many women too joined these and other orders.

St Francis and the wolf

There was once a wolf visiting the city of Gubbio where St Francis lived. The wolf used to attack the people, who wanted to kill it. St Francis understood that the wolf was hungry. He asked the people to feed it every day. He spoke to the wolf too, who promised

A painting depicting St Francis and the wolf

not to attack anyone if it was fed. The wolf visited the village for two years. It was fed everyday and became friendly. Then it died of natural causes, and all the people of Gubbio were sad.

(This is one of the many stories about St Francis.)

Cathedrals and churches

In the towns and cities, cathedrals and churches were built. Some of them had paintings and sculptures and grand architectural styles. People came here to worship and pray to God. Anyone could pray on their own, but at certain times, there were formal types of prayers led by a priest. People prayed and sang hymns together.

Icons and saints

Christians at this time worshipped both icons and saints. Icons were paintings or images of Jesus, Mary or various Christian saints. Saints were those who were considered to have some miraculous powers. The title of saint was given by the Christian Church, usually after the death of a person. The miraculous power of a saint came through their goodness or their close association with God. A saint could be prayed to by an ordinary person, and as the saint was believed to have contact with God, it was through them that the prayers would get results.

Churches and shrines were built on or around the tombs of saints. Relics, any item associated with the saint, such as a book, or the remains of the body of the saint, could also be worshipped. It was believed that their bones left behind, would once again come to life and form a glorious body. They were not just dead or useless things.

Saints could be both men and women. The practice of worshipping saints began around the 2nd century CE, or even earlier.

Feast days

Special days called feast days were holidays for all. Such days made Christianity a part of daily life. Feast days included Christmas, Easter and days dedicated to various saints.

The Western and Eastern Church

What were the main principles of Christianity? As we saw earlier, from the beginning there were arguments about the nature of God and of Jesus, and about various practices such as baptism. Christian Councils were held where high Church officials met and decided on these issues. But often the different groups could not come to an agreement. Some groups began to break away from the central (Western) Church organization headed by the pope. The Syrian and Western Christians split after the First Council of Ephesius in CE 431. A Church of the East was formed with its centre at Ctesiphon. Coptic (Egyptian) Christianity separated from the Western Church after the Council of Chalcedon, CE 451. In Europe a schism (spilt) between the Western and Eastern Churches took place in 1054. The Eastern was known as the Eastern Orthodox Church and was prominent in the Byzantine empire and in Russia.

The Inquisition

For the Catholic Christians, anyone who went against the views of the Councils was called a heretic. At first such people were excommunicated, that is they were not considered Christians and not allowed to worship in churches. But in 1231, at the time of Pope Gregory IX, a person known as an Inquisitor was appointed. His job was to question people about their beliefs and make sure they had the right ones. Sometimes, he would 'persuade' them to have right beliefs, through torture. And if they still did not listen, they would be killed. The usual method was to tie them to a stake and burn them to death.

31

Europe: Kingdoms, Wars and Conflicts
CE 1000–1500

Between CE 1000 and 1500 there were a number of different kingdoms in Europe. There were wars and conflicts and frequent changes in territory. In this chapter we will look at some of the main kingdoms and empires. The two main empires were those of the Holy Roman Empire in central Europe and the eastern Roman or Byzantine Empire.

The Holy Roman Empire had within it a number of independent or semi-independent countries. In eastern Europe, extending into Asia, was the Eastern Roman or Byzantine Empire. There were also independent kingdoms which were not part of either empire.

THE HOLY ROMAN EMPIRE

We saw earlier that Otto I of East Francia (Germany) was given the title of Roman Emperor by the pope. In 1002 Henry II of Bavaria became the Western Roman Emperor. From CE 1024–1125 the

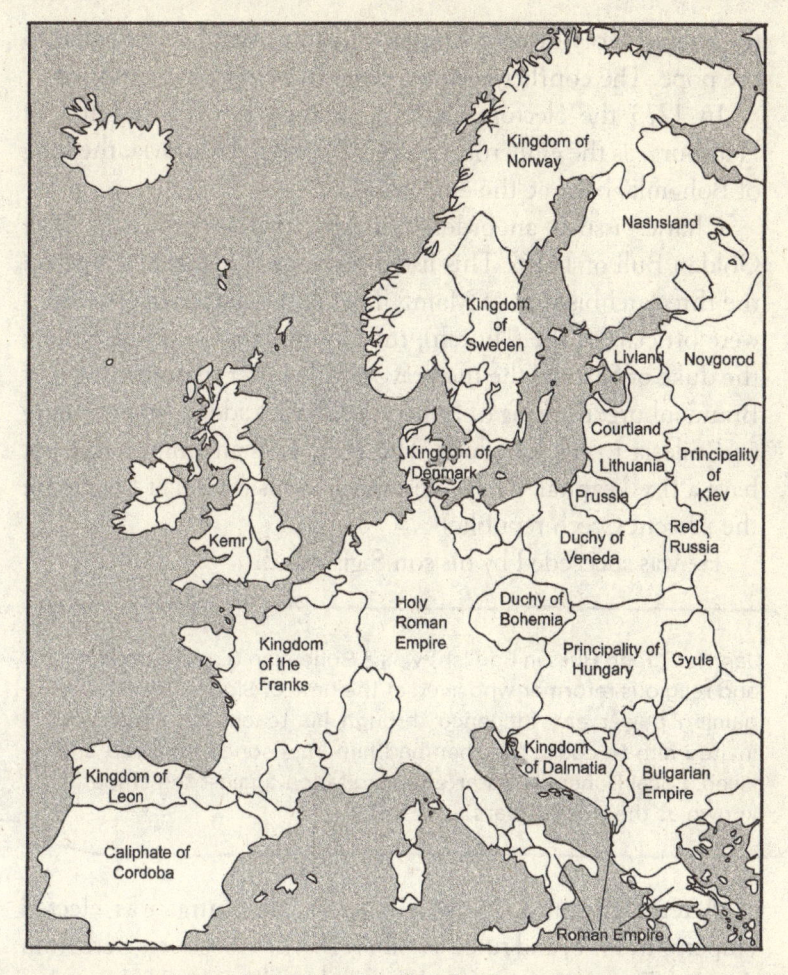

Map of main European kingdoms c. CE 1000

emperors were from the Salians of Franconia who were related to the Saxons.

From 1137–1254 the Hohenstaufens of Swabia were the emperors and the empire reached its peak. Frederick I, called Barbarossa (Red Beard), ruled from 1152–1190 and gave himself the title of Holy Roman Emperor to show that he was equal to the pope. The conflict between pope and emperor continued.

In 1273 the electors chose a Swabian prince, Rudolf I of Habsburg, as the emperor. In 1347, Charles of Moravia, the king of Bohemia, became the emperor.

Charles issued an order or decree that is known as 'The Golden Bull of 1356'. This listed seven electors of the emperor: the three archbishops of Mainz, Trier and Cologne (archbishops were officials of the Church); the Count Palatine of the Rhine; the duke of Saxony; the margrave (a title lower than the duke) of Brandenburg; the king of Bohemia. Charles added Brandenburg and Silesia to his kingdom. The Holy Roman Empire did not have a fixed capital. Charles established his capital at Prague (in the present Czech republic).

He was succeeded by his son Sigismund.

Jan Hus (John Huss in English) was a Bohemian (Czech) preacher and religious reformer who lived at the time of Sigismund. He was gaining power and influence through his teachings. Sigismund invited him to court, but then had him imprisoned, tortured and killed. Local Bohemians started an agitation against the emperor, known as the Hussite wars.

After Sigismund, his son-in-law, a Habsburg, was elected emperor in 1438, and ruled as Albert II. The Habsburgs were from Austria. The emperors after this were hereditary and belonged to the Habsburg line. The Holy Roman Empire lasted till 1806, though during this long period there were many changes in its territory and the extent of its power.

Bohemia

Bohemia was part of the Holy Roman Empire but had its own kings. It was ruled by the Premyslid dynasty (9th-century 1306).

FRANKFURT

Frankfurt, a city and port in Germany, was important even in medieval days. Some of the structures of those times can still be seen, including houses in the Gothic style. The Romerberg is a square around which houses were built. The Leinward-Haus, linen-drapers' hall, belongs to the 14th century.

The Cathedral of St Bartholomew was built in the 13th century. Here the electors met to choose the Holy Roman emperors. Frankfurt became a free imperial city in 1372.

At this time, towns expanded and there was a period of peace. In the 13th century silver was found at the town of Kutna Hora. Both Prague and Kutna Hora became prosperous towns. Silver, glass and paper, were the main industries of Bohemia.

However, there were conflicts over succession. In the 14th century the Premyslid line ended. From 1310-1437 it was ruled by kings of the House of Luxemburg. As we saw earlier, Charles, king of Bohemia from 1347, became the Holy Roman Emperor. He made Prague his capital. At this time Bohemia included Moravia, Silesia, and Lusatia. It was another period of prosperity and peace. The first university of eastern Europe was opened in Prague in 1348.

THE BYZANTINE EMPIRE: CE 1000-1500

The Byzantine empire was expanded and strengthened by Basil II. At the time of his death in 1025, the empire covered an area from south Italy to Armenia in the east. Under the emperor Leo VI, Byzantine law was written down in 60 volumes in Greek. In 1081 the Byzantines suffered a defeat by the Seljuk Turks at the battle of Manzikert. The Seljuks took over Anatolia, and the empire soon became involved in the crusades. Some territories were regained during the early crusades. Up to the late 12th century the empire was prosperous. There were new urban centres, and Constantinople became a great centre of trade. New books were written, and mosaics, icons and frescoes were created. Byzantine art and literature influenced Western Europe.

By the end of the 12th century the empire had begun to decline. Several Byzantine territories were already lost to the rising powers of Hungary, Serbia and Sicily. During the Fourth Crusade, Constantinople was occupied by the Latin or Western crusaders in 1203 and 1204. Many people were massacred and buildings destroyed. Icons and precious items were taken away. A new Latin kingdom was founded around Constantinople. There were three small Byzantine kingdoms—Nicaea, Epirus and Trebizond. In 1261 Nicaea reconquered Constantinople. In 1453 the capital Constantinople was besieged by the Ottoman Turks. After an eight-week siege the city collapsed, and the last Byzantine emperor Constantine XI died fighting.

SOME OTHER KINGDOMS IN EUROPE
France
France or West Francia was under the Capetians. Philip IV was the last direct descendant of Hugh Capet. In 1328 his brother's son came to the throne as Philip VI. Charles, the brother of Philip IV, was the duke of Valois, so Philip VI and his successors are called the Valois dynasty. The Valois ruled till 1589 when they were succeeded by the Bourbons.

Switzerland
Switzerland was under the Romans, followed by the Carolingians, Germans and the Holy Roman Empire. In Switzerland there were several small city states or cantons. In 1291 the Swiss Confederation was founded with three cantons. More states

gradually joined and by 1499 the Swiss Federation was virtually independent.

Eastern Europe

Around CE 1000 Greece and Asia Minor were still ruled by the Byzantine empire. Poland, Bulgaria and Hungary, were some of the separate kingdoms. Lithuanian chieftains and princes of Haliscz were among the other rulers.

Bulgaria

Bulgaria was conquered by the Byzantines, but again gained independence from the Byzantine empire around 1185. It was independent for about 145 years and then was conquered by the Serbs, followed by the Turks.

Poland

Boleslaw I (992-1025), the son of Mieszko, who founded the Piast dynasty, extended the Polish kingdom to Moravia and Ruthenia. Under the next few kings, territories were lost to the Germans of Brandenburg and the Bohemians. There were also internal conflicts. At the same time there was economic growth, new towns and trade. Salt and silver were discovered underground, and mines were set up to use these. The towns had some amount of autonomy. Among the towns were Krakow, Poznan, Wroclaw and Gdansk.

Casimir III (1333-1370) was the last king of the Piast dynasty. He was a strong king and expanded the kingdom. As Casimir had no children, his nephew, Louis I of Hungary, became the king after him. Thus a large empire was created.

The first queen of Poland

After Louis' death his daughter Jadwiga became the first queen. Prince Jagiello of Lithuania married Queen Jadwiga, creating a union of Poland and Lithuania. He took the name Wladyslaw II and began the Jagiellon dynasty which ruled between 1386 and 1572.

Casimir IV (ruled 1447-1492) fought a war against the Teutonic knights, gaining west Prussia, Pomerania and other territories.

Krakow

Krakow is one of the oldest cities of Poland. From the 12th to the 17th centuries it was the capital of Poland. In 1430 it became part of the Hanseatic League. The medieval city was surrounded by high walls. Some of the early structures can still be seen.

A Gothic cathedral here dates back to the 11th century. St Stanislaus is said to have been martyred at the altar here in the time of Boreslav II. The cathedral was consecrated and dedicated to him in 1359.

Polish kings were crowned here and many famous people of Poland are buried here.

> St Stanislaus is the patron saint of Poland.

The Church of St Mary, another Gothic structure, dates to 1223. The altar was made by the 14th-century German sculptor, Viet Stoss.

The construction of the Royal Wawel Castle was begun in the 13th century. The salt mines of Wieliczka nearby date back to the same period. Here there are salt sculptures and even chandeliers made from salt.

A university was opened at Krakow in 1364.

Serbia

Serbia was under the Byzantine empire, but an independent kingdom known as Rascia was founded in 1168. In the reign of Stephen Dushan (1331-1355) it controlled a large area extending into Albania and Greece. Ottoman invasions in the 14th century led to its decline. In 1459 it came under the Turkish Ottoman empire.

Prussia

The earlier settlers of Prussia had been pushed out by the Teutonic knights, and a new state of Prussia was created by German settlers.

Slovenians and Croats

The Slovenians and Croats were independent for a short time in the 11th century, but following this were ruled by various other groups for the next 900 years. However they retained their own language and culture.

> ### VENICE
>
> Venice was a city state that grew powerful through trade. It established centres of trade in the eastern Mediterranean. It was when Venice became involved in the crusades that Constantinople was attacked. After defeating Constantinople in 1453 the Ottoman Turks turned towards Venice. A war was fought between 1463 and 1479. Overall the Ottomans were the winners, as they extracted an annual tribute from Venice.

THE CRUSADES

Crusade comes from the word 'cross'. The crusades were an attempt to recover the holy Christian lands that had been captured by Muslims. There were other reasons too for the crusades.

Knights fought in the crusades to gain fame and power. The Byzantine emperor wanted to regain lost territory. It was he who requested the pope to start the crusades. The kings of

Europe also thought they could increase their territory through these wars.

The plan

In November 1095 Pope Urban II (1042-99) put forward a plan for the crusades. He said that knights and others had to form their own groups, choose their own leaders, and go to Constantinople, the capital of the Byzantine empire. There the Byzantine army would join them, and together they would attack the Seljuk Turks, who had earlier defeated the Byzantine armies.

The eight main crusades

In 1096 five armies of noblemen started for Constantinople. In addition was an army of ordinary people led by Peter the Hermit, as well as some other armies of ordinary people. Peter was a Christian preacher originally from France.

This First Crusade (1096-99) had some success; Nicaea, Antioch and Jerusalem were captured. Jerusalem was then under Egypt, and after its capture, most of the population was killed. The Council of Nablus was set up in 1120 to lay down the first written laws for the Kingdom of Jerusalem, one of the Christian kingdoms established in 1099 by the First Crusade. The others were Tripoli on the coast of Syria, Antioch, and Edessa in present Turkey.

Soon the Turks recaptured Edessa. The Second Crusade (1147-49) started but the crusaders could not achieve anything. Between the Second and Third Crusades, the Seljuks regained Anatolia, and Salah-ad-din of Egypt took Jerusalem.

Unlike the crusaders, Salah-ad-din treated the residents of Jerusalem with kindness.

The Third Crusade (1189-92) set off with a huge force. The Holy Roman emperor, Frederick I, the French king, Philip II and the English king, Richard I joined this crusade, but still not much was achieved. In fact Frederick died on the way.

A crusader castle; the Krak de Chevaliersin Syria was one of the castles built by the crusaders.

The Fourth Crusade (1202-1204) was a total disaster, as the crusaders forgot their aims and instead attacked Constantinople. This led to further enmity between Greek and Latin Christianity, and between the Holy Roman Empire and the Byzantine.

The Fifth Crusade (1218-1221), too, was unsuccessful.

The Sixth Crusade (1228-9) led to a temporary return of Christians to Jerusalem. The Turks captured Jerusalem in 1244.

Two more crusades, the Seventh (1248-54) and the Eighth begun in 1270, were equally inconclusive.

In fact the crusades did not have much effect on religion, but there were other results. Numerous forts, castles and churches were built. Trade developed and new products were brought to Europe. There were many cities and market centres.

Children's crusades

Even though the crusades did not have the desired effect, many were inspired by them. Two groups of children are said to have organized their own crusades. According to one account, in 1212 Stephen, a boy shepherd from Cloyes, in France, headed a group of young crusaders, but King Philip II persuaded them to return. Another unit was led by a boy named Nicholas, from Cologne, in Germany. Some of these reached Jerusalem, a few arrived in Rome, some returned home, but many were lost or killed. Some historians feel these crusades did not take place, or if they did were not organized by children. However, in those days boys of 12 or 13 were not like the children of today. In Asia boys ruled kingdoms often before they reached the age of 12, and it is quite likely that in Europe children went on a crusade.

BLACK DEATH

The Black Death was a term for bubonic plague, a disease carried by fleas on rats. It began in Asia, and reached Europe through trading ships. The plague affected Constantinople by 1347. From here it spread to Sicily, France, Belgium, Luxemburg, the Netherlands, Germany, England, and then to northern and eastern Europe and to Russia. Around 38 million people, half the population of Europe, died between 1347 and 1351. Streets were piled with dead bodies. Attempts were made to bury them in group graves. Poor sanitation and crowding in the cities added to the problems. People did not understand the deadly disease; they did not know what caused it. Some said it was a punishment from God, others that it was the work of the devil. Beggars and the poor were blamed, but some blamed the Jews. Jews were burnt to death and massacred, mainly in the cities of Germany. Many Jews left Germany for Poland, where they were given shelter. There were other plague epidemics, including one in 1361, and later. Despite the death and disaster, there were some benefits for those who survived. As there were fewer people available for work, workers were paid more. Less food was required, hence prices fell. Serfdom began to decline, as peasants were in a position to make demands on the landowners. Many started paying rent instead of providing free labour on the landlord's estate.

HUNDRED YEARS' WAR

A war took place between England and France that has been called the Hundred Years' War. Actually there were a series of battles that took place between 1337 and 1453 with intermittent periods of peace.

The wars were for two reasons: England controlled some territories in France though these were legally under the French king. Gradually France regained most of the territories except for Gascony. Meanwhile Philip IV of France died without an heir. Edward III, king of England, was the son of Edward II of England, and Isabella, the daughter of Philip IV of France.

He thought that he could become king of France since Philip IV had no sons. This did not happen. Philip IV's nephew, Philip VI, became the king.

1337-1360: The Edwardian wars

In 1337 wars started between England and France, as Edward III wanted to become the king of France. These lasted till 1360. England gained victories and territory in France, but Edward III gave up his claim to become king of France.

In 1346 Edward III won a great victory at Crecy in France.

Here his sixteen-year-old son Edward fought a great battle. He was called the Black Prince as he always wore black armour.

In 1356 the Black Prince won another victory against France at Poitiers. He even captured the French king, who at that time was John II.

During the war the soldiers wore armour. If an arrow hit them, the armour provided protection. The armour included a vest or tunic with sleeves made of iron links. It was quite heavy and weighed several kilos.

The longbow

A new type of bow, called a longbow, could pierce this armour from a distance of 180 m. This bow was invented in Wales and used by the English. It led to their victory at Crecy.

The Caroline wars

There were some years of peace, and then the next series of wars started between 1369 and 1389. These are called the Caroline wars. Charles V was the king of France and France won this phase of the war.

The Lancastrian war

There were many years of peace before the third phase of fighting started in 1415. Henry V of England (ruled 1413–22) once again claimed the throne of France. He and his army reached France and won a victory at Agincourt.

In 1420 France acknowledged Henry as the heir to the throne. He married Katherine, who was the daughter of the French king Charles VI.

Henry was to become the next king of France, but he died in 1422. Then fighting started again.

In 1429 the English surrounded Orleans in France. The French defended well but the siege continued for seven months.

Jeanne d'Arc—an extraordinary girl

It was an extraordinary 17-year-old girl who defeated the English. Jeanne d'Arc, daughter of a farmer, was born in Domremy in France in 1412. From the age of thirteen she began hearing voices, which she believed were those of saints from heaven. In 1429 she had a vision or dream in which the saints told her to lead a French army against the English.

Jeanne d'Arc [Joan of Arc]; from a painting, c. CE 1485

Who would listen to a young girl? Charles, son and heir of the king of France, agreed to meet her. He allowed her to lead a force. Dressed in armour and men's clothes, Jeanne went to Orleans leading her army. There she found that there was one place where she could break through the English forces. She and her soldiers entered Orleans, fought against the English, and won.

The brave Jeanne then defeated the English at Patay. She won other battles too. Because of her, Charles was crowned king of France at the cathedral in Rheims. He was now Charles VII. Jeanne attended the coronation and was given a privileged place to sit.

Jeanne wanted to continue fighting against the English, but Charles wanted to make peace. Jeanne took her soldiers and went towards Paris. But here she was captured by soldiers of Burgundy. Burgundy had allied with the English. They handed her to the English forces.

At Rouen she was tried by an ecclesiastical (religious) court for heresy and sorcery. The judges said she should not have worn men's clothes. They also said she should have listened to the Catholic Church, and not claimed to know the word of God. She was sentenced to life imprisonment. In prison Jeanne still wore men's clothes. She was again tried by a secular court. It sentenced her to death. She was tied to a stake and burnt on 30 May 1431 at Rouen. Rouen in France was under the English from 1419-1449. The Tour de Jeanne d'Arc, the tower where she was imprisoned, can still be seen in Rouen.

Perhaps Charles VII could have saved her, but he did not even try. Jeanne died but the ordinary French people and soldiers were inspired by her. They fought fiercely and battles continued till 1435. There were some negotiations for peace, but once again fighting began. The wars ended with the Battle of Castillon in 1453. France had regained all the territories lost to England except for the Port of Calais.

Jeanne d'Arc, known as Joan of Arc in English, was declared a saint in 1920.

In France, no one has ever forgotten Jeanne. At Orleans a special festival, the Fetes Johanniques, is held every year to celebrate her. It lasts from 29 April to 8 May. It begins with a procession led by a horse, on which a woman sits, dressed as Jeanne d'Arc, and ends with a religious ceremony.

Plays, books and poems have been written on Jeanne. She has been depicted in paintings, and music has been composed for her.

SPAIN AND PORTUGAL
Spain
Al-Andalus

Al-Andalus was a medieval state that included parts of Spain, Portugal and France. Between CE 711 and 1492 it was under the Arabs and other Muslim groups. This long period of time can broadly be divided into three phases:

1. The early period under the Umayyad Caliphs, 711–756
2. The emirate of Cordoba, 756–929, and the Caliphate of Cordoba, 929–1031
3. The period of numerous small kingdoms, 1031–1492.

When the Umayyad were overthrown by the Abbasids in 750, a branch of the earlier Umayyad ruled independently from Qurtuba (Cordoba). Cordoba, in Spain, was a great centre of learning and culture and, during the 10th century, it was the largest city in Europe.

At this time Al-Andalus had great philosophers, scientists and scholars. The state was tolerant towards other religions. Both Muslim and Jewish scholars flourished here. A great university and library was set up at Cordoba. There were astronomers, physicians, architects and musicians. New crops were brought here from Asia, and new technology was introduced. These spread from Al-Andalus to the rest of Europe.

During the period of the small kingdoms, 1031-1492, there was some prosperity but also confusion. These small kingdoms were known as taifas, and were invaded by Christian states of the north, as well as by the dynasties of north Africa. The Zirids, Almoravids and Almohads were among the north African dynasties that temporarily ruled here. Meanwhile the Christian states began to conquer various areas. This is known as the *reconquista* (reconquest). Among the various states, Cordoba was conquered in 1236, and the rich state of Seville in 1248. According to some accounts, Granada became a vassal of Christian Castille in 1238, but the Nasrid dynasty continued to rule there till 1492. The great palace complex of the Alhambra at Granada was constructed by the Nasrids. In 1469 Isabella of Castille married Ferdinand of Aragon. Both were Catholics. This marked the last stage of reconquest, and the beginning of the unification of Spain. However Christian Spain lacked tolerance. There were forced conversions to Christianity, and a state-controlled Inquisition, authorized by the pope in 1478.

Portugal—the explorers

Portugal's history was closely related to that of Spain. It became independent under King Alfonso in 1143, but still faced political uncertainties and problems. John I came to the throne in 1385. He defeated Castille and allied with England. His greatest achievements, however, came through his son, Henry the Navigator. In 1416 Henry set up a school of navigation at Segres in Portugal. With well-trained sailors, good maps and navigational aids, the Portuguese began to explore the African coast. Among the notable expeditions were that of Lopo Gonsalves, who crossed the equator in 1472; Bartholomew Diaz who reached the Cape of Good Hope in 1487-88; Vasco da Gama who crossed the Cape of Good Hope and reached India in 1497-98 and Pedro Alvares Cabral, who reached Brazil and then India in 1500.

Christopher Columbus (1451-1506)

The voyages of Christopher Columbus, perhaps the most famous explorer, were sponsored by Spain. He first explored the Caribbean and in later voyages reached Central America and Venezuela.

THE TURNING POINT

By the end of the 15th century, Europe had seen growth and decline, as well as devastation by wars and disease. But things were changing. Stronger states were emerging under kings. Trade began to grow once again. Spain was free of Arab rule. Explorers like Vasco da Gama and Christopher Columbus were setting off across the world. Spain and Portugal brought in a new era of exploration and conquest of distant lands. Soon they were joined by the English, French and other Europeans.

A period was beginning when Europeans would dominate the world, and transform the Americas, Africa and Asia.

32

Europe: Art and Culture
CE 1000–1500

In Europe there were new trends in art, architecture, literature, philosophy and culture. These new developments began from around 1000, but a further change started from the 14th century.

Renaissance means 'rebirth'. It refers to a time in Europe when people studied the art and culture of ancient Greece and Rome, and tried to revive or recreate some aspects of them. The period of the Renaissance is considered to have lasted from the 14th to the 17th centuries. However, transformation had begun even earlier, reflecting the many changes that had taken place in Europe. The crusades, though destructive, had revealed new worlds and ways of life to the Europeans. Trade had brought new products to Europe, and there were new ideas and ways of thinking. There were independent and prosperous cities. The Renaissance began in Italy, in the great cities of Venice, Florence, Urbino, Mantua and Milan. Here rich families commissioned artists who created new forms of art. Florence is considered the main city where the Renaissance began. Cities like Florence and Venice were oligarchies, but had democratic features. They were outside the feudal hierarchy, and generally maintained a spirit of freedom.

UNIVERSITIES

Universities began to be founded in Europe. Universities were the new centres of learning. A great university had been set up by the Arabs at Cordoba in Spain. There were early universities in Morocco and Cairo.

In Europe one of the earliest universities was at Lucerne, Switzerland, founded in 1030.

Some other early universities were:

Oxford: no clear date, teaching began 1096 onwards
Bologna University in Italy: founded 1119
University at Paris: founded 1150
University at Coimbra, Portugal: founded in 1290
University at Prague: founded in 1348

Balliol College, founded in 1263, is one of Oxford University's oldest and most well-known colleges.

University at Krakow: founded in 1364

The Ruprecht-Karls-Universitat at Heidelberg: founded in 1386

University at Basel, Switzerland: founded in 1460

There were many others. With the growth in universities, new ideas and ways of thinking spread.

Scholasticism

Scholasticism was a new branch of learning. It combined Christian ideas with Greek philosophical concepts. It was really a question of seeing whether the faith and belief of Christianity could be reconciled with the logic and reason of Greek philosophy. St Anselm (1033-1109), was a Benedictine abbot and archbishop of Canterbury from 1093-1109. He tried to understand Christian concepts through reason. He was influenced by Neo-Platonism (see below). St Thomas Aquinas composed *Summa Theologica*, between 1265 and 1273. He and others used logic to try and understand religious ideas. Truth could be reached both through reason and logic, and through faith and belief. But spiritual truths could not be known only by reason.

Humanism

Humanism was a new way of looking at the past and present, with a focus on people rather than God. The main idea in it was that people could create a good life on earth for themselves. Pico della Mirandola, an Italian who lived in the 15th century, was one of the main writers on humanism. He stated that people had intelligence, reason and unlimited potential, that is, they could do almost anything if they focused on it. Humanists like Mirandola acknowledged the role of God in creation, but at the same time emphasized the greatness of human beings. He said humans were below god and the angels, but the kings of all other beings. As literature and history focused on humans, they were called 'humanities' and became an important area of study. Mirandola was also an important Neo-Platonist.

Erasmus
Desiderius Erasmus (1466–1536), a Dutch scholar, was another humanist and philosopher. In his work *In Praise of Folly*, he used humour and satire to comment on existing Church practices.

Neo-Platonism
Neo-Platonism was a philosophy based on Plato's ideas, along with other additions. Its focus was on spiritual ideas. Plotinus (CE 205–270) was an early founder of this philosophy. He believed there was one undivided entity, which was beyond all living and non-living things. Neo-Platonism included ideas from Egyptian, Indian, Persian and other religions.

Political theory
There were new ideas in political theory. Most notable was the work of Niccolo Machiavelli (1469–1527) from Florence. His book *Il Principe* (The Prince) discusses how a state should be ruled. He said all decisions should be practical, based on actual situations, and should benefit the state.

Other books
Religious texts, as well as other types of books, including epics, poems and stories of heroes were written. Languages used were Latin, German and other regional languages. Among the many books written, some were popular in several countries. There were new ways of learning and writing, and new ideas.

Literature
Dante Alighieri (c. 1265–1321), was a great poet born in Florence. His best-known work is *La Divina Commedia* (The Divine Comedy). This is both philosophical and thoughtful, but also reflects

current Christian ideas. Dante looks at the Christian concepts of hell, purgatory and paradise, and provides his own vision of what they could be like. In paradise, the main character, who visits these three worlds, meets god. The book was composed in an early form of Italian, and the trend began of writing books in regional languages rather than Latin. Francesco Petrarca (1304–74), also known as Petrarch, and Giovanni Boccaccio (1313–75) were other great writers of the early Renaissance. Petrarch, born in Arezzo in Tuscany, wrote an epic called *Africa*, on the Roman general Scipio Africanus, as well a number of poems. In 1341 he was made the Poet Laureate of Rome, the first to be appointed since ancient days. Petrarch wrote in Latin and in Italian. He also wrote hundreds of letters, both to people in history, and to his friends. Boccaccio may not have been born in Florence, but certainly grew up there, before moving to Naples. He wrote prose and poetry. The *Decameron* is his most famous work. Plague had spread through Florence in 1340 and in 1348. Boccaccio used this as a base for the *Decameron*. In this work ten people narrate 100 stories as they try to escape from Florence at a time of plague.

Plays too were written.

Scholars searched for and recovered early Latin and Greek texts.

REYNARD THE FOX

A series of stories were written in the 11th to 12th centuries, with animals representing people. Stories with Reynard the Fox as the central character were popular in France, Germany and Holland. One of the earliest versions available is *Reinhard Fuchs* (c. 1180), a 2000 line work written in German by Heinrich der Glicherzare, adapted from the French original which is lost. There are several French versions. This was translated into English in 1840 as Reynard the Fox. These stories were actually satires.

RELIGION IN ART AND LITERATURE

Even though the focus was on humans, God and Christianity were important themes, both in literature and in art.

Art and architecture

Romanesque architecture was a style used in Europe from around 1000. It was basically a sturdy structure with round arches and small windows. Romanesque churches were usually in the shape of the basilicas of ancient Rome.

Gothic architecture, a different style, developed from around 1140. The style was used in religious and secular buildings, as well as in sculpture and paintings. Though the style had different regional features, there were some common aspects. The buildings were supported by high pillars. There were tall spires, pointed arches and delicate tracery windows. Stained-glass windows in bright colours were another feature.

Some famous cathedrals, built in this style, can still be seen. Among them are the Notre Dame Cathedral in Paris, France, and the Salisbury Cathedral in England.

Gothic sculpture included large statues attached to columns. The Gothic style continued till the 16th century in some parts of Europe, though simultaneously the Renaissance style began to develop from the 14th century.

THE FLORENCE CATHEDRAL

Among the great cathedrals of the time was the cathedral in Florence of Santa Maria del Fiore, constructed from 1296 onwards. Its great dome was designed by the architect Brunelleschi in the 15th century. Lorenzo Ghiberti created the bronze doors of the baptistry. Paintings in the cathedral were made by several artists including Giotto.

THE LEANING TOWER OF PISA

This tower, which is almost 56 m high, was constructed between 1173 and 1372 in the city of Pisa in Italy. Some additions and repairs were made later. The tower leans to one side because of some fault in its construction. The architecture is a combination of Gothic and Romanseqe elements.

Renaissance styles

In Renaissance architecture the Gothic style declined and was replaced by styles based on ancient Rome. Perhaps the greatest achievement in the new style was St Peter's Church in Rome. This was begun by Donato Bramante (1444-1514) but completed by Michelangelo. Earlier, in the 13th century, Nicola Pisano, an Italian architect and sculptor, integrated classical art into the Gothic style. He is known for the marble pulpit in the Pisa baptistry in Italy.

In sculpture the human form was important, as it was in early Greece and Rome.

In art linear perspective developed. Linear perspective is a technique through which space and distance can be indicated in a painting. A more naturalistic way of painting also developed. Though the greatest Renaissance artists lived in the 16th century, many noted artists lived earlier.

Giotto di Bondone (1267-1337), Lorenzo Ghiberti (1378-1455), Donatello (1386-1466), Masaccio (1401-1428) were among the great artists. Fillipo Brunelleschi (1377-1446) was an architect and engineer.

From this time onwards there was individualism in art. Though great art had been known before, artists were rarely recognized by name. Art had often been a collective effort. Now artists developed their own individual styles. Another new trend was the depiction of major figures of religion such as Jesus and Mary in natural human forms.

As mentioned earlier, the greatest achievements in the Renaissance took place in the late 15th to the 16th century. The greatest Renaissance artists, Raphael, Leonardo da Vinci and Michelangelo belonged to this period. Leonardo da Vinci (1452-1539) was a sculptor, architect, artist, inventor, visionary and engineer. Michelangelo (1475-1564) was an artist, sculptor and architect. Among his great sculptures is that of St Proculus, made in 1494-95, and of David made in 1504.

MUSIC

There were singers and storytellers who wandered from place to place, telling stories, sometimes in verse and song. Minnesinger was a term for a type of German lyric poet of the 12th and 13th centuries who sang about love, or court life, or religion. Minnesingers were similar to the earlier troubadours or trouveres. The troubadour tradition began in southern Europe in a region known as Occitania in the early 11th century. From here it spread to Italy, Spain and Greece. The minnesingers in Germany, travadorismo in Galicia and Portugal, and the trouveres in northern France were similar. From the middle of the 13th century, stories were written and sung about ordinary peasants too. The lai was a form of medieval French poetry with music which developed in the 13th century with the trouveres. These could have several hundred lines, and were sometimes on religious themes. The leich in Germany was another song form similar to the French lai.

There were many other types of popular songs, as well as church and religious music.

Gregorian chants

Gregorian chants were a type of music used to celebrate mass and other church services. It is named after Pope Gregory I but it is thought that the chant actually developed during Carolingian times, from earlier forms. Later, polyphony developed, that is with additional voices being added.

SCIENCE AND MATHEMATICS

This period saw developments in alchemy, astronomy and mathematics. Jean Buridan (1300–some time after 1358) developed the theory of impetus. Georg Purbach (1423-1461) was a mathematician and astronomer. His student Regiomontanus (1436-1476) published a book on astronomy, based on Purbach's work. There were many others who contributed to new developments in science at this time, though the great scientists such as Galileo and Copernicus lived a little later.

FIBONACCI (1170-1240)

Leonardo Pisano Bigello, also known as Leonardo Fibonacci, was a great Italian mathematician. Through him, the use of Indian-Arabic numerals in Europe became more widespread, while earlier the more complicated Roman number system was used. He is also recognized for introducing a number sequence, later called Fibonacci numbers, though this too was known earlier in India.

PRINTING

The technique of printing was first developed in China. Both woodblock printing and printing with movable type first developed there. In Europe (Germany) metal movable type was developed by Johannes Gutenberg in 1438. In England, William Caxton (1422-1492) introduced a printing press. After this numerous books were printed in Europe. Books made knowledge more easily available.

> **ASTRONOMICAL CLOCKS**
>
> Apart from showing the time, astronomical clocks displayed information such as the positions of the sun, moon and planets. The first such clock was made in China. Somewhat later was Al Jazari's castle clock dating to 1206. This showed the time, the zodiac, and position of the sun and moon. Every hour an automatic door opened, revealing a mannequin. By the 15th century there were several such clocks in Europe. Among them was one in the Strassburg cathedral, in the Lund cathedral in Switzerland, in Olomouc, Moravia and in Prague.
>
> The clock in Prague, made in 1410, with later additions. has an astronomical dial and several moving figures. The 12 apostles too are depicted, and appear every hour as the clock strikes. This clock can still be seen.
>
> *The astronomical clock at Prague, with twelve apostles*

330   The Puffin History of the World

33
Great Britain and Ireland
CE 1000–1500

As we saw earlier the Danes again ruled England in the early 11th century, but finally were defeated.

The Battle of Hastings
In 1066, Harold, Earl of Wessex, was made King Harold II of England. William, Duke of Normandy in France, wanted to become the king. Harold was also challenged by his brother Tostig and by the king of Norway. He managed to defeat them. But by that time William had sailed from Normandy and reached England. A battle was fought at Senlac near Hastings, and Harold was killed. William, known as the Conqueror, was crowned king at Westminster Abbey on Christmas day, 1066.

Normans in England
Norman rule followed. French was spoken at the court. The type of French spoken has been called Anglo-Norman. France

and England were now closely connected, but there was rivalry and warfare between the two countries for several hundred years.

William still had to put down various rebellions. Numerous battles were fought and many areas of north England were destroyed. To reduce the power of the rich barons and officials, William took over their estates. Normans and those who supported them were given high positions.

The Bayeau tapestry

The Bayeau tapestry is a beautiful work of art that depicts the Norman invasion. It has 72 embroidered panels that show the events up to the Battle of Hastings.

Part of the Bayeau tapestry

The Domesday Book

A land survey was carried out for tax assessment. The results were put together in *The Domesday Book*. It provides a lot of information about the land and the people who lived there.

Matilda and Stephen

William was succeeded by his son William II, followed by his younger son Henry I. Henry I died in 1135 without a son. He had a daughter named Matilda (also called Maud) and he wanted her to rule England after him. The people of England were not keen on this, and Henry's nephew, Stephen of Blois, made himself king. A series of conflicts between Stephen and Matilda's armies took place. The barons became powerful as they were given land by both sides to ensure their support. The common people suffered as towns and villages were destroyed in these battles. Illegal castles were built and there was a general state of lawlessness. This period has been called the Anarchy. It lasted till 1153.

Finally Stephen was the winner in England, but Matilda still controlled Normandy.

The Angevins or Plantagenets

Matilda was married to Geoffrey of Anjou. Anjou was a region in France. Their son Henry invaded England. He forced Stephen to make him his heir. He became the king of England in 1154 and was known as Henry II. He also controlled a large area of France, as well as Ireland, Scotland and Wales. His dynasty is known as Anjevin from Anjou. But they are also called the Plantagenets. This is because Henry's father always wore the stick of a plant in his cap. This plant was known as *Planta genista*.

Richard—the lion heart

Richard I or Richard Coeur de lion (lion heart) succeeded King Henry. He spent his time in the Third Crusade and in defending his French territories. In 1194 he made England a nominal (in name) vassal of the Holy Roman empire.

King John and the Magna Carta—the beginnings of democracy

King John (ruled 1199-1216) faced a lot of problems. He increased taxes. This made the people unhappy. He was unsuccessful in war. He was defeated in the Battle of Bouvines in 1214, and lost Normandy and many other French territories.

The barons began to unite against the king. They met King John at Runnymede near London on 15 June 1215, and got him to sign the Magna Carta (great charter) that limited the power of the king. Certain laws were laid down that both the king and the barons were to follow. It had some advanced provisions, such as ensuring justice for all. But John broke his pledge to the barons and had the support of the pope for this. A conflict began between the king and the barons. The barons invited Prince Louis of France to become the king.

A painting from the 1800s shows King John signing the Magna Carta

Though this first Magna Carta did not last long, it is considered significant, as it was the first step towards constitutional government.

Father of the House of Commons

The House of Commons is the lower house of the British Parliament.

Henry III became king at the age of nine. He ruled from 1216-1272. The barons controlled the government when he was a child. They made the Magna Carta the basis of law in 1225. Later, he had to fight battles in the country and wars against France. But it was during his reign that the first early 'Parliament' was held in 1264.

The Parliament was actually called by Simon de Montfort. Simon was the earl of Leicester and became leader of the barons. He defeated Henry, but held the Parliament in Henry's name. As he invited the first Parliament to meet, he has been called Father of the House of Commons. Of course this early Parliament was very different from the later House of Commons, but it was the beginning.

OTHER KINGS
Edward I

Edward I (ruled 1272-1307) held the first official Parliament. His Model Parliament of 1295 followed the pattern of that of 1265. It included barons, bishops, abbots and representatives of counties and towns. He was a strong king.

In the 14th century Parliament was divided into two houses, later known as those of Lords and Commons.

Edward II

Edward II (ruled 1308-1327) was a weak king. In 1314 he was defeated by the Scots in the Battle of Bannockburn.

Edward was married to Queen Isabella of France. However, he neglected her. Isabella loved a man named Roger Mortimer. She went to France and along with Roger invaded England. Edward II was defeated and imprisoned, and later killed.

Edward III

Edward III (ruled 1327-1377) was a powerful king. He was the son of Edward II and Isabella. He made England strong, but started the Hundred Years' War with France.

Many other kings followed. Apart from domestic matters, some of them were involved in the Hundred Years War and the crusades.

England lost the Hundred Years War in the time of King Henry VI.

Roses, red and white

A civil war, the War of the Roses took place in England. It is so called because the two groups involved had roses as their symbols. The House of Lancaster, to which Henry VI belonged, had a red rose as its symbol. Richard, Duke of York, wanted to be king. The House of York, to which Richard belonged, had a white rose as its symbol. Richard and Henry were both descended from Edward III. The war lasted for 30 years, between 1455 and 1485. Many battles were fought during these years. The greatest battle was fought at Towton in 1461. After this battle, Edward, son of Richard of York, became the king. He was known as Edward IV. Edward IV was succeeded by his son Edward V. Now another Richard, duke of Gloucester, attacked Edward V and took over the throne. He became King Richard III.

The Tudors

In 1485 Henry Tudor of the Lancastrian line, came to England from France and defeated King Richard III in the Battle of Bosworth. He was known as King Henry VII. The War of the Roses had finally ended. A new rose symbol was chosen for the Tudors. There was a white rose in the middle, encircled by a red rose.

Henry VII ruled till 1509. He started the Tudor dynasty which ruled England for 118 years.

Economy

By the 12th and 13th centuries, England grew her own cereal grains, and had sufficient dairy products, beef and mutton. Wool was exported to other countries. English textiles became important from the 15th century. There were many new towns. The universities of Oxford and Cambridge were established. Cathedrals, abbeys and churches were built, and monasteries were rich.

But in the 14th century England was affected by the disasters that spread across Europe.

In the famine of 1315-17 that spread across Europe about 500,000 thousand people died in England.

The plague that swept through Europe, reached England in 1349, and one-third of the population died.

There were internal problems too as the peasants organized a revolt in 1381.

During this time the economy was changing, and the feudal system and serfdom were coming to an end.

Architecture

The Normans built a large number of castles and churches.

Castles were originally made as temporary motte and bailey types, made of wood, which were later rebuilt in stone. A stone castle had a huge square tower in the centre. This was called the Keep. In the Keep was everything required for a siege. The Tower of London was one of the stone castles built in Norman times. It was begun by William the Conqueror in 1077. Its Keep, called the White Tower, was built between c. 1078 and 1097. Inside is the Chapel of St John.

Romanesque and Gothic styles, which were architectural styles used all over Europe, were also used in Britain. The Normans built cathedrals, abbeys and churches in Romanesque styles with some regional features. The Durham cathedral is one of the great structures in this style.

Romanesque style churches were also made in Scotland and Ireland. The ones in Ireland were somewhat different with round towers.

From the late 12th century to the 16th century, the Gothic style was used, in churches, cathedrals, castles and other structures. Though the basic style remained the same, there were changes made over the centuries. Salisbury Cathedral (built 1220-1266) represents the early style. Gothic castles had thick, high walls, gatehouses and towers.

From the 15th century, many structures were built of brick instead of stone.

Houses in towns were made of stone, brick or wood, and were usually small. Up to the time of the Tudors, most houses of ordinary people were of wood. Beds were made of straw. Roofs were thatched. But after 1213 there was a law that tiles and shingles had to be used on roofs because of the danger of fire.

Art

In art too Romanesque styles were used from the time of the Normans. There were illuminated manuscripts and religious paintings.

The Winchester Bible (1170-1180) is a beautiful hand-painted Bible. Many artists worked on it for several years. Ivory and stone carvings too were made in Romanesque styles. In buildings, doorways, arches and doorjambs were carved.

Later books were illustrated in Byzantine and Gothic styles. Gothic sculptures were made of marble, gilt-bronze and alabaster.

LITERATURE
Geoffrey Chaucer (1343-1400)

Geoffrey Chaucer was a great English poet. He wrote a number of poems, which are actually stories in verse. Among them, *Troilus and Criseyde* is a tragic love story about the Trojan prince Troilus. It has 8000 lines.

WESTMINSTER ABBEY

Westminster Abbey is an important structure located in Westminster. Initially it was a church of a Benedictine Abbey (monastery). The present church was built between the 13th and 16th centuries, with some later additions.

From the time of William the Conqueror, English kings were crowned here. Some are buried here. There are sculptures of kings in bronze and stone. There is also a portrait of Richard II, who abdicated the throne in 1399. It is probably the oldest painting of a British king.

There are tombs of some famous English people, and monuments to others. Geoffrey Chaucer, Sir Isaac Newton and Charles Darwin, are among those buried here. Geoffrey Chaucer was the first poet to be buried here, though this was done 155 years after his death.

The royal court was at Westminster from around 1200. Westminster was then a small town, separate from the city of London. Gradually the area between them became urbanized.

His best-known work is *Canterbury Tales*, a collection of stories, mostly in verse. A group of pilgrims set out on a pilgrimage to the Canterbury Cathedral, where the shrine of St Thomas Becket is located. There is a storytelling contest in which the pilgrims narrate stories. Each story is in the style of the pilgrim who is said to have narrated it. The 24 stories contain more than 18,000 lines of poetry.

Other noted poets

Among other noted poets of this time were William Langland (1332-1400) and John Gower (1330-1408). John Gower wrote poems in three languages, French, Latin and English.

Legends of King Arthur

As we saw earlier King Arthur was a legendary king. He may have lived in the 5th century. There were many stories about him. Sir Thomas Mallory wrote *Le Morte d'Arthur* (The Death of Arthur) in the 15th century (1469-1470). It was written in English prose. It put together the various legends and stories of Arthur.

Sir Gawain and the Green Knight is another book written around 1370. It is about one of Arthur's knights.

Piers Plowman

Piers Plowman is a great book which was probably written by William Langland. It shows through a series of visions, the plight of the poor, the greed of the rich, and the beauty of living a Christian life.

IRELAND

In Ireland, there were a number of different kingdoms. The Vikings, too, had established a number of settlements. As we saw earlier, after the death of Brian Boru, the High King in 1014, Ireland was again disunited, and several different kings ruled. The Normans invaded Ireland between 1169 and 1172, and Ireland came under King Henry II.

Under the Normans a feudal system was established. Manors with their surrounding estates, and towns developed. In 1297 the Parliament of Ireland was founded. By the 14th century Norman control decreased. The Irish and the Normans began to intermarry, and a new culture was created. In 1367, the Statutes of Kilkenny, passed by the Irish Parliament, tried to prevent this. It said that the English in Ireland, that is, the Normans, should speak only English and follow English laws. But Norman influence continued to decline till the end of the 15th century.

Lifestyle

Ireland had its own literature, music and art. Cattle were important in Ireland. People who owned more cattle had a higher status in society. Usually cattle were not killed for meat. But blood was drawn from live cattle, and mixed with butter and milk. Black pudding, eaten at breakfast, was made from blood mixed with barley or other grain. Pork and mutton were also eaten. The potato, later so important in Ireland, was only introduced in the 16th century.

Ireland and Scotland both had early literature in the Gaelic language. Scottish Gaelic developed as a separate language only in the 15th century. Two books composed in Gaelic in the 12th century are *The Book of the Dun Cow* and *The Book of Leinster*. These, composed in prose and poetry, have a number of stories, which were written down at this time but were known earlier. Mythical and religious stories, stories of voyages and of early kings, were among the other types of books composed.

WALES

As we saw earlier, there were four main kingdoms in Wales: Gwynedd, Powys, Deheubarth and Morgannwg. Gwynedd was the most powerful. The Norman conqueror William I invaded and gained control of Wales, but a revolt in 1094 led to him losing most of the lands. The struggle between Wales and England continued until Wales was conquered by Edward I in 1284. Edward built a number of castles to ensure control, the largest being Caerphilly Castle. This has thick stone walls and a wide moat, and is the second largest castle, after Windsor castle, in the whole of Great Britain. There were other rebellions, but by the end of the 15th century, these had ended. Wales at this time was a separate principality, but later was united with England.

Wales' economy was based on cattle and sheep rearing. Flannel, made from wool, was a major industry.

Welsh (*Cymraeg*) is another Celtic language which is the early language of Wales, and is still used to some extent. Literature was composed in Welsh from early days. A number of manuscripts date between the 12th and 14th centuries. Welsh poets enjoyed a high status at the courts of kings. Prose, including stories, were also written.

The *Mabinogion* is a collection of stories in Welsh, written between the 11th and 13th centuries. Among the 11 stories are folk tales, myths, and legends of King Arthur.

SCOTLAND

We saw earlier that Kenneth MacAlpin had united most of Scotland in the 9th century. A number of kings were descended from him. By the 11th century, the whole of Scotland was united under Malcolm II (ruled 1005-1035). Malcolm II was succeeded by Duncan I, Malcolm's grandson through his daughter. Duncan was challenged by Macbeth, another descendant of Kenneth MacAlpin. Macbeth won a battle against Duncan I and ruled from 1040-1057. Scotland was conquered by Edward I of England in 1296. However, Robert Bruce defeated the English under Edward II at Bannockburn in Scotland, in 1314. In 1328 England recognized the independence of Scotland. The Stuart dynasty ruled Scotland from 1371 for more than 300 years.

> *Macbeth*, a play written by Shakespeare in around 1603, is not a historical account of this king of Scotland. Duncan I was killed in battle, and not murdered. There are other inaccuracies too.

The Scots had professional poets called makars who were attached to the court. William Dunbar (1460-1520), a poet and a Franciscan monk, wrote *Lament for the Makaris* in which he provides the names of a number of former poets.

34

The Mongols
CE 1200-1500

Mongols were groups of nomadic people living in Central Asia and Mongolia. They had joined together in confederations from the 8th century onwards. In the 12th century there was a Mongol confederacy led by Khabul Khan. They had many problems and conflicts with the Jin dynasty of Khitan Mongols. Yesukai, grandson of Khabul Khan, was a chief of the Khamag Mongols, but was poisoned. His son Temujin, who was 13 years old, succeeded him. There were many other groups in the region. The Mongols rode horses and kept herds of sheep, and in the dry desert regions, they used camels. They hunted wild animals, but also obtained items through trade. Grain, tea, cloth and metals came from China.

GENGHIS KHAN

In 1206, some Mongol clans met, and chose Temujin, son of Yesukai, as their leader. He was known as Genghis Khan, or the 'Great Leader'. ('Genghis' means lord or precious warrior and khan means leader).

The city of Karakorum became his capital.

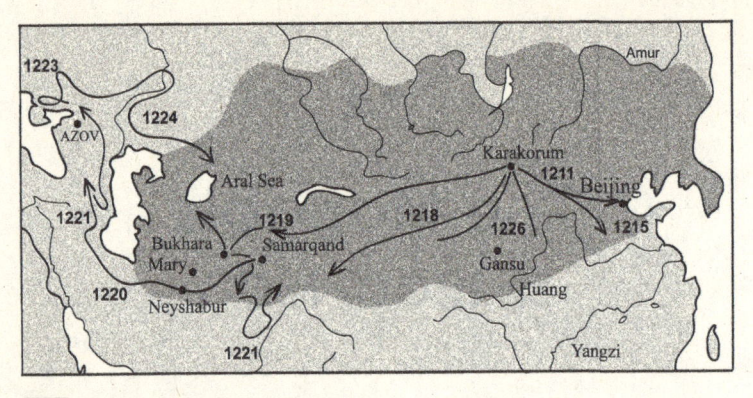

The conquests of Genghis Khan

Genghis had a small but powerful army. His warriors rode on fine horses and were good archers. Led by Genghis, they conquered northern China, then under the Jin dynasty. Next, Korea was captured. They also occupied some states of Central Asia and further invaded Khwarizm, an empire under the Turks, which included the regions of Iran and Iraq. The Mongols also reached Russia.

Genghis died in 1227 having created a huge empire.

In this empire there were people speaking different languages, and following different religions. Buddhists, Christians and Muslims joined his army. All were treated equally. Genghis Khan followed a religion in which nature gods and ancestors were worshipped. Tengri, the sky god, was the main deity. Eje, the earth mother, was also important. Their religion said a person should be honest and respect all people. Genghis also created a system of writing for the Mongolian language. It was based on the Turkish script.

The Great Yasa was a code of government created by Genghis. This was followed by other Mongol rulers who came after him.

THE GREAT KHAN AND OTHER KHANS

After a brief period when Tolui, Genghis' youngest son, acted as regent, Ogadai, the third son, became Genghis Khan's successor. He called himself Khagan or 'Great Khan'. In theory, the Great Khan was supreme, but in practice he did not have absolute power. Even before his death, Genghis had divided his empire among his four sons. The empire was subdivided into khanates. These gradually became independent of the Great Khan.

Ogadai was Great Khan from 1229–1241. As Great Khan, Ogadai expanded Mongol territories further into Russia, China, Iran and even Europe.

He mainly ruled in East Asia. His own territory included part of Mongolia, northern China, Tibet, Korea, Dongbei and northern Indo-China. However, he died in 1241 and the Mongols withdrew from Europe.

Jagatai (Chagatai), Genghis' second son ruled the Turkistan khanate. This included the present Xinjiang Uyghur Autonomous region of China and extended towards the west to Central Asia and north Iran.

Tolui, Genghis' youngest son, ruled the main Mongolian region around Karakorum.

Jochi, Genghis' eldest son, died before Genghis. He had been given Russia. This was divided between Jochi's sons Batu Khan and Orda Khan. They received what is known as the Blue Horde and the White Horde. These regions were combined and formed the Golden Horde, or Khipchak Khanate.

Tolui Khan was the acting or provisional Great Khan from 1227–1229. He was the father of Mongke Khan (also known as Mangu Khan) and Kublai Khan.

From 1242–1246, Toregene Khatun, the wife of Ogadai, acted as regent for the Great Khan.

The next Great Khan from 1246–1248 was Guyuk Khan, son of Ogadai.

Mongke was the Great Khan from 1251–1259.

Conquests

During these years the Mongols made more conquests.

The Mongols defeated the Seljuks of Rum in 1243.

In 1258 the Abbasid caliph at Baghdad was killed by the Mongols. The Mongols then attacked Damascus and Syria. They moved towards the Mamluks in Egypt, but at this time the Great Khan Mongke died. The Mamluks managed to defeat the Mongols in a battle near Nazareth in 1260.

With this the unified Mongol empire came to an end. There was conflict between Kublai and his brother Arik Boke for the title of Great Khan.

> **HORSESHOES**
>
> The Mamluks had been using horseshoes for their horses since 1244. The Mongols had not yet begun. This gave the Mamluks an advantage.

KUBLAI KHAN

Kublai Khan became the Great Khan, but in practice each Mongol territory was now independent. Kublai ruled over China.

Hulagu in Iran acknowledged Kublai Khan as the Great Khan. His territory was known as the Il-Khanate. Berke, a Muslim Khan was against Hulagu and Kublai Khan. In 1263 Berke organized an opposition to Hulagu. The opposers included the Golden Horde of Russia, the Mamluks of Egypt, the Byzantine empire and Italian Genoa. War between the Golden Horde and Il-Khanate continued after the deaths of Hulagu in 1265 and Berke in 1266. Beyond that was the khanate of Turkistan, while the Russian khanate was divided into three. We will look at the Mongol dynasties in Iran, China and Russia in other chapters.

> **THE SECRET HISTORY OF THE MONGOLS**
>
> This is a book written in Mongolian soon after the death of Ogadai. It is not known who wrote it.
>
> The book has 12 chapters, mostly on the life of Genghis Khan, though the last chapter has an account of Ogadai.
>
> It begins with a mythical account of the ancestors of Genghis Khan. Long, long ago, it says, his first ancestors were descended from a blue-grey wolf and a fallow doe.

KARAKORUM

Karakorum is located in Mongolia, near the town of Khorkhorin. In the 12th century Karakorum was under the Khwarizm empire. It became the capital of Genghis Khan around 1220, after he defeated Khwarizm.

Karakorum, the Mongol palace and the silver tree; this is based on an 18th-century painting by a Dutch artist.

William of Rubrick, a Franciscan missionary, was sent here by the pope. He reached Karakorum in 1258.

William said the city was surrounded by walls, and had four gates. At each gate, there was a large sculpture of a tortoise. On its back was a pillar, with beacons that travellers could see from a distance. Apart from the palace, there were two groups of houses. All kinds of people lived there, and all religions were practised there.

There were 12 temples, two mosques and a Nestorian church.

Ogadai built a palace at Karakorum.

Mongke Khan too had a palace there.

The silver tree

The palace of the Great Khan at Karakorum was known as Tumen Amugulang Palace. In front of the palace, or perhaps inside, was a silver tree fountain, described by Rubrick.

The tree, including branches, leaves and fruits, was made of silver. On top was an angel blowing a bugle. Four golden serpents were climbing the tree, and four silver lions sat below it. The lions and the serpents had mouths which acted as fountains, but they were not water fountains. Different drinks came out of their mouths.

From the lions, came airag, a name for fermented mare's milk. The Mongols were very fond of this drink. From the serpents' mouths, different drinks poured out: wine, airag, mead and rice beer.

In the time of Kublai Khan, the Mongol capital was in China. Karakorum remained an administrative centre of the Yuan dynasty. Karakorum declined when the Yuan dynasty ended but was again rebuilt in the 15th and 16th centuries.

YURTS

Yurts were a transportable type of house of the nomads of Central Asia. Yurt is term used in Turkic languages, but Mongolians called them ger. Ger means home.

A yurt on a cart [ger-tereng]

They were round and had a wooden frame. The frame was covered with felt, made from sheep wool. They could be folded up, moved, and re-erected somewhere else.

Ger-tereng was a ger placed on a cart. These carts were huge. They could be 6 m wide, and had to be pulled by 22 oxen.

Tents were also used by the nomads.

FOOD

Mongol food varied in different regions. In Mongolia there was a lot of grilled meat of various animals both domestic and wild, including the marmot. Fermented mare's milk and salty goat milk tea were drunk. Meat, barley or rice added to the tea turned it into soup. Animal fats as well as dairy products, including cheese, dried curds, yoghurt and milk were used. Meat was also used in soup or dumplings. Dumplings could be steamed, boiled or fried. Barley was eaten as porridge.

RELIGION

The Mongols in the time of Genghis Khan worshipped several different gods (see above). The later Mongols adopted different religions. Kublai Khan was a Buddhist. Ghazan, a later ruler of the Il-Khanate in Iran, became a Muslim.

TIMUR

Timur, born in 1336 in Sharisabz, south of Samarkand, was another great warrior like Genghis Khan. Though not related to Genghis, he thought of reviving the glory of the Mongol empire. The son of a landowner, he became a military leader under the Chagatai Khan, of the Turko Mongol tribes between the Amu Darya and Syr Darya rivers and then conquered Khorasan, Sistan, Khwarizm and Mughulistan. (Mughulistan was a region that included parts of present Kazakhstan, Kyrgyzstan and Xinjiang.)

He then went further into Iran, and into Iraq, Turkey and Central Asia.

He defeated Tokhtamysh, ruler of the Golden Horde, invaded India in 1398 and then attacked the Mamluks in Syria and the Ottoman sultan Bayazid I in Turkey. He began to move towards China but died at Otrar on the Syr Darya in 1405. His conquests are said to have led to the death of 17 million people. At the same time he was a patron of art, literature, learning and architecture. He called himself 'guregen', son-in-law of the Chagatai khans, whom he acknowledged as rulers, and with whom he was connected by marriage. He had the title of amir, not of khan. His capital was at Samarkand (present Uzbekistan). Here he erected grand buildings. Among them is the tomb of Ahmad Yesevi, a Sufi saint. Books were produced at the time of Timur. Omar Aqta, a great calligrapher at his court, is said to have written a really large-sized Quran as well as a tiny Quran that could fit on a signet ring.

After Timur

After Timur's death his sons fought over succession. Shahrukh, his fourth son, became the ruler in 1407. Shahrukh moved his capital to Herat in present Afghanistan, then part of Khorasan. Ulugh

Beg, Shahrukh's son, ruled in Samarkand from 1409-1447. There he built an observatory. Samarkand became a centre of science and learning. But his son Abd al Latif had Ulugh Beg killed in 1449.

There were numerous small states in western Central Asia between 1450 and 1500. Most of them were ruled by descendants of Timur. Samarkand and Bokhara were the most important, where art and culture flourished. Literature was composed in Chagatai Turkish. However these states were constantly at war, and were taken over by the Uzbeks.

Shatranj/Chaturang

Timur is said to have created a new form of shatranj (chess), with camels and additional pieces. It is actually not known who created this, but it developed in Iran in his time. It has a larger board with 110 squares, instead of the usual 64 squares. The pawns are of different kinds and have different functions.

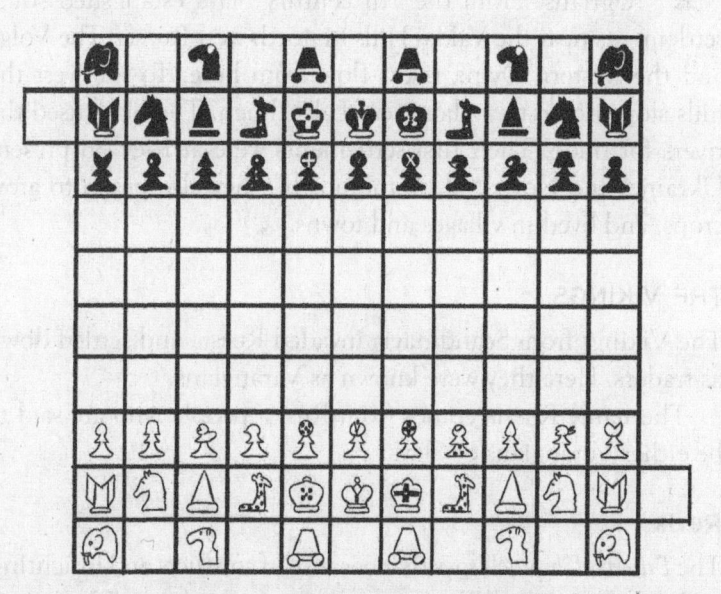

A new form of shatranj: the starting board

35

Russia
CE 1000–1500

There were a number of nomadic groups around the region of Russia. Among them were the Slavs and Finno-Ugrians. From the 7th century Slavs established some settlements near the Valdai Hills in north-west Russia. The Volga and the western Dvina rivers flow from here. To the west the hills slope down to a plain near Lake Ilmen. The Slavs used the rivers for trade. Their first settlements were at Kiev (in present Ukraine) and Novgorod, to the north. They also began to grow crops, and lived in villages and towns.

THE VIKINGS

The Vikings from Scandinavia invaded Russia and settled down as traders. Here they were known as Varangians.

The name Russia comes from Rus, a people who are said to be either Varangians or Slavs.

Rurik

The *Primary Chronicle* says that because of conflicts and infighting, a Varangian named Rurik was chosen as the king of Novgorod

> **THE RUSSIAN PRIMARY CHRONICLE (POVEST VREMENMYKH LET)**
>
> This was probably written by a monk, and tells the story of Russia from the ancient past up to 1110. It is the earliest chronicle of Russia. It includes myths on the origin of the world and about the Russian people, but the later events described are considered to be factual. There were several other Russian chronicles which tell us about life in the country.

in CE 862. It was hoped he would bring unity. Historians feel Rurik may have become the king through conquest.

The *Chronicle* states that two other Vikings, Dir and Askold, ruled in Kiev.

Igor, Olga and Svyatoslav

Rurik died in 879. His son Igor was still a young child. Igor became the king, but Oleg, a relative, ruled as the regent. Oleg expanded and united the region by bringing Kiev under his control. The territory came to be known as Kievan Rus. Igor came to the throne in 913, followed by his widow Olga, and then their son Svyatoslav in 962. Cultural and trade relations with the Byzantine empire were established. Svyatoslav further extended the Kievan Rus territories, creating an empire.

Svyatoslav died in a battle and his empire was divided among his three sons. His youngest son, Vladimir I, defeated his brothers and became king of the whole region in 980.

Religion in Russia

At this time many different gods were worshipped in Russia. Among them were Perun, god of thunder and of war, and Veles, god of water and of the underworld. Veles was also worshipped as the god of cattle. Sometimes one of the gods, particularly Perun, was worshipped as a supreme god. Trees and sacred groves were also worshipped.

VLADIMIR I

Vladimir I, known as Vladimir the Great (CE 980-1015), was interested in religion. He invited both Christians and Muslims to his court. He was attracted to Byzantine Christianity and converted to that religion in 988. Byzantine Christianity became the official religion of Russia. Vladimir I may have converted to Christianity for political reasons. Vladimir I was already married, but he left his earlier wives and married Anne, the sister of the Byzantine emperor Basil II, who was a Christian. Vladimir I had idols of the earlier gods thrown into the river.

The Russian Orthodox Church was the type of Christianity established in Russia. It was similar to Byzantine Christianity, but the language used was Slavic.

A new political system

It was difficult to keep the area united. Sons, grandsons, brothers and uncles all wanted to rule over small states. Vladimir tried to introduce a political system to unite the various regions. According to this system the centre of power would be Kiev, ruled by a Grand Prince. All other areas would be ruled by princes of the same family. There would be an order of seniority from the eldest to the youngest. The princes would govern different places in rotation, and the senior most would finally get power at Kiev. This system worked well for about a hundred years, and was again revived by Vladimir II.

YAROSLAV I

After Vladimir's death, his territories were divided among his sons. His son Yaroslav (1019-54) defeated his brothers and ruled from Kiev. He built a beautiful capital with grand buildings at Kiev. The great cathedral, the Hagia Sophia of Kiev, was constructed. Schools were set up.

But Yaroslav was not able to control the princes in different areas. Vladimir I had 12 sons, and soon there were many grandsons. These sons and grandsons wanted control over their own territories. After Yaroslav the territory began to break up into small states. The princes also had military forces led by leaders known as boyars.

Nomads from beyond the borders also invaded the region. In 1097 a meeting was held at Liubech, to the north of Kiev. The various related princes came to an agreement to divide the territory among themselves and rule separate states.

VLADIMIR II

Vladimir II (ruled 1113-1125) attempted to unite the region, but after him there were again small states. The title of Grand Prince of Kiev and all of Rus still existed, but now it did not mean much.

TRADE

Unity was required mainly for trade. Initially fur, forest and agricultural products were traded. Tribute and tax was taken from the peasants in produce. This agricultural produce was exported and formed the basis for the economy. Later each region traded in different types of items.

THE MANY STATES

Among the states were those centred around Kiev, Novgorod, Vladimir-Suzdal, Galicia, Volhynia and others. They coordinated for defence but at times fought wars against one another. But people in the whole region had cultural similarities. Each of the states had its own history, even though they had many things in common.

Kiev gradually lost its importance. After the decline of Kiev,

Novgorod became an important city. Through Novgorod, furs from the northern Russian forests were transported to other cities. Novgorod was virtually independent from 1136, until its conquest by Muscovy in 1478.

THE MONGOLS

In 1223 the Mongols under Genghis Khan invaded Russia, but retreated after winning a victory. In 1237 the Mongol Batu Khan invaded Russia. He won a number of victories and destroyed Kiev. Beyond Russia, he even reached Poland, Hungary and Moravia. In 1242 he founded the Khipchak Khanate, also later known as the Khanate of the Golden Horde. His capital was at Sarai near modern Volgograd. The Mongols introduced their own form of government. The Russian cities earlier had some sort of representative government, but this came to an end. Much of the Russian population left Kiev, and there were new influences in the region. The Golden Horde in Russia converted to Islam and used the Turkish language but the culture remained Mongolian.

ALEXANDER NEVSKY

Novgorod in north-west Russia remained free of the Mongols, but in 1240 was attacked by a Swedish army. They were defeated by Alexander Yaroslavich, Prince of Novgorod, on the banks of the river Neva. He was then known as Alexander Nevsky, Alexander of the Neva. Alexander was the son of Yaroslav II, Grand Prince of the city of Vladimir, and in 1236 had been

Alexander Nevsky, a later portrait

elected prince of the city of Novgorod. In 1242 the Teutonic Knights led an attack, but were again defeated by Alexander. Yaroslav died in 1246, after accepting Mongol supremacy, and there was a struggle to be Grand Prince. Finally Alexander became Grand Prince of Vladimir and Suzdal. Alexander ruled Novgorod through his son Vasily. He died in 1263, and Russia again broke up into small states. Alexander was one of the most powerful princes. In 1381 he was recognized as a local saint. In 1547 he was made a saint by the Russian Orthodox Church.

MOSCOW

Moscow was located in the province of Vladimir-Suzdal. Once a village, it had become an important city and a subsidiary province. Daniel, a son of Alexander Nevsky, was sent here by his father in 1263. He was the first of the princes of Muscovy. Daniel's son, Ivan I was made Grand Prince by the Mongol Khan Oz Beg in 1328. Ivan moved the capital to Moscow. Ivan and the succeeding princes began to call themselves 'Princes of all Russia'. Moscow also became the new centre of the Russian Church. Ivan collected tributes for the Mongols, and thus increased his power. Ivan I was succeeded by Ivan II (ruled 1353-59).

Under Oz Beg (1313-41) the Mongols of the Golden Horde reached a height, but then their power began to decline. Dmitry, son of Ivan II, defeated the Mongols in 1380 at Kulikovo, on the banks of the river Don. Dmitry came to be known as Donskoy.

After the Ottoman Turks conquered Constantinople in 1453, the importance of Moscow and the role of the Russian Orthodox Church increased. The Church now came under the authority of the Grand Prince. Now the Grand Prince began to call himself Tsar (from the word Caesar). He was no longer a prince, the leader of other princes, but had made himself into a king. He decided that Moscow was now as important as Rome had been and called it the third Rome.

Ivan III (ruled 1462-1505), a descendant of Dmitry, finally succeeded in making Moscow the most powerful. He brought various states including Novgorod under his control. In 1472 he married Zoe (Sophia), the niece of the last Byzantine emperor. In 1480 he stopped paying tribute to the Mongols.

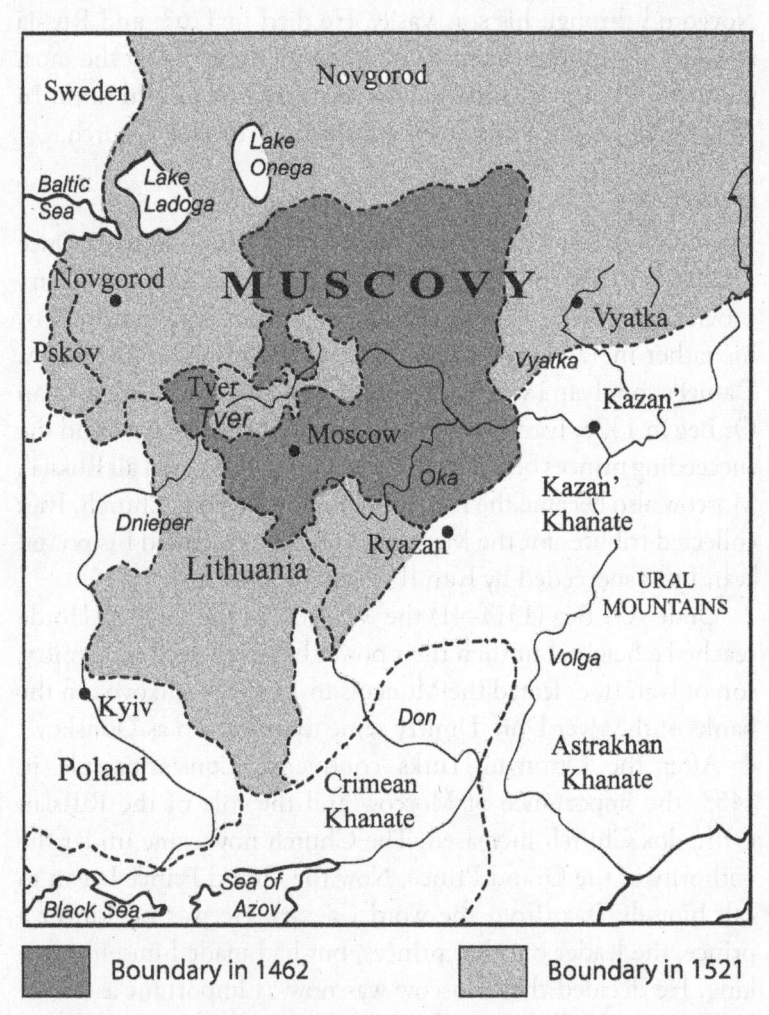

The expanding kingdom of Muscovy

He was now independent. By 1500 Russia had become a great European power.

LIFE OF THE PEOPLE

We learn about life in these times from the Russian chronicles, other books and from archaeology.

There are over 500 books and 100 charters dating between the 11th and 14th centuries. There are also birchbark documents found mainly at Novgorod. Among Russian sites, Novgorod can be considered the equivalent of the Roman Pompeii. The medieval levels are almost perfectly preserved beneath the existing city, because of waterlogging at the site.

Clothes

Men wore tunics, trousers, coats and hats. Women wore long shirts or tunics, and caps. Clothes for the rich were dyed or embroidered and decorated. Jewellery of various types, including glass bangles, beads, and those of gold, silver, other metals and precious and semi precious stones were used. Winter clothing was fur lined. Wool and silk were imported for the rich.

Agriculture and domestic animals

The crops grown at this time in Russia are mentioned in various texts. Horses, cattle, pigs, dogs, sheep, oxen, were among the animals kept. Birds such as chickens and ducks were also domesticated. Beekeeping was known.

Rye, barley, millets and oats were grown. Other crops were beans, lentils, peas, mushrooms, turnips, onions, and garlic. Wheat grew in some areas.

Food

Porridge, eggs, pirogi, kvas, cheese, kasha or kutiya and honey are known from the 12th century. Pirogi is a pie with filling (pirozhki are stuffed buns); kvas is a fermented drink made from rye bread;

kasha is made from buckwheat groats; kutiya is a form of kasha to which nuts, sugar, honey, and raisins are added. Milk was used from the 13th century, and jelly from the 14th century. Rye was used for bread, gruel, porridge and pancakes. The usual food in rural areas would be a stew or soup of vegetables or sometimes meat, or porridge. Peasants drank kvas and ate millet, barley and oats, with some wild game and plants. Around 1300, dried fruit, cabbage, curd cheese and lamb were adopted from the Mongols. Animals were killed for food. Wild forest animals and birds, including bison, elk, stag, bear, boar, rabbit, pheasant, partridge and other birds were used for meat, as well as beef, mutton, pork, chicken, goat, duck and goose. Fish was eaten fresh, salted, smoked and dried. Other foods too were smoked and pickled for storage. Different types of mead were drunk.

Bad weather led to famines that are described in the Russian chronicles.

Trade and travel

Within Russia trade routes mainly followed the rivers. Beyond Russia there were trade routes leading to Constantinople, and to Central Asia and Baghdad. Furs, hemp, honey, rye, salmon and flax were among the items exported, while wine, silk, glassware, jewellery, walnuts, spices and rugs were among the imports. Various metals and semi-precious stones too were imported. Travel was by boats and ships, or on horseback, horse-drawn sledges and skis.

Religion

Though Christianity had reached the region, traditional religious ceremonies still took place which the rulers tried to suppress.

Structures

Structures in Russia included palaces, cathedrals, churches, houses, monasteries and other buildings. Churches were decorated with icons, mosaics and frescoes. Cities had different types of structures, depending on the region in which they were located. Each Russian city had a citadel, a separate area, known as a kremlin.

More or less similar styles in construction and in icon painting existed across Russia. Gothic styles that developed in Europe did not affect Russia.

> **CATHEDRAL OF ST SOPHIA IN KIEV**
>
> A grand cathedral was built in Kiev. Construction for this was begun in 1037 and completed in a few years. The ground plan was a cross within a square and had 13 towers. It had icons, mosaics and decorations. (It was later rebuilt.)

TWO GREAT ARTISTS

Theophanes the Greek (1335-1405) was a painter from the Byzantine empire, who moved to Russia in 1370. He made wall paintings and frescoes in churches and palaces, painted icons and illustrated books. Among the surviving artwork are those in the Church of the Transfiguration in Novgorod (1378). This has depictions of Noah, Abel, St Macarius and others. The most famous painting of this series, known as the *Old Testament Trinity*, is of three angels visiting Abraham. A beautiful icon of his depicts the Transfiguration of Jesus Christ.

Andrei Rublev (1360-1430) is considered the greatest early Russian painter, particularly of icons. He was a monk in different monasteries, and worked with other painters on frescoes and icons. He too painted the Old Testament Trinity (1410). Rublev painted in a different style from Theophanes, and used bright colours.

NOVGOROD—A CITY THAT CAN STILL BE SEEN

Novgorod has archaeological deposits dating back to the 10th century. The site is waterlogged, hence items are well preserved. They include leather, birchbark, plant remains, wood, textiles, and iron, bronze and other metals.

Novgorod is located near the river Volkhov in marshland. The area has a wet climate. The old city was made mainly of wood. The streets were made from logs of wood over the marshy soil.

The Novgorod Kremlin was a fortified complex. South of the Kremlin were houses of wealthy people. Most of the houses were made of wood, the walls of logs, and the floors of planks. Stoves made from clay were used for cooking and heating; ceilings were of wood, but roofs were of different types, mostly sloping. Some of the houses were three storeys tall. In the houses there was wooden furniture, including beds or bunks, tables, benches, chests, cradles and wall hooks. Many of the houses were decorated with icons (religious paintings).

Houses had courtyards with wooden fences.

A recreation of the medieval structures of Novgorod

Apart from houses there were cathedrals, churches and other buildings. The Cathedral of St Sophia at Novgorod was constructed between 1045 and 1052 and had five domes.

Among other buildings were workshops or storage rooms. The city had a system of water ditches and natural channels. In 1372, a wall and ditch were built, to enclose the city.

Other items from Novgorod

Musical instruments have been discovered here including a wooden rebec, a stringed instrument, played with a bow, dating to the 12th century. Metal ornaments in Viking style, pottery, carved bone bird heads on handles of walking sticks, keys, wooden combs, a harp, leather masks, leather footwear, comb cases, knife sheaths, and more than 1000 leather and wooden toys, were among the other items found. Wooden tops, carved animals and balls were some of the common toys. Objects like hockey sticks have been found, and maybe some early form of the game was played. Melnitsa, dice and chess were other games.

> Melnitsa is a board game which in English is called Nine Man's Morris. Known by different names, it was played in many parts of the world.

Birchbark documents

About a thousand texts on birchbark have been found from Novgorod and its neighbourhood. Did this indicate widespread literacy, or were they written by scribes? These birchbark texts included tax documents, lessons, wills, marriage proposals, prayers and spells, accounts of legal conflicts, and orders for icons. Birchbark was boiled to soften it, and writing was done with a stylus. Such documents are also found from other Russian cities. They are mostly written in a vernacular dialect by ordinary people. Some are in Old Church Slavonic, one in Norse, and one in Karelian (Finnic language). About a hundred styluses used for writing were discovered in Novgorod, mostly of iron, but also of bronze and bone.

Osmin—a boy who was bored

Osmin was a young boy. His writing is preserved on a birchbark fragment. He began writing the alphabet but got bored. Then he started drawing. He drew a warrior, fighting another. He gave the victorious warrior his own name, Osmin. Underneath he wrote 'I am a wild beast'.

Children have not changed very much. Maybe you too draw in class when you get bored?

36

India
CE 1000–1500

Across north India there were numerous dynasties which ruled over small kingdoms. Rajput dynasties, which existed from around CE 700, were still important. Among them were the Gahadavalas ruling from Kannauj (present Uttar Pradesh), the Chahamanas who controlled the region of present Delhi and Rajasthan, and the Chandellas in present Madhya Pradesh. The Palas, who were Buddhists, were kings in the region of Bengal. They were succeeded by the Senas (1160–1245). There were other dynasties as well, but there was no unity. The kings of these dynasties granted land to officials, who began to govern almost independently. They had a grand lifestyle, wearing jewellery and gold-bordered clothes. They lived in large houses with many servants.

Agriculture and food

At this time more than a 100 types of cereals, including wheat, barley and rice were grown. Sugar cane, spices and cotton were other important crops. Tanks and wells were dug, and canals provided irrigation. Food included cereals, milk products and vegetables. Some ate meat, including that of wild animals.

Cities, crafts and trade

Cities and trade had declined between CE 600 and 1000. But after 1000 there were new cities, markets and both internal and long-distance trade. There were crafts of all kinds. Pottery, textiles, as well as items of gold, silver and other metals were made. People wore jewellery made from precious and semi-precious stones. Strong swords were made and exported. Textiles were embroidered with gold and silver thread. There was trade with Southeast Asia, China, the Arab empire and north Africa.

Art and culture

Art and culture flourished. Numerous books were written at this time, and new temples were built. Beautiful sculptures were created of Hindu and Buddhist deities and of Jain saints.

Dilwara temples

Among the beautiful temples are a group of Jain temples, located at Dilwara at Mt Abu in Rajasthan. The Adinatha or Vimala Vasahi temple is the earliest, built in 1032, with additions being made later. Constructed entirely of white marble, the inner shrine has an image of Adinatha, the first Tirthankara. There are several other small shrines with Jain images. The pillars and side walls are elaborately carved with deities and scenes

An intricately carved ceiling of a Dilwara temple

from their lives, surrounded by delicate scrollwork. On the ceiling are concentric circles with rows of musicians, dancers, soldiers, horses and elephants.

Next to it is the Neminatha or Luna Vasahi temple, constructed in 1230 and later. It is also of white marble, and even more intricately carved.

These temples are well preserved and still attract numerous visitors and pilgrims.

NEW INVADERS

To the north-west Ghazni and Ghur were two kingdoms in the region of Afghanistan. Mahmud of Ghazni (ruled 997-1030) invaded India a number of times, taking back gold and jewels from the grand temples of north India. Muizuddin Muhammad of Ghur (1173-1206) was not content with invasions. He wanted to conquer India. The Rajput kings, who often fought against one another, joined together to defeat Ghur's armies. After an initial success, the Rajputs were defeated in 1192 in the Battle of Tarain. Following further defeats, a series of sultans began to rule over north India.

THE SLAVE KINGS
Qutbuddin

Qutbuddin Aibak, a general of Muhammad of Ghur, defeated all rivals and established his rule by 1206. His capital was at Delhi. Before he could do much, he died in 1210 after a fall from his horse while playing polo. Qutbuddin was a Turk who had been captured in war, and made a slave by Muhammad, but soon rose to a high position. Because of his origins, he and his successors are sometimes called 'the slave dynasty'.

Queen Raziya (1237-1240)

Qutbuddin was succeeded by his son Iltutmish, who fought wars to establish control over a large region. After him his son ruled briefly, followed by his daughter, Raziya. She was the first woman to rule from Delhi. She wore men's clothes, rode horses, and knew how to fight. But the male nobles did not like to be ruled by a woman. Raziya was defeated and killed by some of them. There were several other rulers after her. Most important was Balban (1265-1287), a noble who became the sultan.

The Khaljis (1290-1316)

The Khaljis were the next dynasty to rule over north India. Jalaluddin Khalji, who founded the dynasty, was an Afghan noble at the court of Delhi. Alauddin Khalji (1296-1336) was the most powerful ruler of this dynasty who created a huge empire. He even extended his conquests to south India.

Section of Siri Fort in Delhi built by Alauddin Khalji

The Tughlaqs (1320-1412)

Ghazi Malik, once a Turkish slave of Balban, took the title Ghiyasuddin, and founded the Tughlaq dynasty. He died after stepping on a wooden platform that collapsed. The platform had been built by his son Ulugh Khan, who became the next sultan with the title Muhammad bin Tughlaq (ruled 1325-1351). Muhammad bin Tughlaq had a number of creative ideas. He moved the capital from Delhi to Devagiri in central India, and introduced paper money. Both these experiments were failures. His good points were that he was tolerant of all religions, and always wanted to learn something new. After the next sultan, Firuz Shah Tughlaq (ruled 1351-1388), there were weak rulers.

Timur of Samarkand invaded India in 1398, and left behind destruction. A very small area remained under Tughlaq control.

The Sayyids and the Lodis

Two more sultan dynasties ruled: the Sayyids and the Lodis. In 1526 the Lodis were defeated by new invaders, who established the Mughal dynasty.

LIFE IN THE TIME OF THE SULTANS

The sultans lived in great splendour in huge palaces. They wore gold-embroidered clothes and jewellery. A special umbrella was held over the sultan when he went out. Behind him a band of musicians played.

The vazir was the main official. He and other officials and nobles lived in huge houses and sometimes in palaces. Merchants, lower government officials and soldiers were also quite wealthy. There were workshops where luxury items were made only for the sultans. For instance Muhammad Tughlaq had 4000 weavers to weave textiles for his clothes and 500 to weave gold brocade. Firuz Tughlaq bought a pair of shoes for 70,000 tankas. But ordinary people lived in simple houses. In rural areas there were mud and thatch houses. A whole family could live for a month on four or five tankas.

There were numerous towns, cities and ports. Delhi was one of the largest cities of the times.

There were new styles in architecture. Mosques, minarets and tombs were built. Arches and domes were used in these. One

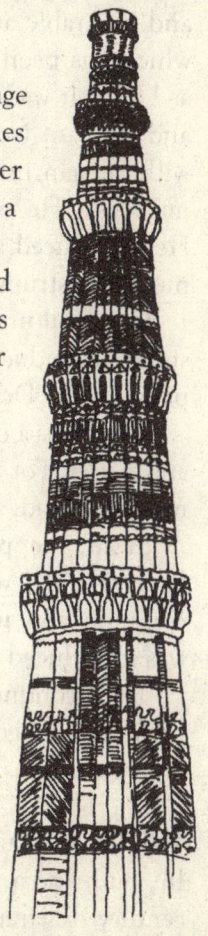

The Qutb Minar

of the most amazing structures that can still be seen is the Qutb minar in Delhi. This is a tapering tower reaching a height of 71.4 m. It is made of red and white sandstone and marble, and might have been meant to be a minaret for a mosque. This structure was completed in the 13th century.

New influences were seen in literature, art and music. There were books in Sanskrit, in regional Indian languages, and in Arabic and Persian. A new language began to develop, which has been called Hindavi, and later came to be known as Urdu. It was a mixture of Hindi, a North Indian language, and Persian. New forms of music and dance, too, developed with Persian influence. Amir Khusrau was a great writer and musician. He wrote books in Persian, Arabic and Hindavi. He introduced a new style in North Indian music, and a new musical instrument, the sitar.

In agriculture, the earlier crops were still cultivated, but some sultans introduced new plants. Firuz Tughlaq had 1200 orchards planted near Delhi with seven varieties of grapes.

There was a continuity in crafts too, but textiles became finer and better. For the first time the spinning wheel was used for making thread, and a loom for weaving.

Sugar, pepper and oil from oilseeds were produced. Papermaking, which had been known earlier became more common and many books were produced. Gunpowder, too, was introduced.

Trade continued. Silk and cotton textiles, spices, sandalwood, perfumes, indigo, precious stones, sugar, rice and coconuts were among the items exported. Imports included gold, silver and horses.

SOUTH INDIA

In south India the Chola dynasty was prominent till the 13th century. Rajaraja I (ruled 985-1014) was followed by his son Rajendra I (ruled 1012-1044). They not only conquered other parts of south India, but even crossed the seas to defeat Sri Lanka, the Maldive Islands, Sumatra and other places in the Malay Peninsula. Chola territory was divided into provinces, further divided into smaller units for efficient government. The villages had a form of self-government. Numerous crafts were produced and there was an extensive network of trade. Chola merchant ships regularly went to China. Beautiful bronze images of gods were made and great temples were built. Among them, the Brihadeshvara temple at Thanjavur was constructed in the time of the Chola king Rajaraja I. It is dedicated to the god Shiva. It has a tower reaching a height of 61 m. Above is a dome weighing 81 tonnes.

A bronze image of Nataraja at the time of the Chola dynasty

There were other dynasties, too, in south India. Among them were the Hoysalas, Cheras, Pallavas and Pandyas. King Jatavarman Sundara Pandya (1251-1272) defeated the Cholas, as well as the other kingdoms. He also defeated Sri Lanka. Marco Polo of Venice, who had visited the court of Kublai Khan in China, visited the Pandya kingdom too. He said the kingdom was very rich, and the king wore a necklace of precious stones, gold, and other jewellery.

Books were written in Tamil, Kannada and Telugu. Malayalam, too, had developed as a new language.

Philosophers
Ramanuja and Madhva were great philosophers of the south. Their philosophies, as well as that of Shankara who lived earlier, are still influential in India.

Ramanuja lived in the 12th century. He said both knowledge and devotion to god (bhakti) were necessary to understand the truth. Madhva, who lived in the 13th century, said that God's essence was in all people, but God and people were not the same.

Bahmani and Vijayanagara

In central India, between the north and the far south, two independent kingdoms were founded in the 14th century. This was at the time Muhammad bin Tughlaq was ruling in the north. The Bahmani kingdom covered parts of the present states of Maharashtra, north Andhra Pradesh and Karnataka, while the Vijayanagara covered south Andhra and south Karnataka. They fought wars to gain control of agricultural land and important ports. At times they allied with each other. Between the late 15th and the 16th centuries, the Bahmani kingdom broke up into five smaller units. The Vijayanagara kingdom was destroyed after a great battle in 1565.

Both kingdoms were very rich. The Russian trader Nikitin visited the area in about 1471. He said that in the Bahmani kingdom when nobles went out, they were carried on silver beds. Twenty horses decorated with gold walked in front. Behind there were 500 men on horseback and 500 on foot. Abdur Razzaq, ambassador to the Vijayanagara kingdom, said that in the king's palace, there were rooms filled with gold.

A royal marriage

All the wealth was displayed when a marriage took place between the sultan Firuz Shah Bahmani (ruled 1397–1422) and the daughter of King Devaraya I of Vijayanagara. When Firuz Shah arrived at the city of Vijayanagara for the wedding, the road from the city gates to the palace was covered with gold, silver and velvet cloth. This was a distance of more than 10 km.

RELIGION IN INDIA

Hinduism, Buddhism, and Jainism were religions that had grown and developed in India. Followers of Christianity, Judaism and Zoroastrianism had reached India between the 1st and 10th centuries. There were Muslim traders in India from the 7th century, and an Arab kingdom in western India in the 8th century. With the invasions from the north-west and the rule of the sultans in Delhi, many more Muslims reached India. Islam became a major religion in the region. Mostly people of different religions lived peacefully. Sufi saints of Islam and Bhakti saints of Hinduism believed that true religion was in one's heart. Guru Nanak (1469–1539) founded a new religion later known as Sikhism. He said that God was unchanging, eternal and without form. He used both Muslim and Hindu names for god and emphasized that there was no difference between the two. Other Sikh gurus (religious leaders) who lived later also contributed to the religion.

NEPAL

To the north, the region of Nepal had close relations with India. It was also connected with Tibet, further north. In Nepal there were a number of different kingdoms. Rajputs originally from India ruled part of the region from the 14th century. Among the many kingdoms was the kingdom of Lo, on the northern border of Nepal.

Lo Manthang

Lo Manthang is a place located within Nepal on the Tibetan border. Founded in the late 14th or early 15th century, it was the capital of the kingdom of Lo. It is on a plateau 3800 m above sea level, on a trade route that follows the Kali Gandaki River. The river cuts a path through the Himalayas. A 6-m-high wall surrounds the settlement that has a palace and monasteries within it.

A view of Lo Manthang

Nearby more than a hundred caves were carved into the cliffs. In these Tibetan religious texts and wall paintings have been found. These date between the 12th and 15th centuries. The paintings include 55 panels which could be a depiction of Buddha's life. Manuscripts have a mix of Bon and Tibetan writings, some of them with illustrations. There were also human skeletons of the same period. Analysis indicates that the caves are six thousand years old.

In English the kingdom is known as Mustang. As it was remote and inaccessible there were many myths and stories about it. It was believed to be the same as Shambala, described in some texts as the place where a future divine leader would be born.

SRI LANKA

Sri Lanka's history was closely connected with that of India. It was earlier known as Sinhala. Kings from south India frequently invaded and ruled the region. In the 12th and 13th centuries there were a number of local kingdoms. In the early 15th century there was Chinese occupation. By the 16th century the Portuguese, followed by other Europeans gained control.

Buddhism was the main religion in Sri Lanka.

INDIAN OCEAN ISLANDS

There are numerous islands in the Indian Ocean. Apart from Sri Lanka, the Andamans, Madagascar, Mauritius and Maldives are among them. Each island or group has a different history.

37

West Asia
CE 750–1500

The Abbasids, who claimed descent from the Prophet Muhammad's uncle Abbas, were the caliphs between CE 750 and 1258. Apart from being caliphs, they were also hereditary kings. They and their supporters were against the Umayyads and wanted members of the Prophet Muhammad's family to rule.

Abu al Abbas was the first Abbasid ruler. In 762 the Abbasids moved the Caliphate, that is, the city from which the caliphs ruled, from Damascus to Baghdad. At this time

Scholars at an Abbasid library: an illustration by Yahyá al-Wasiti, Baghdad 1237

Arab Muslims were no longer the most important, and non-Arabs were welcome at the court. The caliphs began to rule according to Islamic law. The post of vizier was established which was often held by an Iranian. The Abbasids established good relations with the Chinese Tang dynasty.

Other dynasties

By about CE 850, Abbasid power began to decline. By 820 the Samanids were ruling almost independently in Transoxiana and Greater Khorasan; there were other semi-independent local dynasties in Iran and north Syria. Some army officers tried to control the caliphs. The western provinces of Al Andalus were under a ruler of the Umayyad dynasty. In north Africa, the Aghlabids ruled in the Maghreb, and the Fatimids in Ifriqiya.

In 945 the Buyid dynasty of Iran gained control over part of the Abbasid territory, though they acknowledged the supremacy of the caliphs. Other local dynasties too ruled independently. The political control of the Abbasids, and the territory under them was reduced. In 1055 the Seljuk Turks took over the remaining territory of the Abbasids.

However, the Seljuks respected the religious authority of the Abbasids and allowed them to remain caliphs.

In 1258 the rule of Abbasid dynasty finally ended with the invasion of the Mongols. In 1261 the Abbasid Caliph moved to Egypt which was under the Mamluk dynasty.

Baghdad—a centre of learning

The time of Abbasid rule saw great developments in science, technology, medicine, philosophy, literature and architecture. Though the Iranian Sasanians had been defeated by the early caliphs, the Abbasids were inspired by the art and culture that once existed in the Sasanian empire. The caliphs, Haroun al-Rashid (ruled CE 786-809) and Al-Mamun (ruled 813-33) were known for the scholars, artists and scientists at their courts. The Baitul Hikmah or the House of Wisdom was established in Baghdad during their rule. The Baitul Hikmah was a centre for research and learning. Here, literature from various parts of the world including ancient Greece and Rome, was translated into Arabic. Other works, too, were translated, from India and Iran, from China, Egypt, North Africa and the Byzantine empire. Mathematics, astronomy, medicine and other sciences were studied in Baghdad. New literature was written and scholars visited from all over the world. A great library too was set up here. There were four million books in the library. The books were organized according to type and category. Nearby there were stationery shops and bookshops. It is said that thousands of books were sold from these bookshops every day. At this time Baghdad was the greatest centre of learning in the world. It was through Baghdad that the ancient knowledge of Greece, Rome and elsewhere came to be known in Medieval Europe.

Baghdad was a centre of trade and commerce. It had wonderful markets. The book *One Thousand and One Nights* describes markets with produce from all over the world. There were Syrian apples, Osmani quinces, Omani peaches, cucumbers from the Nile, Egyptian lemons, and Sultani citrons. From Iran and India came rice, wheat, sugar, citrus fruits, bananas, mangoes, spinach, and eggplant. Poems in praise of grand meals were recited.

Baghdad was destroyed at the time of the Mongol invasion of 1258.

Book production

There were other huge libraries in Cordoba and in Cairo. How were so many books produced? Paper, made from cloth, began to be produced in large quantities. Thousands of people copied manuscripts, and even illustrated them. For some books, woodblock printing was used. The world's first paper mill was built in Baghdad and later another in Cordoba. In 751 the Abbasids defeated the Tang forces in the Battle of Talas in Central Asia, along the border of present Kyrgyzstan/Kazakhstan. It blocked the Chinese advance into Central Asia. It is said that the Abbasids learnt the technique of papermaking from Chinese prisoners, though paper was already known in Central Asia from the 4th century.

New learning and techniques

Among the great philosophers of this time was Ibn Sina who lived between 980 and 1037. He studied Greek philosophical ideas and introduced new concepts in Islam. His books include the *Kitab-al Shifa*, or *Book of Healing*, which was a philosophical encyclopaedia, and the *Kanun-fit-tibb* or *Canon of Medicine*. He was also famous in Europe, where he was known as Avicenna.

There were new developments in music. Al-Kindi (CE 801–873) wrote 15 works on musical theory. Al Farabi (872–950) wrote *Kitab-al-musiqi al-kabir* (The Great Book on Music).

Algebra was developed by the Persian mathematician Al-Khwarizmi. The system of numerals used in India, later called Arabic numerals, was transmitted to the Western world. Papermaking and gunpowder (both from China) were made known to the world through the Arabs. There were great discoveries in medicine. In the 9th century there were more than 800 doctors in Baghdad.

Water power and windmills were used. Irrigation and farming techniques improved. There were waterwheels with gears for lifting water. New techniques were used for making textiles, ropes and matting, silk, paper and sugar.

Jabir ibn Hayyan (c.721–815) was a great philosopher, chemist and alchemist, who probably lived in the region of present Iraq, at Al-kufah and Baghdad. Over 2000 works are ascribed to him, including works on chemical processes, alchemy, philosophy and mysticism, though scholars believe many of these belong to a later date. He has been called the 'father of Arab chemistry' and influenced European chemistry.

SPECIAL ITEMS MADE
Lustreware

A very fine metallic pottery was made in Baghdad and Basra from the 8th century onwards. A craft guild was responsible for its production. The pottery was glazed with metals, including copper, silver and lead, so that beautiful patterns on the surface glowed and glittered in the light.

This painted lustreware bowl from Syria dates to around CE 1100

Damascus steel

Damascus steel swords were used against the crusaders. They were the sharpest and strongest type of swords. They were made from a fine grade of iron ore, which was melted in a crucible. The impurities were removed and various items added including carbon. This technique was first used in India. The crusaders tried different techniques to make similar swords, but did not succeed. The exact method of making these is still not known. The raw iron for the weapon is known

A Damascus steel sword

as wootz steel. Analysis shows traces of vanadium, chromium, manganese, cobalt, nickel, and rare trace elements. In addition the bark of *Cassia auriculata* and the leaves of *Calotropis gigantea* were added.

SCHEHEREZADE—THE STORYTELLER

Scheherezade is one of the main characters in the book *One Thousand and One Nights*. She was very learned and a great storyteller. The book is generally known as the *Arabian Nights* in English. It is written in Arabic and has stories originally from Persia, India, Arabia and other areas. It was composed between the 8th and 13th centuries, with some later additions.

According to this book, the Persian king Shahryar had lost faith in women after his wife was unfaithful to him. Being a king he had the power to do whatever he liked. He decided to marry a new woman every day, and to kill the one he had married the previous day. Thus he married and killed 1000 women. Then Scheherezade offered to marry him. On the first night she told him an exciting story, but left it unfinished. The king wanted to hear the end, so he did not have her killed that night. The next night Scheherezade finished that story but began another fascinating story leaving it too, incomplete. Again the king was desperate to hear the end, and spared her life. The same thing continued for 1000 nights. Meanwhile the king fell in love with her. They had three sons and lived happily ever after.

The most famous stories she told are those of Aladdin

An illustration showing Sheherezade, Dinarzade and the sultan

and his magic lamp, Sinbad the sailor, and of Ali Baba and the 40 thieves. There are many many more. Among them is the story of Zumurrud, a beautiful slave girl from Samarkand, and of Prince Husain of India, who had a magic carpet.

Scheherezade's younger sister Dinazade married Shah Zaman, the ruler of Samarkand. Shah Zaman was Shahryar's brother. He, too, had been killing one woman every day, after he had found his wife unfaithful. But then he heard of Scherezade's stories and met Dinazade, and fell in love with her.

There are different versions of *One Thousand and One Nights*.

The great Russian composer, Rimsky Korsakov (1844–1908), composed a symphony named *Scheherezade*, based on her story.

ARABIA

Between CE 1000 and 1500 there were different dynasties and small states in the Arabian Peninsula. The Qarmatian dynasty ruled part of the region from 900–1200. The Abbasids, Fatimids, Ayyubids and Mamluks were among the others who ruled the region at different times. The Ottoman Turks conquered Egypt in 1517 and gained influence in Arabia. Despite the different dynasties Arabia was prosperous as important trade routes passed through the region.

IRAN

Hulagu, grandson of Genghis Khan, founded the Il-Khanate (subordinate territory) of Iran, which included areas beyond Iran. Hulagu followed the traditional Mongol religion, with some Buddhist elements. He was succeeded by his son Abaqa, who was followed by his son, Arghun. The war with the Golden Horde ended at the time of Abaqa. Abaqa and Arghun were followers of Buddhism. Buddhist temples were built across Iran and Iraq and Muslims were persecuted. Arghun was succeeded by his brother Gaykhatu. Gaykhatu introduced paper money, which was known in China, but this did not work in Iran. In fact merchants and traders refused to use it and trade was destroyed. He lost power after a rebellion in 1295. Ghazan, son of Arghun, became the khan. Ghazan became a Muslim, and Islam now became the religion of the Il-Khanate. He replaced Mongol law with the Sharia (Islamic law) and converted Buddhist temples into mosques. Buddhists and Christians were persecuted. Ghazan was succeeded after his death in 1304 by his brother Oljeitu, who was a Shiah Muslim, whereas Ghazan was a Sunni Muslim. Oljeitu persecuted the Sunnis. He died in 1316 and was succeeded by his son Abu Said, a Sunni. Another conflict began with the Golden Horde over territory in the Caucasus Mountains.

After the death of Abu Said in 1335 a succession struggle began. The Black Death also swept through the region, killing thousands. Jani Beg of the Golden Horde attacked the Il-Khanate capital of Tabriz in 1357. In 1393 Timur took over the Il-Khanate. At its height the Il-Khanate included most of Iran, Iraq, Turkey, Turkmenistan, Georgia, Armenia, Azerbaijan, west Afghanistan, and south-west Pakistan.

The capital cities were Maragheh, 1256-1265; Tabriz, 1265-1306; Sultaniyeh, 1306-1335.

The summer palace at Takht-i Suleiman (c. 1275) and the Tomb of Uljaytu at Sultaniyya (early 14th century) are some of the outstanding structures.

Mongolian, Persian and Turkish were the main languages used.

Shah Namah

Firdausi (940-1020) was a Persian born in a village near Tus, in the province of Khorasan, in north-east Iran. He wrote the *Shah Namah* (Book of Kings) which he completed in 1010. This book has about 60,000 verses. It contains mythical, legendary and historical accounts of Iran up to the time of the Sasanid dynasty. It includes 62 stories, among which is the popular story of Sohrab and Rustam. This Persian epic became influential in many parts of the medieval world.

Nasir al din al Tusi (1201–1274)

Nasir was a great Iranian scholar, born in Tus, Iran. Tusi wrote on logic, mathematics, astronomy, biology, physics, theology and other subjects. About 150 of his works are known, written in Arabic and Persian. He lived at the time of the Mongol invasion, but was respected even by Hulagu. Nasir persuaded Hulagu to build an observatory near Maragheh, the capital of the Il-Khanate at that time.

Maragheh is known for its special and beautiful building stone, called Maragheh marble, that is formed in spring water. Maragheh is located in a valley below Mt Sahand. There are five tomb towers dating from the 12th to 14th centuries.

FATIMID CALIPHS

While the Umayyads and Abbasids were Sunnis, the Fatimids were Shiahs of the Ismaili sect. Their name came from Fatima, the daughter of the Prophet Muhammad. The Ismailis wanted to overthrow the Sunni caliphs and have their own.

In 909 their imam (leader) made himself a caliph and took the name al-Mahdi (the messiah, or one inspired by god). They made a base in Yemen and then conquered Sicily, northern Africa including Egypt, and the region of Mecca and Medina in Arabia. They wrote books on Ismaili beliefs and sent people to spread these ideas in different parts of the world, including Central Asia and India. Trade was developed through the Red Sea. A huge palace and great library were set up in Cairo.

The Fatimids began to decline in the 11th century.

In 1057-9, a general in Iraq, tried to assert the power of the Fatimid caliph in Mosul and Baghdad. This would have made the Fatimids supreme in the Islamic world, but he could not get enough support, and was defeated by a Seljuk Turk. At the same time the crusades began.

In Syria and Palestine they were attacked by Byzantines, Turks and crusaders. The Fatimid Caliphate ended in 1171.

38
West Asia: The Turks

The Seljuks were Turks from Central Asia, who gradually established an empire. They settled in Khwarizm around CE 950 and in Khurasan in Iran in the 11th century. Their name comes from Seljuk Beg, a soldier who was in the Khazar army. Tughril (Togrul) Beg and Chagri Beg were the grandsons of Seljuk. They fought against the Ghaznavid dynasty who ruled from Ghazni (present Afghanistan). After initial defeats they gained control of part of the territories of the Ghaznavids. In 1055 Tughril Beg captured Baghdad from the Buyid dynasty. Tughril was succeeded in 1063 by Alp Arslan, who was the son of his brother Chagri. The Seljuks led by Alp defeated the Byzantines in the battle of Manzikert in 1071. By the time of Malik Shah (1072-1092), the Seljuks controlled Iran, Iraq, Anatolia, and part of Afghanistan and Central Asia. Over this huge area there were a number of subordinate states under beys or begs.

Malik Shah made Isfahan in Iran his capital. It remained the capital till 1118. Until the Mongol invasion, it became a prosperous city, famous for its crafts, art and literature. The Persian language flourished. Islam began to spread through the

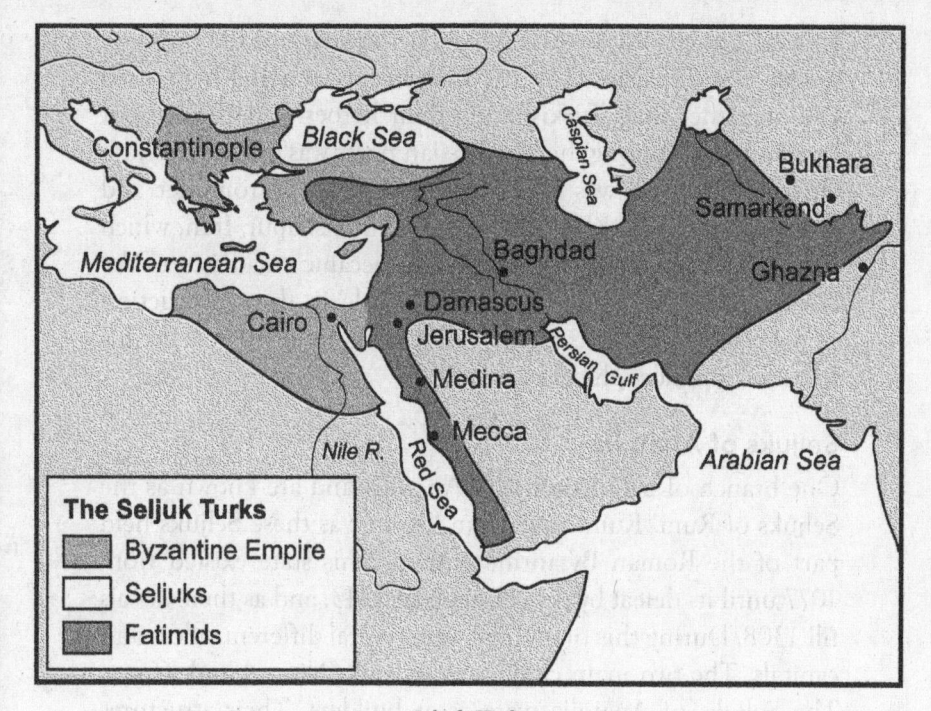

Seljuk Turks

regions under their control. After the death of Malik Shah his brother and four sons fought for control over the territories. Numerous begs too asserted their independence.

The Seljuks were involved in the First and Second Crusades. Ahmad Sanjar, Malik Shah's third son, ruled in Khorasan. In 1118 he gained control of other regions, with the death of his brother, Muhammad I. But by the time of Sanjar's death in 1156 (he ruled only till 1153), most of the former Seljuk territories were virtually independent. By 1194 Seljuk rule had ended except in part of Anatolia.

Three languages were used by the Seljuks—Arabic, Persian and Turkish. Arabic was for religion and law. Persian was the court language, also used for literature. The language of the ordinary people was Turkish. Even the Ghaznavids and Il Khans used Persian rather than Turkish, and their heroes were the ancient Persian kings. Among the best Persian poets was Omar Khayyam (1048-1123), who was also a mathematician, astronomer and philosopher. Omar Khayyam was born in Nishapur, Iran, which was at that time under the Seljuks. He became an advisor of the Seljuk sultan, Malik Shah. He had a role in the construction of an observatory at Isfahan. Today he is remembered for his *Rubaiyat*, a philosophical poem.

Seljuks of Anatolia

One branch of Seljuks ruled in Anatolia and are known as the Seljuks of Rum. Rum came from 'Rome', as these Seljuks held part of the Roman Byzantine empire. This state existed from 1077 until its defeat by the Mongols in 1243, and as their vassals till 1308. During this time there were several different rulers and capitals. The two main capitals were Iznik (Nicaea) and Konya. The Seljuks of Anatolia were great builders. Their structures were made mainly of dressed stone, with some brick. They constructed palaces, mosques, tombs and caravanserais (Hans). These last served as resting places along routes, for traders and merchants. The Sultan Han, built in 1229, located between Konya and Aksaray, is the largest, covering a huge area.

Rumi

The Sufi saint Rumi was born in 1207 in the province of Balkh, then part of Khorasan, but later lived with his father in Konya. His most famous work is his *Masnawi*, which consists of 26,660 couplets. This has stories interspersed with Sufi and mystical concepts. It is written in Persian. Rumi died in 1273 and is buried in Konya, and his grave is a centre of pilgrimage. Love, peace and tolerance are his message to the world.

He founded the Mawlawi (Mevlevi) Sufi order, known for their whirling dances through which ecstasy could be achieved. Rumi has had an influence on Sufi saints in all parts of the world.

THE MAMLUKS

In 1250, the Mamluks took over Egypt. In 1260, though Baghdad had earlier (1258) been taken by the Mongols, and the caliphate had ended, it was restored by the Mamluks, in Cairo. (For more details on the Mamluks see Chapter 45.)

A portrait of Rumi

OTTOMAN TURKS

As the Seljuks of Rum declined, several small states emerged. Among them were those ruled by Turks later known as the Osmanlis or Ottoman Turks. Osman is considered the founder of the Ottoman dynasty. A leader of the Turks, he began to organize them into a kingdom on the Black Sea coast around 1300. They had a strong military organization. Osman died in 1326, but the dynasty founded by him created a huge empire. It was at its height in the 16th century, but continued to exist till 1922. Osman's son, Orkhan, took the title of sultan. He created the janissaries, a new type of infantry. The declining Byzantine empire often asked him for help and he married a daughter of the Byzantine emperor. Soon after the time of Orkhan, Serbia and Bulgaria were defeated. A later crusade, known as the Crusade of Nicopolis sent against the Ottomans in 1396 was defeated. They then conquered Greece. In 1391 Constantinople was besieged for six years. The region of Anatolia, too, was made part of their kingdom.

There were also diplomatic relations with a number of states including those considered vassals. The Ottoman sultan Bayazid I tried to bring these under direct control. But Ottoman power was temporarily checked by the great warrior Timur. Bayazid was defeated by Timur in 1402. In Anatolia, the local chiefs were once again powerful.

Sultan Muhammad II

Sultan Muhammad II revived the empire and made several more conquests. His greatest achievement was the conquest of Constantinople in 1453. With this the Byzantine empire came to an end. The Ottomans were well known for their efficient army. They had two types of cavalry, that is horse-mounted soldiers, and the very disciplined infantry, the janissaries. They also had artillery, and engineers. There were special forces for different campaigns, and for guarding their fortresses.

Muhammad II launched a fierce attack on Constantinople. He had a force of 1,50,000. He also had a huge cannon which used gunpowder. A Hungarian engineer had built it, but this huge cannon needed 100 oxen to move it and could be fired only seven times a day. Muhammad II used infantry. He even had 70 ships transported across land to position them behind the Byzantine ships guarding the region.

The emperor Constantine XI died fighting. Muhammad occupied Constantinople and made it his capital. St Sophia was converted into a mosque. Serbia which had been invaded earlier, was finally conquered in 1459. It remained under the Turks for almost 350 years. Other conquests included Trebizond, followed by the Peloponnese (part of Greece), Bosnia and Herzegovina, Albania and the Ionian islands. The Khan of the Crimea became his vassal. In 1475 Kaffa, which was under Genoa, was conquered. With these conquests the Ottomans had gained control over the Black Sea. Venice was defeated in 1499–1502. Syria, Iraq, Algiers and Egypt and Belgrade, were added to the empire in the 16th century. Conquest continued up to the 18th century. The Ottomans created an empire as large as the earlier Roman empire or the Byzantine empire.

Though Muhammad had turned the Church of Sophia into a mosque the Ottomans were tolerant of all religions. Jews and Christians were free to practise their religions.

Constantinople remained a flourishing city. In 1600 it had a population of 7,00,000.

Muhammad also laid down new law codes for the people in the empire.

Muhammad came to be known as the 'Sovereign of two worlds and two seas'. The two worlds were Rumelia and Anatolia, and the two seas were the Mediterranean and the Black Sea.

Another later great ruler was Suleiman I.

Other achievements

In all parts of the vast Ottoman empire books were written in Turkish, Arabic, Persian and other languages. Mosques, tombs, palaces and other structures were built. There were different types of art and different crafts practised in the various parts of the empire. Carpets were woven with beautiful designs. Gold and silver were used to make special items.

An Ottoman carpet

39

China

CE 1000-1500

After the decline of the Tang dynasty, there was a period of conflict and turmoil in China. Between CE 907 and 960 when the Sung dynasty came to power, five dynasties ruled successively in north China, while in the south there were ten kingdoms, each ruling a small area.

The south remained relatively peaceful, while the north was involved in struggles and conflicts.

SUNG (OR SONG) DYNASTY

Zhao Kuangyin (Chao Kuang-yin), an army officer of the later Zhou dynasty, was persuaded by his fellow officers and troops to take control, and in 960 became the emperor Taizu, founding the Sung dynasty. Taizu ruled from 960-976, conquered the various dynasties and kingdoms, and unified China. The capital was at Bianjing (modern Kaifeng). The Sung had to fight against the Khitan Mongols of the Liao dynasty in the north-east and the Tanguts of the Western Xia dynasty in the north-west. In 1005 they made a peace treaty with the Liao.

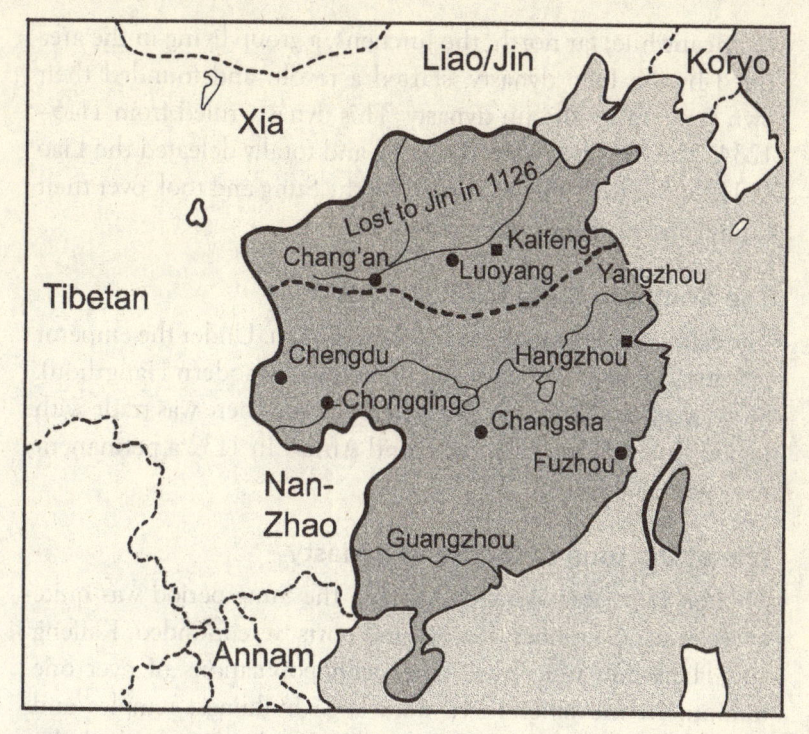

The territory of the Sung dynasty

From 1075, wars were fought with the Li dynasty of Vietnam, but peace was agreed to in 1082.

The civil service examination continued. Government officials were recruited through this. At the time of the emperor Shenzong, who ruled from 1067–1085, the structure was changed so that more people from different backgrounds could sit for the examination. These were part of the reforms introduced by the chancellor Wang Anshi, who also modified the system of education. Some people were opposed to his reforms, and there were two groups at the court.

Meanwhile, far north, the Jurchens, a group living in the area ruled by the Liao dynasty, started a revolt, and founded their own state under the Jin dynasty. This dynasty ruled from 1115-1234. The Jin allied with the Sung and totally defeated the Liao in 1125. But then the Jin turned on the Sung and took over their capital and northern territories.

The Southern Sung (CE 1127-1279)

The Sung dynasty moved to southern China. Under the emperor Gaozong, a new capital was set up at Linan (modern Hangzhou). Ships were built and new ports were set up. There was trade with Japan, Korea, West Asia, India and Africa. In 1132 a permanent navy was established.

Life at the time of the Sung dynasty

Though there was so much warfare, the Sung period was quite prosperous. A number of cities and ports were founded. Kaifeng and Hangzhou were huge cities with populations of over one million. In the cities there were large buildings, temples and pagodas. Wood, bamboo, stone and mortar, brick and glazed tiles were used in buildings. These were often decorated and painted.

Pagoda towers were built. Some of these were very tall. The Liaodi Pagoda at Heibei, built in 1055, reached a height of 84 m.

Royal pyramidal tombs were made and can be seen at Gongxian in Henan province and elsewhere. Avenues leading to the tombs had statues of officials, guardians, animals and various creatures.

The Sung government even had programmes for the poor. Free medical centres and homes for the old were set up. New methods were used in agriculture to increase food production. The postal service, first founded at the time of the Han dynasty, was expanded.

Canals were built and used for transport. Bridges were

constructed across rivers and ravines, some of them more than 1000 m long. Money consisted of copper coins and paper notes. China was the first country to use paper money.

Iron production increased. Textiles of silk and cotton were woven. Fine celadon wares and other types of pottery were made. Other crafts included fine lacquerware. Iron, swords, silks, textiles, velvet, porcelain and tea were among the items exported.

There were teahouses, restaurants, taverns and various clubs where people met. Plays were performed in theatres, and there were music performances and other forms of entertainment.

In art, delicate and beautiful landscape paintings were made. Ma Yuan and Xia Gui were two great court painters. Poetry and literature flourished. Weiqi (known in Japan as Go) and Xiangqi (a type of chess) were among the board games played.

Food

Food for the ordinary people mainly consisted of rice, pork and fish. The rich ate a variety of different items including birds such as pheasants, partridge and duck, as well as hare and deer, fruit and vegetables. Milk and its products were usually not eaten.

Books and printing

Books were written and printed, not merely copied by hand. While earlier woodblock printing existed, now in addition, printing with movable type was invented. Movable type meant that each letter was made separately and could be placed in different ways to form words and sentences. Ink was put on the letters and pressed on to paper. At this time movable type was made from pottery and later from metal.

Printing spread to Europe later. Right up to the time when computers were developed, most printing in the world was through movable type.

In China printing made books and learning available to more people. Men from higher and middle classes were educated, and many women too. Li Qingzhao (1084–1151) was a notable woman writer and poet. A huge number of books were written, including encyclopaedias and those on technical subjects. The *Zizhi Tongjian* was a history in 1000 volumes.

Other inventions

There were other new inventions, as well as developments in mathematics, geometry, science, and cartography (the science of making maps). The abacus was invented. Forensic science, including the method of performing autopsies and determining how a person died, was developed.

Coal began to be used as a fuel in the 11th century.

Military science was well developed. In war, fire rockets and gunpowder bombs were used. Books on war and weapons were written. The book *Wujing Zongyao* (1044) provided methods of

THE CLOCK TOWER OF KAIFENG

The first mechanical clock was made in China in the 8th century. Around 1050 Su Song constructed and described in a book, a 12-m-high astronomical clock tower located at Kaifeng. It was hydraulic powered and had a chain drive and rotating gear. There were 133 rotating mannequins that rang bells and played drums at certain times. Su Song also composed a celestial atlas, that is, an atlas of the stars.

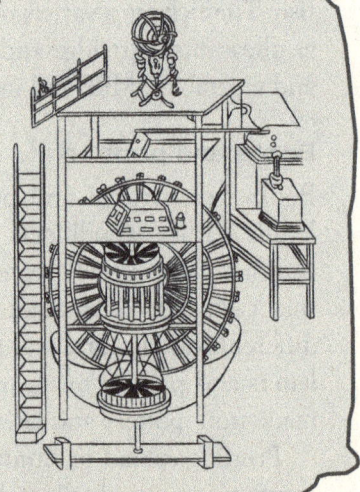

The clock tower of Kaifeng

making gunpowder bombs. Landmines, grenades and cannon were also known.

Religion

Daoism and Buddhism were among the main religions, but Buddhism showed some decline. Neo-Confucianism was a new type of philosophy, a combination of Confucian and Buddhist principles. Local deities and ancestors were worshipped.

YUAN DYNASTY

In Mongolia, the Mongols united under Genghis Khan and began invasions in the north. Later in 1229 at the time of Ogadai Khan, the Jin and Western Xia territories were conquered. Finally Kublai Khan defeated the Sung and founded the Yuan dynasty in China.

Kublai Khan (1215-1294) was the grandson of the great Mongol Genghis Khan. He first helped his brother to conquer part of China and even reached as far south as Tibet. In 1259-1260, after the death of Mangu, Kublai became the Great Khan. He gradually gained control over north China and in 1264 set up his capital at Khanbalik (present Beijing; it was also known as Dadu). Khanbalik was a well-planned city with 11 entrance gates. His summer capital was at Shangdu. By 1279 Kublai defeated the southern Sung dynasty and conquered the whole of China. He conquered Myanmar and Korea, but failed in his attempts to conquer Java and Japan. Kublai reorganized the administration in China.

Kublai Khan, A portrait: from a painting made in 1294, by Anige, a Nepalese artist and astronomer

Mongols were given the important positions. New roads were constructed across the country. Paper money continued to be made in China. Kublai became a Buddhist and Buddhism was made the state religion. Trade and communications improved and travel between Europe and China became easier. Christian missionaries and traders reached China from Europe.

Though there was a change in government, production of the traditional crafts continued. Some new techniques were used. Crafts included porcelain, bronze and copper items, and silk and other textiles. There were new types of literature and art.

After Kublai the Yuan dynasty began to decline. Mongol rule was resented by the Chinese who could not become high officials. There were heavy taxes and between 1330 and 1350 there were floods and famine. Revolts started all over China. The Mongol leaders too were fighting with one another.

The travels of Marco Polo

Marco Polo (1254-1324) was the son of a Venetian merchant, Nicolo. Nicolo and his brother Maffeo had travelled to Bukhara (in present Uzbekistan) and then proceeded on the Silk Route to China where they reached the court of Kublai Khan at Shangdu (Xanadu). They were welcomed by the emperor and encouraged to return. On their second trip, the young Marco Polo went with them. They reached Shangdu in 1275, and Marco Polo was employed by the emperor to visit distant lands as his agent. He travelled to many lands including Karakorum, Tibet, Myanmar and India. Possibly he visited Siberia, and for a few years was governor of a province in China. His father and uncle remained as military advisors to Kublai Khan. In 1292, the three left China as escorts of a Mongol princess, sent to the Persian khan. Finally, they reached Venice in 1295. But Marco Polo's adventures had not ended. War broke out between Venice and Genoa. Marco commanded a section of the Venetian navy, and was captured and imprisoned. In prison he narrated an account of his travels. These were written down and formed an exciting book. Returning to Venice in 1299, he married and lived peacefully till his death at the age of 70.

XANADU

The great poet Samuel Taylor Coleridge was inspired by Marco Polo's account. After a visionary dream he wrote the poem 'Kubla Khan', which began with the lines:

> In Xanadu did Kubla Khan
> A stately pleasure dome decree
> Where Alph the sacred river ran
> Through caverns measureless to man
> Down to a sunless sea.

THE MING DYNASTY (1368-1644)

Zhu Yuanzhang overthrew the last Yuan emperor and founded the Ming dynasty. In the 1360s Zhu gained power over the Yangzi valley. In 1368 he set up his capital at Yintiang (Nanjing). By 1371 he overthrew the last Yuan emperor and captured Khanbalik (Beijing). The government was again reorganized. Chinese officials were placed in charge of the government. There was a new system of justice. China was divided into 15 provinces, each under three main officials who took care of finance, justice and military affairs. The states of East Asia once again acknowledged the supremacy of China and paid them tribute. China became prosperous. The length of the Great Wall was increased to protect the country. The Grand Canal was repaired. Buildings were constructed in Yintiang and the population reached one million. It was at that time the largest city in the world. Soozhow

(Soochow) in southern China was another big city. Silk and cotton textiles were made here.

Mongolia continued to attack China but was defeated at the beginning of the 15th century. In 1421 the capital was moved to Beijing. Here new buildings including a palace complex and temple were built. Trade expanded. Zheng He (1371–1433) who was in charge of the Ming navy, made several journeys across the seas to ports in Southeast Asia for trade. He even reached India, Madagascar on the coast of Africa, and Jeddah in Saudi Arabia. Items exported included silk and cotton textiles, porcelain and other ceramics.

In 1644 the Ming dynasty ended and was replaced by the Qing. But a decline had begun by around 1450.

LITERATURE, ART AND CULTURE

Literature, art and culture flourished at the time of the Yuan and Ming dynasties.

Yuan dynasty

Chinese drama developed in the 13th century. It included dialogue and song. Both poetry and prose was written. Among the prose works, *Xiyouji* (Journey to the West) was a fictional account of the Chinese pilgrim Xuanzang's journey to India. It was written in the 14th century.

Chinese artists were still attached to the royal court. They mainly painted birds, flowers and landscapes in traditional styles. The four great artists of this time were Huang Gong-wang, Ni Zan, Wu Zhen and Wang Meng. Wang Meng (1310–1385) specialized in landscapes, trees and mountains. Among other artists Zhao Mengfu (1279–1368) made paintings of horses.

Calligraphy developed as an art form with several different styles.

New techniques were used to create decorated and coloured porcelain. Copper oxide was used to get a red colour.

Ground cobalt mixed with water was painted on unbaked porcelain. When baked it turned blue. Blue and white porcelain vases, bowls and other items were popular both in China and in other countries.

Ming dynasty

At the time of the Ming dynasty, a Royal Painting Academy was established. Great artists included Sen Zhou and Weng Zhengming (1470-1559). Dong Qichang (1555-1636) was a painter, art critic and scholar. He analysed Chinese painting dividing it into northern and southern styles. Ceramic production improved. Porcelain was now more decorative with enamel painting in different colours, including green, yellow, purple and pink. Copper objects, too had enamel decorations.

The Bodhisattva Manjushri in gilt brass. This Ming dynasty statue is 19.1 cm high and dates to the early 15th century.

Beautiful silk tapestry and textiles were woven. Special robes were designed to wear at court. These were decorated with dragons. The emperor's robes were distinctive. They were decorated with Dao symbols.

Lacquer items continued to be produced. They were painted with flowers, dragons, people, animals, and with

A porcelain cup with enamel glaze, of the Ming dynasty, dated between 1465 and 1487

PAO

Pao was the name of a robe worn by both men and women in China. It was worn from the time of the Han dynasty up to the end of the Ming dynasty. It had broad sleeves, and was wide and loose, reaching down to the ground. It was tied with a sash at the waist.

Different designs were used to indicate different ranks at court. In the Tang period the emperor wore a dark robe with 12 imperial symbols. Officials wore red robes with squares in which animals and birds were painted. The Japanese kimono developed from this.

various designs. Jade was used to make vases and small images of gods and goddesses. Bronze vessels recreated earlier styles.

KOREA

Within the present region of Korea, Koryo was the name of a new state established in CE 918 by Wang Kon. Wang Kon united the region, extending his territory up to the north. Here he came into conflict with the Liao dynasty of the Dongbei Khitans. They fought numerous wars but peace was maintained after 1022.

Koryo became a very prosperous kingdom. The government was based on the Chinese system of administration. Buddhism was the main religion. Literature, art and craft flourished. A beautiful type of pottery was made, a grey-green ware with a glaze.

Problems arose in the 12th century, as there was a struggle for power, along with a threat from the Jurchen dynasty in the north. In 1170 army officials gained power and began to control the king.

In 1231 there was a Mongol invasion and by 1259 Koryo was conquered. It remained under the Mongols till 1356, when the Mongols were defeated. By 1392 the Koryo state had declined.

The Choson or Yi dynasty was founded by Yi Songgye in 1392. It was based on a Neo-Confucian philosophy and influenced by China, but at the same time had its own distinct culture. The Korean alphabet known as Hangul was created in 1446 by King Sejong. The country was prosperous and peaceful up to around 1600, after which there were some problems. Even so the dynasty lasted till 1910.

40

Japan

CE 794–1500

There were new trends in Japan after CE 794.

HEIAN PERIOD: CE 794–1185

As we saw earlier, the Emperor Kanmu (ruled CE 781–806) shifted his capital twice. The second move was to Heian-kyo (later known as Kyoto). The time after the capital relocated to Heian-kyo in 794 is called the Heian period.

The emperors extended their territories over many islands, but the large northern island of Hokkaido remained under Ainu occupation.

Fujiwara control

Gradually the Fujiwara family, that had been founded by Nakatomi, began to rise in power. They were among the numerous nobles at the court. Many women of the Fujiwara family married the emperors, and thus Fujiwara control increased. The emperors lost their authority. As they were considered the heads of the Shinto religion, they had to perform Shinto rituals. If they did not perform these, it was believed that Japan would suffer from some misfortune.

The emperors used to retire or abdicate early, and leave a child on the throne. The Fujiwaras became regents for the child emperors.

In 858 Yoshifusa of the Fujiwara family began to influence the government. Fujiwara Mototsune, who controlled Japan from 884, was officially known as the kampaku or civil ruler. Fujiwara Michinaga was an important minister at the court.

Apart from the Fujiwara, other noble families, as well as some temples, began to govern large areas of land.

Fujiwara Michinaga (CE 966-1028)

Fujiwara Michinaga had five daughters. All of them married emperors, who ruled in name from 995 to 1028. Michinaga was a lively participant in social affairs at the court. He wrote a diary, *Mido kampaku ki*, which still exists.

Japanese culture

At this time Japanese culture began to develop in its own way, and Chinese influence decreased. The Chinese script was simplified to create a new script or system of writing for the Japanese language. Several new books were written,

Fujiwara Michinaga: from a drawing by Kikuchi Yosai (1781-1878)

including literature and poetry. The *Kokinshu* was a collection of poems, put together in CE 905. Murasaki Shikibu, a court lady, wrote *Tales of Genji*, a novel about life at court. Genji was a prince, who was fond his wife but he also had many other lovers. Fujiwara Michinaga was a friend of Murasaki. The character of Genji is thought to be based on him. Sei Shonagon, another court lady, wrote *The Pillow Book*. Paintings were made in new Japanese styles. Art was both religious and secular.

Kibi no Mabi (CE 693–775)

Many Japanese visited China.

Among them was Kibi-no-Mabi, in the 8th century. He spent 17 years in the Chinese capital of Changan. He studied Confucianism, the art of warfare, astronomy and folk arts. When he returned to Japan he lectured on Confucianism, and became an official at the Japanese court. From there, he brought to Japan a musical instrument, the biwa, which was a four string lute; he also brought with him the game of Go, and the art of embroidery.

> **THE GAME OF GO**
>
> Go (known in China as Weiqi) is a board game that originated in China. According to legend it was created by the Chinese emperor Yao (2337–2258 BCE), for his son Danzhu. It was to help Danzhu to learn concentration and discipline. There are other theories about its origin, but it was well known by the 4th century BCE. From China it spread to Korea and Japan. Go is played between two people with black and white stones on a board with 19x19 grid lines (originally there were 17 by 17 grids). It is known as Baduk in Korea. Go is a complex game that is now played in all parts of the world.

Cloister government: CE 1086–1156

Fujiwara Michinaga died in 1028 and Fujiwara control began to decline. The emperor Go-Sanjo came to power in 1068. But in 1086 he abdicated. A new system of government developed, called 'cloister government' (insei government).

Some retired emperors had joined Buddhist monasteries. They began to rule from there while the actual emperors still had no power.

Samurai

The noble families who controlled land developed their own armies to protect themselves. These were known as samurai. Among the samurai leaders were warriors who belonged to the Taira and Minamoto clans. The Taira were prominent in the south-west, the Minamoto in the east. Each of the two groups wanted to be the most powerful in Japan.

A painting of the Samurai Suenaga facing the Mongols, dated to c. CE 1293

YORITOMO

Meanwhile in 1156, and again in 1159–60, there were conflicts between the emperors and the Fujiwara family, who were still trying to remain in control. The Taira clan took advantage of this and gained power. But in 1185 the Taira were defeated by Minamoto Yoritomo. Yoritomo became the new leader.

Shogun

Shogun was a term that meant the supreme military commander. A shogun was appointed in 720 to bring the Ainu, living in Hokkaido, under the control of the government.

Yoritomo was given the title of shogun by the emperor in 1192. After this various shoguns ruled as military dictators till

1868. The Minamoto shoguns inherited the title till about 1300. They were followed by shoguns from the Ashikaga family, till about 1600.

Kamakura shoguns

Yoritomo set up his government at Kamakura. The time when the shoguns ruled from Kamakura has been called the Kamakura Shogunate. It lasted till 1333. The emperors continued to live at Kyoto. They had very little power. Yoritomo's centre of government was called the bakufu (tent government). Bakufu was originally the term for the house of the shogun. Yoritomo appointed his own officials to govern the provinces. He married Hojo Masako of the Hojo clan. She was an expert in kyudo and kendo, two martial arts.

THE HOJO SHIKKENS

Soon after Yoritomo died in 1203 the Hojo clan began to rule as regents (shikken) for the shogun. Now even the shoguns had little power, while the shikkens ruled. The Hojo continued to be the real rulers for more than a hundred years. They ruled from their bakufu at Kamakura. Their own officials became powerful. The Hojo and their officials formed new military clans, known as daimyo.

THE MONGOLS

The Mongols invaded Japan in 1274 and again in 1281. The daimyo supported and helped the Hojo rulers to defeat the Mongols. A typhoon at sea also led to the defeat of the Mongols, as it destroyed 200 of their ships. These great winds have been called Kamikaze, or divine winds.

MUROMACHI PERIOD: CE 1333-1573
Emperor Go Daigo (ruled 1333-1336)

In 1333 Emperor Go Daigo led a revolt against the Hojo. Go Daigo was helped by some of the daimyo. Among them was

Ashikaga Takauji, leader of the Ashikaga family. Go Daigo ruled from Kyoto. He briefly restored the emperor's power, but he could not retain his authority for long.

Ashikaga Takauji wanted to be shogun. The emperor refused to appoint him, and Ashikaga started a revolt. Go Daigo left Kyoto and went to Yoshino in the south. Ashikaga made Komyo the emperor in 1338. Komyo was forced to appoint Ashikaga as the shogun. Ashikaga set up his bakufu at Kyoto. As the government buildings were in the Muromachi district of Kyoto, this is known as the Muromachi period.

During the period 1338-1392 conflict continued between Daigo and the succeeding emperors at Yoshino, and the Ashikaga, with their line of emperors at Kyoto. Finally the Ashikaga won.

Onin war: CE 1467-1477

There were different groups in the Ashikaga family. The daimyo too were aiming to gain more power. Ashikaga Yoshimasa was the shogun from 1449-1474. He appointed his brother Yoshimi as his successor, but later he had a son. A succession war began in which daimyo groups supported the rival claimants. The Hosokawa daimyo and allies fought against the Yamana daimyo and allies.

Yoshimasa abdicated in 1474. He began building the Ginkakuji (silver pavilion) in Kyoto, as a place where he could live peacefully among beautiful gardens. After his death in 1490 it became a Zen Buddhist temple.

The daimyo armies kept fighting till 1477. Kyoto was ruined and the Ashikaga bakufu lost its power.

This is called the Onin war as 1467 was the first year of the Onin era, which lasted from 1467-1468. Japanese era names were based on the Chinese system and were introduced in Japan in 645. The names were given by court officials, based on some event that had taken place, and were changed frequently.

Sengoku (warring states)

The next stage in Japanese history is referred to as a period of warring states. New daimyo families arose. The Ashikaga shoguns lost their power, though they continued to be shoguns in name till 1573. Some of the daimyo ruled well in the provinces. There were new towns built around castles, new ports, and increased trade. Art and culture flourished. Sesshu was a great artist. Sogi was among the great poets.

Language

The modern Japanese language began to develop in the 12th century.

Houses and gardens

Japanese houses were usually simple structures, but from about the 11th century rich people began to build large houses surrounded by gardens. This type of house was called shinden-zukuri. The samurai had a different kind of house called shoin-zukuri.

Food

From the earliest days rice was the main food item in Japan. It was usually eaten boiled, called gohan or meshi, along with side dishes called okazu. Poorer people and peasants also ate millet. Pounded rice cakes called mochi were made from steamed glutinous rice. Meat was often banned by the emperors, because of the Buddhist concepts of non-violence. The emperor Temmu was the first to pass a decree or order in 675 against killing and eating of cattle, dogs, monkeys, horses and chickens. Other emperors of the 8th and 9th centuries passed similar orders, and killing and eating of all land animals were banned. Noodles were eaten from the 8th century, because of Chinese influence. They became popular from the 14th century. Milk and dairy products were hardly used, as in Korea and China.

Cattle were used mainly for drawing carts and ploughing. Spices were rarely used in food. Pepper and cloves began to be imported from the 8th century, and garlic was grown, but these were mainly for medicines.

Fish was eaten in different forms except by Buddhist monks. Eating thinly sliced raw fish with sauces was popular. Sushi too was made though initially this was used to preserve fish through fermentation. A variety of sea plants, as well as soya bean and the tofu made from it, were widely eaten.

Food was eaten with chopsticks in lacquered wooden bowls.

Clothes

The kimono was a type of clothing worn by both men and women in Japan. It was introduced during the 7th century, and was based on a long robe that was worn in China. The kimono is a long gown with wide sleeves and a V-neck. It folds over the chest, and is tied in place by a sash called the obi. In the 14th century a short-sleeved kimono was introduced, that was worn by women on top of other clothes. The kimono was worn mainly at court. Ordinary men usually wore jackets with trousers, and women jackets with skirts.

Elaborate robes with many layers were worn by the royal family at coronations and special functions. The outer robes had patterns and decorations. The empress wore a golden comb on her hair, and a gold-lacquered chrysanthemum. From the 12th century, baggy trousers with long

A portrait of an emperor in a kimono

jackets were the daily or ordinary wear of courtiers. These were also worn for hunting. The samurai had their own form of dress.

BUDDHISM IN JAPAN

In Buddhism, the Tendai, Shingon and other sects became prominent.

Kukai (774-835), founder of the Shingon Buddhist sect, is believed to have developed the syllabic script, known as Kana. He built a great Shingon monastery on Mt Koya, and wrote about 50 books on Shingon Buddhism. Shingon focuses on the cosmic Buddha Vairochana, and on the method of identifying with Vairochana. It also advocated Ryobu Shinto, Shinto with a dual aspect. This identified Vairochana with Amataresu.

Tendai Buddhism was founded by Saicho (767-822). Pure Land or Jodo Buddhism was another form, founded by Honen in 1175. It gained followers as it was a simple form of Buddhism. According to this all could attain salvation by worshipping and believing in Buddha Amida (Amitabha). Jodo-Shinshu (True Pure Land) was another branch founded by Shinran, successor of Honen.

At the end of the 12th century, Zen Buddhism was introduced in Japan, and soon became the religion of the samurai. According to Zen each person can attain enlightenment through meditation.

Nichiren Daishonen started the Lotus Hokke sect in 1253. There are many branches of this today.

Buddha Amida (Amitabha)

A huge bronze Buddha was erected at Kamakura in 1252. It is an image of Buddha Amitabha,

Statue of Amida Buddha at Kamakura

known as Amida in Japan. It is 11.4 m high and weighs 93 tonnes. It is known as the Kamakura Daibutsu. (Daibutsu is the Japanese term for great Buddha).

NOH THEATRE

Dance dramas used to take place at temples and shrines, depicting stories of the gods. Noh theatre, a special form of storytelling through dance, developed from this in the 14th century. The Japanese actor and playwright Zeami wrote about 50 plays. Noh plays were of different types. Some were on the kami, or gods, or on other supernatural beings. Others were about ordinary people, or about love, death and disaster. Special music developed for Noh theatre, known as yokyaku. This included songs and instrumental music.

A Noh actor: a painting of c.1820s by the artist Ashiyuki

THE TEA CEREMONY

Tea reached Japan from China. According to records, in 815, the emperor Saga drank a cup of specially prepared tea. Yeisei, a Japanese Buddhist monk, visited China and brought back a new method of preparing tea. Tea was initially associated with Zen Buddhism, but gradually became popular in teahouses. In the 14th to 16th centuries, it was again associated with Zen Buddhism, and an elaborate Tea Ceremony was devised, that is still in practice today.

IKEBANA

Ikebana, the art of flower arrangement, began when flowers were arranged as offerings to Buddhist deities. In the Kamakura period, samurai houses had a small sacred alcove called the tokonoma, where there were flowers, incense and candles. The first ikebana manuscript dates to 1486 and is called *Kao irai no Kadensho*.

41

Southeast Asia: Myanmar, Thailand, Laos, Cambodia, Vietnam

Southeast Asia is a region that can broadly be located between India and China, extending further south and southeast. Today the countries in this region, from west to east are Myanmar, Thailand, Laos, Cambodia, and Vietnam. To the east and south are the islands of the Philippines, Malaysia and Indonesia. Brunei, Singapore and Timor Leste are smaller countries in the region. There are other islands too.

Early kingdoms in the region did not follow modern boundaries. These developed later. Each country has its own history, yet at the same time the area has some common aspects. Its early history was influenced by India and China. Trade between India and China crossed the region. We will look at some aspects of Southeast Asia in this and the next chapter.

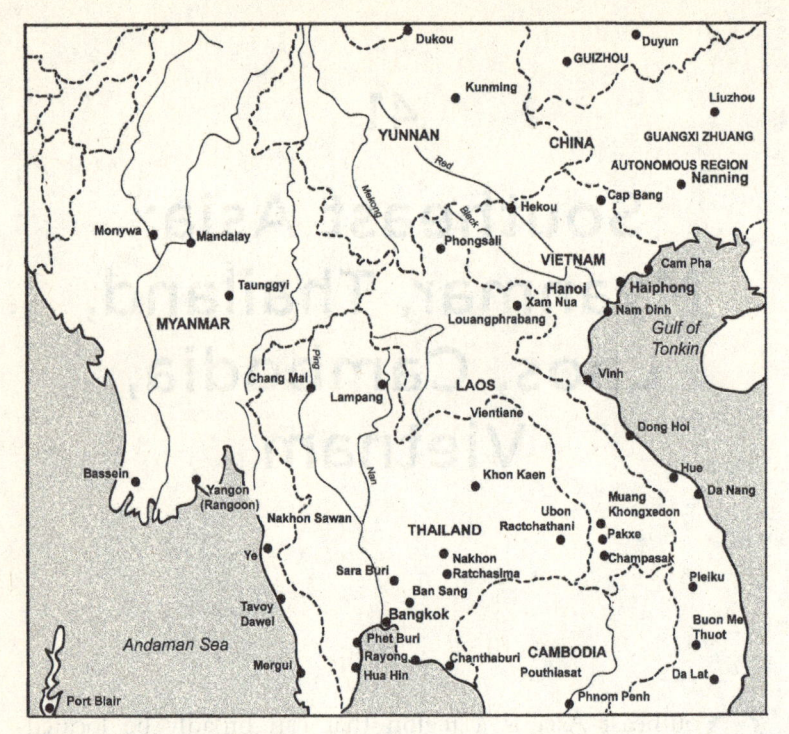

Map of the region: Myanmar, Thailand, Laos, Cambodia, Vietnam

MYANMAR

In Myanmar, crops were cultivated and animals domesticated as early as 10,000 BCE. This was known as the Anyathian culture. By 500 BCE some large villages had developed. Copper, bronze and iron were used. Rice was grown. Pigs and chickens were kept.

The Pyu culture

By the 2nd century BCE small city states had developed, and more emerged over the centuries. This was known as the Pyu culture, as it was established by the Pyu people, who came from the Chinese region of Yunan. Buddhism reached the Pyu states from India. The Pyu people already had their own language and script. The Pyu states continued to exist till the 9th century CE. According to Chinese records there were 18 states in the valley of the Irrawaddy river. The largest was Shri Kshetra.

The Mon people

In the 6th century CE, the Mon people entered Myanmar from Thailand. By the 9th century they established two small kingdoms, the kingdom of Pegu and of Thaton. The Mon were Buddhists.

King Anahwrata

The Mranma, also known as Burmans, horsemen from the north, entered the region in the 9th century CE. They came from the Nanzhao kingdom of Yunnan. They defeated the Pyu and established a small kingdom at Bagan (earlier called Pagan). Around CE 1050, King Anawhrata expanded the kingdom into an empire. It included areas around the Irrawaddy valley, which were united for the first time. Anawhrata built canals and irrigation channels, increasing food produce. He constructed forts along the eastern foothills to guard the empire. By the 12th to 13th centuries, Bagan expanded further and included most of the region of modern Myanmar. The Burmese language and culture replaced earlier languages. Buddhism was the main religion, and more than 10,000 Buddhist temples were built. Theravada Buddhism was the main form, though Mahayana and other religious cults existed. There was Vajrayana Buddhism too, as well as forms of Hinduism, and local cults, including Nat (spirit) worship. Tax-free lands were given to Buddhists. The empire had a good army. The city of Bagan had a population of around 2,00,000 people. There was trade with India and China. The Burmese language and script developed. Pali, the language of Theravada Buddhism, was used by Buddhist scholars.

But after this there was a decline, with invasions by different people including the Mongols. There were also internal rebellions.

Pagodas

There were two types of temples, pagodas or stupas and Gu temples. Pagodas were structures built around the relics of the Buddha. Gu temples were those with halls for worship and meditation.

Dhammayazika Pagoda

The Dhammayazika is a circular pagoda built in 1196 during the reign of King Narapatishtu. It is located at Pwasaw, east of Bagan. It is circular and has three terraces. These are decorated with terracotta tiles, depicting stories from the Jatakas.

Nats

Nats are local Burmese deities or spirits of various kinds, who continue to coexist with Buddhism. Nats include guardian deities and legendary or heroic people, as well as nature spirits. Nats who live in nature are believed to be invisible, and images

Nat images from Shwe Zigon pagoda near Bagan

of them are not made. Other Nat images are worshipped usually outside Buddhist temples. King Anawhrata made a list of 37 Nats for worship. The Shwe Zigon pagoda at Nyaung-yu has images of all 37 in the pagoda courtyard. Some of the images are new, but a large image of Sakka, chief of the Nats, can be dated to between the 9th and 13th centuries. The name Sakka comes from Shakra, a name of the god Indra. Indra was an important god in the ancient Indian texts known as the Vedas. The Shwe Zigon is still one of the most popular places of worship in Myanmar.

An eight-day week

A week is considered to have eight days in Myanmar. There are actually only seven, but Wednesday is divided into two. Each day is associated with an animal. Pagoda compounds usually have eight shrines, one for each day of the week. In each are a Buddha image and the animal of the day.

THAILAND

Thailand is between Myanmar on the west and Laos and Cambodia to the east. Malaysia is to the south. Around its main river, the Chao Phraya, is fertile agricultural land. In the north and west are mountain ranges. On the coasts are tropical forests and swamps. Early *Homo erectus* fossils have been found in Thailand in the Lampang province, dated to between 1 million and 5,00,000 years ago. By 3000 BCE rice cultivation began in the region. There are numerous sites in Thailand that can be dated between 1500 BCE and CE 500. Some of these in the north-east, around the Mun and Chi river valleys, have been excavated. Near the Mun river are mounds surrounded by ditches and ramparts.

The Thai people are believed to have migrated to the region from China around the 1st century BCE. There are other groups including the Lao people, who may have come here from Laos. In the 3rd century CE, after the collapse of the Chinese Han dynasty, the kingdom of Nanzhao was founded in Yunnan in China by Tai-speaking people. This came under the Mongol empire in the 13th century.

Funan and Chinese records state there were early trading settlements in the south. These extended into present Malaysia.

Sukhothai

Sukhothai was one of the kingdoms in Thailand. At first it was under the Khmer kingdom of Cambodia, but became independent in CE 1238, under King Sri Indratit. The kingdom expanded and reached a height during the time of King Ramkhamhaeng (ruled 1275-1298). At this time it reached present Laos in the east and the Malay Peninsula in the south. Sukhothai was a Theravada Buddhist kingdom, known for its Buddhist images and Buddhist art. Unique walking images of the Buddha were made here.

Ayutthaya

Among the other kingdoms in Thailand was Ayutthaya. Its capital city, too, was called Ayutthaya. The kingdom existed from c. CE 1350-1767 and was founded by Rama Tibodi, a local prince. It began to expand after 1400. Ayutthaya often attacked the Khmer kingdom of Cambodia. Because of this the site of Angkor there was abandoned in c. 1431. The older Thai kingdom of Sukhothai was taken over in 1438. Ayutthaya was influenced by Cambodian and Indian customs. Theravada Buddhism was the main religion. Ayutthaya was a rich and powerful kingdom. The remains of the old palace and temple complex can still be seen.

Wat phra Mahathat was a great temple site of Ayutthaya.

LAOS

Laos is a mountainous region. The Mekong is the main river here.

The early people of Laos, known as the Kha, came under the kingdom of Funan, and later of Chenla. Both these kingdoms were in present Cambodia and Vietnam. The region also came under the kingdoms of Thailand, and the later Cambodian kingdoms.

Lan Xang

The kingdom of Lan Xang was founded in Laos in CE 1354 by Fa Ngum. Lan Xang means 'million elephants'. This kingdom extended into Vietnam and Thailand and lasted till 1707.

CAMBODIA

Cambodia was occupied at an early date by the Mon-Khmer people.

Funan

Around the 1st century CE, the kingdom of Funan was formed. It was located in the Mekong delta, including part of Cambodia and south Vietnam. Funan was influenced by India. It is said that Kaundinya from India came here, married a local princess named Soma, and founded the kingdom. Another story in the Chinese *Book of Liang* says it was established by a person named Huntian, who came from a foreign land.

Funan's capital may have been at the present city of Angkor Borei or at a place called Vyadhapura, further to the east. Oc Eo was a port of the kingdom. Oc Eo and Angkor Borei were linked by canals. Trade between China and India took place through this port. Funan is described in Chinese records. It is said to have had a number of ports. The cities had brick walls. Precious items from different countries were found in its markets. Trade also crossed through the ports of the kingdom to Rome. Sanskrit, the language of India, was the court language. Hinduism and later Buddhism were the religions practised.

Chenla

Chenla was a small kingdom within Funan, a kingdom that existed from the 1st century CE. In the 6th century its power began to grow and gradually it conquered Funan. Chenla covered the region of north Cambodia and south Laos. In 706 it was divided into two parts, and later came under the Sri Vijaya empire of Sumatra.

Angkor

In Cambodia the Khmer dynasty ruled the kingdom of Angkor from CE 802-1432. Jayavarman II (ruled 802-850) was the founder of the dynasty. Jayavarman freed the region from the Sri Vijaya kingdom. King Suryavarman I (ruled c. 1004-c. 1050) expanded his territories into Thailand. Suryavarman II (ruled 1113-1150), sent expeditions into Thailand, Vietnam, and the kingdom of Champa. Champa managed to conquer the Khmer kingdom, but was defeated by 1171. The next Khmer king, Jayavarman VII (ruled 1181-c. 1219), restored the power of the kingdom. After him there was some decline. Finally Angkor was defeated by Ayutthaya in 1432. Though later the Khmer kingdom revived to some extent, it had lost its importance.

Religion

The Khmer kings traced their origin to India. Hinduism was the main religion in India. The Khmer kings had Indian names and they worshipped Hindu deities. The Devaraja cult was followed, in which the kings were identified with gods.

A number of Hindu temples were constructed here from the 9th to the 12th centuries CE. Among these were several temples to the god Shiva, including the Preah Ko (sacred bull) Shiva temple of the 9th century, the Bakong Shiva temple and the Lolei Shiva temple, also of the 9th century. The Baphuon Shiva temple was constructed in the middle of the 11th century. The greatest and best-known monument, however, is the temple of the Hindu god Vishnu at Angkor, known as Angkor Wat (Wat means temple). It was constructed by King Suryavarman II (ruled 1112-52).

Angkor Wat

This huge temple, built in south Indian style, covered an area of 210 hectares.

Buddhism was important from the late 12th century. Jayavarman VII was a follower of Mahayana Buddhism. He constructed a large Buddhist temple at Angkor. Angkor Wat became a Buddhist temple too. Theravada Buddhism became prominent in the 14th century. More Buddhist temples were built at this time.

Theatre in Thailand and Cambodia

The kingdoms of Thailand and Cambodia fought many wars, but their culture was similar. The dance drama known as Lakon Nai in Thailand was similar to Lakon Kbach Boran of Cambodia. Both these were at that time performed only by women. Khon, another dance drama of Thailand, was similar to Lakon Khol of Cambodia, and both these were enacted by men. Khon was based on the Ramayana, an Indian epic, which had a slightly different version in Thailand. Men wore masks and high crowns on their heads while performing Khon. The dance dramas were accompanied by music. Musical instruments included gongs, cymbals and drums.

Nang Yai in Thailand and Nang Shek in Cambodia, were shadow puppet dramas, somewhat similar to the Wayang Kulit of Malaysia and Indonesia.

VIETNAM

Vietnam is on the east of the Indochina peninsula. In the northwest it is connected with China. In the past it included three regions known as Tonkin, Annam and Cochin China. There were early farming communities in this area. According to traditional accounts, there was an ancient kingdom of Van Lang. One of its kings founded a small kingdom called Au Lac in the Song Hong (Red River) valley. In 221 BCE the Qin dynasty of China conquered the region. After the death of the Chinese emperor Shi Huangdi, the Qin dynasty soon declined. A Chinese commander, ruled a small state in south Vietnam called Nam Viet, or in Chinese, Nan Yue. The kingdom of Au Lac too became part of this.

But then in 111 BCE, at the time of the emperor Wudi of the Han dynasty, once again the region came under China.

The Vietnamese had their own language and culture. But now the Chinese language, Chinese art, and Chinese music came to the region. There were Chinese governors, and a Chinese type of administration.

Many people in Vietnam did not like this. They wanted their own culture and government.

The sisters revolt

The Trung sisters led a revolt in CE 39. They were two widows of rich families. Trung Trac became the ruler of an independent state till CE 43 when she was defeated by the Chinese.

Trieu Au

Trieu Au was a woman who led an army against the Chinese in the 3rd century. She had some success but was defeated in CE 248.

Trieu Au was a strong personality who declared: 'I will not resign myself to the lot of women, who bow their heads and become concubines. I wish to ride the tempest, tame the waves, kill the sharks. I have no desire to take abuse.'

There were many other rebellions. But the Chinese suppressed them. Then in CE 939 Ngo Quyen defeated the Chinese and created an independent state. After his death there were conflicts, but finally, the Ly dynasty was founded in 1010.

Ly dynasty: CE 1010-1225

The Ly dynasty continued with many of the Chinese traditions and systems. The examination system was the same. Confucian classics were studied. The elite followed Chinese fashions. But in rural areas, there were Vietnamese traditions and culture.

At the time of the Ly dynasty agriculture was important. Rice was the main crop. But there were also local crafts, markets and trade.

Tran dynasty: CE 1225-1400

The Ly dynasty was succeeded by the Tran dynasty. During this time, China under Kublai Khan attacked Vietnam but after many battles, China was defeated.

The Vietnamese state was a small one, including the Hong Song river valley and neighbouring hills. On the central coast was the kingdom of Champa.

Champa also had frequent conflicts with Vietnam. In the 15th century Vietnam captured the capital and finally took over Champa. Their forces then reached the Mekong delta where the Khmer kingdom (present Cambodia) was located.

This kingdom was in a state of decline, and by the 17th century Vietnam conquered the lower Mekong delta.

Meanwhile, in 1407 the Ming dynasty of China attacked Vietnam.

Le dynasty
In 1428 Le Loi led an army against the Chinese and defeated them. He started the Le dynasty of Vietnam and became its first emperor. The Le dynasty declined in the 16th century.

Portuguese
The Portuguese reached Vietnam in 1516.

Culture
Vietnamese culture was a mix of indigenous and Chinese elements.

Hat Boi
Hat Boi is a type of classical opera performed in Vietnam. It dates back to the 13th century and was influenced by Chinese opera.

Water puppets
A unique type of drama in Vietnam is through water puppets. These are wooden puppets, placed on floats in water. The attachments through which they are moved are below the water. The puppeteers too stand in water but are hidden behind a screen. The puppets therefore look as if they are moving by themselves.

FOOD
By the 15th century, food in this region was similar to what it is today. Some food items such as chillies and tomatoes only reached the region later, and were not used at this time. On the whole, though there were regional variations, food was a mix of Indian, Chinese and local influences. Curry, rice, pickled vegetables, noodles, tofu, soy sauce were among the main food items, along with various types of meat and fish. Fish sauce and fermented fish were made. Spices such as black pepper were used. Coconut milk was used in curries.

42

Southeast Asia: Philippines, Malaysia, Indonesia

The Malay Archipelago is a large group of islands. Though today they are divided among different countries, their history is closely linked. The archipelago countries include the Philippines, Indonesia, Papua New Guinea, Brunei and the states of Sarawak and Sabah which are part of Malaysia.

PHILIPPINES

The Philippines has 11 main islands and thousands of others. The main islands are Bohol, Cebu, Leyte, Luzon, Masbate, Mindanao, Mindoro, Negros, Palawan, Panay, and Samar. Some of the islands were occupied 2,50,000 years ago. Later, different types of people reached here. Before 10,000 BCE, they probably walked to the region, as the islands were then not under water. Later, more came from China, Vietnam, Malaysia and Indonesia. By around the 1st century BCE, textiles, glass and iron tools were made here. By the 5th century CE the mingling of different groups of people led to a new type of culture. Various items including coins were made.

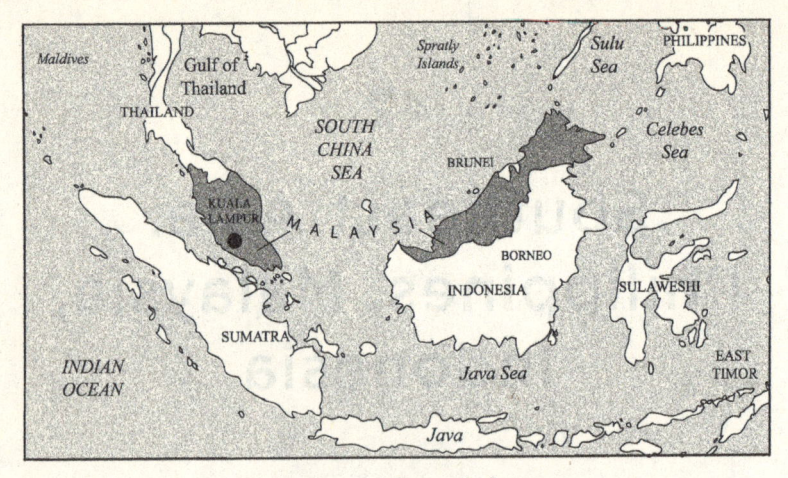

Philippines, Malaysia, Indonesia

In the 12th century the Philippines came under the influence of the Sri Vijaya kingdom of Sumatra (present Indonesia).

Islam reached the region in the 13th century.

The Ming dynasty of China had trade and other relations with the islands in the 15th century.

MALAYSIA

Malaysia is a federation of 13 states as well as other territories. Malaysia is in two parts, separated by 650 km of sea. Eleven states form the first part, located on the Malay Peninsula with Thailand to the north, while two states, Sabah and Sarawak are on the island of Borneo across the South China Sea.

Malaysia had a number of small kingdoms. These were influenced by India and China. At times, some came under the empires of Sumatra or Cambodia.

There were some Malay kingdoms that came under Funan. Among them were Langkasuka and Tambralinga. These even traded with Rome. Langkasuka is said to have been founded at Kedah, in the 1st or 2nd century CE, and much later moved to

Pattani. Its capital was described in Chinese records, as a city surrounded by walls and gates.

Langkasuka continued to exist till the 15th century, when it came under the kingdom of Pattani.

But it is not known where exactly Langkasuka was located. Chinese records indicate it was on the east coast of the Malay Peninsula, but Malay accounts place it on the west coast.

Malacca

The kingdom of Malacca was formed on the Malaysian mainland in CE 1400. Islam had reached the area through traders from India, and the king became a Muslim. Malacca was large and prosperous. It expanded its territories fighting against the neighbouring kingdoms of Johor and Achin. In the 15th century Europe imported spices from the Moluccas or Spice Islands. Malacca was a point on the trade route between the Moluccas and Europe.

In 1511 the Portuguese conquered the territory.

INDONESIA

Indonesia consists of thousands of islands. Out of these 6000 are inhabited. Sumatra and Java are among the main islands. Bali is another important island.

Java is known for finds of *Homo erectus*, early human beings, dating back to 5,00,000 BCE. It has Palaeolithic, Mesolithic and Neolithic settlements. Many different types of people came to the region. By 1000 BCE there was rice cultivation in the coastal areas. Bronze was used by 300 BCE. India began to influence the region from the 1st century CE. There was trade with India from around this time. Brahmanas (priestly caste) from India were invited to the courts of kings. Chinese trade started by the 3rd century CE. Cloves, tree resins and camphor were exported to China. In the 5th century, Faxian, a Buddhist pilgrim who travelled from China to India, said that ships regularly sailed between west Indonesia and China. But some local cultural aspects and art forms, including Wayang or shadow puppet theatre, the gamelin orchestra, and batik art on cloth, may have existed before this.

There were numerous Indonesian kingdoms.

Tarumanagara

Tarumanagara was a large kingdom with its centre near present Jakarta, which was influenced by Hinduism. It existed from around CE 350 to 669. In the time of King Purnavarman, who ruled 395–434, it controlled 48 smaller kingdoms. Inscriptions of Purnavarman and other kings have been found. Other kingdoms in the area had Buddhist influence.

Sri Vijaya

Sri Vijaya was the main kingdom on the south-east coast of Sumatra which existed from the 7th to the 12th centuries. It had trade relations with India and China. It is described in the works of Xuanzang, the Chinese Buddhist pilgrim of the 7th century, and is known from other Chinese sources and from inscriptions. Its capital was at Palembang. It became prosperous through the control of sea trade. It expanded into Java and the Malay Peninsula and even reached Cambodia and Thailand. However, its influence was mainly in the coastal areas. Buddhism was the main religion. The Old Malay language was used in Sri Vijaya, which spread through the region. Later Indonesian and Malaysian languages developed from it.

Java kingdoms

In Java, kingdoms rose and fell. The kingdoms of central and east Java were based on rice cultivation. They had Hindu and Buddhist temples that can still be seen. These date back to

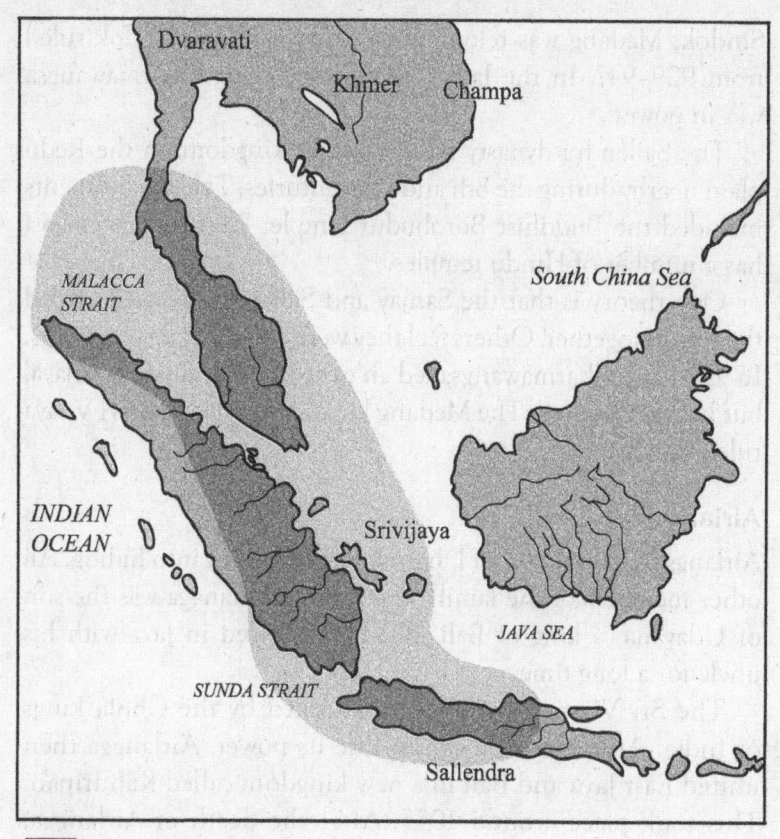

The territory of the Sri Vijaya kingdom

the 8th and 9th centuries. The Devaraja cult of god-kings was prominent in them. Inscriptions tell us about these kingdoms.

Sanjay and Sailendra dynasties
On the Dieng plateau, the kingdom of Medang, with its capital at Mataram in Central Java, existed under the Sanjay dynasty. King Sanjay reigned from CE 732–778. Later, at the time of King

Sindok, Medang was relocated in east Java. King Sindok ruled from 929-947. In the late 10th century, King Dharmawangsa was in power.

The Sailendra dynasty ruled another kingdom on the Kedu plain nearby during the 8th and 9th centuries. Their monuments included the Buddhist Borobudur temple. Prambanam in Java has a number of Hindu temples.

One theory is that the Sanjay and Sailendra dynasties ruled the region together. Others feel they were two separate kingdoms. In 990 King Dharmawangsa led an expedition against Sri Vijaya, but he was defeated. The Medang kingdom ended and Sri Vijaya ruled Java.

Airlangga

Airlangga, the nephew of Dharmawasanga, went into hiding. All other members of the family were killed. Airlangga was the son of Udayana, a king of Bali. But he had lived in Java with his uncle for a long time.

The Sri Vijaya kingdom was attacked by the Chola kings of India. After this it began to lose its power. Airlangga then united East Java and Bali in a new kingdom called Kahuripan. This took place around 1035. After the death of Airlangga, the kingdom declined. Airlangga is considered a great hero in Java, as he freed Java from the rule of Sumatra and created a strong kingdom.

Sunda, Kediri and Singosari

Other kingdoms in the region included the Sunda kingdom (669-1579) and the Kediri kingdom (1045-1221).

The Kingdom of Singosari was founded in Java by King Angrok, who ruled from 1222-27. At the time of King Kertanagara (ruled 1268-1292) Java ruled over some parts of Sumatra. Vijaya (ruled 1293-1309) was the next king after Kertanagara.

Majapahit

Vijaya, who was the son-in-law of Kertanagara, founded the kingdom of Majapahit. Majapahit was attacked by the Mongols, but managed to defend its lands. Majapahit reached its height at the time of King Hayam Wuruk (reigned 1350-1389). At this time it included most of Indonesia and part of Malaya. Gajah Mada, chief minister from 1331-1364, was mainly responsible for this expansion. Majapahit declined by 1520.

Sultanates

Arab and Indian traders had been in the region for a long time. Gold and timber products were exported from Sumatra and spices imported from India. Rice from Java was exchanged for spices from the Moluccas. Gradually Islam began to spread, and by the 13th century, some north Sumatran states were under its influence. Sultan Malik al Saleh ruled at Pasai at this time. The Pasai sultanate was conquered by the Portuguese in 1521. There were many other kingdoms in Java. Among them were Tuban and Gresik. These were influenced by Islam and had close relations with Malacca.

Relationships and routes changed in the region with the coming of the Portuguese in the early 16th century.

Temples

This region had many Buddhist and Hindu temples. One of the most significant is the Buddhist temple, also known as a stupa, at Borobudur.

Borobudur was constructed in Java in the 9th century by the rulers of the Sailendra dynasty. It is the most elaborate stupa ever built and has five terraces, with images of the five celestial Buddhas. On the first four terraces, are the Buddhas Akshobhya, Ratnasambhava, Amitabha and Amoghasiddhi in their respective directions, while the fifth terrace has only Vairochana, the Adi

The Temple of Pura Besakih on the slopes of Mt Agung in Bali probably dates back to the 14th century.

Buddha or first Buddha. All around the stupa are scenes from Shakyamuni's life, and from the Jatakas and Mahayana texts. From the base to the top, the stupa represents the journey to nirvana. The stupa remains an important centre of pilgrimage for Buddhists from all over the world.

> Bali has numerous Hindu temples where festivals take place throughout the year. The odalan or birthday festival of the deity is particularly important. Many of the temples date back to between the 11th and 13th centuries. The Gao Gajah cave shelter is Buddhist and belongs to an earlier period.

GAMES, THEATRE AND MUSIC
Sepak takraw

Sepak takraw is a game still played today. It originated in Southeast Asia. It was played in varied forms using a woven ball of cane. It was played in Malaysia from at least the 15th century. In this region it is known as Sepak raga. The ball has to be kept in the air by kicking or bouncing it with the head. In different forms the game was played in most of the countries in the region.

Wayang Kulit

Wayang kulit is a shadow puppet play, a form of theatre in Malaysia that dates back to early times.

It also existed in Indonesia. Stories were shown through the shadows of puppets, projected on a cloth screen. There were several other types of plays and dances. In one form in Bali, masks were used.

Gamelan orchestra

Gamelan was a type of music used in Bali, Java and elsewhere, both at religious festivals and on other occasions. An image of a gamelin orchestra can be seen in the Borobodur temple, and included gongs, bamboo flutes, drums and stringed instruments. Later there were different types of gamelin orchestras.

43

North America
CE 1000–1500

Across North America, settlements expanded and became numerous. There were many different cultures. Cities and towns had developed, and large structures were built in them. We will look at the main types of cultures in this region.

NORTHERN COASTS

On the northern coasts of Alaska and Canada, people lived mainly by fishing and hunting caribou. The Inuit people were prominent in Alaska, and around CE 1000 some Inuit groups migrated to Greenland and settled there. South of the northern coasts, across most of Canada, there were Native American groups speaking various Algonquin and Athabascan languages. Here too people lived mainly by fishing and hunting. Moose and caribou were the main animals hunted. From the northern coasts to about 300 km north of the present USA border, the region was too cold for agriculture.

NORTH-WEST PACIFIC COAST

The north-west Pacific coast had its own distinctive culture. This region extends from southern Alaska to northern California, a narrow strip of land with the ocean to the west and mountains to the east. Plants grew on the mountain slopes, including berries and tubers that could be used for food. Sheep, goats and elk from the mountains and fish from the sea were used for food. There were villages in the region with long wooden houses. In winter groups gathered together to watch plays based on stories of the gods. Feasts known as potlatches were organized, where gifts were exchanged. The people traded with other regions and made beautiful wooden carvings and other objects. Native American groups here included the Tlingit, Chinook and several others.

PLATEAU REGION

Other groups of people lived in the plateau area which included parts of Idaho, Oregon, Washington, Montana and an adjoining part of Canada. Fish from the rivers, camas (edible plants) and other naturally growing plants were eaten and dried for the winter. People mostly lived in villages, but there was at least one market town on the lower Columbia river.

MOUNTAIN SLOPES

In the mountain slopes and valleys of Utah, Nevada and California, people lived by hunting, fishing and catching birds. They also ate pine nuts and grains that grew wild, but in addition grew some crops. They lived in villages with thatched houses, and made various items, including baskets. They traded with other regions using shell as a form of money. The Paiute, Ute, Shoshone, Modoc, Yurok and Wintun were among the many Native American groups in the region.

PLAINS

In the North American plains there were grasslands extending from Canada to Mexico. Here herds of bison roamed. They formed the main food for people in this region. Initially the people in the plains were nomadic, but by CE 1000 many had settled in villages and towns along the rivers. Various crops were grown.

EASTERN WOODLANDS

The Eastern woodlands culture area includes the eastern United States and Canada, from Minnesota and Ontario up to North Carolina in the south and the Atlantic Ocean in the east. The early cultures here included the Adena and the Hopewell.

Around CE 1000 there was a Viking settlement in the region of Newfoundland, present Canada. This did not last long.

MISSISSIPPI CULTURE

The Mississippi culture existed in this region from around CE 1000-1500.

There was continuity with the earlier Woodland period. This culture had local variations. The general features were the construction of settlements with a plaza or open space in the centre. Around this there were raised earthen mounds with various structures including temples and large houses. Ordinary people lived in simple houses. The most important of these centres was at Cahokia in Illinois and Moundville in Alabama.

At its height, Cahokia had a population of at least 20,000 people. Cahokia had over a 100 mounds. On some of these wooden temples were built, and there may have been streets along them. The chiefs were buried in tombs, along with grave goods, and their families and servants. Among other burials were those of 50 women, all around the age of 21.

Most other settlements were small, with about 500 people. The settlements were surrounded by ditches and wooden fences.

The people of this culture grew maize, beans and squash, as well as other plants such as sunflower, chenopodium and smartweed. They domesticated turkeys. Pottery, tools and arrowheads of stone, as well as items of shell and copper, were made.

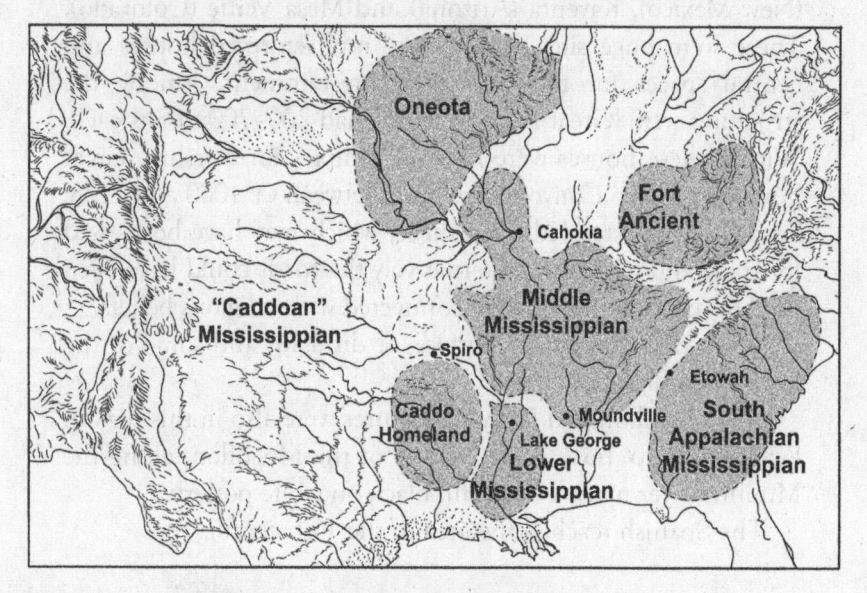

Mississippi culture

THE SOUTH-WEST

The South-west, also known as Oasisamerica includes the south-west states of Arizona, Utah, New Mexico, Colorado, Nevada and part of California in the USA. It extends into Mexico.

The Pueblos

The Early Pueblos were among those who lived in this region. Pueblo means village in Spanish and was a name given to them by Spanish explorers, because they lived in a particular type of village. The Navajos referred to them as the Anasazi. Pueblo settlements existed from c.CE 100. After c.CE 1050, the Pueblos were known for their stone and adobe structures built along cliffs. Adobe was a special kind of material. It was made of sand, clay, water, organic material and some other substances. Three main branches of the Pueblos were in Chaco Canyon (c. 900–1150) (New Mexico), Kayenta (Arizona) and Mesa Verde (Colorado). These were huge sites. There were multi-storeyed houses and central spaces for meetings and entertainment. Among the structures were 'Great Houses' which had 200–700 rooms each. Within these houses were kivas or temples for worship. Great houses at Chaco Canyon were built between CE 1000 and 1125. Several roads extended from these, which may have been used for trade and transport. Alternatively the roads could have been used for ceremonies, or were connected with religious beliefs.

After 1275 there were periods of drought, and some of the towns were abandoned.

The Mogollon and Patayan Cultures were also in this region, extending into Texas. One branch of the Mogollon, along the Mimbres river made a beautiful black on white pottery.

The Spanish reached the area in the 16th century.

Chaco Canyon houses

South-east

A different type of culture existed in the South-east, north of the Gulf of Mexico along the Atlantic coast extending towards the west to central Texas. Here there were extensive pine forests and herds of deer. Deer were hunted, and crops, particularly maize, were grown. There were towns, trade and crafts. The Cherokee, the Choctaw, the Chickasaw, the Creek, and the Seminole, were the main Native Americans here. The Spanish reached here in the 16th century.

CARIBBEAN ISLANDS

The Caribbean Islands consist of an archipelago which separates the Caribbean Sea from the Atlantic Ocean. They are located east of Central America and north of South America. American Indian groups settled in the region. Christopher Columbus reached the islands between 1492 and 1502. Their culture changed with the coming of the Europeans in the 16th century. The islands are in groups which form 27 territories. These territories are under different countries including Britain, France and USA. There are 13 independent nations (see Chapter 1 for the names). The largest independent nation is Cuba.

Each nation or island group has its own history and culture. The Ciboney were early inhabitants of Cuba, the Bahamas and Greater Antilles. They were replaced in Cuba by Guianas who, when Christopher reached there, called themselves Tainos, and now are known as Arawak. The Carib were the Native American group in Dominica at the time of Columbus. There were other groups in the different islands. The Tainos in Cuba lived by farming, fishing and hunting. They grew food crops such as cassava, yam, maize and beans. They also grew cotton which was woven into cloth. They made pottery, ropes, baskets and items of wood, stone, shell and coral. Strong boats were made and used for fishing. People lived in small family groups, while

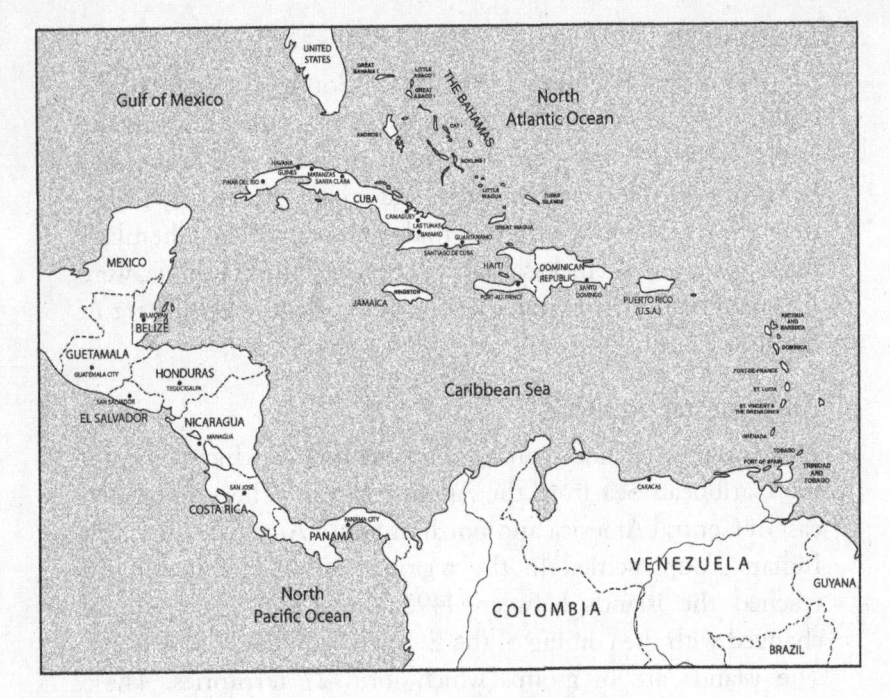

Map of Caribbean Islands

larger groups were headed by a chief. The way of life in the other islands was similar.

The island of Barbados had been abandoned when the British reached there. Archaeological excavations reveal early settlements.

Settlements in Antigua date to 2400 BCE.

Routes to Peru and Mexico passed through the islands.

44

South and Central America

CE 1000–1500

In Central America, the Zapotecs continued to occupy the Oaxaca valley in Mexico. Their main centre of Mt Alban reached its height between CE 600 and 900. The Zapotecs then declined and were followed by a people known as the Mixtecs.

THE MIXTECS

The Mixtecs had lived in southern Mexico from before 1500 BCE. They spoke numerous different Mixtec languages. Living on hillsides, valleys and coasts, they grew various crops including cacao, cotton, maize, beans and chillies. They made jewellery from gold and precious stones, decorated pottery and other items. They lived in a number of small kingdoms which at times fought with one another, and at other times made alliances. In the 11th century CE, the ruler of the Mixtec kingdom of Tilantongo united this with the kingdom of Tutupec. They occupied Mt Alban and neighbouring areas from the 12th century till the 16th century. A Mixtec tomb at Mt Alban, dated between CE 1400 and 1500

> **MIXTEC CODICES**
>
> Before the Spanish reached the region, the Mixtecs and other people made books that are called codices. A codex (plural, codices) is a folded book written on sheets of bark or deer skin. There are three Mixtec codices which tell us about their history and beliefs.

had a number of beautiful items in the grave. There was gold and silver jewellery, skulls inlaid with turquoise, carved jaguar bones, and fine pottery.

Mixtec cities had central plazas surrounded by houses and other buildings, pyramids, tombs and ball game courts. The Mixtec and Zapotecs were conquered by the later Aztecs.

MAYA

In Central America, the Maya civilization continued. The period after CE 900 until the Spanish conquest

A Mixtec image

A Mixtec king and warlord meets another: an illustration from an early codex

saw a decline of some cities and temples, and of written records. However, there were still flourishing Maya cities. Chichen Itza, Uxmal, Ednza, Coba, Mayapan, Iximche and Utatlan were among the important city centres at this time. After the decline of Chichen Itza and Uxmal, Mayapan was the most important. Different Maya groups ruled these cities. Among the groups were the Kaqchikel Maya and the Kiche Maya. The Spanish began to conquer the Maya city states from 1517 onwards. But it was not until 1697 that all the states were conquered.

Popul Vuh

Popul Vuh, a book about the Mayas, was composed by the Kiche Maya.

It includes an interesting story of twins whose names were Hunahpu and Xbalanque.

Once their father and uncle were playing a ball game. The sound of the ball bouncing and being hit reached Xibalba, the world below the ground. The lords of Xibalba were angry at the noise. They called the two, and using some trickery, they killed them. Hunahpu and Xbalanque planned to bring their father and uncle back. They started playing a ball game, making a big noise. Again the sound reached Xibalba and they were called there. But this time the twins managed to defeat the leaders of Xibalba. Later the twins became the gods of the sun and moon.

Chichen Itza

Chichen Itza, a Maya site, located near two natural cenotes (waterholes) was founded in around the 6th century CE, and continued to be occupied till 1540. Chichen was probably invaded around the 10th century, by a Maya group known as Itza, or by the Toltecs.

A step pyramid with the temple of Kukulcan referred to as El Castillo, in the centre of the Chichen Itza site

There are numerous structures here. In the central plaza was the Castillo (great pyramid), with a height of 30 m. A temple with a carving of a plumed serpent on the top of the pyramid represents the god Kukulcan, the same as Quetzalcoatl of the Toltecs and Aztecs.

Within the pyramid was a jade-studded red jaguar throne. Nearby, there is a ball court. It measures 166 by 68 m, the largest in the whole region. At one end is the Temple of the Jaguars.

Maya gods

Kukulcan, Chaac, a rain god, and a maize god were some deities worshipped.

CHOCOLATE

Chocolate and cocoa are made from the beans of the cacao tree. This tree, *Theobroma cacao* grows naturally in the Amazon region of South America. It was planted in Central America by about 2000 BCE. The people in this region, including the Olmecs, Zapotecs, Mixtecs, Maya, Aztecs and Toltecs, all made various types of drinks from the beans. These were used as medicines, and also in ceremonies and rituals. By the 15th century, a chocolate drink,

> sweetened or spiced, sometimes mixed with maize, was served at weddings and on other occasions.
>
> Hot chocolate?
>
> Some of you may like a drink of hot chocolate. But in those days there was a different type of hot chocolate. It was spiced with chilli peppers, and was therefore chilli-hot!

THE TOLTECS

The Toltecs were another people who reached Central Mexico from the north in around CE 900 or according to some theories, even earlier, around 750. They influenced the culture of the Maya cities and occupied some Maya centres. Maya decline could have been due to Toltec invasions, though other possibilities are natural disasters, drought, or overpopulation combined with the failure of crops.

The Toltecs were Nahuatl-speaking people. Their capital was at Tollan, usually identified with Tula. The Toltecs defeated and destroyed Teotihuacan which was already declining. The Toltecs were warriors. They had military orders known as the Coyote, the Jaguar and the Eagle. They are known mainly from the work of the later Aztecs, and accounts of them are often exaggerated and mythical. The Toltecs are said to have been skilled craftsmen, who invented all kinds of wonderful things, including the art of medicine. They were extremely wise, understood the movement of the heavens, and sang great songs. In some accounts, they are described as giants. Hence some historians doubt whether they existed at all and attribute the structures at Tula and elsewhere to mixed groups of people.

Tula has a number of buildings of this time. Among these are three pyramid temples. On the largest temple are huge standing figures, each with a height of 4.6 m.

Chichen Itza and Tula have some similarities. Some archaeologists feel Chichen Itza was a later Toltec capital, others that Chichen Itza influenced Tula.

> Based on these legendary accounts, in modern times the famous mystical writer Carlos Castaneda used the term Toltec to signify a sage or 'spiritual warrior'.

Gods

Mixcoatl, Tezcatlipoca and Quetzalcoatl were among their gods. The last two were also Aztec gods.

AZTECS

The Aztecs arrived in the Valley of Mexico in the 13th century CE.

The main Aztec group was also known as the Mexica, but the name Aztec is often applied to other groups in the region as well. Here we are using the term Aztec for the Mexica.

According to their stories, they came from Aztlan, the place of white reeds. One of their leaders had a dream or vision. In this he was told that they would one day come to a marshy land. There they would see a cactus plant growing out of a rock. On the cactus an eagle would be perched. In the mouth of the eagle would be a snake. If the Aztecs built a city there, it would become the centre of a great civilization.

When they reached the Mexico valley, there were many different kingdoms and city states in the region. In the marshland around Lake Tezcoco they saw the rock, cactus, eagle and snake.

Chinampas

In this marshy region they collected mud, mixed it with vegetation and made it into small islands known as chinampas.

Trees were planted to keep these stable, and crops were grown on this fertile land.

Cities, kings and conquests

In 1320 the Aztecs began to build their city of Tenochtitlan. It was located near Tezcoco Lake. Tenochtitlan soon grew into a large settlement. (This was the site of present Mexico City.) Pyramids, temples and other buildings were constructed here. Bridges and canals were built. There were huge markets. By about 1500, over 60,000 people visited the markets every day. Nearby another city was built, known as Tlatelulco. The Aztecs gradually expanded and created a large empire.

There were numerous Aztec kings. An early king was called Tenoch. Acamapichtli was the king of Tenochtitlan from 1372-1391. He was followed by Huitzilihuitzil (1392-1415). Huitzil made an alliance with the Tepanecs. In 1430, at the time of king Itzacoatl, the Mexica Aztecs joined with the Tepanecs of the city of Tlacopan and the Acolhua of the city of Texoco, forming a Triple Alliance. Together they conquered the city of Azcapotzalco. In 1486 when Ahuitzotl was the Mexica king, they conquered the Guarrero and Oaxaca people. The Mexica Aztecs now ruled a large area. All other states or kingdoms came under them and paid them tribute. Their territory was divided into 38 provinces.

Montezuma II (also known as Motecuhzuma) ruled from 1502-1520. Hernan Cortes, a Spanish soldier, reached the region in 1519. Montezuma welcomed him, but was taken hostage. According to a story, Montezuma thought Cortes was the god Quetzalcoatl, but this story, which was narrated by the Spanish, is now thought to have been invented. Montezuma did not realize just how dangerous the Spaniards were. Cuitahuac became the next Mexica king. Cortes gathered together other local people to fight against Cuitahuac, but this was not necessary. The Spanish had brought with them germs and diseases that had been so far unknown. A smallpox epidemic soon began, and Cuitahuac was among those who died. Cuauhtemoc (Guatemotzin) was the next king, but in 1521 he as well as Tenochtitlan was captured by the Spanish. The Aztec empire came to an end.

Food

The basic Aztec food, as for most others in the region, was maize. This was cooked in different ways. Maize was often made into tortillas, a type of flat bread. Beans, chillies and meat were eaten with it. Tomatoes, squash, avocadoes, and different types of fruit were also eaten. In addition they ate types of cactii and algae from lakes. They used chocolate and vanilla in drinks. Though meat and fish were eaten, they do not seem to have formed a major part of their diet. The kings and high officials ate rich food. According to Bernal Diaz, a Spaniard who wrote about the Aztecs, Montezuma was served with elaborate meals every day, with more than 30 types of dishes.

> **THE TURKEY**
>
> The turkey was domesticated in most of South and Central America, by the Aztecs and others. Turkey meat and eggs were eaten. Their feathers were used for decoration.

Language and writing

The Aztec language was known as Nahuatl. They maintained administrative documents in this language. The documents were written on barkcloth paper. This was made from the inner bark of fig or mulberry trees. Sometimes animal skins were used for writing.

Calendar

The Aztec calendar was similar to that of the Maya. One year had 18 months of 20 days each. Five more days were added to this to reach 365 days. Another calendar used for foretelling the future had 13 months of 20 days each.

Religion

The Aztecs had numerous ceremonies and sacrifices. They worshipped several gods.

Gods

Among the gods were:

Tezcatlipoca (the smoking mirror): god of the night and a jaguar god; he was invisible and had a mirror. In this he read people's thoughts, and saw the future.

Huitzilopochtli (humming bird of the south): sun god and most important god of the Aztecs. He gained strength through the hearts and blood of humans. He was also the god of war and sacrifice. He was the guide of the Aztecs during their migration, and led them to Tenochtitlan.

Coatlicue: earth goddess, mother of Huitzilopochtli

Coyolxauhqui: moon goddess, sister of Huitzil and conquered by him. Huitzil also conquered his 400 star brothers.

Mictlantecuhtli: ruler of lowest level of the underworld, usually in the form of a skeleton

Ehecatl: god of the wind, a form of Quetzalcoatl.

Tlaloc: the rain god; he was also the god of agriculture. The Olmec and Maya worshipped a similar god.

Chalchiuhtlicue: goddess of water

Centiotl: god of maize

Tonatiuh: a sun god and patron of warriors

Quetzalcoatl (the 'feathered serpent'): a very important and benevolent god. He was a creator and a patron of knowledge and learning.

Templo Mayor

This was a great temple constructed at Tenochtitlan. The main shrine was to the god Huitzil. This shrine was coloured red and decorated with skulls. A second shrine was dedicated to Tlaloc. This had blue bands on it representing water and rain. Here 10,000-50,000 people were sacrificed every year. Near the Templo Mayor was a temple of Tezcatlipoca.

THE FIVE SUNS

According to the Aztecs there were five periods of creation, each ending in disaster.

Period 1. The First Sun, called Four Jaguar. The main god was Tezcatlipoca. The world was full of giants, but at the end they were killed by jaguars.

Period 2. The Second Sun, Four Wind. The main god was Ehecatl. This world ended because of hurricanes. All the people living at this time became monkeys.

Period 3. The Third Sun, Four Rain. The main god was Tlaloc. Fiery rain ended this world. All the people living became dogs, turkeys and butterflies.

Period 4. The Fourth Sun, Four Water. Chalchiuhtlicue was the main goddess. Floods destroyed this world and all the people became fish.

Period 5. The Fifth sun, Four Movement, the present times. This world will be destroyed by earthquakes.

INCAS

The Incas lived in Peru. Their main city was Cuzco.

Origin

Their own accounts say that they came from Tiahuanaco which was located near Lake Titicaca. But they have other stories of a legendary origin. These stories say that Manco Capac was the first king. His father was the sun god Inti. Manco Capac lived in a cave along with his three brothers and ten other Inca groups. Inti told him to go out and build a city at a place where a golden staff could be pushed right into the ground. He went from place to place, and finally found the right spot at Cuzco. Here he founded the city of Cuzco around CE 1200.

Kings

There were many other kings. Their kings were known as Sapa Inca, or 'unique Inca'. In around 1390 Hatun Tapac became Sapa Inca, and called himself Viracocha, which was also the name of one of the main Inca gods.

In 1430, when Cuzco the capital city was invaded, Viracocha Inca handed over power to his son, who took the name Pachacuti. Pachacuti and his son Topa Inca (1471-93) further expanded the empire. In 1532 the Spaniard Francisco Pizarro invaded

An Incan fortress on a hilltop near Cuzco

the region and defeated the Incas. Inca power was destroyed. However, the Incas continued to rule a small area further north-west up to 1572.

Inca territory and language
Inca territory was along the Andes mountains and the Pacific coast. At its height the Inca empire covered a huge area of almost 1 million sq km and extended over a length of 4000 km. At least 100 different groups living in mountains, coasts and forests were included in the empire. The different groups accepted Inca supremacy and paid them tribute.

The Incas used a form of the Quechua language. Many different dialects of this language were used in the areas where they ruled, along with some other languages. In this language they and their empire were also called Tawantinsuyu (this means 'four parts together').

Important places
Among the important Inca sites were:
   Cuzco, the capital
   Pachacamac, in Peru
   Machhu Pichu in the Andes mountains. This had a large palace and other buildings, and was constructed at the time Pachacuti ruled.
   Llullaillaco, a burial site in Argentina
   Chan-Chan, earlier the capital of the Chimu kingdom
   Adobe bricks and shaped stones were used for construction.

Roads
The Incas constructed roads right across the empire. The main road had a length of 8500 km, and there were 30,000 km of smaller roads. These roads were used for trade and transport.

Agriculture and domestic animals

In different parts of the kingdom, maize, potatoes, quinoa, squash, tomatoes, beans, and cotton were the main crops grown. Alpacas, llamas and guinea pigs were the domesticated animals. Potatoes were frozen underground for future use.

Beer was brewed from maize.

> **GUINEA PIGS**
>
> Guinea pigs, which are small rodents, were first domesticated between 5000 and 3000 BCE. They were reared for food and also used in medicine and in rituals all over South America. They are still eaten in South America, and used in traditional medicine and religious ceremonies.

Items made

Cotton and wool textiles were made, as well as woollen tapestries. The wool of alpacas and llamas was used. The textiles had beautiful patterns. For the kings they were interwoven with gold thread. Feathers in different colours were used for decoration. Polychrome pottery, as well as items of wood, stone, shell, tin, copper, silver and gold were made.

Quipu was a term for dyed and knotted strings. These were probably used for counting or even for memorizing certain things. The Inca did not have a form of writing. Their history and myths were preserved in songs and stories, and also painted on wooden tablets.

Medicine

They had an advanced system of medicine and even performed skull surgeries.

Religion

Temples and shrines known as huacas were made. Huacas could also be natural structures like caves.

There were priests who conducted many ceremonies and rituals.

Viracocha was the main god. He made people from clay. Then he made the sun, moon and stars.

Inti was the sun god. He was also called Apu Panchau.

Mama Kilya was the moon goddess, the wife and sister of Inti.

Ilyapaa-aa was the god of thunder, or of the weather.

Mama Alipa was goddess of the harvest.

Chasca was goddess of the planet Venus, who protected young girls.

Supay was the god of death.

> **CORICANCHA TEMPLE**
> This was a huge temple built in Cuzco. Inti's images were on the walls and were covered in sheets of gold.

CHIMU

Among other kingdoms in Peru, was that of the Chimu, along the coast. Chimu culture probably flourished from around the 11th century CE to 1450. In 1465-70, they were conquered by the Inca under Pachacuti and his son. Chan Chan, their capital covered an area of about 36 sq km.

45

Africa
CE 1000–1500

EGYPT

The Ayyubid dynasty

Salah-ad-din had been a general of Nur-ad-din of Aleppo in present Syria. The Fatimids appealed to Nur-ad-din for help during the crusades, who sent an army headed by Salah-ad-din. Salah-ad-din was made the vazir (vizier) of the Fatimids. In CE 1171, he overthrew the Fatimid dynasty, founded the Ayyubid dynasty and ruled over Egypt. The Ayyubids had to protect the region from the European crusaders.

Salah-ad-din defeated the crusaders and regained Syria and Palestine. He was the most powerful ruler of the region at this time. His nephew Sultan al Kamil (ruled 1218–1238) prevented a crusade attack on Egypt. During the Ninth Crusade there was another attack in 1249. The

A portrait of Salah-ad-din, c. 1180

Mamluks, who were slave-soldiers under the Ayyubids, helped in their defeat. In 1250 the Mamluks defeated the Ayyubids and became the rulers of Egypt.

> Vazir or vizier was a high official like a prime minister.

Mamluks

The Mamluks ruled in Egypt from CE 1250-1517. There were two main dynasties known as the Bahri Mamluks (1250-1382) and the Burji Mamluks (1382-1517). The Bahris were Khipchak Turks in origin. Baybars I was a strong ruler, who defeated the Mongols in 1260. Mamluk control extended over Syria, Palestine and Arabia including the holy cities of Mecca and Medina. During the time of the Bahri Mamluks, the amirs or military commanders often took over the throne and made themselves sultans. Al-Nasir was the last great Bahri sultan, who died in 1341. The Black Death (plague) reached Egypt in 1348 and affected the land. Many people died.

The Burjis were of Circassian origin. During their rule there were numerous power struggles. Qaitbay (ruled 1468-96) is considered the greatest of the later sultans. In 1517, Egypt was conquered by the Ottoman Turks. Meanwhile the Portuguese were gaining control of the trade routes.

At the time of the Mamluks there was widespread trade. Cairo became an important and flourishing city. Beautiful items were made including carpets, textiles, metal and wood items, as well as gilded and enamelled

A vase of the Mamluk period

glasswork. A huge number of buildings were constructed, including houses, warehouses for storage, mosques, tombs and madrasas or Islamic schools, and monasteries of Sufi saints.

In 1260, though Baghdad had earlier (1258) been taken by the Mongols, and the caliphate ended, it was restored by the Mamluks, in Cairo.

THE ETHIOPIA REGION
Shewa

The mosque of the Mamluk sultan Hasan, CE 1356

Shewa, a historic kingdom of Central Ethiopia, lies on high plateau country, with the Blue Nile to the north-west and the Omo river to the south-west. It had a local kingdom from c. CE 950-1400.

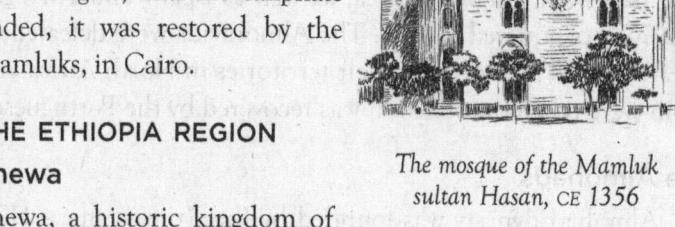

The Zagwe

Gudit, a queen, killed the emperor and conquered the declining Aksum state around CE 960. Not much is known about her, but she is said to have ruled for 40 years. She destroyed Christian churches and monasteries. Her descendants ruled till 1137. A new dynasty, the Zagwe, then began to rule the region of the Aksum state. They were in power till 1270. The Zagwe were Christians. Their capital, Adefa, was later named Lalibela, after one of their greatest kings. Lalibela (ruled c. 1185-1225) had 11 rock-cut churches built in his capital. These can still be seen.

The Amhara

The Amhara began to rule Ethiopia from CE 1270. Amhara princes, like the early Aksum kings, claimed descent from

Solomon and Sheba. Up to 1974, most of the Ethiopian emperors were Amhara.

SOME OTHER KINGDOMS
The Almoravids

The Almoravid dynasty was founded by Yahya ibn Ibrahim and his religious teacher Abdullah bin Yasin. It became powerful in CE 1040 in the Sahara region. From this base it conquered a large part of north-west Africa, as well as Spain and Portugal. In 1076 it conquered Ghana. The Almoravids were defeated by the Almohads in 1147, and their territories in North Africa and Spain were taken over. Lisbon was recovered by the Portuguese.

The Almohads

The Almohad dynasty was founded by Ibn Tumart in CE 1121. They began their conquest under the succeeding ruler Abd-al Mumin al Kumi. They extended their territories over North Africa and Spain, after defeating the Almoravids. However, they lost power by 1267. The Almohads constructed mosques and other buildings.

> **MARRAKESH**
>
> Marrakesh, in present Morocco, was the capital of the Almoravid dynasty. It was founded in 1062. Its importance continued in the time of the Almohads. It was one of the largest cities of Africa. Poets and scholars gathered there at the time of Yaqub al Mansur, the third Almohad sultan.

Marinids

The Marinid dynasty succeeded the Almohads. They were Berbers, like the preceding two dynasties. They first ruled in Morocco in c. 1217 and later expanded their territories. Sultan

Abu Yusuf was the first king. He was originally from Ifriqiya. Fez al-Jadid (New Fez) was constructed as the capital city, and unified with old Fez through fortifications. Fez had been the capital of the earlier Idrisids. The Almohad mosques at Taza and Tlemecen were enlarged and new mosques built. The mosques had tall minarets and were decorated with carved wood, tiles and stones. They built a number of madrasas to propagate Sunni teachings. These were elaborately decorated.

The al-Attarine madrasa at Fez has a rectangular courtyard opening into a square prayer hall. There are glazed tiles, stucco ornamentation, carved and painted wooden arches and marble columns.

The Marinids declined by 1465.

Hafsids

The Hafsid dynasty was founded by an Almohad governor Abu Zakariyya Yahya in about CE 1229. The dynasty ruled in Ifriqiya till around 1500. They were another Berber dynasty. They had conflicts with the Marinids. Tunis was the capital.

Zayyanids

The Zayyanids, a Berber dynasty, initially vassals of the Almohads, governed western Algeria from CE 1236-1554. They ruled independently from 1269.

Another group of Berbers, the Abd al Wadid dynasty, controlled part of the region from the 1230s.

Wattasids

The Wattasids, who had been ministers of the Marinids, ruled in northern Morocco from 1465.

Bornu

Among the kingdoms in the Sudan region, was that of Bornu which existed from the 8th to the 17th centuries. It was powerful in the 16th century.

Islam

There were numerous Islamic dynasties. Initially Islam was a religion confined to the ruling classes and urban centres, but from the 15th century it began to spread to the ordinary people. Islamic dynasties declined for a while, but later revived in the 18th century.

Sufis

Dhul-Nun al-Misri, born in Upper Egypt near Sudan, is regarded as the founder of Sufism. Sufis are still prominent in southern Egypt and Sudan.

Soso

We saw earlier that the kingdom of Ghana, also known as Wagadou or Aoukar, was located in north-west Africa, south of the Sahara. In the late 11th century, it was conquered by the Almoravids. South of Ghana was the kingdom of Soso, also ruled by Soninke people. In the 12th century Soso occupied the region of Ghana and of Malinke. Soso was conquered by Mali in 1240.

Mali

According to traditional accounts, there were 12 brothers who were heirs to the throne of Kangaba, a state on the upper Niger river. All except Sundiata, a weakling, were murdered by Sumanguru, the ruler of a neighbouring state. But Sundiata organized an army, defeated Sumanguru in c. 1235 and began to expand his kingdom, founding the Mali empire. The region of the Niger and Senegal rivers formed the core area of the empire. The kingdom of Soso was conquered around CE 1240. Sundiata became a Muslim, and all future kings were Muslims. Mansa Musa (c.1307–32) was the greatest king. He made a pilgrimage to Mecca, and carried a huge amount of gold with him to give as gifts and in charity. He conquered Timbuktu and Gao. Trade through these cities crossed west Africa. Timbuktu was also a centre of learning and culture. Mali, Kirina and Jenne were other major cities. Mali sent ambassadors to the states of northern Africa, including Egypt and Morocco. Egyptian scholars came to the kingdom. But by 1400, the decline and break-up of the empire started, and by 1550, it was complete. Gold and trade contributed to the economy of this rich kingdom.

Songhe empire

The Songhe state was located near the river Niger, with its capital at Gao. It existed from before the 9th century CE, but Gao and other parts of the state had been conquered by Mali. The Songhe kingdom became their vassals. As Mali declined Songhe grew in power. King Sonni Ali (1462-92), otherwise known as Sunni Ali, took over part of the Mali empire. Gao once again became the capital. Timbuktu, Jenne and Gao, became part of the Songhe kingdom. Askia Muhammad (1493-1528) expanded the empire. He made a pilgrimage to Mecca, distributing gold there. Morocco attacked the Songhe kingdom and took over Gao, its capital in 1591. After this a number of small kingdoms emerged in western Sudan, which often fought against one other.

Engaruka

In the east there were several local cultures. Among them were the Engaruka, who flourished in c.CE 1400. They lived in the northern region of Tanzania, near the river Engaruka. They grew millet and corn on terraced hillsides, and lived in circular houses made of wood, mud and thatch. Stone walls were constructed around groups of houses. Canals were dug to irrigate their fields.

Coastal cities

Along the coast of east Africa, extending from the present regions of Somalia in the north to Tanzania in the south, were a number of towns and cities. Among these were Kilwa, Malindi, Sofala, Mogadishu and Mombasa. These trading centres included islands and inland cities, that were prosperous between around CE 900 and 1500. Goods from the interior of Africa reached these cities for export, and ships from across the oceans brought items from West Asia, India and China. Many of these cities were under the overall control of the Kilwa sultan, but retained considerable independence. With numerous Arab settlers here, the Swahili language developed as a mixture of Arabic and Bantu. Bantu was the local language.

The Hausa

In Nigeria there were a number of city states of the Hausa people. According to legendary stories Bayajidda, a prince of Baghdad, came to Daura, located north of Kano in Nigeria, after a fight with his father. At Daura, a huge snake kept the inhabitants in terror. Bayajidda killed it. In gratitude, the king married his daughter to Bayajidda. There were seven main states which were said to be founded by their sons. Additional states were founded by sons from a concubine of Bayajidda.

There are other theories of the origin of the Hausa people. It is thought they may have migrated from the area around Lake Chad, or from Ethiopia, or may have had some connection with early Egypt.

Among the oldest states were Daura, Gobir and Rano. These states were formed from existing villages around CE 1000. Other states included Katsina, Zazzau, Kano and Biram. Beautiful textiles, as well as glass and metal items were made in these states. Traders and merchants from different regions were among those who lived in the cities. Ivory, gold, textiles, leather and salt were some of the items of trade.

Yoruba

In south-west Nigeria, the Yoruba culture flourished with its centre at Ife. Ife was important between the 12th and 15th centuries. It continued to be occupied later, but the main centre then shifted to Oyo. Remains from Ife include bronze and terracotta figures. The Yoruba are also known for woodcarving, textile designs, and sacred theatre, combining songs, music and dancing.

Yoruba gods

Among the Yoruba gods are:

Olorun: the creator and sky god
Orunmila: the eldest son of Olorun
Obatala: creator of land and of people
Olokun: god of the sea and waters
Shango: god of thunder and lightning
Ifa: god of healing and prophecy
Eshu: a messenger god; he is a mischievous deity who brings trouble and has to be pacified.

A YORUBA STORY

Once the whole world was covered in water. Obatala thought of creating land there. For this, he got permission from the god Olorun; then Orunmila, who had a lot of knowledge, told him how to do this. He was to get a long gold chain, long enough to reach the water from the sky above. Then he was to take a snail shell filled with sand, a white hen, and a black cat, put them in a bag, and carry them with him when he climbed down the chain.

It was a real problem to make that chain. All the gods and the goldsmiths gave him gold. Finally the chain was made. Obatala climbed down. He threw the sand out of the shell, and then the white hen came out and scratched it, scattering sand. In this way land was created. Obatala lived happily on the land along with his companion, the black cat. He loved the cat, but he thought he needed more company and so he made some people out of clay. Olorun breathed life into them. Thus the Yoruba people were created.

46

Southern Africa

CE 1000–1500

A new kingdom arose in the 14th century, around CE 1395 with its capital at Mbanza Kongo. Located between the Congo, Loge and Kwango rivers, the kingdom occupied the region of modern Angola. Banana, millet and sorghum were grown. The kingdom had rich iron ore resources and controlled trade in copper, from mines across the Zaire river. The Portuguese reached here in the 1480s and converted the rulers to Christianity.

Thulamela

Thulamela is located in the present Kruger Park in South Africa. Here a rich city surrounded by walls flourished from CE 1200–1600. People specialized in making gold items, including gold jewellery, gold beads and gold thread. They also made bronze jewellery, ivory bracelets and iron objects. Thulamela traded the items it made for goods from distant lands. Glass beads from India and porcelain from China have been discovered at the site. Cloth, too, was imported.

Mapungubwe

Mapungubwe, located on a hilltop in southern Africa near the Limpopo river, was one of the many places occupied in the region. People lived here from around CE 1000. Mapungubwe is thought to have been the capital of a large kingdom. It lasted till around the 14th century. There were similar settlements in eastern Botswana.

At the bottom of the hill was a court, and on the hill a graveyard. Here, people were buried in a seated position, and must have been members of the royal family. In the graves were items of gold and copper, glass beads and other items. There was a small rhinoceros of gold foil, wrapped around wood. A golden sceptre and a golden bowl have also been found. The rhino symbolizes leadership for the Shona people, who are among those who live in the region today.

A gold rhino from a burial site at Mapungubwe

Floods made the land fertile, and in the neighbouring villages millet, sorghum and cotton were grown. Cattle, sheep, goats and dogs were domesticated.

Objects were made of iron, copper, gold, ivory, wood, ostrich shells as well as snail and mussel shells, and of bone. Pottery and textiles were made. Between 1200 and 1300 it was the main centre for trade in south Africa. There was trade with China and India. Chinese ceramics have been found here.

Mapungubwe probably had a population of around 5000. Around CE 1300, as the climate changed and became drier, there were migrations out of the area. As Mapungubwe began to decline, Great Zimbabwe rose in importance.

Great Zimbabwe

Great Zimbabwe is located on the Zimbabwe plateau in south central Africa, between the Zambezi and Limpopo rivers. It was once the centre of a great civilization. The Bantu-speaking ancestors of the Shona people of the region had settled in the region around the 4th century CE. In the 9th century they began to extract gold from mines and to trade with other areas. By around CE 1100 structures were built on a hill and in the valley below. On the hill there was a ritual enclosure and an area for smelting and keeping iron. In the valley was the Imba Huru, the great enclosure where the king lived. Settlements were surrounded by thick stone walls. These were built with granite blocks, fitted together without mortar. The stone walls surrounded huts of daga, mud and thatch, which were located adjacent to each other around courtyards. In some courtyards, seats were built. There was trade in gold and copper. Iron, tin, cattle and cowry shells were also traded. Among the imported items found here were a coin from Kilwa in Tanzania, glass items from Syria, and ceramics from China and Persia. Birds were carved from soapstone and erected on columns, representing the spirits of departed rulers. Great Zimbabwe covered an area of 1800 acres. It is estimated that about 18,000 people lived here.

The Great Zimbabwe site: the conical tower can be seen

Remains of other centres, built in the same style, have been found in the region. After CE 1500 Great Zimbabwe declined. The people moved north and founded other kingdoms.

Portuguese

African trade was prosperous. In the late 15th century the Portuguese discovered the sea route around Africa and in the 16th century established trade centres on the east coast. Henry the Navigator, prince of Portugal, organized numerous voyages of exploration from 1434 onwards. In 1497-98, Vasco da Gama followed the route around the Cape of Good Hope and reached India. The Portuguese then established trading settlements. El Mina, founded on the west coast in 1482, was one of the most important. There were also Portuguese settlements in East and Central Africa. Portuguese occupation increased in the 16th century.

One of the eight soapstone bird sculptures found at Great Zimbabwe

---

LANGUAGES

Today more than 2000 languages are spoken in Africa, which belong to four different language families or groups. Most of these, except for the European languages, were in Africa at this time.

The main language groups excluding European, Arabic and Malagasy are:

Niger-Congo: 1436 languages; among these are 500 Bantu languages.
Afro-Asiatic: 371 languages
Nilo-Saharan: 196 Languages

47

Australia and New Zealand: Up to CE 1500

Long ago Tasmania and New Guinea were connected to the mainland of Australia. The whole early region has been given the name Sahul. Nearby was another large land area that has been called Sunda. Sunda is now the region of Southeast Asia. At that time the sea level was about 150 m lower. The Sahul and Sunda continental shelves, the land sloping down into the oceans, were once partly above water. Today there are Pacific and Indonesian islands on these shelves. People in those early days could walk across land and reach these islands. But they could not easily cross between Sunda and Sahil, as there was a deep channel between the two. This deep channel has been called Wallacea.

Early occupation of Australia

The early history of Australia is known from archaeology and art, and from stories and legends. There was no written language, but there are cultural records found in their rock art. The art shows plants and animals, including animals that were extinct 20,000–40,000 years ago.

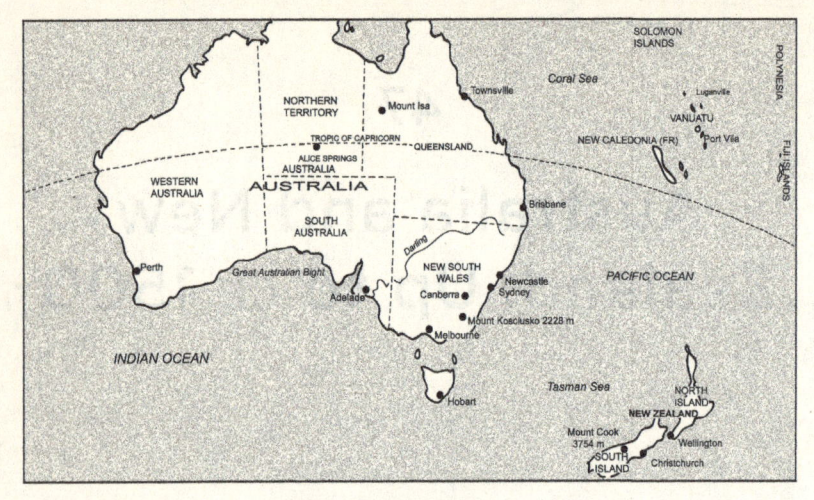

Australia and New Zealand

How did the early people reach here? As sea levels were lower, people could have walked across what are now islands on the Sunda Shelf, or perhaps made some short sea crossings. Then they had to cross the Wallacea channel by sea. They may have come from the Indonesian islands. One theory is that the early people were blown here by tsunamis, but this is unlikely. The first settlers seem to have been *Homo sapiens* who must have arrived here from Africa.

Estimates of when people reached here are constantly changing. There are even theories that there was a separate line of evolution in Australia, but as no primate fossils have been found here, there is no possibility of this.

At present there are different versions of when people first came here.

Some theories are based on DNA studies. These suggest that modern humans, *Homo sapiens sapiens* travelled from Africa to the Middle East 1,20,000 years ago, then into Asia and on to Australia at least 60,000 years ago. Other DNA studies relate the people of Australia and New Guinea, to those who left Africa 70,000–50,000 years ago. They either came here directly from Africa or via Asia.

Stone tools found at Rottnest Island may date to 70,000 years ago. In south-east Australia there were a number of fires around 1,20,000 years ago. Were these the result of people being there? Some think so, but it is not clear.

Australian archaeologists such as Richard Fullager, state that ochre samples from the Jimmium monolith in the Northern Territory of Australia indicate a date of 1,76,000 years ago. Petroglyphs on the monolith and surrounding boulders are dated 75,000 years ago. Other archaeologists have contradicted these findings.

Though an earlier date is uncertain, Australia was certainly occupied around 60,000–40,000 years ago. There is early evidence of art that dates to this period. Rock art has been found at Ubirr and Uluru. There are also archaeological sites that date to 40,000 years ago. Among the sites are Devil's Lair, Lake Mungo, Nauwalabila, Malakunanaja and many others. There are more than 150 such sites. Some of these are on the Swan river in western Australia.

The land

Australia has a number of unique animals and birds. There were many more in the past.

Around 60,000 years ago there were thick forests and a number of large animals. Among them were those of the Diprotodon family. These were very large marsupials. The biggest, *Diprotodon optatum* was almost 4 m long, 2 m high, and could weigh 2800 kg. It became extinct about 25,000 years ago. There was also a large kangaroo, 2 or 3 m tall and a huge tortoise, the size of a car. There was a monitor lizard *Megalania prisca*, up to 5 m long. And there were lots of large birds who walked around but couldn't fly. The *Dromonis stirtoni* was a bird 3 m high. It weighed 500 kg. But between 40,000 and 20,000 years ago, all these, as well as other creatures, disappeared. Were people responsible for the extinction of the megafauna? Some scientists feel this is so, but it is more likely that it was related to climate change. Around 30,000 years ago there were forests, lakes and snow-covered mountains. Around 20,000 years ago, the climate became colder, as the ice age started. In Australia, temperatures were about 10 degrees less than today. Rainfall was reduced. Cold winds blew across the desert regions. This affected both animals and people. Possibly 80 per cent of the population died. Others moved into the mountainous regions of Pilbara, Kimberley, the south-east coast of Australia, and the patches of rainforests in Arnhem Land and Kakadu. But as the tree cover was reduced, a larger area was available for hunting. Caves at Carpenters Gap and Purit Jarra in central Australia indicate this. Warmer conditions began 14,000 years ago. New plants and trees grew. By 10,000 years ago the climate was approximately what it is today. People burnt down the thick forests. New trees such as eucalyptus, acacia and tall grasses grew. The sea level reached its present height around 6000 years ago.

Lifestyle

The centre of Australia has deserts. Along the coasts are rainforests. In the north is tropical vegetation and flowing rivers. The aborigines lived all over the country. Over the thousands of years before European contact and occupation, changes did take place in the way of life, but these were not as major as those taking place in the rest of the world. Apart from art, archaeology and legends, we get an understanding of their lifestyle through their later contacts with Europeans. The Europeans had recorded what they observed.

Food

The early people mainly lived by hunting animals and collecting wild plants to eat. Wild yams and edible roots were dug out with special digging sticks. Fruits, berries, seeds, some other wild vegetables and insects, honey ants, grubs and moths were eaten, as well as taro, coconuts, and nuts. Plaited bags or wooden baskets were used to collect these foods.

They also ate lizards, bandicoots, birds, possum and snakes. Large animals were killed with spears, clubs, boomerangs or stones. Emu, wombat and kangaroo were killed and eaten. Different hunting techniques were used. Sometimes the hunter tried to look like an animal or bird by wearing skins or feathers, or by hiding behind a bush. Animals were trapped in snares or pits.

Animals domesticated

Dingoes (wild dogs) were probably brought to Australia from Southeast Asia and domesticated around 3500 BCE. There was no other domestic animal on the mainland. Some mainland and Torres Strait islands used the dingo as a companion and hunter. Torres Strait islanders also domesticated pigs.

Houses

Houses were simple, usually made of bark, branches and leaves, or bushes. People also lived in caves and natural shelters. In a few places there were houses with circular stone walls covered with branches or leaves for the roof.

Tools and other items used

Most of the tools were made of stone and wood. Metal was not used.

Stone axes were used 40,000 years ago in Papua New Guinea. In the mainland of north Australia they began to be used 20,000 years ago. They were used in southern Australia much later, perhaps from around 2500 BCE. They were never in Tasmania. Stone choppers and flakes were made consistently from early days. Stone blades were made from 4000–3000 BCE. There were stone spear points, barbs, knives and scrapers. Stone tools actually formed a small part of the items used. There were implements made of wood. Resin, shells, precious stones, seeds and feathers were made into various items. String and rope were made, and bags and baskets were woven. In the deserts small wells and natural waterholes provided water. There were no trees in these regions, but spears were made from roots of desert shrubs.

There were different phases and types of existence. Between 3000 and 1000 BCE, Henry Lourandos and others suggest there was a change in activity, accompanied by population growth and more trade. New types of stone tools were made, consisting of finer points and scrapers. Some new methods to get food were used, such as making eel traps. Spear throwing developed. There were differences in various parts of the continent. The boomerang, a special type of tool that returned when thrown, was only found in south-east Australia. The didgeridoo (musical instrument) was used in ceremonies only in the far north.

Trade in the form of exchange took place across the different regions of Australia. These exchanges were made at large gatherings, where there were other festivities as well. There was also trade with New Guinea via the Torres Strait islands. Later, probably from around CE 1400, there was trade with Sulawesi and other Indonesian islands. People from Makassar (now known as Ujungpandang in Sulawesi) came in large fleets of praus (sailboats) for trade. According to tradition, the Baiini were earlier traders who came in ships from Indonesia. Some historians feel that even these people even began trading in the 15th century, while the Makassar came later.

Society

Aboriginal people refer to themselves by the name of the tribe or clan to which they belong, or the name of their language. There were once separate 'nations' and 600 language groups. Different dialects were spoken within each language group. At the time when Europeans began to settle here, they spoke about 250 different languages. Nation or country refers to a region occupied by a clan or a number of related clans. A clan or tribe consisted of about 500 people. Within this there were smaller groups and families. The people of the country moved from place to place within this territory, and were thus semi-nomadic. They carried a few possessions such as weapons and digging sticks. Later they cleared some land with fire to allow edible plants to grow. Fire was also used to get rid of insects and for ceremonies and warfare.

In general, women gathered food and cared for young children. Men went out hunting. At the age of six the boys started going with their fathers to learn how to hunt. The girls learnt the women's tasks.

The various tribes had their own customs and ways of life. There were laws and rules according to which people had to live, including specific rules for marriage. Among the many clan groups are the Pintupi, Pitjantjara, and the Warlpiri, which is also a language, the Anmatyerr or Alyawarre, and the Arrernte. The Ngunnawal, Eora, Dieri are among the many others.

The society of a tribe was divided into two or more groups. Each group had its own ancestral spirits as well as sacred places, plants and animals. Each person was connected with one or more of these objects known as totems. Groups could be divided into sections and subsections. There could be four sections or eight subsections based on relationships.

Each person had a relationship with a number of other people in the tribe, sometimes up to 70. These relationships included parents, grandparents, uncles, cousins and others. People from different clans and groups came together in large gatherings. At these, items were traded, various ceremonies took place accompanied by dance and music, and weddings were arranged.

Art, songs, dances and stories were important in daily life.

No speaking to your mother-in-law

One of the odd customs is that no one, man or woman, should speak directly to his or her mother-in-law. This must have been a rule which helped to maintain harmony. If a woman, for instance, wanted to say something to her husband's mother, she had to ask her husband to convey the message.

Art

Art and decoration were of different types. Paintings and carvings were made on rocks, trees and bark. Bodies were painted and

Early rock art dated c. 28,000 years ago from Nawarla Gabarmang in the Northern Territory. Thousands of such images have been found in this rock shelter.

decorated for ceremonies. Each region had different art styles. They also changed and evolved over the centuries. Weapons, vessels, and other objects were also decorated. Sometimes feathers and different substances were used in art. There were also sculptures and carvings, and designs made in sand. Gods, people and hunting scenes were depicted in art, as well as various designs. Some art, that has been called X-ray art, showed the internal organs of an animal. Such paintings began about a thousand years ago. Aboriginal art is largely connected with totems.

Religion

Archaeology and art indicate that several deities were worshipped. There are a number of stories about creation and different deities for each tribe. Sometimes the deities were depicted as animals, plants and rocks. They believed the spirit reincarnates in different bodies, including in animals and plants. Each deity has its own story which is narrated in words, and through dance, music and painting. Creator deities were involved in creation. Ancestor deities or ancestral beings were ancestors who taught the people how to hunt, collect food, and live. There were also totemic beings or ancestors of a different type. Each person had one or more totemic ancestor, which could be a plant such as the yam, or an animal or bird. Every clan had several totems, hence even related people could have different totems.

Their spiritual system revolved around the theory of the interconnectedness of life. Ceremonies included music, song and dance and sand and body paintings.

Dreamtime

Dreamtime stories were a very important part of aboriginal life. Through dreaming and narrating their dream stories, the people brought the distant past to life. There were dream stories about the origin of the world, the creation of the land and living beings, and the origin of each tribe. Social and religious customs were often woven into these accounts. Many focus on an animal, reptile or bird. Some are secret, only for a few, others are for all.

Ceremonies and rituals

Ceremonies and rituals in which various deities were invoked were also important. Apart from these there were initiation ceremonies when boys and girls reached adulthood, as well as funeral ceremonies. Funeral practices also varied among tribes. Sometimes it consisted of two stages of exposure of the body and then collection of the bones.

The Rainbow Serpent

The Rainbow Serpent mythology is painted on rocks in the Kakadu National Park region. This is believed to be 7000 years old. This deity is still worshipped by people in the area. There are many different Rainbow Serpent stories. He lives in permanent waterholes, and represents water.

Memories

Many of their stories preserve memories of the past. These stories must have been transmitted from generation to generation. Even the extinct megafauna are preserved in their stories such as Waugal, Rainbow Serpent and Bunyip. Many groups from Arnhem land, the Kimberley and the south-west of west Australia have stories about the rising waters.

Tasmania

Tasmania was occupied around 30,000 years ago.

Tasmania separated from the mainland 11,000 years ago. They did not use new technology like spear throwing. They were an isolated community until the Europeans reached there.

Torres Strait Islands

The people of the Torres Strait Islands in the far north of Queensland had a distinct culture that is a mixture of aborigine and that of Papua New Guinea to the north.

NEW ZEALAND

New Zealand has two main islands, North Island and South Island. It also has other dependencies.

Before the Europeans reached here, New Zealand was lived in by people who later called themselves Maoris. They were Polynesians in origin, who may have reached here via Cook Island in CE 900–1000.

The first European, Abel Tasman, reached the islands in 1642. Before that the Maoris were the only people settled there.

According to their oral history, Maoris came from Hawaiki, their legendary homeland. Kapu is remembered in their stories as the first person who reached the islands. He returned to Hawaiki and brought other settlers. It is not clear where Hawaiki was.

There are a number of different Maori groups. Each has its own history narrated through songs, legends and stories. Maoris had a social structure that was similar to other Polynesians. The basic social unit was the tribe, and sub-tribe. The term for these was iwi and hapu. Within the sub-tribe were large families.

Maoris built single room structures. They used several such rooms for different purposes. A separate room was used for cooking.

Tools were carved out of stone, and weapons were made of stone, wood and bone. They had different types of boats and sailing vessels made from wood, and specialized in woodcarving. They used flax for making clothes as well as baskets. They wore ornaments and decorated themselves with tattoos.

Among the important food items was the kumara (sweet potato). They also hunted and ate the moa, a flightless bird, other birds, seals and fish.

> **A STORY OF CREATION**
>
> Maoris have a number of different gods. Rangi, the sky, and Papa, the earth, came from Po, which is the origin of everything. Rangi and Papa didn't want to be separated. But they had several children and hence the children were trapped between them and couldn't get out into the world. But finally they pushed their parents apart and moved into the world. These children were the gods, known as atua. Among the many gods, Tane is the god of trees and vegetation as well as the giver of light. Rongo is the god of agriculture. Tu is the god of war.

PACIFIC ISLANDS

In the Pacific Ocean there are more than 25,000 islands. (See Chapter 1 for names of some of the island groups.) The Pacific islands are divided into three groups: Melanesia, Micronesia and Polynesia. The Melanesia and Micronesia islands were first settled about 30,000 years ago, while the Polynesian islands were settled much later, between about CE 500 and 1200. Some of the islands were on the Sunda and Sahil continental shelves and the first people may have reached by crossing the land from Southeast Asia. At that time the islands had land connections and were not under water. Later, after the seas levels rose, more people reached the islands by crossing the water in boats or canoes.

Though each island group has its own history, there are some aspects in common. There were originally very few animals on most of the islands, but a number of birds and insects.

At least 1200 languages are spoken across the many islands, apart from the languages brought in by later colonizers. Before the coming of the Europeans, people generally lived by farming and fishing. Crops grown included taro, cassava, yams, sweet potato, breadfruit, bananas, other fruits, sago and coconut palm.

Crafts included pottery and textiles, objects made from shells, stone and wood. Baskets, mats, canoes and fishing implements were also made. In Fiji and some other islands, a special type of material was made from the bark of the mulberry tree. This is known as tapa cloth.

Houses were usually simple, consisting of one thatched room. Sometimes there was a separate room for cooking. A number of gods were worshipped. Religious and other ceremonies included dances and songs.

Megaliths

Megaliths were made on many of the islands of all three groups. These consisted of platforms known as ahus, on which huge stones were erected. Mostly these stones were cut out of rock, but sometimes they were made out of different materials. In some cases statues were made.

Easter Island in the south-eastern Pacific was settled by the Polynesians in the 6th century. Between CE 700–850, stone statues (actually made from compressed volcanic ash) were erected here on rectangular platforms (ahus). Even larger statues

Easter Island statues

were made after CE 1200. There are over 600 huge statues. Each is between 3 and 12 m high. These statues are extremely heavy and a complex technology of ropes and ramps would have had to be used to put them in place. This shows that though the islanders lived simple lives, they were able to use special techniques for difficult tasks.

Among different types of megaliths were those at Tinian on Mariana Islands where pillars made of coral were grouped together.

In Micronesian islands, huge stones in the shape of rings have been found.

Conclusion

We have looked at the history of the world up to around 1500. A new era was about to start as Europeans began to colonize and dominate the world. Asia, the Americas, Africa, Australia and various islands all came under the control or influence of Europeans.

Index

Abaqa, 382
Abbasid dynasty, Abbasids, 247, 250, 284, 285-86, 318, 346, 376-77, 379, 382, 384
al-Abbasiyya, 286
Abd al Latif, 351
Abd al Malik (ruled 685-705), 249-50
Abd-al Mumin al Kumi, 460
Abd al Wadid dynasty, 461
Abd ar Rahman, 249
Abdullah, 243
Abdullah bin Yasin, 460
Abraham, 150, 151, 245, 361
Abric Romani, Catalonia, Spain, 43
Abu al Abbas, first Abbasi ruler, 376
Abu Bakr, 246, 247
Abu Hureyra, 52-54
Abu Ibrahim Ahmad (856-863), 286
Abu Simbel, Egypt, 74, 181
Abu Sufyan, 248
Abu Talib, 243
Abu Yusuf, Marinid sultan, 460-61
Abu Zakariyya Yahya, Hafsid king, 461

Acamapichtli, king of Tenochtitlan (ruled 1372-1391), 449
Achaean League of Greece, 132
Achaemenes, 163
Achaemenid empire, Achaemenids (Hakhamanishya), 115, 116, 150, 153, 162-66, 171, 172
Acheulian (stone tools), 33
Achin kingdom, 429
Acolhua, 449
Acts of the Apostles, 160
Adena culture, Ohio, 186-87
administration system, Chinese CE 581-1000, 278, 402
Aeneas, Trojan warrior, 143
Aeschylus (525-456 BCE), 110
Afghanistan, 80, 82, 154, 167, 169, 213, 257, 273, 277, 350, 383; India, trade, 86
Africa, 8-10, 21; Arabs, 284-85; the first people, 28, 29, 34, 36, 472;— moved out, 32, 472; (up to CE 500), 176-83; (CE 500-1000), 284-91; (CE 1000-1500), 457-66; other kingdoms and people, 291

Africanus, Scipio, 325
Afro-Asiatic languages, 470
Agamemnon, king of Mycenae, 106
Aghlabid dynasty (CE 800-909), 286, 287, 377
agriculture and domestic animals, 52; in Africa CE 500-1000, 285; in ancient Europe, 121; in India (3500 BCE-500 BCE), 84; in India (500 BCE-CE 500), 216; in India (CE 1000-1500), 365, 370; in Iran, 169; of Maya civilization, 198; in North America, 185; in Russia, 359; in South and Central America, 455
Ahmad ibn Tulun, Turkish governor, 285
Ahmad Sanjar, 387
Ahmose I, king of Egypt (1540-39 BCE), 73
Ahuitzotl, Mexica king, 449
Ahura Mazda, 154, 165, 170, 174
Aihole, 272
Airlangga, 432
Ajanta and Ellora caves and temples, Maharashtra, India, 217-18
Akhesenamun, queen of Egypt, 75
Akheteton (Amarna), 74
Akipana, 198
Akkad, Akkadians, 67, 164
Aksum kingdom of Ethiopia, 181-82, 183, 286, 459
Al-Andalus, 318
Alaric I, Germanic king, 136
Alaska, 436, 437
Alban Mt, 443
Albania, 311
Albert II, 306
Alcuin (c. 732-804), 236
Alexander, king of Macedonia, 72, 73, 110, 115-20, 177, 250;

Alexandrias, 119; conquered Damascus, 250; conquered Egypt, 72, 176-77; conquered Iran, 171; death (323 BCE), 117, 119-20, 166, 176; defeated Darius III, 116-17, 166; invaded north-west India, 117, 212; CE 500-1000, 270-75; North India, 270-72; South India, 272-73; other kingdoms, 273-74
Alexander IV, 118, 120
Alexandria, Egypt, 78, 112, 176, 177, 178, 285
Alfonso, King of Portugal, 319
Alfred I, Saxon king, 255
Algeria, 9, 134, 176, 286, 287, 461
Algiers, 284
Alhambra, Granada, 319
Ali, 243, 244, 246-47, 248
Alighieri, Dante (c. 1265-1321), *La Divina Commedia* (The Divine Comedy), 324
Almohads, 319, 460, 461
Almoravids, 319, 460
Alphaeus (Apostle), 159
Altamira, Spain, 45
Amataresu, sun goddess, 224, 229-30, 412
Amenemhet I, king of Egypt, 73
Amenhotep II, king of Egypt (ruled c.1426-1400 BCE), 74
Amenhotep IV (Akhenaton), king of Egypt (ruled 1353-1336 BCE), 74
America: Clovis culture, 56-57; the first people, 40-41; village settlements (10,000-5000 BCE), 49
Amhara, king of Ethiopia, 459-60
Amida (Amitabha) Buddha, 412-13
Amyntor, 115
Anahita, 174

Index 487

Anahwrata, King of Myanmar, 417
Anasazi, 439
Anatolia, 104, 386-91; Seljuk Turks took over, 307, 312
ancestor worship, 54
Andamans, 375
Andrew (Apostle), 159
Angkor kingdom of Cambodia (CE 802-1432), 420, 422
Angkor Wat (Vishnu temple), Thailand, 422-23
Anglo-Norman, 331
Anglo-Saxons in England: (CE 450-1066), 253-56, 258, 259, 261; chronicle, 258; language, 160
Angola, 467
Angrok, king of Java (1222-27), 432
animal species, animals and birds, new, 24-26, 29; in Africa, 179; animal skin as clothes, 34, 36; changing patterns, 39-40; in Australia (up to CE 1500), 473-74, 475; domestication, 43, 49, 51-52, 54, 55, 56, 58, 91, 122, 190, 195, 359, 416, 439, 455, 468, 475; in early Egypt, 78; in India (3500 BCE-500 BCE), 85; migration in 10,000-5000 BCE, 48-49, 56; in North America, 184, 190, 437; in South Africa, 468, 469; in Southeast Asia, 30
Anjevin dynasty, 333
Anmatyerr or Alyawarre (an Australian tribe), 477
Anselm, St (1033-1109), 323
Anshan, Iran, 149, 162-63, 164
Antarctic Ocean, 2
Antarctica, 14, 21, 22
Antigonus, 120, 156
Antioch, 312
Antony, Mark, 134, 177

apes and humans, 26
Aphrodite, 106, 114
Apostolic Fathers, Apostles, 159
Aqta, Omar, 350
Aquitaine, 232, 233, 238
Arab(s) (Bedouins), 169, 242-43, 248, 297, 322; in Africa, 284-85, 286; coinage, 249; conquered Byzantine territories, 239; Muslims, 250, 377; Quraishi tribe, 243
Arabia, 148, 242, 247; (CE 1000-1500), 382
Arabian Nights. see One Thousand and One Nights
Arabic numerals, 329, 379
Aral Sea, 154
archaeology and history, xi-xii; Central Asia, 154; North America, 184
Archimedes (287-212 BCE), 112
Arctic islands, 10, 12, 184
Arctic Ocean, 16
Arctodus, 40
Arcy-sur-Cure site, 47
Ardashir I, Sasanian ruler, 168-69
Ardeche river, 45
Ardipithecus: *Ardipithecus kadabba*, 28; *Ardipithecus ramidus*, 28
Argentina, 197, 454
Arghun, 382, 383
Arianism, 161, 231
Ariaramnes, son of Tiespes, 164
Arik Boke Khan, 346
Arikamedu, 215
Aristotle (384-322 BCE), 108, 110-11, 115
Arius, 161
Armenia, 167, 169; conquered by Trajan, 135; under Byzantine, 307; under Il-Khanate, 383

Arnhem Land, 474
Arpad dynasty, 240
Arrernte (an Australian tribe), 477
Arridaeus, Philip, 117
Arridaeus, Philip III, 120
Arsaces I (Arsaks), 167
Arsacid (Arshakani) dynasty, 167, 172
art and architecture, art and culture across the world (50,000-10,000 BCE), x, 44; in Africa CE 500-1000, 285; in Australia, 37, 471, 478; in China, 98, 277, 400; in early Egypt, 80; in Europe (CE 500-1000), 235, 240; (CE 1000-1500), 308, 321-30; in Great Britain, 337-38; in ancient Greece, 109, 111; in India (500 BCE-CE 500), 217-18; in India (CE 1000-1500), 366, 370; in Japan, 228, 229, 410; in Korea, 402; in Mesopotamia, 61, 69; Mongols, 351; Roman, 143, 308; Romanesque and Gothic styles, 337-38; in Southeast Asia, 424; in West Asia, 377, 386, 391
Artabanus V, Parthian ruler, 168
Artaxerxes III, Persian princess, 118
Artemis temple, Ephesus, Greece, 114
Arthur (Artorius), King of England, legends, 257-58, 340, 342
Aryabhatta, 218
Ashikaga Yoshimasa, 409
Ashikaga Yoshimi, 409
Ashikaga, Takauji, 409
Ashoka (r. 269-232 BCE), 213-14, 217, 221; XIIIth Rock Edict, 213; conquered Kalinga, 214, 221
Ashurbanipal (ruled 668-627 BCE), 68
Asia Minor, 69, 120, 132, 240, 267, 309

Asia, 4-5, 21, 223, 318, 320, 485; animal domestication, 51; Black Death, 314; children's crusades, 314; the first people, 29, 30, 31, 32, 34, 40, 472-73; Greek culture, 120; land, changes, 48; metals, use, 69; Roman empire, 129, 138, 304; village settlements, 48, 52
Askia Muhammad, Songhe king (1493-1528), 463
Askold, Viking ruler of Kiev, 353
Assyria, Assyrians, 68, 73, 152, 156, 180
Astarte, 124
astronomical clocks in Europe (1000-1500 CE), 330
astronomy. *see* mathematics and astronomy. *see also* science
Astyges, king of Medes, 163
Asuka valley, Yamato, Japan, 226-27
Atharva Veda, 88
Athelstan, king of Wessex (ruled CE 924-39), 255, 257, 259
Athens, 108-113; invaded by Xerxes I, 166
Atlantic Ocean, 2, 438, 441
Atlas (Titan), 114
Atlityam, 58
Au Lac, kingdom of Vietnam, 424
Augustine, St, 261
Augustus (Octaviaus, Octavian), 134, 237
Aurochs, 51
Australia, 1, 13-14, 21, 41; animal domestication, 475; art, 37, 45, 473, 478-79; burials, 43; ceremonies and rituals, 480; early occupation, 471-73; the first people, 31, 40; food, 475; houses, 475; land, 473-74; lifestyle, 474;

Mungo man, 42; and New Zealand (up to CE 1500), 471-84; religion, 479; society, 477-78; tools, 475-76; Tores Strait island, 481
Austrasia, 232
Austria, 233, 238, 306
Avars, 238
Avatamsaka Sutra, 283
Avesta, 174
Avignon, France, 300
Ayutthaya kingdom of Thailand (c. 1350-1767), 420
Ayyubid dynasty, 382, 457-58
Azcapotzalco, 449
Azerbaijan, 167, 383
Azhar University, al-, 286
Aztecs, 444, 446, 447, 448, 449-50, 452; calendar, 451; five suns, 452; food, 450; language, 450; religion, 451

Babylon, Babylonians, 67, 117, 120, 163; conquered by Alexander, 116
Bactrian Greeks, 214
Baghdad, 257; a centre of learning, 377-78; Mongol invasion, 378; paper, 379
Bahamas, 441
Bahmani, Firuz Shah (ruled 1397-1422), 372
Baiini (traders), 476
Baitul Hikmah (House of Wisdom), 378
al-Bakri, 288
Balban (1265-1287), 368
Bali, 432, 434
Balkans, 69, 238-39
Balkash Lake, 154
ball game, 192, 197, 444
Baltica, 20

Baluchitherium, 26
Banabhatta, *Harshacharita*, 272
Banana, 467
Bannockburn, Battle of, 335, 342
Bantu, 290, 291, 464, 469
Barbados, 442
Barsine (Statira), Persian princess, 118
Bartholomew (Apostle), 159
Barygaza, 216
Basil I, Macedonian emperor, 240
Basil II, Byzantine emperor (CE 963-1025), 240, 307, 354
Basketmaker, 189-90
Basra, 247, 380
bathhouses in Roman empire, 140
Batu Khan, 345, 356
Bavaria, 235, 237
Bayajidda, a prince of Baghdad, 464
Bayazid I, Ottoman sultan, 350, 390
Baybars I, 458
Bayeau tapestry, 332
Bede, Benedictine monk (CE 673-735); *Historia Ecclesiastica Gentis Anglorum*, 258
Beg, Chagri, 386
Beg, Jani, 383
Beg, Seljuk, 386
Beg, Tughril, 386
Behistun inscription, 165
Bei Qi (550-577), 205
Bei Zhou (557-581), 205
Belize, 198
Benedictine Abbey, 339
Beowulf, an epic poem, 258
Berbers, 183, 250, 285, 460, 461
Berekhat Ram site, Israel, 37
Bering Bridge, 48
Berke Khan, 346
Bessus, Persian leader, 117

Bharata, *Natya Shastra*, 221
Bhrikuti, a princess from Nepal, 280
Bible, 150, 152, 163, 246; Hebrew, 160; Jewish, 153
Bigello, Leonardo Pisano. *see* Fibonacci, Leonardo
Bindusara, 213
bird goddesses in ancient Europe, 122
Black Death: in Asia, 314; in Egypt, 458; in West Asia, 383
Black Sea, 389, 391
Blackwater Draw, New Mexico, 56
Blanchard, France, 46
Blombos Cave, Cape Town, South Africa, 37
Bluefish Caves, Yukon Territory, 41
Boccaccio, Giovanni (1313-75), *Decameron*, 325
Bodhidharma, 280
Bohemia, Bohemians, 241, 306-7, 309
Boleslaw (992-1025), 309
Bolivia, 197-98
Bologna University, 322
Bon religion, 281
Boniface VIII, Pope and Philip IV, king of France, conflict, 300
Book of Kells, The, 261
Book of Leinster, The, 341
Book of Revelation, 160
Book of the Dun Cow, The, 341
book production, books and printing: in China (CE 1000-1500), 394-95; in India, 371; in West Asia, 378-79. *see also* writing
Boreslav II, 310
Boris I, 240
Bos primigenius, 25
Bosnia, 390

Bosworth, Battle of, 336
Botswana, 468
Boudicca of England, revolt against Romans, 137
Boukephalus, Alexander's horse, 119
Bourbons, 308
Bouvines, Battle of (1214), 334
Bramante, Donato (1444-1514), 327
Brandenburg, 306, 309
Brazil, 40, 319
Brian Boru, the High King of Ireland, 260, 340
Brittany, 125
Bruce, Robert, 342
Brunei, 415, 427
Brunelleschi, Fillipo (1377-1446), 326, 327
Bruniquel cave, France, 47
Brutus, Marcus Junius, 134
Brythonic, 259
Buddhas and bodhisattvas, 217, 221
Buddhism: in Cambodia, 423; in China, 208, 221, 271, 280, 282, 397-98; Hinayana, 221, 275; in India, 87, 88-89, 90, 220, 221, 271, 275, 373; in Iran, 382, 175; in Japan, 226-27, 228, 230, 280, 412-13; Jodo sect, 412; Jodo-Shinshu, 412; in Korea, 211, 280, 283, 402; Lotus Hokke sect, 412; Mahayana, 221, 271, 275, 281, 417, 423, 434; in Myanmar, 417; Shingon sect, 412; in Southeast Asia, 416, 417, 418, 420, 421, 423, 430; in Sri Lanka, 375; Tendai sect, 412; in Thailand, 420; Theravada, 417, 420; in Tibet, 281; Vajrayana, 275, 281, 417; Zen, 412, 413
Bukhara (Bokhara), 351, 398; invasion by Abd al Malik, 249

Bulgaria, Bulgars, 121, 122, 239, 240-41, 309
Burgundians, Burgundy, 232, 233, 238, 317
burials across the world (50,000-10,000 BCE), 43, 50; in Argentina, 454; in China, 202; in Great Britain, 256; in Mongolia, 210; North America, 186-87, 188, 438; Oseberg ship burials, 264-65
Buridan, Jean, 329
Buyid dynasty of Iran, 377
Byzantine empire. *see* Roman Empire, Eastern

Cabral, Pedro Alvares, 319
Cactus Hills, Virginia, 56
Caddo Indians, 187
Caerphilly Castle, 341
Caesar, Julius, 133-34, 143, 144, 177; invaded Britain, 252
Cahokia, 438
Cahuachi, Peru, 196
calendar of Aztec and Mayas, 200, 451
California, 437, 439
calligraphy in China, 400
Cambodia, 415, 419, 425, 428, 430; kingdoms, 421-22; theatre, 423-24. *see also* Southeast Asia
Cambridge University, 337
Cambyses II, 163, 164, 173
Camelids, 190
Canaan (Israel-Palestine), 73, 150-51
Canada, 10, 11, 436, 438; the first people, 41
Canterbury Cathedral, 339
Cao Wei (CE 220-265), 205
Cape of Good Hope, 319, 470
Caracalla, Roman emperor, 252

Caribbean Islands, 10, 11-12, 441-42
Caribbean Sea, 441
Caroline wars, 316
Carolingian dynasty, Carolingians, 233, 235, 236, 237, 264, 308, 329. *see also* Roman empire
Carolman, 233
Carpenters Gap caves, 474
Carthage, 132, 143, 178-79, 284
cartography in China, 396
Casimir III (1333-1370), 309
Casimir IV (ruled 1447-1492), 310
Caspian Sea, 163
Castaneda, Carlos, 448
Castillon Battle, 317
castles in Europe (1000-1500), 295-96
Catal Huyuk, 54-55
Catallus, Gaius Valerius (c 84-54 BCE), 144
Cathedral of St Sophia in Kiev, 361
cathedrals and churches in Europe (1000-1500), 302
cattle, 51-52; genom, 52
cave paintings across the world (50,000-10,000 BCE), 44-45, 50. *see also* Ajanta
Caxton, William (1422-1492), 329
Ceiba tree, 200
Celtic, Celts: in Britain, 251, 253, 259, 260; culture, 125; in ancient Europe, 124, 125-26; languages, 124-25, 259, 342; religion, 261
Central America: early, 10, 11, 191-200, 320, 441; (CE 1000-1500), 443-56
Central Asia, the region, 154-55, 167, 203, 343, 344, 350, 379; the early period, 148-55

Cernnunos, 126
Chad Lake, 464
Chagatai Khan (Jagatai), 345, 350
Chahamanas, 365
Chaldean dynasty (Neo-Babylonian), 152, 156, 163
Champa, kingdom, 425
Chamundaraya, 273
Chan (Zen), 280, 412, 413
Chan Chan, Inca capital, 456
Chanakya, 212
Chandellas, 272, 365
Chandragupta, Maurya, 212-13, 215
Changan city. *see* Xian
Changan, Han emperor, 203
Chansons de geste and *Chanson de Roland*, 235-36
Characene kingdom, Mesopotamia, 168
Charaka, 218
Charlemagne, 233, 234-35, 236, 237, 254
Charles of Moravia, the king of Bohemia, 306, 307, 308
Charles the Bald (Charles II), 237
Charles V, king of France, 316
Charles VI, king of France, 316
Charles VII, king of France, 317
Charlie Lake Caves, British Columbia, 57
Chatelperronian culture in Spain and France, 47
Chaucer, Geoffrey (1343-1400): *Canterbury Tales*, 339; *Troilus and Criseyde*, 338
Chauvet Cave, France, 45
Chavin culture, Peru, South America, 194-95
Chavin de Huantar, Peru, 194
Chenla kingdom of Cambodia, 420, 421-22
Cheras, 215, 371. *see also* India
Cherokee, 441
Chichen Itza, a Mayan city, 445-46, 448
Chile, 197
chimpanzees and humans, 19, 27
Chimu kingdom in Peru, 456
China, 297, 415, 427; (221 BCE-CE 581) early Mongoilia and Korea, 201-11; three kingdoms and six dynasties (CE 220-589), 205; (CE 581-1000) Monglia and Korea, 276-83; (CE 1000-1500), 392-403; city civilization, 61, 278; early, 91-100; early dynasties, 92; early settlements, 52; India, trade, 216; Indonesia, trade, 429; Iran, trade, 170; and Japan, trade, 228; under Kublai Khan, 346; legalism, 99; literature-Wu Ching, 99-100; philosophy, 98; religion, 208, 221, 271, 275, 280, 282, 397-98; Romans, trade, 138; South Africa, trade, 467, 468, 469; system of government, 228; travels of Marco Polo, 398-99; warring states (481-222 BCE), 96
Chinampas, 448-49
chocolate and cocoa in South and Central America, 446-47
Choctaw, 441
Cholas, 215, 220, 273, 370, 371, 432. *see also* India
Chonson (Yi) dynasty of Korea, 403
Christan Bible The, 160
Christian Church and monasteries,

159, 459; in Europe (500-1000), 232, 233, 238; (1000-1500), 299, 300-2; Western and Eastern, 303
Christianity, Christians, 156-61, 250; in Africa (up to CE 500), 181; (CE 500-1000), 289, 291; Arianism, 161, 231, 232; in Bulgaria and Moravia, 241; Catholics, 159, 232, 233, 303, 319; in China (CE 581-1000), 280; conflicts, 161; conversions to, 240, 319, 467; Coptic (Egyptian), 303; in Egypt, 178, 179; in Europe, 125, 233, 299, 302, 303; in Great Britain and Ireland, 253, 258, 261; in India (CE 1000-1500), 373; in Iran, 175; Nicene Creed, 146, 161; in Roman empire, 145, 146; in Russia, 354; in Scandinavia, 266; Syrian, 303
Church of St Mary, Poland, 310
Church of the Transfiguration, Novgorod, 361
Ciboney, 441
Cicero, Marcus Tullius (106-43 BCE), 144
Circus Maximus, 139-40, 142
Cishan culture in early China, 91
Cistercians, 300
cities and towns, city civilization (5000-1500 BCE), 60-69; in Africa, 181, 464; Chinese, 278; in early Egypt, 75; in Europe (1000-1500), 296-97, 321; ancient Greek, 107-8; in India (3500 BCE-500 BCE), 82-84, 87; (500 BCE-CE 500), 215; in India (CE 1000-1500), 366; in Iran, 149, 169, 173; Mixtec, 444; in North America, 441; in Roman empire, 139; in South and Central America, 449-50
Claudius, Roman emperor (ruled CE 41-54), 134, 252
Clement I of Rome, 159
Cleopatra, 134, 177
Cleopatra VII, 177
climate change, xiv, 22, 39, 468, 474
clock tower of Kaifeng, 396
Clonard Abbey, monastic school, 261
Clontarf Battle, 260
Clotaire I, King, 232
Clotaire II, King, 232
clothes and shoes across the world (50,000-10,000 BCE), 44; of the first people, 36; in Japan, 411-12; in Roman empire, 141; in Russia, 359
Clotilda, 232
Clovis (Chlodovic) culture, 56-58, 184, 231-32
Clovis I, ruler of Western Franks, 231-32
Cnut (Canute II), king of Denmark and Norway, 255
coastal cities of Africa, 464
Coatzacoalcos river, 191
Cochin China, 425
coins: in India (3500 BCE-500 BCE), 87; in India (500 BCE-CE 500), 216; in Iran, 165, 171
Coleridge, Samuel Taylor, 399
Colosseum, amphitheatre of Rome, 139, 141
Colossus of Rhodes, 79
Columba, St (521-597), 261
Columbia, 20
Columbus, Christopher (1451-1506), 320, 441

Comb Ceramic culture in south-east Europe, 121
Commodus, Roman emperor, 135
community boundaries, 59
Comoros, 10
Confucianism, 203, 226, 280, 397, 406, 425
Confucius (551-479 BCE), 98, 227; *The Analects*, 98
Conrad I, Duke of Frankonia, 237
Constantine, Roman emperor (CE 306-337), 135, 142, 146
Constantine XI, 390
Constantinople, 135, 238, 308, 311, 312, 313, 357, 390-91
continental shelf, 16
continents, 2
Cook Island, 481
Copan, a Mayan city state, 198, 199
Copernicus, 329
copper, 57; in Iran, 171; in early Egypt, 70, 80; in ancient Europe, 121, 122; in Mesopotamia, 69
Cordoba, Spain, 318-19, 378-79; emirate (756-929), 318; Caliphate (929-1031), 318
Coricancha temple, Cuzco, 456
Corsica, conquered by Romans, 132
Cortes, Hernan, 449
Council of Chalcedon (CE 451), 303
Council of Nablus, 312
Coyote military order of Toltecs, 447
crafts and trade. *see* trade. *see also* art and architecture Creek, 441
Crassus, Marcus Licinius, 133
Crete island, 32, 101, 103
Crimea, 390
Croats, 311
Cro-Magnon and others, 41-42
Cronus (Titan), 114
Crusades in Europe (1000-1500), 298, 307-8, 311-12, 321; Children's, 313-14; eight main, 312-13; Third, 333; Fourth, 308, 313; Ninth, 457; of Nicopolis, 389
Ctesiphon, 167, 169, 174, 303
Cuauhtemoc (Guatemotzin), an Aztec king, 450
Cuba, 441
Cucuteni and pre-Cucuteni culture in Romania, 121
Cuicuilco valley, Mexico, 193
Cuitahuac, Mexica king, 449-50
culture: Chinese (CE 581-1000), 277, 278-79; in ancient Greece, 109-10; Japanese, 405; Romans, 143
cuneiform writing. *see* writing
Cuzco, Peru, 453, 454, 456
Cynethryth, 255
Cyprus, 8, 55, 80, 104, 176
Cyril, 241
Cyrus cylinder, 164
Cyrus I (Kurush), 163
Cyrus II (Kurush) the Great, Achaemenid (ruled 559-c.529 BCE), 153, 163, 173
Czech republic, 241

da Gama, Vasco, 319, 320, 470
da Vinci, Leonardo (1452-1539), 328
Dacia, conquered by Trajan, 135
Dagobert I, king of Austrasia and Franks, 232-33
Dai Ping Dao (Yellow Turbans), 208
daimyo, military clan of Japan, 408, 409
Daishonen, Nichiren, founder of Lotus Hokke sect of Buddhism, 412

Dajokan (governing council in Japan), 228
Damascus (Syria), 248, 249, 250, 284, 376; Mongol invasion, 346; steel, 380-81
Danelaw, 255, 263
Danes, 237, 255, 258, 331
Daniel, son of Alexander Nevsky, 357
Danube river, Serbia, 122
Daoism; *Daodejing* (*Tao-tse-Ching*) in China, 98, 208, 280, 397; in Japan, 226
Darius I, 163-65, 166, 171, 173
Darius III, Achaemenid king, 116, 117, 118, 166
Darwin, Charles, 18, 19, 339
Darwinius masillae (Ida), 27
dating techniques, xii; dendrochronology, xiii, 265; obsidian hydration dating, xiii; radiocarbon dating, xii; seriation dating, xiii; stratigraphy, xii; thermoluminescence dating, xii-xiii
Dausi, an epic, 289
David, 151
De Architectura (On Architecture), 144
de Guzman, Dominic, 300
Deheubarth, Wales kingdom, 259, 341
Deipkloof rock shelter, South Africa, 37
Demetrius, 120
Denisova cave in Siberia, 31
Denmark, 16, 262, 233
Devaraja cult of god-kings, 422, 431
Devaraya I, king of Vijayanagara, 372
Devil's Lair, 473
Dhammayazika Pagoda, Myanmar, 418
Dhanananda, Nanda king, 212
Dharmawangsa, king of Java, 432

Dholavira, 84
Dhul-Nun al-Misri, 462
di Bondone, Giotto (1267-1337), 327
Diaz, Bartholomew, 319
Diaz, Bernal, 450
Dido, Queen, 143
Dieri (an Australian tribe), 477
Dilwara temples, Mt Abu, Rajasthan, 366-67
Dinosaur, 23; bones in Antarctica, 22; great disaster—65 million years ago, 24
Diocletian, Roman emperor, 135, 138
Diprotodon family, 473
Dir, Viking ruler of Kiev, 353
diseases, a medical discovery, 58
Djeitun culture, Turkmenistan, 154
Dmitry (Donskoy), son of Ivan II, 357, 358
DNA, DNA studies, 19, 31, 36, 58, 75, 472
Dokyo, 228
dome of the rock (Qubbat as-Sakrah mosque), 249-50
Domesday Book, The, 332
Dominicans, 300
Domitian, Roman emperor, 141, 144
Donatello (1386-1466), 327
Dong Qichang (1555-1636), 401
Dong Wei (534-550), 205
Dong Wu, Han emperor, 205
Dongbei, 345; Khitans, 402
Dordogne, France, 45
Dorians, 106
Doumenzhen, 96
drainage system: in ancient Greece, 103; in India (3500 BCE-500 BCE), 84
dreamtime stories, 479-80
Dromonis stirtoni, 474

496   Index

Druids, Celtic priests, 126
Drypetis, 118
Du Fu (Tu Fu) (712–770), 278
duchies, 235, 237
Dunbar, William (1460–1520), *Lament for the Makaris*, 342
Duncan I, king of Ireland, 342
Durandel (sword), 236
Durham cathedral, 337
Dyed flax fibres, 47
Dzudzuana cave, Georgia, 47

Eadred, king of Wessex, 255
Eagle military order of Toltecs, 447
early ancestors, 28
early art, 37
earth, changing, 19–20, 21
earthquakes and volcanoes, 21, 22
East Anglia, conquered by Vikings, 253, 255, 256, 263
economic system in Europe (1000–1500), 292–93
economy: of Great Britain (CE 1000–1500), 336–37; of Russia, 355
Eddas, 267
Edessa, Turkey, 312
Edubba schools; in Mesopotamia, 66
education, education system; in China, 393; in early Egypt, 79; in Europe, 235; in India (CE 500–1000), 271; in Mesopotamia, 65–66; in Roman empire, 142
Edward I (ruled 1272–1307), 335, 341, 342
Edward II (ruled 1308–1327), 315, 335, 342
Edward III (ruled 1327–1377), 315, 335, 336
Edward IV, 336
Edward V, 336

Edward the Confessor, 256
Edward the Elder, 255
Edwardian wars (1337–1360), 315
Egbert (ruled 771–839), Saxon king, 255
Egypt, 57, 104, 150, 151, 158, 238, 248, 284, 285–86; city civilization, 61; conquered by Arabs, 239; conquered by Romans, 178; early period, 70–81; Greece, trade, 73; (up to 500), 176–77; (CE 1000–1500), 457–59, 462, 463, 464; hieroglyphic writing system, 70, 79, 178; Mesopotamia, trade, 70; Middle Kingdom, 72–73, 180; New Kingdom, 73, 180; Old Kingdom, 72; religion, 178
Eirik the Red, 265
El Fustat, 285
El Mina, 470
El Palmilo, Mexico, 193
El Salvador, 198
Elam civilization, 149–50
Ellora. *see* Ajanta and Ellora
Elymais (Elam), 168
endosymbiosis, 19
Engaruka river, 463
English language, 253
entertainment and games: in India (3500 BCE–500 BCE), 85; Romans, 141
Enuma Elish, 68
environmental factors, 19
Eora (an Australian tribe), 477
Epirus, 308
Equidae (horse family), 40
Erasmus, Desiderius (1466–1536), *In Praise of Folly*, 324
Eritrea, 176, 179, 181
Erlitou culture (1900–1600 BCE), 93, 94
Ethiopia, 152, 179, 181, 459–60

Index 497

Etruscans, 126-28, 129, 130
Euclid (323-283 BCE), 112, 176; *History of Mathematics*, 112
Euphrates river, 52, 61, 62, 67, 116, 248
Eurasia, 7-8
Euripides (484-406 BCE), 110
Europe, 5-7, 21, 257; ancient, 121-28; (CE 500-1000), 231-41; (CE 1000-1500), 292-303;—art and culture, 321-30;—decree (The Golden Bull of 1356), 306;—feudalism, 292-93;—four kingdoms, 232-33;—guilds, 297;—icons and saints, 302;—later emperors, 237-38;—political theory, 324; Christianity, 232, 299, 302, 303; Eastern, 309; the first people, 29, 30, 31, 32, 36; kingdoms, wars and conflicts, 240, 304-20; and Moluccas, trade, 429; village settlements (10,000-5000 BCE), 49
European languages, 470
evolution theory, 18-19
examination system of Han dynasty, China, 203
Ezana (Aezianas), 181

famine (1315-17), Europe, 337
Fangshan, 96
Al-Farabi (872-950), *Kitab-al-musiqi al-kabir* (The Great Book on Music), 379
Farghana, 203; invasion by Abd al Malik, 249
farming settlements: in early China, 91; in ancient Europe, 121; in Europe (1000-1500), 296; in Greta Britain, 251; in early Greece, 105; in Iran, 149; in North America, 185, 442; in South and Central America, 191
Fatima, 243, 244
Fatimids, 250, 285-86, 377, 382, 384-85, 457
Faxian, a Buddhist pilgrim, 429
Feng river, 96
Fenghaocun, 96
Fengxi, 96
Fetes Johanniques, 318
feudalism and serfdom in Europe (1000-1500), 274, 292-93, 299, 322, 337
Fez al-Jadid (New Fez), 461
Fibonacci, Leonardo (Bigello, Leonardo Pisano, 1170-1240), 329
Fimbulwinter, 267
Finian, St of Clonard (470-549), 261
Finland, 262
Finno-Ugrians, 352
Firdausi, *Shah Namah* (Book of Kings), 383-84
fire, 35-36, 477
First Council of Ephesius, 303
first forms of life, 18-19
Five Pecks of Rice, 208
Florence, 296, 321, 324, 325, 326
Flores, Indonesia, 41
Florida, 185
food across the world (50,000-10,000 BCE), 42; in Australia (up to CE 1500), 475; in China (CE 1000-1500), 394; in early Egypt, 79; in Europe (1000-1500), 298; of the first people, 35; in India (CE 1000-1500), 365; in Japan, 410-11; of Mongols, 349; in Russia, 359-60; in South and Central America, 450; in Southeast Asia, 426

food plants, early, 50
forests in 10,000-5000 BCE, 48
Formorians, 260
fossils, xi, 19, 22, 27, 29, 30, 31, 35, 42
Foxes, 56
France (West Francia), 29, 233, 237, 238, 308, 318; and Great Britain, rivalry and warfare, 331-32; invaded by Magyars, 240
Francis, St, 301; and the wolf, 301-2
Franciscans, 300, 301
Franconia, 235, 237
Frankfurt, 307
Franks, 231; Eastern, 232; Western (Salian), 231, 232
Frederick I (1152-1190), 305, 312
French territory of St Pierre and Miquelon, 10
Frey and Freya, 266
frieze of archers, 173
Frigg, 266
Frumentius and Edesius, 182
Fujiwara (Nakatomi no Kamatari), 227-28, 404-5
Fujiwara, Michinaga, (CE 966-1028), 405
Fujiwara, Mototsune, 405
Fujiwara, Yoshifusa, 405
Fullager, Richard, 473
Funan kingdom of Cambodia, 420, 421, 428
Futhark, 268

Gaea, 114
Gaels, 259; Gaelic Celts, 260; language, 341
Gagaku music of Japan, 230
Gahadavalas, 365
Gajah Mada, chief minister of Majapahit, 433
Galicia, 328
Galileo, 329
Galiliee, 156, 158
Gamelan orchestra in Southeast Asia, 435
games and sports in ancient Greece, 113
games, theatre and music in Southeast Asia, 434-35
Ganweiwala, 84
Gaozu, Han emperor (BCE 206-195), 203
Gathas, The, 154, 174
Gaugamela battle (331 BCE), 116, 166
Gaul (France), 134, 136, 231; conquered by Julius Caesar, 133
Gaulish, 124
Gault, Texas, 56, 57
Gaykhatu, 383
Gaza, 116
genetic changes, 19
Genghis Khan, 343-44, 345, 348, 350, 356, 382, 397. *see also* Mongols
Genoa, 346, 390
Geoffrey of Anjou, France, 333
Georgia, 167, 169, 383
Germanic alphabet, 268
Germanic tribes, 114, 135, 136, 231, 232, 233, 238, 253, 268
Germans, 308, 309
Germany (East Francia), 233, 237, 238, 328; invaded by Magyars, 240
Ger-tereng, 349
Ghana, the kingdom of gold, 287-88, 289, 462
Ghazan Khan, 350, 383
Ghazi Malik (Ghiyasuddin), 368
Ghaznavid dynasty, 386, 388

Ghazni kingdom, Afghanistan, 367
Ghiberti, Lorenzo (1378-1455), 326, 327
Ghur kingdom, Afghanistan, 367
Gigantopithecus (a vegetarian ape), 30
Gildo of Africa, revolt against Romans, 137
Gilgamesh, king of Uruk, 66-67
Giotto, 326
Giza, pyramid, 78
glacial periods, 22
Gladiators, 141-42
Glicherzare, Heinrich, 325
Go (game), 406
Go Daigo, emperor of Japan (ruled 1333-1336), 408-9
Gao, 463
Gol Mod, Mongolia, 210
Golden Horde of Russia and Il-khanate, war, 346
Gondwana, Gondwanaland, 20, 21
Gonsalves, Lopo, 319
Go-Sanjo, Japanese emperor, 406
Gothic sculpture, 337-38
Goths, 114, 135
Goturks, 282
Gower, John (1330-1408), 339
Granada (Spain), 287, 319
Grand Canal, 276, 399
Granicus river, 116
grasses, 24
grassland mammals, 25
Great Barrier Reef, 13
Great Britain and Ireland, 29; (up to CE 1000), 251-61; (CE 1000-1500), 331-42; democracy, 334; House of Commons, 334-35; megaliths, 251; two houses of Parliament, 335; was made a vassal of Holy Roman Empire, 333

Great Schism of the Church, 300
Great Wall of China, 210, 276, 399
Great Yasa, 344
Greater Antilles, 441
Greece, Greek(s), 78, 121, 122, 165, 177-78, 239, 309, 311, 321, 328, 378; ancient, 101-14; city states/ civilization, 61, 107-8; coins, 171; culture, 109, 127; and Egypt, trade, 73; gods and goddesses, 103, 113-14; Iran, wars, 166, 167; language, 108; and Latin Christianity, enmity, 313; literature, 110; Minoan civilization (3000 BCE-1450 BCE), 101, 104, 106; Mycenae, 105-6; palaces, 103, 105; philosophers, 110-11; wars, 109
Greenland, 10, 264, 265
Gregory VII, Pope, 299
Gregory IX, Pope, 303
Gregory, Bishop of Tours, 232
Grendel, 258
Guarrero, 449
Guatemala, 198
Gudit, queen of Ethiopia, 459
Guhilas, 272
Guinea pigs, 455
Guinevere, 257
Gulf of Oman, 169
gunpowder: in China, 396; invention of Tang dynasty, 279; in West Asia, 379
Gupta dynasty, 214-15, 216, 270; sculptures, 217
Gutenberg, Johannes, 329
Guyuk Khan (Great Khan, 1246-48), 346
Gwynedd, Wales kingdom, 259, 341

Habsburgs, 306

Hadrian, Roman emperor (ruled CE 117-80), 135, 253
Hadrian's wall, 252-53
Hafsid dynasty of Africa, 461
Hagar Qim temples of ancient Europe, 128
Hagia Sophia (Church of Holy Wisdom), 238, 355
Hakhamanishya. see Achaemenids
Haliscz, 309
Hallstatt culture (800-500 BCE), 124
Hamangia culture in Romania and Bulgaria, 121
Hammurabi of Babylon, 67-68
Han dynasty of China, 96, 98, 202-4, 209, 210, 388, 402; decline, 208, 419; Eastern or later (CE 25-220), 204-5; new developments, 206
Han river, 95
Hanging Gardens of Babylon, 78
Hangul, 403
Haniwa sculptures, 225-26
Hanseatic League, 297-98, 310
Hao, 95, 96
Harappan (Indus-Saraswati) civilization, 82, 83, 84, 87, 212, 213; decline, 87
Harold II, king of England (Earl of Wessex), 256, 331
Haroun al-Rashid (ruled CE 786-809), 286, 377
Harrogate, Yorkshire, buried treasure, 257
Harshacharita (Banabhatta), 272
Harshavardhana, Indian emperor (ruled 606-647), 270-71
Hasan, 248
Hasmomneans, 156
Hastings, Battle of, 331, 332
Hat Boi, classical opera of Vietnam, 426
Hatsheput, queen of Egypt, 74, 179
Hatun Tapac, 453
Hausa, 464-65
Hawaiki, 481
Hayam Wuruk, king of Indonesia (ruled 1350-1389), 433
Hebrews, 150-51, 153, 156, 160, 183
Hegira, 243-44
Heian period (CE 794-1500), Japan, 404-7
Heian-kyo (Kyoto), Japan, 229
Heimdall, 266
Heimskringla (Snorri Sturluson), 266
Helen, 106
Helmand river, 150
Henry I, duke of Saxony, 237
Henry I, king of England, 333
Henry II of Bavaria, Western Roman emperor, 304
Henry II, king of England, 333, 340
Henry III (1216-1272), king of England, 334
Henry IV, King of Germany, 299
Henry V of England (ruled 1413-22), 316
Henry VI, king of England, 336
Henry VII, 336
Henry VIII, 336
Henry Tudor (of Lancastrian line), 336
Hephaestion (c. 357-324), 115, 118
Heracles, 104
Herculaneum city, 137
Hermione, 106
Herod, Roman governor of Galilee, 156, 157
Herodotus (c. 484-425 BCE), 113; *History*, 113
Heuneburg, 125
hieroglyphic writing system *see* writing

Himiko (Pimiko), Queen, 225
Himyarites dynasty of Arabia, 148
Hinayana. *see* Buddhism
Hindu Kush, 117
Hinduism, 373, 417, 421, 430; in Cambodia, 422; in India (3500 BCE-500 BCE), 87, 88; in India (500 BCE-CE 500), 222; (CE 500-1000), 274-75
Hippocrates (460-370 BCE), 111-12; *The Complicated Body*, 112
hippopotamus, 25
Hissarlik, Turkey, 107
Hittites dynasty, 68
hobbit, 41
Hohenstaufens of Swabia (1137-1254), 305
Hohokam culture, North America, 189
Hojo Shikkens, 408
Hokkaido island, Japan, 223, 404, 407
Homer, 106
Homo antecessor (Pioneer Man), 29
Homo erectus and other early humans, 29-30, 31, 40, 91, 419, 429
Homo ergaster, 29, 35
Homo floresiensis, 41
Homo habilis (handy man), 28-29, 35
Homo heidelbergensis, 29
Homo sapiens neanderthalensis. see Neanderthals
Homo sapiens sapiens, 31, 40, 41, 472
Homo species, 28-29
Honduras, 198, 199
Honen, founder of Jodo Buddhism, 412
Honshu island, Japan, 223, 224, 225
Hopewell culture, Ohio, 185-86; people, 187-89

Horace (65-8 BCE), 144
horseshoes, 346
housing and shelter of across the world (50,000-10,000 BCE), 42; in 10,000-5000 BCE, 55; in Australia (up to CE 1500), 475; in Europe (1000-1500), 298; of the first people, 33, 35, 42; and gardens, Japan, 410; in Novgorod, 362-63; rock shelters, 33
Hoysalas, 371
Hruodlandus (Einhard), 236
Huanbei Shang city, China, 94
Huang (Yellow River), 91, 94
Huang Gong-wang, 400
Huari civilization (CE 600-1100), Peru, 197
Hugh, Duke of Francia, 238
Huitzilihuitzil (1392-1415), Aztec king, 449
Huitzilopochtli, Aztec god, 451
Hulagu, 346, 382, 384
humanism in Europe (1000-1500), 323
humans, earlier and modern, relationship, 38
Hundred Years' War between England and France, 314-17, 335-36
Hungary, 239, 308, 309, 356
Huns, 136-37, 169, 270
hunter-gatherers, 29, 53, 185, 290
hunting, 474, 477
Husain, 248
Huss, John (Jan Hus), 306
Hydaspes (Vishtaspa), governor of Parthia, 163
Hywel Dda, Wales king (ruled 942-950), 259

Ibiza, 284

Ibn al Zubayr, 249
Ibn Sina, *Kitab-al Shifa* (*Book of Healing*), 379; *Kanun-fit-tibb* (*Canon of Medicine*), 379
Ibn Tumart, Almohad sultan, 460
Ibrahim ibn al Aghlab, 286
ice age, 22, 28, 474
Iceland, 16, 262, 266; invaded by Vikings, 264
IDA fossil, 27
Idris dynasty, Idris II (ruled 803-828), 287
Ifriqiya, 284, 286, 287, 377, 461
Igbos, 288
Igbo-Ukwu, 289
Ignatius, St of Antioch, 159
Igor, king of Russia (Novgorod), 353
Ikebana, 414
Il Khans, 388
Il-Khanate, 346, 350, 382, 383
Iliad, 106
Illinois, 187, 438
Iltutmish, 367
impetus theory, 329
Inca empire, Incas, 197, 453-56; kings, 453; origin, 453; territory and language, 454
India, India-Pakistan, 21, 57, 297, 319, 415, 428; (3500 BCE-500 BCE), 82-90; city civilization, 61; conquered by Darius I, 165; great empires (500 BCE-CE 500), 212-22; (CE 500-1000), 270-75; (CE 1000-1500), 365-75; and Indonesia, 429; Iran, trade, 170, 216; invasion by Timur, 350; new invaders, 367; Romans, trade, 138; slave kings, 367-69; South India, 272-73, 370-72
Indian Ocean, 2, 10; Islands, 375

Indiana, 186, 187, 188
Indo-China, 345, 425
Indonesia, 41, 427, 428, 429-30; China, trade, 429, 430; Indian influence, 429; India, trade, 433; islands, 472; kingdoms and dynasties, 430-31
Indo-Parthians, 214
Indo-Sasanians, 270
Indricotherium, 26
Indus river, 82, 117
Ingolfur Amarson, 264
Inquisition in Europe (1000-1500), 303, 319
insects, animals, birds, reptiles, 23, 24; diversity, 25
Inuit people, 436
Ionic, 108
Ipsus battle, 120
Iran (Persia), 57, 68, 247, 248, 350, 382-83, 386; Elam civilization, 149-50; empires, Achaemenids, Parthians and Sasanians, 162-75; India, trade, 170, 216
Iraq, 167, 350, 383, 386, 391
Ireland, 6, 259, 260, 264, 333, 340-341; invaded by Vikings, 260, 264; Parliament, 340
Irrawaddy river, 417
irrigation and farming in West Asia, 379
Isabella, queen of France, 315, 335
Iscariot, Judas (Apostle), 159
Islam, new religion, 242-50; in Africa CE 500-1000, 289, 291, 462; the Caliphs, 247-48; in China (CE 581-1000), 280; conversions to, 250; Hadis and Sunnah, 246; in India, 373; in Indonesia, 433; in Malacca, 429; in Philippines, 428;

in Russia, 356; schools of law, 246; Sharia, 247; Sunni and Shiahs, 246-47, 285, 286, 383, 384
Islands, 14-16
Israel, 54, 57, 73, 150, 152, 156, 167; lost tribes, 152
Isthmian Games, Corinth, 113
Italy, 29, 127, 128, 129, 233, 238, 321, 328; invasion by Celts, 125; invaded by Magyars, 240
Itzacoatl, an Aztecs king, 449 Tepanecs of
Ivan I, 357
Ivan II (ruled 1353-59), 357
Ivan III (ruled 1462-1505), 358

Jabir ibn Hayyan (c. 721-815), 380
Jacob, 150
Jadwiga, first queen of Poland, 309-10
Jagatai Khan. *see* Chagatai Khan
Jagiello, Prince of Lithuania, 309-10
Jaguar military order of Toltecs, 447
Jainism: in India (3500 BCE-500 BCE), 87, 89-90; (500 BCE-CE 500), 222; (CE 1000-1500), 373; Tirthankaras, 89
James (Apostle), 159
Japan, 280, 397; (up to CE 794), 223-30; (CE 794-1500), 404-14; and China, trade, 228; Chinese influence, 226, 228, 405, 410; Cloister government, 406; constitution, 226-27; early settlements, 52; era names based on Chinese system, 409; Fujiwara control, 404-5, 407; Heian period (CE 794-1500), 404-7; Murumachi period (CE 1333-1573), 408-12; Onin war (CE 1467-1477), 409-10; religion, 221;—Shinto, 225, 226, 229-30, 404, 412; Sengoku (warring states), 410; Yorimoto, 407
Jatakas, 221, 222
Java, Indonesia, 397, 429, 430, 432
Jayavarman II, Khmer king of Cambodia (ruled 802-850), 422
Jayavarman VII, Khmer king of Cambodia (ruled 1181-c. 1219), 422, 423
Al Jazari, 330
Jeanne d'Arc, 316-18
Jericho and Catal Huyuk, two early towns, 54-55
Jerusalem, 152, 156, 250, 312; captured by Turks, 313
Jesus Christ, 146, 157-59, 160-61, 245, 250, 301-3, 328, 361
Jews, 157-58, 163, 242, 250, 391; and Christians, 159-60; in Iran, 175
Jiahu culture, China, 50
Jianking (Nanjing), 205
Jiao Zhongqing, 209
Jimmium monolith, 473
Jin dynasty, Dong or Eastern (317-420), 205, 282, 344
Jin dynasty (ruled 1115-1234), 393-94, 397
Jinmu, emperor of Japan, 224
Jochi Khan, 345
John (Apostle), 159, 160
John, king of England (ruled 1199-1216), and the Magna Carta, the beginning of democracy, 334, 335
John I, King of Portugal, 319
John II, French king, 315
Johor kingdom, 429
Jomon culture of Japan, 223-24

Jordan, 57, 167
Joseph, 150, 158
Joshua, 151
Judah, 152, 156, 157
Judaism, 160; in China (CE 581-1000), 280; in India (CE 1000-1500), 373; in West Asia and Central Asia, 151, 153
Judas (Apostle), 159
Jupiter, 131, 145
Jurchens, 394
Justinian I (ruled CE 527-65), 238
Jutes, 253
Jutland, Denmark, 253

Kaba, 242-43, 244
Kahuripan kingdom, 432
Kairouan (al-Qayrawan), 286
Kakadu, 474
Kalasasaya, 198
Kalibangan, 83, 84, 86
Kalidasa, 220; *Abhijnana Shakuntalam*, 220; *Meghaduta*, 220
Kamakura, 412; Daibatsu, 413; Shogunate, 408
Kamarupa, 274
Kangaba, 462
Kanishka (ruled CE 78-120), 214
Kanmu (ruled CE 781-806), Emperor of Japan, 228-29, 404
Kannauj, 271, 365
Kanvas, 214
Kara-Khitan khanate (Western Liao), 282
Karakorum, 343, 347-48, 398
Karanovo culture in Bulgaria, 121
Karbala, battle, 248
Kashmir, 273
Katherine, 316
Kavadh I, Sasanian king, 175

Kaya, kingdom of Korea, 211
Kazakhstan, 4, 154, 350, 379
Kea Island, 101
Kediri, kingdom of Java, Indonesia (1045-1221), 432
Keep (White Tower), 337
Kent, Anglo-Saxon kingdom, 253
Kerma, 180
Kertanagara, king of Java, Indonesia (ruled 1268-1292), 432, 433
Khabul Khan, 343
Khadija, 243
Khalji, Alauddin (1296-1336), 368
Khalji, Jalaluddin, 368
Khaljis (1290-1316), 368
Khan Krum, 240
Khanbalik, 397, 399
Khangai mountain range, 210
Khangai, 210
Khazner Firaun temple, 149
Khipchak Khanate (Khanate of Golden Horde), 356, 357, 382
Khipchak Turks, 458
Khitans. *see* Mongols
Khmer kingdom of Cambodia, 420, 422, 425
Khoisan, 290
Khon, dance drama of Thailand, 423
Khorasan, 247; conquered by Timur, 350
Khufu, Pharoah (king) of Egypt, 73, 77
Khumarawayh, Tulunid ruler (884-896), 285
Khunuin river, 210
Khusrau I, Sasanian king of Iran (ruled 531-579), 169
Khusrau II, Sasanian king of Iran, 169, 272
Khusrau, Amir, 370

Khwarizm, 347, 386; conquered by Timur, 350; invasion by Abd al Malik, 249; invasion by Genghis Khan, 344
Al-Khwarizmi, 379
Kibi-no-Mabi (CE 693-775), 406
Kiche Maya, 445
Kiev, 353, 354, 355, 356
Kimberley, 474
Al-Kindi, (CE 801-873), 379
Kinich Yax Kuk Mo, Maya king, 199
knights in Europe (1000-1500), 292, 293-94, 311; orders, 294-95
Knossos island, 101, 103, 104
Koguryo kingdom of Korea, 211, 283
Kojiki (Record of Ancient Matters), 229
Kokinshu, 405
Komyo, emperor of Japan, 409
Korea, 345, 402-3; (221 BCE-CE 581), 203, 211; (581-1000 CE), 283; Mongol invasion, 344, 402; religion, 221
Krakow, Poland, 310
Kruger National Park, South Africa, 291, 467
Ku Kai Chi (painter), 206
Kublai Khan (1215-1294), 281, 345, 346-47, 348, 350, 371, 397, 398-99, 425
Kufa, 247, 248
Kukai (774-835), founder of Shingon Buddhist sect, 412
Kukulcan, 200, 446
Kush kingdoms, 180-81, 183
Kushans of Central Asia, 214, 216, 217, 221, 273
Kyoto, 409
Kyrgyzstan, 154, 350
Kythera Island, 101

Kyushu island, Japan, 223, 224, 225

La Tene, Celtic phase (500 BCE-1 BCE), 125
La Venta, 191
Labrador, 12
laquerware. *see* pottery
Ladhra, 260
Lakon Kbach Boran, dance drama of Cambodia, 423
Lakon Nai, dance drama of Thailand, 423
Lalibela, king of Ethiopia (ruled c. 1185-1225), 459
Lan Xang kingdom of Laos, 421; Mon-Khmer people, 421
Lancastrian war, 316
Lancelot, 257
Landnamabok (Book of Settlements), 264
landownership system in Europe (1000-1500), 292-93
Langkasuka kingdom, Malaysia, 428-29
Langland, William (1332-140), 339; *Piers Plowman*, 340
language of the first people, 36, 46; in 10,000-5000 BCE, 49; in Africa, 470; in Australia (up to CE 1500), 477; in India, 87; in Iran, 165; Japan, 410; in Mesopotamia, 65-66; in West Asia, 383, 388
Laos, 282, 415, 419, 420-21, 422
Laozi (Lao-Tzu), 98, 99
Latins, 129
Laurasia, 21
Laureate, 325
Laurentia, 20
Lavinia, 143
Lavinium, 143

Le dynasty of Vietnam, 426
Le Loi, 426
Leaning Tower of Pisa, 327
Lebanon, 167
Lebor Gahala Erenn (Irish Book of Conquests), 260
Lechfield, Battle, 240
Leinward-Haus, 307
Leo III, Pope, 234
Leo VI, Byzantine emperor, 307
Lepidus, 134
Lesbia, 144
Li Bai (Li Po) (701-762), 278
Li dynasty of Vietnam, 392
Li Qingzhao (1084-1151), 395
Li Shimin (Taizong) 627-49), 276
Li Yuan, Tang ruler, 276
Liao dynasty, 282, 392, 394, 402
libraries in Mesopotamia, 68-69
Libya, 176
lifestyle: across the world (50,000-10,000 BCE), changing patterns, 39-47; (10,000-5000 BCE), 49-50; in Australia (up to CE 1500), 474; in early, China, 97;—(CE 1000-1500), 394-95; in early Egypt, 77-78; in India (3500 BCE-500 BCE), 84-87; (500 BCE-CE 500), 215-16; (CE 500-1000), 274; in India (CE 1000-1500), in the time of Sultans, 369-70; in Ireland, 341; in Japan, 224; Romans, 137-39; in Russia, 359
Liji or The Book of Rites, 100
Limpopo river, 469
literature in China (221 BCE-CE 581), 208-9, 400-2;—Han dynasty, 204; in Europe (500-1000), 235-36; in Europe (1000-1500), 308, 324-25; in Great Britain, 258, 338-39;

in India (500 BCE-CE 500), 218-20; in Ireland, 341; in Japan, 229; Mongols, 351; of Romans, 143-45; in Scandinavia, 266-67, 352; Welsh, 342. *see also* writing
lithosphere, 20
Lithuanian chieftains, 309
Liu Bang, Han emperor, 202-3
Liu Sheng, Prince, 207
Liu Xu (Guangwudi), Han emperor of China, 204
Liubo, a board game, 206
Liu-Song (420-479), 205
Livy (c. 59 BCE-CE 17) *Ab urbe condita* (History of Rome), 144
Llama, 190
Lo Manthang, 373-74
Lodi dynasty, 369
Lombards, 234, 239
longbow, 315
Longinus, Gaius Cassius, 134
Lorraine, 235
Lothair I, 237
Lothal, 84
Louis I of Hungary, 309
Louis II, 237
Louis the Pious, Roman emperor, 235
Louisiana, 185
Lourandis, Henry, 476
Lubeck, Germany, 297
Lucius Tarquinas Superbus, Roman king, 131
Lucretius (c. 99-55 BCE) *De rerum Natura* (On the Nature of Things), 144
Lugalbanda, Mesopotamian king, 66
Lui Lanzhi, 209
Luke, 160
Luoyang, Henan (Hunan), 96, 205

Ly dynasty of Vietnam (CE 1010-1225), 425
Lydenburg, Mpumalanga province, South Africa, 290-91
Lydians, 163

Ma Yuan, 395
Mabinogion, 342
MacAlpin, Kenneth, 259, 342
Macbeth, king of Ireland (ruled 1040-1057), 342
Macedonia, 109, 115-16, 120, 122, 239; conquered by Darius I, 164; India, trade, 216; and Romans, war, 132
Machiavelli, Niccolo (1469-1527), *Il Principe*, 324
Madagascar, 10, 375
Madhva, 371, 372
Magadha, 212, 214
Maghreb, 284
Magyars, 239, 240
Mahabharata, 218-19
Mahayana. see Buddhism
Al-Mahdi, 384
Mahmud of Ghazni (ruled 997-1030), 367
Majapahit kingdom of Indonesia, 433
Majorca, 284
Makassar (Ujungpandang), 476
Makuria kingdom, 289
Malakunanaja, 473
Malay Archipelago, Malaysia, 427, 428-29, 433
Malcolm I of Alba, 259
Malcolm II, king of Ireland (ruled 1005-1035), 259, 342
Maldives, 375
Mali al Saleh, sultan of Pasai, 433

Mali, 462-63
Malik Shah (1072-1092), 386-87, 388
Mallory, Thomas, *Le Morte d'Arthur* (Death of Arthur), 340; *Sir Gawain and the Green Knight*, 340
Malta, 128, 179
Malwa, 270
Mamluks of Egypt, 346, 377, 382, 389; (CE 1250-1517), 458-59; Bahri (1250-1382), 458; Burji (1382-1517), 458; defeated Mongols, 346 in Syria, 350
Mammallapuram, 272
mammals, 23, 24, 25
Al-Mamun (ruled 813-33), 377
Manco Capac, Inca king, 453
Mangwancun, 96
Manichaeism: in China (CE 581-1000), 280, 282; in Iran, 175
Manimekhalai, 220
man-made things, remains, xi
Mann site, Hopewell, 188
Mansa Musa (c. 1307-32), Mali king, 462
Manyoshu (Anthology of a Myriad Leaves), 229
Manzikert battle (1071), 307, 386
Maoris, 481, 482
Mapungubwe, 468
Maqar culture, 55, 148
Maragheh (1256-1265), 383, 384
Marathon Battle (490 BCE), 109, 165
Marco Polo (1254-1324), 371, 398-99
Marcus Aurelius, Roman emperor (ruled CE 161-180), 135
Marcus Vitruvius Polio (80 or 70 BCE-15 BCE), 144

Marduk, god of Babylon and Mesopotamia, 68
Mariana Islands, 484
Marinid dynasty of Africa, 460-61
Mark, 160
Marksville culture, 185
Marrakesh, 460
Marsian war, 133
Marwan I, 249
Mary, 157, 245, 302, 308
Masaccio (1401-1428), 327
Masako, Hojo, 408
Massagetae, 163
material culture, xii
material remains, xi
mathematics and astronomy: early, 46, 59; in China, 396; in early Egypt, 69, 80; in Europe (1000-1500), 329; in Mesopotamia, 69; in West Asia, 378, 379. *see also* science
Mathew (Apostle), 159, 160
Matilda (Maud) and Stephen, 333
Mauritania, 284, 287; conquered by Claudius, 134
Mauritius, 10, 375
Mauryas, 212-13, 217
Mausoleum, Halicarnassus, 79
Maximian, Roman emperor, 135
Maximus, Pontifex, 146
Maya civilization of Central America, 198-200, 444-45, 447, 451; agriculture, 198; calendar, 200, 451; cities, 445; decline, 200, 445, 447; gods, 446; three worlds and a Ceiba tree, 200
Mazdak, 175
Mbanza Kongo, 467
Meadowcroft, Pennsylvania, 40

Mecca, 242-44, 248, 249, 384, 462
Medang kingdom, Indonesia, 431, 432
Medes empire of Iran, 150, 163
medicine system in South and Central America, 455
Medina, 247, 248, 250, 384
Meditations, 144
Mediterranean region, 29, 53, 61, 311; islands conquered by Romans, 132
Mediterranean Sea, 70, 123, 176, 284, 381
Megalania (giant monitor lizard), 39
Megalania prisca, 473
Megaliths, 58-59; in Australia, 483-84; in ancient Europe, 123; in Great Britain, 251; in India, 87; in Southeast Asia, 100; in Turkey, 59
Megasthenes, a Greek ambassador, 213
Mehrgarh, 86
Mekong river, delta, 420, 425
Melnitsa game (Nine Man), 363
Mencius (372-289 BCE), 98
Menelaus, king of Sparta, 106
Menes, king of Egypt, 70, 73
Mentuhotep II, Pharaoh (king) of Egypt, 72
Mercia, Anglo-Saxon kingdom, 253, 255, 263
Merlin, 257
Meroe, Kush city, 181
Meroitic script, 183
Merovech, 232
Merovingian(s), 231-32, 233; monasteries, 233. *see also* Clovis
Mesoamerica, 189, 192; city civilization, 61
Mesopotamia, 87, 150, 169; (5000-1500 BCE), 51, 60-69; conflict and confusion, 67; conquered by

Arabs, 239; conquered by Trajan, 135; Egypt, trade, 70; golden goats, 65; India, trade, 86
Metamorphoses (Ovid), 144
Methodius, 241
Mexico, 10, 11, 24, 189, 191, 193, 441, 442; Aztecs, 448; Maya civilization, 198; Mixtecs, 443-44
Michelangelo (1475-1564), 327, 328
Micronesian islands, 484
Middle East, 472
Mieszko, 309
Mieszko I, 241
Mihiragula, 270
Milesians, 260
military science in China, 396
millennium man, 27-28
Milos Island, 101
Mimbres river, 441
Minamoto clan of Japan, 407, 408
Minatogawa Man, 42
Minean kingdom (1200-650 BCE), 148
Minerva, 261
Ming dynasty, of China (1368-1644), 399-400, 425; literature, art and culture, 401-2
Minnesinger, 328
Minoan civilization (3000 BCE-1450 BCE), 101, 104, 106
Minorca, 284
Minos, king of Knossos, 104
Minotaur, 105
Mirandola, Pico della, 323
Mississippi river, 184-85; Mississippi culture (CE 1000-1500), 438-39
Mithra, 146, 174, 261
Mithridates I (Mithradata) (c.171-138 BCE), Parthian emperor, 167, 170
Mithridates II (c.124-88 BCE), Parthian coins, 171

Mitras, 216
Mitzvah, 153
Mixcoatl, 448
Mixtecs, 443-44, 446; codices, 444
Mnajdra temples of ancient Europe, 128
Moche culture (CE 100-800), Peru, 196
modern humans, 31
Mogollon culture of North America, 189, 190, 441
Mohenjodaro, 84, 86
Moluccas, 429, 433
Mon people of Myanmar, 417
money in Europe (1000-1500), 297
Mongke Khan (Mangu Khan, the Great Khan, 1251-1259), 345, 346, 348, 397
Mongols, Mongol empire, Mongolia, 420, 459; (221 BCE-CE 581), 209-11; (581-1000 CE), 282-83; (CE 1200-1500), 343-51, 397, 400; China, war, 400; invaded Russia, 356; Khamag, 343; Khitan, 343, 392; defeated Seljuks of Rum, 346; dynasties in Iran, China and Russia, 347; food, 349; religion, 349-50; secret history, 347; writing system, 344
Montenegro, 122
Montezuma II (also known as Motecuhzuma) (ruled 1502-1520), 449
Moravia, 50, 241, 306, 307, 309, 330, 356
Morgannwg, Wales kingdom, 259, 341
Mornu kingdom of Sudan, 461
Morocco, 176, 284, 287, 322, 460, 463
Mortimer, Roger, 335
Moscow, 357-59

Moses, 151, 245
Mound city, Ohio, 188
Mranma (Burmans), 417
Muawiya I (ruled 661–680), 248
Muawiya II, 249
Mughulistan, 350
Muhammad I, 387
Muhammad II, Ottoman Sultan, 390-91
Muhammad, prophet, 242, 243-44, 246-47, 249, 376, 384
Muizz, Fatimid ruler of Egypt, 286
Muizuddin Muhammad of Ghur (1173-1206), 367
mummies (embalmed bodies) of Egypt, 75-76
Mungo Lake, Australia, 42, 43, 473
Mungo Man, 41-42, 43
murex snail and other items in ancient Europe, 123-24
Murray Springs, Arizona, 56
Musa bin Nusair, the governor of Ifriqiya, 284
Music: in 50,000-10,000 BCE, 46; in China, 97, 209; in Europe (CE 1000-1500), 328; in Japan, 230
Muslim(s), 244, 246, 250, 311, 318, 383; in Russia, 354; traders in India, 373
Myanmar, 281, 398, 415, 416, 417; an eight day week, 419; nats, 418-19; pagodas, 418, 419; trade with India and China, 417
Mycenae, 105-6
Mycenaeans, 104

Nabatean kingdom of Arabia (400 BCE-CE 200), 148, 149
Nagaoka, Japan, 229
Nahal kana cave cemetery, Israel, 69

Nalanda, 271
Nam Viet, 424
Nan Chen (557-589), 205
Nan Liang (502-557), 205
Nanak, Guru (1469-1539), 373
Nanda dynasty of India, 212
Nang Shek (shadow puppet play), Cambodia, 425
Nang Yai (shadow puppet play), Thailand, 425
Nanzhao kingdom of Yunnan, 280, 281-82, 417, 420
Napata, 180
Naples, 137
Napoleon, 178
Nara period (CE 710-794), 228-29
Narasimhavarman I, Pallava king, 273
Al Nasir, 458
Nasrid dynasty, 319
Natufian culture, 53, 54
natural selection, theory, 19
Nauwalabila, 473
Navajos, 439
Nayanars and Alvars, 275
Nazareth, 346
Nazca culture (CE 100-800), Peru, 196; lines, 196-97
Neanderthals, 30-31, 40, 43
Nefertiti, Queen of Egypt, 74
Nemean Games, Nemea, 113
Nemeds, 260
Neo-Babylonian dynasty. see Chaldean dynasty
Neolithic culture, settlements, 58, 91, 429
Neo-Platonism, 323, 324
Nepal, 273, 373-74; Lo Manthang, 373-74
Nero, Roman emperor, 134
Netherlands, 7, 238, 314

Neustria, 232
Nevsky, Alexander, 356-57
New Guinea, 471, 473
New Zealand, 481-82
Newfoundland, 10, 12, 264, 438
Newton, Isaac, 339
Ngo Quyen, defeated Chinese (CE 939), 425
Ngunnawal (an Australian tribe), 477
Ni Zan, 400
Nicaea, 308, 312
Nicholas, 313
Nicolo, 398
Nicomedia, 135
Niger river, 462
Nigeria, 182, 464, 465
Nihon shoki (Chronicles of Japan), 229
Nikitin, 372
Nile river, 52, 70, 71, 77, 78, 180, 180, 378, 459
Nilo-Saharan languages, 470
Nimrud, 67
Nineveh, 67, 68
Ninian, St (c.360-c.432), 261
Nippur, 63
Nisa (Turkmenistan), 167
Njord, 266
Nobatia kingdom, 182, 289
Noh theatre of Japan, 413
Nok culture of West Africa, 182-83
Normandy, 238, 256, 264, 333
Normans in England, 331-32, 337, 340
North Africa, 176, 178, 231, 238, 319, 460
North America, 1, 10, 11, 12, 20, 21, 48; (CE 1000-1500), 436-42; Caribbean Islands, 10, 11-12, 441-42; early, 184-90; Eastern woodlands, 438; the first people, 40, 57; mountain slopes, 437; Northern Coasts, 436; North-West Pacific Coast, 437; Plains, 438; Plateau region, 437; the South-West, 439-41
North Pole, 21
Northumbria, conquered by Vikings, 253, 255, 258-59, 263
Norway, 16, 262
Nova Scotia, 10
Novgorod, 352, 355-56, 357, 358, 359, 361; archaeological deposits, 362-63; birchbark documents, 363-64
Nsibidi script, 183
Nubia, 72, 73, 180, 181, 182, 289-90
numeral system in India, 379
Nur-ad-din of Aleppo, 457

Oasisamerica, 189, 439
Oaxaca valley, Mexico, 192, 193, 443, 449
Occupations; in Great Britain, 251; in early Egypt, 78-79
oceans, 2, 15-16, 20, 22, 48, 263, 464
Octaviaus. *see* Augustus
Odin (Woden), 265
Odyssey, 106
Offa, King (ruled 757-796), 254-55
Ogadai Khan (Great Khan), 345-46, 348, 397
Oglay Hay treasure, 256-57
Ohio river, 186-87
Okinawa Island, Japan, 42
Old Crow Flats, Canada, 41
Old Testament Trinity (1410), 361
Olduvai (Oldupai) Gorge, 35
Olduwan (stone tools), 33
Olga, 353
Oliphant (horn), 236

Oljeitu, 383
Olmec civilization, 191-92, 193, 198, 199, 446, 451
Olympic Games, 113
Omar Khayyam (1048-1123), 388; *Rubaiyat*, 388
Omar and Osman, 246
Omphis (Ambhi), king of Taxila, 117
Ona Nagast, 181
One Thousand and One Nights, 378, 381-82
Onmyodo belief system, 226
Opone, 182
oracle bones, 94-95
Orda Khan, 345
origins, 17-26
Orkhan, 389
Orleans, 316, 317, 318
Orrorin tugenensis, 28
Oseberg ship burial, 264-65
Osmin, 364
Ostrogoths, 231
Otto I, king of East Francia (Germany), 237, 239, 304
Otto II, king of East Francia (Germany), 238
Otto III, king of East Francia (Germany), 238
Ottoman Turks, 308, 311, 357, 389-90, 458
Ouachita river, 185
Ovid (43 BCE-CE 17) *Metamorphoses*, 144
Oxaca valley, Mexico, 193
Oxford University, 322, 337
Oxus (Amu Darya), 154, 155, 172
Oxus civilization (Bactria Margiana Archaeological Complex, BMAC), 154-55
oxygen, 19
Oz Beg Khan (1313-41), 357

Pachacuti, Inca king, 456
Pacific islands, Pacific Ocean, 2, 14, 41, 454, 471, 482-83; north-west coast, 437
Paekche, kingdom of Korea, 211, 283
painting across the world (50,000-10,000 BCE), 44, 45, 46; (10,000-5000 BCE), 50, 55; at blombos cave, 37; China, 204, 206, 208; Egypt, 70, 77, 80-81; in ancient Europe, 127; Greece, 103, 111; India, 85, 218; Ireland, 261; Mayan, 199; Mesopotamia, 64, 65; Roman, 139; early in South and Central America, 192-93, 194, 197
Pakistan, 169, 273, 383. *see also* India
Palaeolithic (Stone Age), 32-33, 209, 429
Palas, 365
Palestine, 5, 54, 72, 73, 152, 167, 240, 248, 249, 385, 457, 458
Pallavas of Kanchi, 272-73, 371
Pandya, Jatavarman Sundara, king (1251-1272), 371
Pandyas, 215, 272, 371. *see also* India
Pangaea, 21
Pannotia, 20
Panthalassa, 21
Pantheon, 147
Pao, 402
Papal States, 299
paper money in China, 278, 397; in West Asia, 368
papermaking; in later Han China, 206; in Korea, 211; in West Asia, 378, 379
Papua New Guinea, 475
Paracas culture (1000 BCE-CE 400), Peru, 195-96

Index   513

Paraceratherium, 25, 26
Parachas (Faras), 289-90
Parahu, king of Egypt, 179
Paramaras, 272
Paranthropis boisei, 35
parchment, 112
Parthian dynasty, Parthians, 134, 135, 162, 167-68, 170, 171, 174, 214
Partholon, 260
Parysatis, 118
Pasai sultanate, 433
Pasargadae, Iran, 173
Pasiphae, 104
Pataliputra (Patna), 213
Patayan Culture, 441
Patrick, St, 261
Pattadakal, 272
Pattani kingdom, Malaysia, 429
Paul (Saul) of Tarsus (c. CE 10-67), 146, 151
Paul, St, 159, 250
pebble stone tools, 30
Pedra Furada rock shelters, Brazil, 40
Pegu kingdom of Myanmar, 417
Peloponnese, 390
Pentateuch, 153
people (the first people) 26, 27-38
Pepin the Short, 233
Perdiccas, 120
Pergamum, Asia Minor, conquered by Romans, 132
Pericles, 108
Persepolis, 117, 165, 173
Persia, 116, 469; attacked Greece, 109
Persian empire, 134, 388
Persian fallow dear, 56
Persian Gulf, 165
Persians, 116
Persis (Fars, Iran), 168
Peru, 194-97, 442

Perun, Russian God, 353-54
Peter the Hermit, 312
Peter, Simon (Apostle), 159
Peter, St (Apostle), 159
Petrarca, Francesco (1304-74), 325
Petroglyphs, 50, 473
Petronius (CE 27-66), 145
Phagmodrupa dynasty, 281
Phaistos, 103
Phalaborwa, 291
Pharos lighthouse, Alexandria, 79, 177
Philip (Apostle), 159
Philip II, king of Macedonia, 109, 115, 312, 313
Philip IV, king of France, 300, 308, 315
Philip VI, 308, 316
Philippines, 427-28
philosophy six systems in India, 90
Phoenicians, 178-79; occupied the island of Malta, 128; traders in ancient Europe, 123, 124, 127
Piast dynasty, 241, 309
Picts from Scotland, 253, 259
Pindar (518-438 BCE), 110
Pingming, 96
Pintupi (an Autralian tribe), 477
Pisano, Nicola, 327
Pitjantjara (an Autralian tribe), 477
Pizarro, Francisco, 453
plants and animals, 17, 23, 24; migration in 10,000-5000 BCE, 48-49
Platea Battle (479 BCE), 109
Plato (424-348 BCE), 110; *The Republic*, 110
Pliny the elder (CE 23-79) *Historia Naturalis*, 144
Plocnic, 122

Plotinus (CE 205-270), 324
Poetic Edda (Snorri Sturluson), 267-68
Poland, 241, 309, 356; the first queen, 309-10; Krakow, 310; and Lithuania, 310
political theory, Europe (1000-1500), 324
Polycarp, St, 159
Polynesians, 481, 483
Pomerania, 310
Pompeii, 137
Pompey the Great of the Optimates, 133
Pontius Pilate, 158
Pope, 159, 232, 233-34, 299, 303; and emperor, conflict, 306
Popul Vuh, 445
population bottlenecks, 19
Portugal, Portuguese, 136, 318, 319, 328, 375, 426, 433, 458, 460, 467, 470
Porus (Puru), King, 117
Poseidon, 104
Potnia (goddess), 103
Potporanj, 122
pottery: in 10,000-5000 BCE, 49, 55; in Central Asia, 155; in China, 93, 400-1;—lacquerware in Han dynasty, 203-4; in Cuicuilco, 193; in early Egypt, 70; in ancient Europe, 122, 124; in ancient Greece, 103, 106, 109; in India (3500 BCE-500 BCE), 86; in Iran, 172; in Japan, 223-24; in Mesopotamia, 62, 63; in North America, 189, 190, 439, 442; in South and Central America, 193, 196, 443, 444, 455; in West Asia, 380

Poverty Point, Loisiana, 185
Powys, Wales kingdom, 259, 341
Prabhakaravardhana, 270
Prague and Kutna, 307
Prague University, 322
Pratiharas, 272
Premyslid dynasty, 241, 306-7
Primary Chronicle (*Povest Vremenmykh Let*), 352-53
primates, 24, 25, 26
printing in Europe (1000-1500 CE), 329-30
Prometheus, 114
Proto-Sesklo culture in Greece, 121
Provinces in Roman empire, 138
Prussia, 310, 311
Ptolemy II, 176
Ptolemy III, 176
Ptolemy IV, 177
Ptolemy V, 178
Ptolemy XIII, 176-77
Ptolemy, 120, 176
Pueblo culture of North America, 189, 190, 440-41; Chaco Canyon (c. 900-1150), 440; Kayenta (Arizona), 440; Mesa Verde (Colorado), 440
Pulakesin II (ruled CE 608-642), 272
Pumapunku, 198
Punic wars, 132
Punt (Pwenet), Egyptian kingdom, 179-80
Purbach (1423-1461), 329
Purit Jarra caves, 474
Purnavarman, king (CE 395-434), 430
Pushyabhuti dynasty, 270
pyramids and tombs of Egypt, 70, 75-76, 77, 78, 181; in South and Central America, 191, 193, 196, 198, 446, 447, 449

Pythagoras (582-500) and Pythagorean Theorem, 111
Pythian Games, Delphi, 113
Pyu culture, 416-17

Qaitbay (ruled 1468-96), 458
Qin dynasty of China, 96, 201-3, 424
Qing dynasty, 400
Quechua language, 454
Quetzalcoatl, Aztec god, 448, 451
Quran, 244-46, 350
Qutb Minar, 369-70
Qutbuddin Aibak, 367

Rainbow Serpent mythology, 480
rainforests in Australia, 474
Rajamalla IV (977-985), 273
Rajaraja I, Chola king (ruled 985-1014), 273, 370
Rajendra I, Chola king (ruled 1012-1044), 273, 370
Rajput dynasties, Rajputs, 272, 365, 367
Rajyashri, 271
Rama Tibodi, Ayutthaya king of Thailand, 420
Ramanuja, 371, 372
Ramayana, The, 219, 423
Rameses II, king of Egypt (ruled from c.1279-1213 BCE), 74
Ramkhamhaeng, Sukhothai king of Thailand (ruled 1275-1298), 420
Raphael, 328
Ras Hafun, 182
Rascia kingdom, 310
Raziya, Queen (1237-1240), 367-68
Razzaq, Abdur, 372
Red Eyebrows, 204
Red Sea, 32, 72, 149, 384
Regiomontanus (1436-1476), 329

Reinhard Fuch (Reynard the Fox), 325
religion: in Africa CE 500-1000, 289, 291; in Australia (up to CE 1500), 479; Cambodia, 422-23; in early China, 95, 97; in China (221 BCE-CE 581), 208; in China (CE 581-1000), 280, 281, 282, 283; in China (CE 1000-1500), 397, 398; in early Egypt, 80-81; in Europe, 232;—ancient, 124, 126; in ancient Greece, 113-14; in Great Britain, 253, 261; in India (3500 BCE-500 BCE), 86, 87; in India (500 BCE-CE 500), 221-22; (CE 500-1000), 274-75; in India (CE 1000-1500), 373; in Iran, 174; in Japan, 227, 228; of Mayas, 199-200; in Mesopotamia, 65; of Mongols, 349-50; of Olmecs, 192; Roman, 145-46; in Russia (CE 1000-1500), 353-54, 360; Scandinavian gods and goddesses, 265-66; in South and Central America, 455; West Asia and Central Asia, 153-54
Renaissance, 144, 321; styles, 327-28
Reunion Islands, 10
Rhea (Titan), 114
Rhodes Island, 101
Rhodri Mawr, king of Gwynedd (ruled CE 844-878), 259
rice cultivation: in Indonesia, 429; in Thailand, 429
Richard I (Richard Coeur de lion), king of England, 312, 333
Richard II, 339
Richard III, King of England (Duke of Gloucester), 336
Richard, Duke of York, 336
Rig Veda, 88
Ritsu-ryo system in Japan, 228

roads: in China, 278, 397; in Damascus, 249; Inca, 454; in India, 84; in Nazca culture, 197; in North America, 440; Roman, 139, 142; Iran, 165, 169
rodents, 24
Rodinia, 20; from Rodinia to today, 20-21
Roland, 236
Roman Colchester, 252
Roman empire, Roman world, Romans, 126-28, 129-47, 156, 168, 169, 175, 177, 179, 205, 231, 240, 259, 261, 321, 378, 428; early kings, 130-31; Eastern (Byzantine), 135, 233-35, 238-39, 240-41, 284, 287, 304, 307-8, 309, 310, 311, 312, 313, 338, 346, 353, 354, 358, 361, 378, 385, 386, 388, 389, 390-91;—invasion by Abd al Malik, 249; conquests, 132-33; conquest of Britain, 134, 135, 252; conquered Egypt, 178; collapsed in Great Britain and Europe, 125, 253; conquered Nabatean kingdom, 149; defeated Celts, 125; destroyed Jewish temples, 160; divided into two, 135; festivals, 147; Holy, 237, 241, 304-6, 307, 308, 312, 313, 333; India, trade, 215; Iran, trade, 170; invaders, 136-37; new, 231, 233-35, 238; Optimates and Populares, 133; problems and conflicts, 133; religion, 145-46, 156; Roman Republic, 131-32; tetrarchy system, 135; Western, decline, 231, 233, 235
Romania, 121, 122, 239
Romulus and Remus, 130
Rosetta stone, 178

Roshanak, Sogdian princess, 118
Rottnest Island, 473
Rouran Khaganate, 282
Royal Painting Academy, China, 401
Royal Wawel Castle, 310
Rublev, Andrei (1360-1430), 361
Rudolf I of Habsburg, 306
Rumi, Sufi saint, *Masnawi*, 388-89
Runes, 268-69
Rurik, king of Russia (Novgorod) (CE 862), 352, 353
Russia, Russian(s), 16, 241; (CE 1000-1500), 352-64; and Byzantine, cultural and trade relations, 353; invasion by Vikings of Scandinavia, 352; khanate, 347; new political system, 354; many states, 355-56; Orthodox Church, 354, 357
Rustamid dynasty, 287
Ruthenia, 309

Sabaean kingdom of Arabia (930 BCE-115 BCE), 148-49
Saga, emperor of Japan, 413
sagas, 266
Sahelanthropus tchadensis, 27
Sahul Shelf, Australia, 41, 471, 482
Saicho (767-822), founder of Tendai Buddhism, 412
saint worship in Europe (1000-1500), 302
Salah-ad-din, 312, 457
Salamis Battle (480 BCE), 109
Salians of Franconia (1024-1125), 305
Salisbury Cathedral, 326
Sama Veda, 88
Samanids, 377
Samaria, 156
Samarkand, 257, 351; invasion by Abd al Malik, 249

Samoa island, 111
Samudragupta (c. CE 335-380), 215
Samurai, 407, 410, 412, 414
San Lorenzo Tenochtitlan, 191
Sangam literature, 220
Sanjay and Sailendra dynasties, 431, 433
Sanshin, 211
Sanskrit epics, 218-19
Santa Maria del Fiore, cathedral, 326
Sappho (c.650-590 BCE), 110
Saracens (Arabs), 236
Saraswati river, 82
Sardinia, 179, 238; conquered by Romans, 132
Sargon I, 67
Sasanian Persian dynasty, 135, 162, 168-69, 171, 172, 174, 175, 270, 377; coins, 171; defeated by caliphs, 377; statues, 169-70
Satavahanas, 215
Saturnalia, 147
Saxons, 305
Saxony, 235, 237
Sayyid dynasty, 369
Scheherazade, the storyteller, 381-82
scholasticism in Europe (1000-1500), 323
science: in China, 396; in Europe (1000-1500), 329; in ancient Greece, 111-12; in India (500 BCE-CE 500), 218; in Mesoptamia, 69; in Roman empire, 142-43; in West Asia, 378
Scotland (Caledonia), 125, 252, 258-59, 333, 342; invaded by Vikings, 264; England recognized independence, 342
script and writing. *see* writing
sculptures and paintings. *see* paintings

sea trade in ancient Greece, 104
sea travel, 32
seals: in India (3500 BCE-500 BCE), 85-86
seeds, plants, trees and pollen remains, xi
Seleucid Greeks, 156, 166, 168
Seleucus Nikator, Seleucid Greek ruler, 120, 213
Selevac, 122
Seljuk Turks, 250, 307, 312, 377, 385, 386-88; of Anatolia, 307, 388; defeated Byzantines, 307, 312, 386; of Rum, 346, 389
Sen Zhou, 401
Senas (1160-1245), 365
Senegal river, 462
Septimius Severus, Roman emperor (ruled CE 193-211), 134
Septum Severus, Roman emperor (ruled CE 193-211), 135
Serbia, Serbs, 240, 308, 309, 310-11
Sesklo culture in Greece, 121
seven wonders of the ancient world, 78, 177
Seville, 319
Seychelles, 10
Shabuhragan, 175
Shahiyas, 273
Shahrukh, son of Timur, 350
Shakespeare, William, *Macbeth*, 342
Shamanism, 282, 290
Shang dynasty, 92, 93-94, 95, 97
Shangdi, 97
Shankara, 275, 371
Shanxi, 96, 202
Shapur I (ruled CE 241-272), Sasanian ruler, 169, 175
Shapur II (ruled CE 309-379), Sasanian ruler, 169

Shar-i-sukhteh city of Iran, 150
Shatranj (Chaturang), 351
Shawnee Minisink, Delaware, 56
Sheba, queen, 152, 460
Shenzong, Sung emperor of China (ruled 1067-1085), 393
Shewa, kingdom of Central Ethiopia, 459
Shi Huangdi, Qin emperor of China, 201, 202, 424
Shijing (Shih Ching) or The Book of Poetry, 99
Shikibu, Murasaki, *Tales of Genji*, 405-6
Shikoku island, Japan, 223
Shilappadigaram, 220
Shillourokambos, a pet cat, 55-56
Shinran, founder of Jodo-Shinshu form of Buddhism, 412
Shinto, religion of Japan, 225, 226, 229-30, 404, 412
ships of Vikings, 263
Shoguns, 407-8; Kamakura, 408; Minamoto, 408
Shomu (ruled CE 724-49), emperor of Japan, 228
Shona people, 469
Shonagon, Sei, *The Pillow Book*, 406
Shotuko, Prince of Japan, 226-27 (spl variation)
Shravana Belagola, 273
Shri Kshetra of Myanmar, 417
Shu Han, Han emperor, 205
Shujing (Shuh Ching) or The Book of History, 99
Shungas, 214
Shwe Zigon, Myanmar, 419
Siberia, 20
Sicily, 128, 179, 238, 308; conquered by Romans, 132, 134

Sigismund, 306
Siimiformes, 25
Silesia, 306, 307
Silk Route, 203, 205, 228, 398
Silla, kingdom of Korea, 211, 283
silver coinage in Britain, 255
Simeon, emperor of Greeks and Bulgars, 241
Simon de Montfort, earl of Leicester, 335
Sind, invasion by Abd al Malik, 249
Sindok, king of Java (ruled 929-947), 432
Singapore, 415
Singosari kingdom of Java, Indonesia, 432
Sintashta culture, 154
Sistan, conquered by Timur, 350
Slave dynasty, 367-69
Slavic tribes, Slavs, 239, 240, 352
Slovenians, 311
Smerdis (Bardiya), 164, 165
Smilodon, 25, 40
snakes, 25
Snorri Sturluson (CE 1172-1241), 266, 267
society in Australia (up to CE 1500), 477-78
Socrates (c.469-399 BCE), 110
Soga clan, 226, 227, 228
Sogdiana, 117, 118
Solomon, King, 151-52, 460
Somalia, 10, 176, 179, 181, 464
Song Hong (Red River) valley, 424, 425
Song of Mulan, The, 208-9
Songhe empire of Africa, 463
Songtsen Gampo, Tibetan king (CE 608-650), 280
Soninke people, 289

Sonni Ali, Songhe king (1462-92), 463
Sophocles (496-406 BCE), 110
Soso kingdom, 462
Sotho, 291
South Africa (CE 1000-1500), 290, 467-70
South America, 12, 13, 21; and Central America, early, 191-99; (CE 1000-1500), 443-56
South China Sea, 428
South Pole, 21
Southeast Asia, 221; Myanmar, Thailand, Laos, Cambodia and Vietnam, 415-26; Philippines, Malaysia, Indonesia, 427-36
Southeast Asia Minor, 239
Southeast the Peacock Flies, 209
Spain, 29, 134, 136, 231, 233, 236, 238, 318-19, 328, 460; conquered by Romans, 132; invasion by Abd al Malik, 249
Spaniards, 449
Spanish, 441
Sparta, 108-9, 166
Sparatacus, a Roman slave and gladiator, 133
species change, 19
Spitamenes, 117
Sri Indratit, Sukhothai king of Thailand, 420
Sri Lanka, 216, 221, 370, 371, 374-75
Sri Vijaya kingdom of Sumatra (Indonesia), 422, 428, 430, 432
St Peter's Church, Rome, 327
Stanislaus, St, 310
Starcevo Cris culture in south-east Europe, 121
Statira, 118
Stegodon, 30

Stephen Dushan (1331-1355), 311
Stephen, king of England, 313, 333
Stephen I, 239
Stone Age, 33, 52, 82, 209
Stoss, Viet, 310
Strabo (63 BCE-CE 24), 113; *Geographica*, 113
structures in Russia, 360-61
Stupendemys, 25
Su Song, 396
Sudan, 182, 289, 462, 463
Suetonius, *De Vita Caesarum*, 144
Sufis, 247, 373, 459, 462
Sui dynasty, 205, 276
Suiko, Empress of Japan (CE 593-628), 226
Sukhothai kingdom of Thailand, 420
Sulawesi island, 476
Suleiman I, Ottoman Sultan, 391
Sultan al Kamil (ruled 1218-1238), 457
Sultanates of Java, Indonesia, 433
Sultaniyeh (1306-1335), 383
Sumanguru, 462
Sumatra, Indonesia, 429, 432, 433
Sumer, Sumerians, 63, 65, 69, 164
sun, earth and solar system, 17-18
Sunda kingdom of Java, Indonesia (669-1579), 432
Sunda Shelf, Southeast Asia, 41, 471, 472, 482
Sundiata, 462
Sung (Song) dynasty, 280, 392-97; Southern Sung (Ce 1127-1279), 394
Suryavarman I (ruled c. 1004-c. 1050), Khmer king of Cambodia, 422
Suryavarman II (ruled 1113-1150), 422 (year variation 1112-1152)
Susa (Shush), 118, 149, 165, 173-74; conquered by Alexander, 116, 117

Sushruta, 218
Sushun, Yamato emperor of Japan, 226
Sussex, Anglo-Saxon kingdom, 253
Sutton Hoo, a ship grave, 256
Svyatoslav, king of Russia (Novgorod), 353
Swabia, 235, 237
Swabian Alb region, Germany, 46
Swahili, 464
Sweden, 262
Swiss Confederation, 308
Swiss Federation, 309
Switzerland, 233, 238, 300, 308-9
Symposia, 108
Syr Darya, 154, 350
Syria, 54, 72, 167, 176, 239, 248, 312, 377, 385, 391, 457, 469; India, trade, 216; and Romans, war, 132

Tabriz (1265-1306), 383
Tacitus (CE 56-117), 145
Taharqa, King of Egypt, 180
Tahert, Algeria, 287
Taika reforms-Ritsu-ryo system in Japan, 228
Tainos in Cuba, 441
Taira clan of Japan, 407
Taizu, emperor of China (ruled 960-976), 392
Tajikistan, 117, 154, 167
Takht-i Suleiman (c. 1275), 383
Talas Battle, 379
Tambralinga kingdom, Malaysia, 428
Tamil literature, 220
Tamiryn Ulaan Khoshuu, 210
Tang dynasty of China (CE 618-907), 271, 276-77, 278, 279, 280, 283, 377, 379, 392, 402
Tanguts of Western Xia dynasty, 392
Tantrism, 275

Tanzania, 35, 463, 464, 469
Tao Qian (Tao Yuanming), *Peach Blossom Fountain*, 208
Tarain Battle (1192), 367
Tarquinia, early Roman city, 127
Tarumanagara kingdom of Indonesia, 430
Tarxien temples of ancient Europe, 128
Tashkent, invasion by Abd al Malik, 249
Tasman, Abel, 481
Tasmania, 471, 476, 480
Taurine cattle (*Bos Taurus*), 52
Tawantinsuyu, 454
tea ceremony of Japan, 413
Tell Brak and Tell Hamoukar, Mesopotamia, 62
Temmu, 410
Temple Mayor, Tenochtitlan, 452
Temple of Artemis, Epheseus, 79
temples: in Africa, 289; in China, 208, 280, 394, 400; in Egypt, 74, 75, 78, 80, 178, 181; in Europe, 124, 127, 128; in Great Britain, 253, 261; in Greece, 103, 108, 112, 114; in India, 86, 217-18, 272, 274, 366-67, 371; in Indonesia, 433-34; in Iran, 382-83; in Japan, 227, 228, 405, 409, 413; in Korea, 211; in Mongolia, 348; in Mesopotamia, 63, 65, 66; in North America, 438; 440; Roman, 131, 139, 147, 253; South and Central America, 194, 195, 197, 198, 445-46, 447, 449, 452; in Southeast Asia, 417, 418-19, 420, 422-23, 430, 432, 433-34, 435; in West and Central Asia, 149, 152
Temujin, a Mongol leader, 343

Tenji, emperor of Japan (prince Naka no Oe) (ruled 626-672), 227-28
Tenoch, an Aztec king, 449
Tenochtitlan, an Aztec city, 449, 450, 452
Teotihuacan, Mexico, 194
Tepanecs, 449
Terence (Plubius Terentius Afer), (195 or 185 BCE-159 BCE), 144
Terracotta warriors in China 221 BCE-CE 581, 202
Teshik-Tash, a Neanderthal or Homo sapines child, 43-44
Teutonic knights, 310, 357
Texoco, 449
Tezcatlipoca, Aztec god, 448, 451
Tezcoco Lake, 448, 449
Thailand, 282, 415, 417, 419-20, 422, 428, 430; kingdoms, Sukhothai and Ayutthaya, 420, 421; theatre, 423-24
Thaton kingdom of Myanmar, 417
theatre; in Malaysia, 435; in Thailand and Cambodia, 423-24
Thebes, 73, 77
Theodosius, Roman emperor (ruled CE 372-395), 146, 161
Theophanes the Greek (1335-1405), 361
Thera Island, 101; volcano, 103
Theravada. *See* Buddhism
Thermopylae, 166
Theseus, 105
Thessalonika, Macedonia, 241
tholoi, 106
Thomas (Apostle), 159
Thomas Aquinas, St, *Summa Theologica*, 323
Thor, 266
Thucydides (460-400 BCE), 113

Thulamela, 467
Tiahuanaco (Tiwanaku), Bolivia, 197-98, 453
Tiber river, 129, 130
Tiberius, Roman emperor, 134
Tibet, 273, 280, 281, 245, 373, 374, 397, 298
Tibetan writings, 374
Tiespes (675-640 BCE), king of Anshan, 162, 164
Tigris river, 61, 62, 67, 167
Tilantongo, Mixtec kingdom, 443
Timbuktu, 463
Timor Leste, 415
Timur, Mongol emperor, 350, 368; after Timur, 350-51
Titans, 114
Titicaca Lake, Bolivia, 197, 453
Tlacopan, 449
Tlatelulco, an Aztec city, 449
Toba Wei kingdom, northern China, 211, 282
Tobacco in Americas, 188
Tokhtamysh, ruler of Golden Horde, 350
Toltecs, 445, 446, 447-48
Tolui Khan, 345
Tomb of Uljaytu, Sultaniyya, 383
tombs and graves in later Han China, 207
Tonkin, 425
tools: of the first people, 32-33; in 50,000-10,000 BCE, 46-47; in 10,000-5000 BCE, 49, 54; in Australia (up to CE 1500), 475-76; chopping tool, 34; handaxe, 33, 34, 35, 36; stone tools, 32-33, 35, 475-76
Topa Inca (1471-93), 453
Toraman, a Huna, 270

Toregene Khatun, wife of Ogadai Khan, 345
Torres Strait islands, 475, 476, 481
Tostig, 331
Totonac people, 194
Tou Wen, princess and prince Liu Sheng, 207
Toumai and millennium man, 27
Toumen, 210
Tower of London, 337
Towton battle, 336
trade and commerce, trade and craft: in Africa, 179, 181, 464-65; in Australia (up to CE 1500), 476; Chinese (CE 581-1000), 278; and contacts in later Han dynasty, China, 205; in early Egypt, 78, 79-80; ancient Europe, 123; in Europe (1000-1500), 296, 297, 298, 308, 321; in ancient Greece, 104; in India (3500 BCE-500 BCE), 85, 86; in India (500 BCE-CE 500), 216; in India (CE 1000-1500), 366, 370; between India and Tibet and China, 273; in Iran, 150, 170, 171-72; Japan, 228; of Mayas, 199; in North America, 441; in Roman empire, 138, 252; in Russia, 355, 360; Vikings, 264; in West Asia, 384
Trajan (CE 98-117), Roman emperor, 134, 135, 141
Tran dynasty of Vietnam (CE 1225-1400), 425
Transoxiana, 377
Treasure hoards, 256-58
Trebizond, 308, 390
Tribal Hidage, The, 253
Trieu Au, 424-25
Tripoli, 9, 312
Triumvirate, 133-34

Trojan war, 106-7
Trung sisters, revolt in Vietnam, 424
Trung Trac, ruler of Vietnam, 424
Tuatha de Danann, 260
Tudors, Tudor dynasty, 336, 338
Tughlaq dynasty, Tughlaqs, (1320-1412), 368
Tughlaq, Firuz Shah (ruled 1351-1388), 368, 369, 370
Tughlaq, Muhammad bin (ruled 1325-1351), 368, 369, 372
Tula, 447-48
Tulunid dynasty, 285
Tumen Amugulang Palace, Karakorum, 348
Tunisia, 10, 176, 286
Turk empire, 210
Turkey, 7, 55, 68, 167, 350, 383, 450; megaliths, 59
Turkish Ottoman empire in Serbia, 311
Turkistan, 345, 346
Turkmenistan, 154, 167, 383
Turks, 169, 309, 312, 385, 390
Tusi, Nasir al din al, 384
Tutankhamun, (ruled c.1332-1323 BCE), 74, 75, 77
Tuthmosis I, king of Egypt (1493-c. 39 1482 BCE), 74
Tutupec kingdom, 443
Tyre, 116
Tyrins, 104

Udayana, king of Bali, 432
Ui Sang, 283
Ulugh Beg, ruler of Samarkand (1409-1447), 350-51
Ulugh Khan. *see* Tughlaq, Muhammad bin
Umar al-Khattab, 247
Ummayad dynasty (CE 661-750),

Ummayads, 247-50, 284, 287, 376, 377; architecture, 249; caliphs, 247, 318
universities in Europe (1000-1500), 322-23
Upanishads, 88, 89, 90
Ur (c. 2700 BCE), 63, 64, 65, 150
Urals, 154
Uranus, 114, 146
Urban II (1042-99), Pope, 312
Urewe culture of East Africa, 183
Uruk, 63, 66
USA, 10, 11, 185, 189, 436, 438, 439, 441; Clovis culture, 56
Uxmal, a Mayan city, 445
Uyghur Khaganate, 282
Uyghurs, 282
Uzbekistan, 43, 117, 154, 350, 398
Uzbeks, 351

Vaclav of Premyslid dynasty, 241
Vairochana Buddha, 412, 433
Vajrachchhedika Sutra, The (Diamond Sutra), the oldest printed book, 279
Vajrayana. *See* Buddhism
Vakatakas, 215
Valac, 122
Vale of York, treasure, 257
Valerian, Roman emperor, 135, 169
Valmiki, 219
Valois dynasty of France, 308
Van Lang, kingdom of Vietnam, 425
Vandals invaded Roman Empire, 136, 178, 231
Varangians, 352
Vardhamana Mahavira, 89-90
Vatapi, 272
Vedanta, 90, 275
Vedas, 88, 89, 90, 222, 419

Venice, 296, 311, 321, 391; and Genoa, war, 398
Venus of Hohle Fels, 46
Verdun Treaty (843), 237
Vespasian, Roman emperor, 135
Vetulonia, early Roman city, 127
Victoria lake, 183
Vietnam, 203, 205, 277, 415, 421, 422, 427; and China, 392, 424-26; dynasties, 425-26; water puppets, 426
Vijaya, king of Java, Indonesia (ruled 1293-1309), 432, 433
Vijayanagara empire, India, 372
Vikings from Scandinavia, warriors of the North: (CE 750-1100), 257, 260, 262-69, 438; invaded England, 255, 259, 263-64; in Ireland, 340; invaded Russia. 352-54; women, 263
Villa estates in Roman empire, 140
village settlements, early, 52
villages and towns (10,000-5000 BCE), 48-59
Vinca Belo Brdo site, 122
Vinca copper culture in ancient Europe, 122
Viracocha, Inca king, 453
Virgil (70-19 BCE), *The Aeneid*, 143
Visigoths, 136
Vladimir I (Vladimir the Great), king of Russia (CE 980-1015), 353, 354
Vladimir II (ruled 1113-1125), king of Russia, 354, 355
Volga river, 352
Vologases VI, Parthian ruler, 168

Wagadou (Aoukar) kingdom of Africa, 287

Wales, 125, 252, 333, 341-42; and England, struggle, 341; four kingdoms, 341; occupied by Celts, 259
Walila (Ce 789-791), 287
Wallacea channel, 471, 472
Wang Anshi, 393
Wang Kon (CE 918), Korean state, 402
Wang Mang, the Xin dynasty, 204
Wang Meng (1310-1385), 400
Wang Wei (699-759), a Chinese painter and poet, 278-79
War of Roses (1455-1485), 336
Warlpiri (an Autralian tribe and language), 477
warring states: of China, 96; of Japan, 410
wars and conflicts in Europe (1000-1500), 304-20
Wat phra Mahathat, Ayutthaya, Thailand, 420
water power and windmills in West Asia, 379
water puppets of Vietnam, 426
water wells in Cyprus, 55
Watson brake and other places in North America, 185-86
Wattasids, ministers of Marinids, 461
Wayan Kulit (a shadow puppet play) of Malaysia, 435
weapons in Europe (1000-1500), 294
Wedmore, Treaty, 255
Welsh laws, 259
Wen, founder of Zhou dynasty, 95-96
Wencheng, Tang Princess, 280
Wendi, Han emperor (180-157 BCE), 203
Weng Zhengming (1470-1559), 401

Wessex, Anglo-Saxon kingdom, 253, 255, 257
West Asia: early, 148-55; (CE 750-1500), 376-85, 464; new learning and techniques, 379-80; special items made, 380-82; the Turks, 386-91. *see also* Central Asia
Westminster Abbey, 339
Wieliczka salt mines, 310
Willendorf, Austria, 46
William I, 341
William II, king of England, 333
William of Rubrick, a Franciscan missionary, 348
William, the Conqueror (Duke of Normandy, France), 256, 331-32, 333, 337, 339
Winchester Bible, The (1170-1180), 338
Windsor castle, 341
Won-hyo, 283
woodblock printing; in China CE 581-1000, 278-79, 394; in West Asia, 379
Woolley, Leonard, 64
woolly rhinoceros, 39
writing in Africa, 183; in early China, 94-95, 97; cuneiform in Iran, 149, 164; in ancient Europe, 124; hieroglyphic system of Egypt, 70, 79, 178; in ancient Greece, 104; in India (3500 BCE-500 BCE), 86-87; of Mayas, 199; in Mesopotamia, 65-66, 69; in North America, 184; Olmecs, South and Central America, 192, 450
Wu (222-280), 205
Wu Ching (Wu Ching) literature of early China, 99-100

Wu Zhao, Tang empress (690-705), 277
Wu Zhen, 400
Wu, Zhou king, 95
Wudi, Han emperor (140-87 BCE), 203, 424
Wujing Zongyao (1044), 396

Xanadu, 398, 399
Xerxes I (Khshayarsha), 166
Xi Wei (535-556/7), 205
Xia dynasty of China, 92, 93, 392, 397; Western, 392, 397
Xia Gui, 395
Xian (Changan), 95, 96, 202, 203, 205, 276, 278, 406
Xianbei, 210-11
Xianrendong cave, China, 47
Xie He, 206
Xingjian, 283; conquered by Timur, 350
Xinjiang Uyghur Autonomous region of China, 345
Xiongnu, 210
Xiyouji (Journey to the West), 400
Xuanzang, 271-72, 280, 400, 430
Xuanzong (Minghuang) (712-756), 277
Xunzi, 98

Yahweh, 153, 158
Yahya ibn Ibrahim, Almoravid king, 460
Yajur Veda, 88
Yakamochi, Otomo no, 229
Yamato period (CE 300-710), 225
Yan, vassal state of Zhou, 96
Yang Guifei, 277
Yang, Sui emperor, 276

Yangtze, 91, 94, 95
Yao, Chinese emperor (2337-2258 BCE), 406
Yaqub al Mansur, Almohad sultan, 460
Yaroslav I, king of Russia (1019-54), 354-55
Yaroslav II, Grand Prince of Vladimir (Tsar), 356-57
Yaroslavich, Alexander, Prince of Novgorod, 356
Yayoi culture, 224-25
Yazdagird III, 169
Yazid, 248, 249
Yeisei, Japanese Buddhist monk, 413
Yemen, 148, 286
Yen Leiben, 279
Yenesei Kirhgiz, 282
Yesevi, Ahmad, a Sufi saint, 350
Yesukai, chief of Khamag Mongols, 343
Yi river, 93
Yi Songggye, emperor of Korea, 403
Yijing (I Ching) or The Book of Changes, 99
Yin-Yang, 98, 208, 226
yokyaku (music for Noh theatre), 413
Yoritomo, Minamoto, 407
Yoruba culture, 465-66; gods, 465
Yuan dynasty, 280, 397-99; literature, art and culture, 400-1
Yuefu (Imperial Music Bureau), 209
Yurts, transportable houses of Central Asian nomads, 348-49

Zagwe dynasty, 459
Zambezi river, 469
Zapotec culture of Mexico, 193, 194, 199, 443, 444, 446

Zarathushtra, 154
Zayyanid dynasty of Africa (CE 1236-1554), 461
Zeami, 413
Zelotes, Simon (Apostle), 159
Zeus statue, Olympia, 79, 111
Zhangjiapo, Fengxi, Changan, Shanxi, China, 96
Zhao, China, 96
Zhao Kuangyin. *see* Taizu, emperor of China
Zhao Mengfu (1279-1368), 400
Zheng He (1371-1433), 400
Zhenxun, 93
Zhou dynasty (1046-221 BCE), 92, 94, 95, 392; decline, 201; Eastern (c 771-481 BCE), 96, 100; religion, 97-98; Western (1046-771 BCE), 95-96, 97
Zhou Hsin, 94
Zhoukoudian caves, China, 30
Zhu Yuanzhang, 399
Zhuangzi (Chaung-tzu), 99
Zimbabwe, Great Zimbabwe, 468, 469-70
Zirid dynasty, Zirids, 287, 319
Ziyadat Allah (817-838), 286
Zizhi Tongjian, 395
Zoe (Sophia), 358
Zoroastrianism, 154, 165, 174, 250, 373
Zoser, king of Egypt, 73
Zun, 97

Acknowledgements

Among the many people who have contributed to the book, I would particularly like to thank the following: Sohini Mitra of Penguin India, for suggesting that I write this book, which I thoroughly enjoyed doing; Mimi Basu for editing it, and for the lively discussions we had; all others at Penguin India involved with the design and production of this book; and finally Kallol Majumdar for expertly drawing the maps and illustrations.